Cyngor Bwrdeistref Sirol

Pen-y-bont ar Ogwr

BRIDGEND
County Borough Council

Bridgend Library & Information Service ᴼᵁᴬ

Gwasanaeth Llyfrgell a Gwybodaeth
Pen-y-bont ar Ogwr

Please return/renew this item by the last date below

Dychwelwch/Adnewyddwch erbyn y dyddiad olaf y nodir yma

www.bridgend.gov.uk/libraries

Piers Griffith

Pirate of Penrhyn

1568 – 1628

Piers Griffith

Pirate of Penrhyn

1568 – 1628

Glenys Mair Lloyd

Published in 2015 by
Humphreys Signs Ltd.

ISBN 978-0-99326-270-8

A CIP record for this title is available from the British Library.

Printed and bound in Wales at
Gomer Press, Llandysul, Ceredigion

A quest for PIERS GRIFFITH, pirate-poet, lord of the manor of Penrhyn and descendant of the Welsh Princes, an Elizabethan courtier and merchant adventurer who led a double life on Her Majesty's Secret Service in the fledgling MI5/6 network of Sir Francis Walsingham, Spymaster.

"*Ventures he hath squandered abroad. Yet ships are but boards, sailors but men: there be land-rats and water-rats, water-thieves and land thieves, – I mean pirates – and there is the peril of waters, winds, and rocks.*"

William Shakespeare, 'The Merchant of Venice', 1597

"*Piers Griffithe, a notable pirate ...*"

State Papers, 1603

"*It is a kind of trap, I know, this life of piracy but one that has its own unbeatable thrill.*"

Piers Griffith, Poet

Contents

Prologue

There is opposite Anglesey
A fortress of oak that favours minstrels,
... a house, ...
Of white stone-work the colour of a swan,
A dwelling-place that is a hundred times better as regards
The wood and the excellence of its construction
... than the sad
Greystone Tower of the Eagle, seat of anger ...

Demolishing the English castle of Edward I at Caernarfon with a word or two, this is how Rhys Goch Eryri, a Welsh poet in the fifteenth century described the superiority of Old Penrhyn, one of Wales's fortified manor-houses once standing on the site now occupied by Penrhyn Castle near Bangor, North Wales. It was from here in the great Elizabethan Age of Voyaging and Discovery that a young man set sail for a life of adventure on the high seas.

His name was Piers Griffith, destined to become one of the more colourful and mysterious characters in history.

A rare manuscript poem dedicated to the adventurous young Penrhyn heir by his pirate friend Thomas Prys in the 1590s, gives an insight into Piers's elusive character:

To a Dolphin

Go on a journey from Menai …
towards Lisbon …
and swim then a while
towards Spain, heart of the world.
Swim as if on a chase,
You are such a spirited adventurer …

History tells us that Piers Griffith was born in 1568, the son of Sir Rhys Griffith, High Sheriff of the County of Caernarfon and of Lady Catherine, in their turreted medieval castle on the wild, windswept shores of the Menai Strait.

Myth, poetic licence and hearsay show that Piers lived a life of adventure as a pirate aboard his ship, the *Grace*. He was in reality a privateer sailing with Sir Francis Drake and Sir Walter Raleigh under Letters of Reprisal from Queen Elizabeth I who took a percentage of the profits.

> *A gentleman of considerable abilities in body and mind. When the Spanish Armada threatened the destruction of his queen and his country, he bought a ship, and providing himself with all manner of warlike stores, he sailed from Beaumaris the twentieth of April, fifteen eighty eight, and arrived at Plymouth the fourth of May following.*

Fact or fantasy, we wonder? From these bare bones of the basic plot, I was drawn to seek the truth that lies somewhere in between and to ask who was this shadowy figure grinning at me boldly through the mists of time …

> *… and upon his arrival in Plymouth, Sir Henry Cavendish sent him an invitation to dine at Sir Francis*

*Drake's ship, where he was treated honourably, and
highly commended for his loyalty and public spirit.
He followed the above-mentioned commanders till the
Armada was defeated; and after that, he went with
Drake and Raleigh to cruise upon the Spanish Coast.*

That was the intriguing fragment I found in a decaying old book
in a back room at the local library, by a certain John Thomas M.A.
Oxford, Headmaster of Beaumaris Grammar School in 1764, with
later additions by William Williams of Llandegai, Land Agent to
Lord Penrhyn. Suddenly I felt I just had to find out more about
Piers Griffith the Pirate.

*A gentleman … the Spanish Armada … all manner of
warlike provisions … the twentieth of April … the fourth
of May.*

These specific dates have a ring of truth about them, as if recorded
from some earlier source now lost, as historian David Thomas has
noted, or gleaned from official Port Books perhaps, but impossible
now to check since all such records for 1588 were 'lost' or 'removed'
nationwide during the war-time crisis of the Armada.

Young Captain Griffith was only nineteen years old. Two weeks
… So it took him two weeks to reach Drake in Plymouth, with
the wind in his sails and a gang of oarsmen rowing like mad for a
penny a day,

… and upon his arrival in Plymouth …

What a scene that would have been, with such echoing images
even today. Hundreds of ships, thousands of people, panic-stricken.
Drake coolly playing bowls. An island people prepared for the
worst.

> *... all manner of warlike provisions ... till the Armada*
> *was defeated ... and after that, he went with Drake and*
> *Raleigh to cruise upon the Spanish coast ...*

APRIL 20, 1588

Britain is in crisis.

The Spanish Armada of the Duke of Medina Sidonia is fast approaching our Western seaboard.

A galleon sails from a hidden creek beneath the pirate's castle on the Menai Strait, with a black-market consignment of guns from Ireland to join Sir Francis Drake in Plymouth, fast. Morning sunlight dazzles on the young captain's helmet and breastplate as he navigates the *Grace* towards the Caernarfon bar and out to sea, yelling his orders,

> *Give way, heave, you water-rats! Hoist the sails, you*
> *gang of thugs!*

Swearing, they scramble to their places, his hired crew of adventurous locals, give or take a captured black galley-slave or two, or Arabian cut-throats freed from merciless Barbary pirates off the African coast when Piers is only fifteen with Captain Koet, a crew shipwrecked still manacled from Spanish treasure ships in Santo Domingo and Mexico, or else, according to legend, such creatures as are washed up exhausted on the rugged shores of Anglesey across the water from the pirate's power-base, like devils seized as witches from the sea.

This pirate arena is but a sword-slice of the whole Elizabethan World Picture, which encompasses not only legitimate trade, politics and scientific exploration (Hakluyt's *Principall Navigations*, the quest for the North-west Passage and the cartography of alchemist-astronomer Dr John Dee) but also the mysterious conflicts of espionage and religion (the Spanish

Inquisition and conspiracies like the Babington Plot to assassinate Protestant Queen Elizabeth and replace her on the throne with Catholic Mary Queen of Scots.)

Treasure-hungry adventurers like Piers Griffith would fit well into this context, licensed to roam and frankly, commit "robbery with violence on the high seas," as Professor John Guy of Clare College, Cambridge has said. Reprisal is necessary for survival. The Spanish onslaught on the golden territories of America, not to mention their savage war-crimes against the native inhabitants, is challenged by the murderous raids of the English fleets of Hawkins and Drake from Europe to the Caribbean, pausing only to capture profitable cargoes of African slaves *en route*.

So here is Piers, brought up since boyhood on the exploits of his chivalrous ancestors and the classical Greek and Roman heroes of his tutored schooldays like Perseus his namesake, now following in the wake of his role-models Drake and Raleigh, granted Letters of Reprisal from the Admiralty with the tacit encouragement of the Queen, one of the chief investors. "Returns could vary", Professor John Guy has estimated, "from a huge 5,000% profit to disastrous losses, which infuriated her. If you were lucky enough to gain her favour, she still expected you to equip and supply your own ship, pay your crew and so on."

Even Sir Walter Raleigh would eventually bankrupt himself on such expeditions in search of exotic El Dorado, desolate Roanoke, or up the Orinoco, let alone Piers. Both are cultured courtiers, dashing favourites of the Queen, true Renaissance men meeting all the exciting new challenges of the Age, both with pretty young wives waiting at home under the shadow of crumbling estates and grasping bankers, yet both husbands are hell-bent on risk and enterprise.

How easy would it be for a handsome, rich young country gentleman typical of the 'Hamlet Generation' born into the 1560s like Piers, to get started as a pirate? Going up to Oxford and

London for the first time, seeking big business investors in the City, attracting the Queen's attention?

"Oh quite easily," Julia Fox has suggested, an expert on the political and romantic intrigues of the Tudor court and author of *The Infamous Lady Rochford* and *Sister Queens*, "given Piers's royal Tudor connections, good looks and charm. He was a protégé of the Earl of Leicester who had an affinity with North Wales."

Welsh gentry, or nobility like the Cecils, Mostyns, Bulkeleys, Griffiths and the Lords of Powys were noted for their rampant ambition since the rise of the Tudors, gaining land, favours, riches and status, while their young relatives secured staff appointments in royal households as trusted bodyguards, soldiers, secretaries, ladies-in-waiting, servants and musicians, as David Starkey has noted.

Given too, Piers's remarkable CV, being sent to sea as a boy with Captain Koet, then Drake, plundering Hispaniola on the Spanish Main, looting ladies' jewels, despoiling Catholic churches, bombarding Cartagena. And inevitably, there would have been his useful knowledge of shipping movements from Wales to Newfoundland, Ireland and Antwerp; then down to La Rochelle and Lisbon with the fishing and fur trades; haunting the secret coves of French corsairs around St Jean de Luz; or distinguishing himself in Drake's 1587 raid on Cadiz; but certainly against the Armada in 1588; and finally on Drake's last voyage of 1595, as several Welsh manuscript poems tell us. There were plenty of others: Captain Owen and cousin Captain John Salesbury for instance, were praised for taking another shot at Cadiz with Lord Essex in 1596 when Britain was still under threat of invasion by Spain.

At these Tudor high-points of swashbuckling adventure, Piers Griffith seems to have led a daredevil life as one of the great privateers of the Elizabethan Age. Suddenly I found myself being drawn down an irresistible detective trail.

I

An Introduction to the Poems

The Legend of Piers Griffith, boy and man

1568 – 1628

SEPTEMBER 25, 1568, PENRHYN OLD CASTLE, NORTH WALES
Piers is born to Lady Catherine Griffith, and as future lord of
the old domain inherited from his father, Sir Rhys Griffith, the
child is descended from Welsh Princes, related to the Tudors of
Penmynydd, with other powerful connections at the English court.
He has the good fortune to be a distant kinsman of Queen Elizabeth
herself; he will become her ward indeed, and a protégé of the Earl
of Leicester. The boy seems to have had everything he could wish
for, as other adventuring poets sometimes remind him, like Siôn
Mawddwy, Thomas Prys and Ifan Llwyd Sieffre. But his life, even
from childhood, is marked by tragedy and loss, both personal and
financial.

Piers is to live dangerously, sailing close to the wind. He
may well have been a spy in the Intelligence network of Sir
Francis Walsingham, then of Sir Robert Cecil. After consulting
experts and studying documents, including unpublished Welsh
manuscript poems of the Tudor and Jacobean times, one may
conclude that Piers is at least a seasoned gunrunner, possibly doing
arms deals with both sides in the Rebellion of the Earl of Tyrone
against English rule. He is very likely a paid intelligencer to Queen
Elizabeth, bringing her the latest information on ship movements
and on Catholic plots against her life from Spain to the Caribbean,
from Venice to London, what with his expert knowledge of foreign
harbours and his smattering of European languages. His fellow
poets, who know him only too well and who provide a valuable
source of evidence previously neglected, have written that he
is a handsome charmer, heroic soldier, shrewd merchant and
courageous adventurer, *"in danger of being arrested as a spy"* in
foreign parts, but nevertheless *"an honourable ambassador for
his country"*. Other tributes describe him as a generous and witty
friend who always stands up for the underdog and is popular with
his crew, *"an armed gang who never left his side"*, wrote Thomas
Prys the pirate-poet, a close ally of Piers and a primary witness

who provides some of the best evidence we have about the young lord.

By all accounts, Piers Griffith's parents, Sir Rhys and Lady Catherine, seem to have lived it up in London at the glittering court of Queen Elizabeth, seeing at first hand the glamour of Gloriana, "… in these days one of the most renowned and magnificent courts that are to be found in Europe," wrote William Harrison in his *Description of England* (1577.) The boy Piers may well have gone too. It was quite usual for children to be pushed forward to gain royal favour, to serve as the Queen's page or as a useful messenger-boy for a time. Like Piers's grandparents and great-grandparents before them at the royal courts of the Tudors (King Henry VII, Prince Arthur, King Henry VIII, King Edward VI, Queen Mary I and Queen Elizabeth I) this Knight of the Shire and his Lady must have returned to their castle full of excited eye-witness accounts of key-events: courtly splendour, awesome pageantry, scandalous gossip, political intrigue, magnificent clothes and jewels, music, dancing, jousting, heraldic-emblazoned ceremonies and bloody executions.

During Piers's boyhood, Sir Rhys has an important role as High Sheriff of the County of Caernarfon, representing his people in the London Parliament, a man of status commanding enormous respect both locally and nationally, with family traditions rooted in the Age of Chivalry, its codes of honour and fealty to the Crown, conditions ideally suited to courting royal favours, and in Piers's case, part of his inherited expectations in life.

1580 North Wales

Back home in Old Penrhyn, Piers soon has to face worse family problems than many a child today. Confidentially, this is a dysfunctional family.

Piers is twelve years old and tutored at home, possibly by Roland Thomas, Dean of Bangor Cathedral, also serving as chaplain to the

Castle family, like one Harry Hughes noted in the Penrhyn Papers. The boy is made a ward of Queen Elizabeth by his mother Lady Catherine when his father, Sir Rhys falls *"sycke in body"*, makes his Will on his deathbed with a wavering signature and soon dies one summer's day, after adding good-humoured last-minute memos to his wife, priest and lawyer:

> That they *shall provide by and set up in the steeple of the sayed parish church three competent and sufficient bells ... and ... my sayed executrix* [Lady Catherine] *shall with the ayde, contribution and assistance of my kynsmen, neighbors, frendes and countreyemen make up, repayre and reedifye the Ruynous and decayed bridge of llan Tegay with all possible expedicion.*

So Sir Rhys Griffith, Knight, courtier to Queen Elizabeth, is buried as requested with his long-dead first wife,

> *the Lady Gruffith, otherwise knowne as the Ladie Phynes,*

who had been laid to rest in the stone-carved, cobwebbed Penrhyn Crypt, now sealed and embedded in the dank, decaying, leaf-fringed depths of Llandegai churchyard.

Two years pass, and when Piers is fourteen, his 'scheming uncle' Thomas, lord of Mostyn in Flintshire, dashing and rich young widower, rides into the estate, oversees Piers being made a ward-of-court, freezes the boy's assets (which he cannot inherit until he is twenty-one, an annual income of at least £15 million in today's money) and promptly engages the attentions of Piers's widowed young mother, Lady Catherine. Meanwhile teenage Piers, younger brother William and elder sister Alys lurk about sulking in the candle-lit shadows. Later William is to feud with Piers, while Alys, with her two small sons, is to disappear from the records after marrying a tragic young gentleman, Mr Williams of Bodlew manor, Anglesey, only to suffer the consequences at the rapacious hands of her vengeful in-laws.

In the case of Piers, a boy who is already promisingly brave and academic, as one elegy to his father confirms, and a boy keen to go to sea, the Penrhyn heir is now expected to marry his new teenage step-sister and cousin Margaret Mostyn. Here is a vulnerable girl who has just lost her own mother, dead in childbirth, the *"lovely lady"* Ursula Mostyn, neé Goodman, heiress daughter of the rich Tudor Merchants of Chester, Sir William Goodman, Knight, Mayor of the City and Lady Margaret. Both were status-empowered figureheads of a Welsh dominated monopoly of coastal trading, pirating and Foreign Exchange along the north-west seaboard. No one bothers to ask this dutiful girl what she feels, as such blatant property deals are quite usual. But Margaret Mostyn, the Pirate's child-bride, will have plenty to complain about later. At the moment, a nerve-racking teenage marriage lies ahead of her. Or is this a Romeo and Juliet affair?

So on the very same day they see their ill-assorted parents married, Piers and Margaret are also united in a quick-fix double wedding, either at Llandegai Church or possibly in the private chapel at Penrhyn, the relocated remains of which are still to be seen as a picturesque ivy-clad ruin in the woods.

True to tradition in Tudor times, the two couples are 'married at the church door', that is, publicly in full view of the Castle servants and tenant-farmers from the estate, muttering a few home-truths no doubt, a scene with poignant links to the boy-heir's lost father, the popular Sir Rhys Griffith, descendant of knights and princes.

Meanwhile, are the children aware – not to mention the lord of Mostyn – that their mother, Lady Catherine (a recusant Catholic, which makes things more complicated) is hiding a Catholic priest, Father John Bennet, in her grand house at Gloddaith, Llandudno, a heretic's crime punishable by excruciating torture and death? The alternative is a hefty fine or bribing the magistrate, which may have happened in this case, as noted by Dr Anthony Carr, former 'Brain-of-Britain' and Professor of Welsh History at Bangor University.

Fortunately after many hair-raising twists and turns, recorded in *The Catholic Martyrs of Wales* by T.P. Ellis, partly from Vatican primary sources, the priest escapes from a hideaway cave high above the sea on the craggy Little Orme headland at Llandudno, to a waiting ship for Ireland and Spain, but unfortunately new step-parents Thomas and Catherine have lots of rows and hardly ever live together.

No wonder the young heir runs away to sea almost immediately, or is sent off, as has been suggested by distinguished maritime author Aled Eames and by Dr Cecil Jones, the marine archaeologist. Piers, like any adventurous local boy, is soon despatched for naval training with an experienced mentor from within the family, in this case possibly the famous privateering fleet-owner, Captain Hugh Griffith of Cefnamwlch on the Llŷn Peninsula, one of the founders of the East India Company, trading ally of the Turks against the Spaniards, gun-runner and intelligencer. Who better to teach Piers the superb navigational skills that are to make him a force to be reckoned with from St Malo to St Jean de Luz amongst the French corsairs, and from Venice to the Azores, to Santo Porto and Santiago de Leon in the West Indies, to Barbados, Venezuela, Cuba and the Gulf of Mexico?

These links in Piers Griffith's life between other leading North Wales families with pulling-power at Court, are to prove important in forging his destiny. His direct inheritance also becomes part of that dynamic Tudor concoction of energies: Noble blood and rich Trade.

Piers is also in a position, through his education at University College, Oxford and the New Learning, through social rank and pedigree, to acquire valuable leads and connections in his aspiring drive to fortune and adventure. Who are these likely to be? Rich Tudor merchants of the East India Company like the Middletons of Wales and Cheapside, the Goodmans of Chester, Ruthin and London, uncle Hugh Griffith (who worked for Walsingham) or the entrepreneurial and aristocratic Bulkeleys of Anglesey. Another influential force of the times, according to Eames and Jones, is the famous Alchemist and Astronomer, Dr John Dee at his mansion on the Thames, a man so useful to Elizabeth Tudor's claim to the Americas. Then there is the evidence of links to patrons like Cavendish, Leicester, Drake and Raleigh. Not to mention the Queen herself.

Other possibilities present themselves:

> "Piers may well have followed, like many other sons of the gentry, in the wake of explorers Preston and Somers or the more flamboyant Earl of Cumberland," Professor John Guy has commented.

Add to that Piers's born role as a man of the people in North Wales with hundreds of loyal tenants and servants on his vast estate; his notorious bodyguards; his valiant ship's crew. The Pirate of Penrhyn is now on course for a series of swashbuckling adventures thereby gaining a local, national, and international reputation.

The view has been that he squandered his ancient inheritance and "bankrupted his estate to pay his pirate fines". The real story reveals more than that.

Was he misjudged?

1583 UNDER SAIL FROM THE CANARIES TO THE WEST COAST OF AFRICA

Piers Griffith begins his pirating career young, immediately after his teenage marriage it would seem.

At fifteen, he is a trainee naval officer privateering with his mates: Thomas Prys of the Plas Iolyn estate in the Conwy Valley, an older boy who is also his cousin, and with Will and Huw Middleton of Denbigh, all adventurous poets and soldiers of fortune with convenient jump-leads to the rich Tudor Merchants of London,

> *seeking a bubble reputation*
> *Even in the cannon's mouth.*

Is it now that Piers first cuts his teeth as an Elizbethan hero, a pirate of the Queen?

An enemy galleon looms ahead through the exotic heat-haze, swarming with Arabian cut-throats terrorising the African coast for slaves and plunder.

Captain Koet yells his orders as thunderous cannon-fire blasts the enemy. He leaps aboard leading the charge, quickly despatching the pirate chief in a bloody swordfight, according to Thomas Prys, as all the lads follow, thrilling to the chase and the kill, seizing the ship and her gleaming treasure.

> *Give way, heave, you water-rats! Hoist the sails, you*
> *gang of thugs!*

1585 THE NETHERLANDS CAMPAIGN WITH THE EARL OF LEICESTER AND SIR PHILIP SIDNEY, THE ELIZABETHAN COURT POET

Two years later Piers is in the thick of things again, accompanying his patron, the Earl of Leicester, the Queen's favourite and quite possibly her lover of some sort, on the Protestant Netherlands Campaign against the invading Catholic Spaniards who are unpopular with the ordinary Dutch people against whom they have committed atrocities of the worst order, as seen in the days of the blood-thirsty Haarlem Engravings. Once again, along goes Thomas Prys, ("*I was in Flanders too,*") eye-witness to the dying Sir Philip Sidney at Zutphen with many other young Welsh professional soldiers, *"a brave hand on a golden sword"* as his poetic source observes. Piers's brother, Will Griffith also serves Elizabeth with Leicester and there is some evidence, Professor John Guy has suggested, of the ship *Grace* in this scenario ferrying troops across the Channel to help the beleaguered Dutch. With his contemporaries as part of the action, Piers would hardly have wanted to be left out, however dangerous the mission.

It is a disaster.

At this point, according to Thomas Prys's unfinished memoir, Piers Griffith *"left off seafaring to buy himself a good education at Oxford."*

1586 MOSTYN HALL, NORTH WALES

Back home the following year, we can imagine the ever-brooding presence of uncle/step-father Thomas Mostyn muttering over his account books, with regard to his rich ward.

> *"Money laid out in the twenty eighth year of the Reign of Elizabeth for my son Pyrs Gruffyth for his journey to Oxford."*
>
> Bangor/Mostyn Manuscript 6476.

In March 1586 as a young gentleman of eighteen, Piers sets off for University College on horseback accompanied by a servant. By December and his return home, his step-father has despatched money to him sixteen times in sums of five shillings to forty-eight shillings and sixpence, totalling £51 17s 10d., an average expense account for the son and heir of a knight of the realm, at least £30,000 by today's reckoning, not ungenerous it would seem – albeit out of Piers's own pot of gold – but his father Sir Rhys would have provided for all these costs, of course. Meanwhile, with ghostly irony, Thomas Mostyn, less control-freak than custodian of the Penrhyn family interests, and now husband of the dead Sir Rhys's widow, would be including the boy's tuition fees, registration, lodging, food, fashionable clothing, horses, servants, and the entertaining of rich, influential friends for getting-on-in-life. Cash is sent periodically to Oxford for Piers by a local *"carrier of Llŷn"*, Caernarvonshire, and when the undergraduate arrives home for Christmas, his step-father gives him a further thirteen shillings and fourpence, with £2 to pay the servant's wages, about £1,000 in today's money, for months of devoted labour. As yet, there is no evidence that Piers gains his degree, nor that he develops any sort of Hamlet-style hang-up about his mother and step-father, but one does wonder.

In meticulous detail, the Mostyn Papers record that Piers is provided with all the rich necessities of a stylish, ambitious young gentleman mingling amongst the élite, 'the smart set' of Oxford and London in a sophisticated academic and courtly milieu. This is vital to avoid ridicule and exclusion:

– *shirts, 16 shillings and eight pence* …
– *a pair of jersey stockings, eight shillings and sixpence* …
– *fustian to make a doublet, twelve shillings and sixpence* …
– *five yards of grosgram to make a cloak at £3, six shillings and eight pence* …
– *lace for the said cloak, six shillings and ninepence* …
– *taffeta hat, ten shillings*

… (from fashionable merchants like the Goodmans or the Edwards family in Chester perhaps.)

Total Cost: £9, at least £6,000 in today's money but not an unusual sum for a member of a seriously high-spending 'High Society', even today.

Uncle/step-father Thomas Mostyn seems to be taking his duties seriously, but then, it is he who holds the purse-strings of a fortune rightly belonging to Piers, a young man with a penchant to 'spend, spend, spend'. Life is fragile in Tudor times, so it could be that this particular uncle, as Julia Fox suggests, has already laid his plans for controlling the Penrhyn Estate, should his precious ward perish of the plague in Oxford or London, or even at sea, as many young students did, having survived the perils of Africa and the Netherlands.

Once at Oxford, like his hapless cousin Thomas Salusbury, Piers is lucky not to be drawn into murderous plots, for the young Penrhyn heir is soon immersed in the cauldron of ideas and debates on politics and religion that are part of Renaissance student life, an ideal scenario for the recruiting of daring young men by the lurking espionage network of Sir Francis Walsingham, the Queen's Spymaster.

1586 ALUMNI OXONIENSES

> *Piers Gruffyth of the County of Caernarvon, militis filius, University College, matriculated fifteenth of April, fifteen eighty six, aged seventeen.*

Walsingham's cold-blooded speciality is turning double agents to his own purpose: the personal safety of the Queen and the defence of the realm. Officially he is Her Majesty's Private Secretary, but covertly he is out to destroy any student, priest, crook, messenger or sea captain caught plotting to assassinate the Protestant Elizabeth and restore the Catholic faith by placing Mary Queen of Scots on the throne of England. Think of the sinister fate of so many gifted young men. Think of the mystery of Christopher Marlowe.

In this dark academic underworld of intrigue and brutality, young Thomas Salusbury, Piers's cousin, is preyed upon by the Catholic plotter, Anthony Babington. A devout Catholic boy of good family, Salusbury is incriminated and publicly executed, along with Edward Jones, son of a Ruthin lawyer whose manor-house near Denbigh is raided one night by officers and secret agents of "*spiery*", when the boy is seized and dragged away. Both students fall victims to the far-curling tentacles of Walsingham's octopus-like network from Douai to Salamanca. An unfortunate event indeed, especially for young Edward Jones, an innocent friend and by-stander condemned for merely lending Salusbury his horse and cloak to escape, according to that fascinating old gossip, Sir John Wynn of Gwydir. The Queen's favourite, the Earl of Leicester knew personally the 'misled' *"little Thome Salusbury"* (as his mother, Piers's Aunt Catrin called him) well enough to write on the boy's behalf to his step-father Morys Wynn, protesting against the arranged marriage his parents had in store for the boy. Could Salusbury have had secret plans to become a priest before his involvement with Babington? Consummate torturer Richard Topcliffe and henchman Nicholas Jones certainly had their work cut out, in the butchery of six young men followed by seven hangings, although 'little Thome' is said to have suffered the more 'merciful' death of beheading.

Not surprisingly, Piers now seems to drop out of Oxford (possibly through his connection with some rakish crowd – he knew Henry Cavendish, wild son of that dazzling aristocratic lady, Bess of Hardwicke – *"my bad boy,"* as she famously called him); or with some fashionable Oxford/London street-gang of Leicester's perhaps, schooled in skulduggery and timely watchfulness. Or has Piers here, in company with such firebrands, got wind of another exciting expedition, like Drake's S.A.S. style raid on Cadiz, soon to be notorious for "singeing the King of Spain's beard"?

DRAKE TO SIR WILLIAM CECIL, LORD BURGHLEY, APRIL 2, 1587

> *The wind commands me away. The ship is under sail, God grant that we may so live in this fear, as the enemy may have cause to say that God doth fight for her Majesty as well abroad as at home … for a great store of warlike provision is being made at CADIZ … I sent word to the Marques of Santa Cruz that I was ready to exchange certain bullets with him!*

I entered the harbour where I was assailed by six galleons …

We set fire to five great ships of Biscay taking in the King's provision of victuals for the furnishing of his fleet at Lisbon laden with iron spikes … burnt, sunke and brought away about 1,000 tonnes of shipping.

DRAKE TO SIR FRANCIS WALSINGHAM

The enemy will now seek revenge with all the devices and traps he could devise … stop him now, and stop him forever.

In the tension-mounting run-up to the Armada invasion that is looming on the horizon, Queen Elizabeth and her people are terrified of being murdered in their beds by cut-throat foreign pirates, hooded priest-assassins and the cruel armies of King Philip II of Spain.

1587

In Wales, always vulnerable to attack, we are nowhere near prepared for an invasion, with cannon and powder in short supply. Our coastal defences are poor and we are already suffering that age-old problem of more pirate attacks than we can cope with around our rocky, treacherous shores.

The inhabitants of Lundy Island in the south have been kidnapped, a boy stolen from Nefyn in the north-west during the night, and the people of Holyhead threatened by a villainous gang of escaped jailbirds from the North of England who cheekily kidnap their women and escape to the Orkney islands to get their washing done.

Meanwhile panic is spreading around the Welsh and English coasts towards Penrhyn.

Who will save the day?

1587 MADRID   NOVEMBER
Secret report to King Philip of Spain by an unknown spy based on the Welsh coast:

> *In Wales the captains and soldiers for the defence of Milford Haven have been appointed although no munitions have yet been sent thither, with very little powder. They are afraid to collect a large body of troops in any one part for fear of a revolt … Great difficulties are experienced in carrying through the musters for Carmarthenshire owing to the poverty of the country.*

Meanwhile back in London, on the eve of wartime, Piers is drawn to live dangerously as a man-about-town in company with richer young blades and his daredevil cousin, Thomas Prys, who records their rebellious exploits. They begin spending wildly on an expensive life-style: theatres, taverns, girls, bear-baiting, gambling with dice, cock-fighting, the odd bout of tennis, possibly as part of Leicester's street-gang; then calling in *en passant* at the rich Thames-side residence in Mortlake of Dr Dee, favourite Tutor of the Queen in Science and Mathematics. The same kind of social circle would also be gathering at the grand town-house near Temple Bar of Sir Gelli Meurig, later implicated with other young Welshmen in the Essex Revolt, a house under surveillance, rumoured to be the drop of foreign agents like the home of the French Ambassador in Salisbury Court. In company with other reckless young rakes, and in a curious action-replay of Sir Rhys's former youthful antics, Piers and Thomas now become embroiled in the shady Elizabethan underworld of dockside tavern haunts like the *Mermaid*, or the *Blue Boar* in Holborn, perhaps mixing with the likes of William Shakespeare, Ben Jonson, John Webster, John Chapman, translator of Homer, and the enigmatic Christopher Marlowe:

… home of all the knavery and bawdery in the world, luring you into dens of vice and gambling with faked dice … smoking tobacco … carousing with a tart as boldly as you like, stripping you of all your wealth … swearing and brawling with naked weapons. London is Hell.

Paraphrase of *Uffern yw Llundain* by Thomas Prys.

1588 ARMADA YEAR

From January onwards reports start flooding in from Queen Elizabeth's intelligencers and from Breton and local fishermen down the coast: the great Spanish Armada is on its way. News spreads fast with Piers eager to volunteer for the defence forces, as beacons are lit on headlands throughout England and Wales, if not Scotland.

In South Wales, Sir John Perrot, the Queen's Agent and possibly her half-brother, struggles to spearhead operations with his squadron of ships that will be useful to her later for harrying the enemy. In North Wales, other local heroes like young Captain John Roberts of Anglesey aboard the *Charles*, 70 tons, is recruited into the official Navy and sails south to join his Commander, Lord Howard of Effingham, Admiral of the Fleet.

Meanwhile, cousin Thomas Prys, soldier of fortune with Leicester and many other young bloods, is an eye-witness to the Queen's disputed speech at Tilbury before her defending troops, an event which *did* happen after all, as Prys's Welsh language memoir confirms:

There never was such a lady in Christendom, and she came personally amongst us at Tilbury camp when the Spaniards crossed the sea, in great force to try to invade England in the year of our Lord 1588.

MS 14,872 PRO

And now Captain Piers Griffith, armed to the hilt aboard his re-fitted ship *Grace* with his gallant crew of Bangor lads, laced with that exotic but deadly cocktail of ex-galley slaves, sets sail from his secret creek at Abercegin where Porth Penrhyn is today. *Grace*, an armed pinnace, painted a brilliant azure blue by all accounts, ventures bravely out to sea flanked by cheering crowds, past the Caernarfon Foryd Estuary, over the bar and south-west towards Plymouth to join Sir Francis Drake, Lord Howard and Piers's old associate, Sir Henry Cavendish. Now the huge galleons of the terrifying Spanish fleet are advancing in crescent formation nearer and nearer to the "*sceptred isle*", spearheaded by the magnificently gilded *Reale* of the Duke of Medina Sidonia, reputedly seasick all the way.

The Bangor/Beaumaris Port Books for 1588, annoyingly lost in Time, together with the records for all the Western harbours Piers may have called in along the way, hold no record of *Grace* and Piers, nor do the official naval lists of 34 ships and pinnaces of at least 200 tons. However, it is now suggested amongst maritime experts that "Piers could easily have been one of the 163 or so unrecorded vessels of about 40 tons pouring in from far and wide, brave little ships to support the main naval force …

"So we think it's quite possible that he could have joined Sir Henry Cavendish, as the Thomas and Williams source says," adds Nigel Overton, Maritime Heritage Officer at Plymouth, "or else a squadron of the ships ordered by the Queen to harry the remnants of shipwrecked Spanish sailors around the stormy coasts of Ireland, Wales and South West England, once the Autumn gales set in,"

> … *thereafter to keep constant vigilance against the enemy abroad.*

Piers Griffith is once again where the action is.

1590-1600
Urgent missions by Drake and others to and from the Caribbean, challenging Spanish domination of the gold and silver treasure-fields of South America, not to mention the vast pearl fisheries around Puerto Rico. At home we are under threat of a second Armada attack.

1595 Despatch sent with the *Pelican* from the West Indies

> *Tell the Queen and Sir Roger Williams that we have been victorious in every chase, wherever her Grace's enemies were ... Off the coast of Spain, the Enemy's old country, we harried his ships as a hawk harries crows and chickens. Then we sailed to Porto Santo, burnt the city and spoiled the land ...*
>
> *... In Jamaica, the Derling, wherein was Captain Jones sent to discover some secret matter, in which discovery the gallant gentleman lost his life ...*
>
> *... In Cuba we fell in with Raleigh returning from Trinidad and from thence sailed to Newfoundland.*
>
> *... On the 10th of September 1595 we dropped anchor at Milford Haven.*

Such riveting events strangely echo a sixteenth century Welsh sailors' ballad by one Lieutenant Peilin of the *Pelican*, Drake's ship before being re-named *The Golden Hind*. The name of Piers Griffith is not included amongst the others listed in the poem as sailing with the Lieutenant and Captain Billings; but this may not be significant, for he may well have been aboard another ship, more likely a pinnace, for messaging or supplying purposes. In any case, Drake was well known for sending tactically diversionary ships in different directions in order to mislead the Spaniards, on some dangerous *"secret matter"*.

Piers himself is fully aware of the hardships of a seafarer's life, as he writes poetically to his fellow adventurer, Thomas Prys: *"the cold, the wet, the risks"*, a curious foreshadowing of Drake's Last Voyage, along with the stalking presence of ruin and death.

Popular amongst his crew, always standing up for the underdog, Piers Griffith's fame as a daring adventurer with his *"familiar laughing face"* spreads amongst the busy local harbours around the Western coast of Britain and exotic seaports abroad. Like other privateers so adored by Queen Elizabeth, his roving life goes with a licence to kill and spy.

After the euphoria of deflecting the Armada threat, (blighted by the death of the Queen's favourite, the Earl of Leicester, and the shocking sight of hungry, unpaid sailors dying in dockland streets), Piers's absences from home become longer and longer throughout the 1590s, much to the distress of his wife Margaret. By now she is *"sad and ill and growing cold-hearted"* towards him, as family friend and poet-priest Sir Huw Roberts appeals to him in *Ode to the South Wind*.

Could Piers be busy throwing himself vigorously into planning his next daring expedition? Often he seems to be away for three or four years at a time. Where is he? What is he up to? Perhaps in his obsessive quest for treasure and glory he is so caught up in the spirit of the age, of voyaging, discovery, adventure and defence of the realm, that he is willing to risk all he has, financially and personally, challenging *"outrageous Fortune"*. This imprint of the 'Hamlet Generation' leaves its mark on Piers, boy and man.

Clearly he is determined not to be left behind.

1595 – 1597 Drake's Last Voyage

Documentary evidence in other Welsh poems (see later) points to Piers's part in this ill-starred secret expedition to the Caribbean, to Santo Domingo, Puerto Rico and Cartagena, with all those famous horrors of wading through foreign swamps, suffering blood-curdling attacks by Spaniards and 'savages', leading to that devastating loss of life so typical of the tragic side of raw adventure.

Captain Thomas Maynarde, one of the many volunteers willing like Piers to follow his hero Drake to the ends of the earth, wrote the following account of a confrontational scene with Sir Francis, now desperate to revive the Queen's lost favour:

> *Here died many of our men …*
> *us to adventure for their glory. I asked, 'why sir?'*
> *He answered, 'It matters not, man. To give her Majesty*
> *good service and make us rich. We must see gold before*
> *we see England'.*

Dysentery, the dreaded *"fluxe of the bellie"*, soon breaks out amongst the sailors, weak from malnutrition. Five hundred men die, are tossed overboard and washed up on beaches. Drake himself now falls fatally ill. Drake's drum is brought back without its master to a desolate reception in Plymouth. Piers the messenger, aboard his pinnace *Grace* or another vessel, we may rely upon it, plays a crucial part in this scenario of shocking news.

Captain Thomas Maynarde records the death of Sir Francis Drake, the great explorer so far from home:

> *He died of the fluxe six leagues to sea and now rests with*
> *the Lord.*

A year later in 1597, William Shakespeare's *The Tempest*, dramatises graphic scenes of shipwreck in authentic, eye-witness terms:

> *Scene One: On a ship at sea; a tempestuous noise of*
> *thunder and lightning heard …*
> *Boatswain: Down with the topmast. Yare, lower, lower!*

Bring her to try wi' th' maincourse ... A plague upon this
howling! ... Yet again! ... Shall we give o 'er, and drown?
Have you a mind to sink?

Throughout this decade of adventure in the 1590s, young
Captain Griffith starts taking out mortgages, we notice, as
soon as he inherits his estate in 1591 at the age of twenty one.
In one transaction for instance, he is clearly trying to regularise
rent arrears amongst his tenants for the support of his wife and
growing family, possibly while he is away on long 'secret' voyages
risking life, limb, and capital. The changing fortunes of Piers
Griffith, at home and abroad, become subject to the same vagaries
of the Tudor and Jacobean economies that force many other
members of the gentry and the nobility to take out mortgages
on land and property from wealthy middle-class merchants of
the provinces with footholds in London and fingers in the pie of
piracy. These city moguls have ready money, like the Goodmans,
Middletons, Trevors and others busy in the dynamic hotbed of
high finance: Welsh, Venetian, Jewish, Armenian, Dutch and
other international bankers around Cheapside, Westminster Hall
and the Royal Exchange.

Now friends like Thomas Prys and Sir Huw Roberts urge Piers
to leave the sea altogether and attend to his estate, fast falling into
rack and ruin.

MESSAGE TO PIERS GRIFFITH FROM THOMAS PRYS, URGING HIM TO GIVE UP SEAFARING C. 1599

To a Dolphin

Go on a journey from Menai ...
towards Lisbon ...
and swim then a while
towards Spain, heart of the world.

Swim as if it were a chase,
You are such a spirited adventurer …

Seek at the water's edge
… a warrior
Pyrs Gruffyth …
… of pure, clean heart.

… Six years! How weary I am since he went abroad
by ship to the seas beyond the Voryd, over the bar and
across the world.

Who could resist?

Where is the Pirate? There are clues here, detected even in paraphrase translation. Nor can his absence simply be explained by hints at "Ladies of Spain" or "rich courtesans in London", as has been suggested, still less by a romantic figure like the former Jane Dormer who married a prominent courtier to Philip II and became the powerful widow Juana Suárez de Figueroa, Duquesa de Feria. At her house in Madrid and her fortified palace in Zafra, this influential lady lived in exile until 1612 with "an unceasing network of conspiracy and espionage amongst supporters of the Emperor, supporters of the Pope, exiled Catholics and agents of Queen Elizabeth's spymasters," as Christopher Howse wrote cryptically in the *Daily Telegraph* (*Sacred Mysteries*, 15 September 2012.) The Duquesa's trusted household servant until her death was Henry Clifford. Was he anything to do with George Clifford who happened to be the third Earl of Cumberland, a possible associate of Piers Griffith?

The Penrhyn Pirate's own poetry, when closely examined for evidence, is fragmentary to say the least; but what we do have gives us a rare, tantalising glimpse into the personal thoughts of an Elizabethan Adventurer.

Here he replies to companion verses by Thomas Prys urging him to abandon his pirate life and return home, or else *"all will be lost"*:

Pirates at Plymouth

Piers Griffith: Why do I do it?
The thrill of the chase,
the freedom, the adventure, the risk,
the promise of riches!

Then there is the beauty of the sea
in all its magical moods
despite the storms and icy weather,
plunging half-drowned, soaking wet ...
Yes, it is a painful choice to make, love of the sea
or love of a woman.

But all is not lost. Piers the risk-taker still has another card to play

1600

The Menai Strait, North Wales. A hidden creek in Penrhyn waters
Piers Griffith's great stunt now is to bring the Spanish galleon, *Esperanza of Ayamonte*, into his private hideaway at Bangor, Port of Beaumaris, loaded with treasure to be inspected by officers of the Admiralty, doubtless to the consternation of crowds of astounded onlookers along the foreshore of Abercegin Creek: young and old, family, friends, servants, tenants, townspeople, traders, clerics, paupers:

> *... a Spanish treasure ship loaded with olive oil, silks, spices and earthenware which he captured in the West Indies.*

The *Esperanza of Ayamonte*, from the heart of the Spanish ship-building industry, is a fine galleon built from the rich woodlands of Doña Aña, wife to the Duke of Medina Sidonia, commander of the terrifying Armada of 1588. This is a prize indeed for Piers and his crew, gained not without blood-loss, daring, nor cruelty, not to mention sheer sadism as victims choked to death or were swallowed into the chill fathoms of the sea. A prize fit for the delight of the Queen herself, *"our Elspeth", "our lady"* as Welsh poets call her. A prize too, symbolising for Piers his own individual trophy, his rebellion against Old Penrhyn, his triumphal breaking-free from the shackles of family tradition rooted in the old-fashioned Age of Chivalry with all its pageantry, honour and social responsibility staying close-to-home, to re-forge instead his own individuality on a fortune-hunting trail as a recognised star of the new Age of Piracy.

The Queen may well have favoured the Welsh at court and Piers may have his feet comfortably in both camps (sophisticated London society and traditional country community) but there are still those who mock and disparage his countrymen for their strange garb, language and ways. Now Piers can impress. His fame spreads at home and abroad until he becomes an international celebrity, feared, respected, adored, missed, *"a notable pirate"*.

But at the very pinnacle of his success, the sands beneath Piers's feet are shifting. The tide is turning on the changing fortunes of Piers Griffith.

1599 – 1601 THE ESSEX REVOLT
Mostyn Harbour, North Wales

Piers is to have another close shave with death at the time of this furore: events surrounding the power-hungry Robert Devereux, Earl of Essex, a rebellion spreading from Ireland, through North Wales, and on to London, less against the Queen herself than against her advisers and hangers-on. Lord Essex is the adopted (and possibly the 'natural') son of the late Earl of Leicester and like him, the Queen's favourite. Now ageing and vulnerable, she is pinning her hopes on the dashing young lord for settling once and for all the 'troublesome Irish'.

In 1599 the fleet of Lord Essex and his retinue lies at anchor in

Mostyn waters, strategically placed in the dazzling sea-light of the coast for embarkation to Ireland.

The ambitious hero with his entourage and rumbustious army are lavishly entertained at nearby Mostyn Hall to a memorable feast by Piers's mother, Lady Catherine Griffith Mostyn and by her estranged husband Thomas, who is now flattered to receive secret sealed letters from Her Majesty and be dubbed a Knight of the Realm by Essex on the Queen's behalf, an occasion celebrated in Welsh poetry of the time, amidst the oak-panelled splendour and crested mullioned windows of the Hall. Such random dubbings are soon to prickle and irritate the Queen.

On his return two years later in 1601, Essex makes other unwise miscalculations, following his disastrous Irish expedition and an uneasy peace treaty with the Earl of Tyrone, unauthorised by his Sovereign.

Beleaguered and war-weary with his desperate soldiers, he lands back in Wales, at Mostyn possibly, but soon moves on to Chester as the report of his hell-bent ride from there to London confirms. Whether Essex allows himself the respite of a sleep-over at Mostyn or not, he is reputedly as hot-footed as can be on his hard day's ride to that dreaded bed-chamber confrontation with the Queen in London that looms ahead of him, so immortalised on screen by Bette Davis and Errol Flynn (1939) and by Helen Mirren (2005.) We know he will soon lose his head, along with that notorious fellow-adventurer Sir Gelli Meurig, hero of Cadiz, another mate of Piers (who may be ferrying troops to and fro across the Irish sea, including his brother Will Griffith, cousin Thomas Prys and friend Ifan Llwyd Sieffre, all known to have served in Ireland from time to time, along with other young sons of the Welsh gentry now being busily recruited into the Essex Revolt.)

There is not a shred of evidence that the Mostyns are involved in this attempted *coup d'état* – to the contrary, as Elizabethan court poet Siôn Tudur confirms in his verse to his patron, the newly knighted Sir Thomas Mostyn. The absolute loyalty to the Crown of Piers's powerful father-in-law is renowned, indeed relied upon, the poet says, in order to secure favours for Wales from *"our Elspeth"/ "our girl"*. There is also Sir Thomas's affinity with the son of his old friend Burghley, the now powerful Secretary, Sir Robert Cecil, a political animal already on the scent of another agenda, courting Scotland and Spain during the last worrying days of Good Queen Bess, as some Welsh poems suggest. Piers should know. His cousin John Owen is one of former Spymaster Walsingham's secretaries, in other words a "keeper of secrets" who has probably stayed on in the service of Robert Cecil too.

Meanwhile, as for Piers, he is more likely to be winging his way to foreign parts by now, because he swears at his arrest in Cork two years later in 1603 that he has been *"near three years out of* [the] *country"*. But if he *is* allied to Essex, he is now plunging headlong into the perilous turmoil of the Queen's displeasure. Another secret agent of Essex at this time is Thomas Phelippes, the codebreaker who once worked for Walsingham, like Uncle Hugh Griffith. Bearing in mind the constant conflict between Essex and Cecil, the plot thickens.

When Essex is executed on his return to London in 1601, the remnants of this audacious raft of rebel officers, as documented, are let off with heavy fines when the Queen relents, distressed and ageing as she is. And when it is brought to her notice that they are but the misled sons of respectable and loyal North Wales gentry, some known to her personally, she soon lets the boys out of jail, as Professor A.H. Dodd has attested.

1603 THE STUART COURT IN LONDON

It has been a miserable winter and by the turn of the year the Queen is dead.

As soon as *"Elspeth, our lady"* is no more, and King James I, VI of Scotland is on the throne with Sir Robert Cecil running the country, both men are keen to make peace with Spain putting a complete ban on piracy, as they will later assure the Spanish Ambassador in London by 1616, Don Diego Sarmiento de Acuña, Count of Gondomar, who is out for Piers's blood.

H.M.S. Tramontana under sail from Cork to London, on the orders of Sir Robert Cecil

Naval account by Captain Charles Plessington, February the 22nd, 1603:

At my last being at court my Lord Cecil commanded me to haste away with my ship from Bristol to Cork to arrest there Captain Pierce Griffith, a notable pirate ... I have examined him concerning the goods taken by him in the ship, most of which were sold and made away with before my coming. The remainder is not worth more than £1,000 at the most. There was a rumour of great sums of money in her when she was taken, but all he will confess is that some of his company in breaking up chests got some forty pounds, which was shared among them, yet says he thinks that there may be money in her, which will not be found before she is unladen. It is not likely, for the flyboat has been near three years out of her country, as appears by her cockets and bills of laiding, and by letters written in Dutch directed to be delivered in Hamburg. Many of them are sealed, and I propose to send them up to his Lordship.

... The goods now in the ship are oils, ginger, logwood and shoemaking leathers, the first much damaged by leakage and the ginger nearly rotten ...

Marine archaeologist Dr Cecil Jones of the University of Wales, Bangor, and maritime historian Aled Eames, have always considered that evidence amongst their diving fraternity points to gun-running and even to Piers's role as a double agent.

Significantly, the arrest by Plessington takes place soon after the Essex Revolt in London and the Rebellion of the Earl of Tyrone in Ireland, with a history of English atrocities by the armies of Essex and Leicester before him, putting to the sword hosts of bedraggled, piteous rebels. Eyewitnesses like poets Thomas Prys and Ifan Llwyd Sieffre are shocked to see starving, skeletal men, women and children crawling desperately out of wild woods on to the barren wastes of merciless, wind-blasted heathland.

Curiously at Cork that day, in the very same place and at the very same time, Captain Plessington has just captured another prize: the ship of Captain Griffith's famous associate, lady pirate Grace O'Malley who is masterminding a protection racket from her coastal fastness, Rockfleet Castle.

The Queen's Private Secretary, Sir Robert Cecil (surviving son of Sir William Cecil, the late Lord Burghley) is now also head of the Secret Service after Walsingham dies in 1590 and an equally nasty piece of work. The family have strong Welsh roots (the Seisyll family anglicised their name to the posher 'Cecil') but Piers can expect no favours there, despite his toadying cousin John Owen, who may even have betrayed him. (Thomas Prys's "Woodcock" poem is full of mysterious innuendo. See later.)

Could Piers be involved in gun-running via Ireland here? This was an age-old practice of the Penrhyn lords according to family tradition, admits Edmond Douglas Pennant M.Litt., a younger son. And could Captain Griffith, as has been suggested, be acting as a paid spy/intelligencer/courier in the service of the Crown? A *"Mr Griffith"* is mentioned several times in State Papers, but this may be Uncle Hugh Griffith according to Aled Eames.

Meanwhile Grace O'Malley, after sharing Piers's fate, flees with the help of her bodyguards to continue her escapades around the Irish Coast as chieftain of her clan, making herself at home again in

Rockfleet despite an overbearing husband and brother, for whom she once risked all to save their rebellious necks on a daring visit to Queen Elizabeth in London, when the two ladies apparently conversed together in Latin.

Now, after Elizabeth's death, and when other pirates are being lynched on cliff tops or imprisoned, Piers has to pay a punishing fine to buy a pardon from King James I and surrender some of his lands to Lord Grey at a loss of about £500,000 a year by today's prices.

Griffith's risky bid for vast fortunes from *"across the world"* have not paid off.

In the new reign of James I, Piers is now an illegal operator, a criminal.

Can the legitimate side of his family business in coastal trading save the day? Hardly. Consider his options: the possible development of the rich mineral, gold and slate reserves of his large Snowdonia estate, like the coal, copper and lead exporting industries of Mostyn, Cilcain and Halkyn, as his shrewd lawyer brother-in-law, Sir Roger Mostyn has succeeded in doing on his Flintshire estate. (There were grinding coal-mines within sight of the front door at Mostyn Hall.)

Or more likely, perhaps Piers considers investing abroad like other Merchant Adventurers in Jamaica or Barbados, fast developing into the modern age as exploitable territories, if only they can be seized from the grip of the Spaniards.

The Penrhyn lord, always reluctant to raise rents and upset tenants, might never have been content to live simply in the manner of the reformed Thomas Prys up in the crags of Snowdonia. It is not in Piers's character to settle down and retire to the life of a country squire like cousin Thomas with his *"beloved horses and hunting dogs"*. So why not just aim for better estate management, as Richard Thomas, Land Agent to the present Lord Mostyn has usefully suggested. Develop the fruitful agriculture and fisheries of Penrhyn. Breed cattle, or sheep for the profitable European meat and wool markets. Write his memoirs.

LONDON, 26 JUNE, 1610

There is worse to come: the sudden tragic death of Piers's son and heir. William Griffith, aged 20 is down from 'Hart Hall', Oxford, possibly for the royal ceremonial induction of Prince James as Prince of Wales and heir to the throne of his father, King James I. Crowded London in June is rife with heat, filth, flies and disease, notably an outbreak of 'the sweats' which can attack in the morning and kill by the afternoon. The previous year, 1609 has been a Plague Year.

Death creeps in through the window of William's lodging house in St. Giles that day.

"Evil struck down the heir of Penrhyn" wrote Thomas Prys in an anguished elegy to his own son and heir, Ellis, who died with William Griffith, *"a shared loss"*, *"a shocking stab of pain"* that would change the lives of their inter-related families forever.

1610 – THOMAS PRYS TO PIERS GRIFFITH
Elegy upon the death of our two sons in London, during a short summer vacation after Oxford.

> *Both our fine young heirs have lost their fragile lives,*
> *in one shock horror before they have begun.*
> *Side by side in the dark night*
> *like two ashen-faced angels lying in the same grave.*
> *Sons, you both died the same morning*
> *and went to Heaven,*
> *two promising young men, twenty years old,*
> *faithful in friendship,*
> *in the year of our Lord, son of Mary,*
> *Sixteen hundred and ten.*

(G.L. Paraphrase Translation.)

Later, in his verse and in his memoir, Thomas Prys is to record again and again the echoes of his contempt for city life:

London – … home of all the knavery and bawdery in the world … swearing and brawling with naked weapons. London is Hell. Uffern yw Llundain.

It is a view shared by many country-people throughout the land, including a group of stricken poets, courtier Siôn Tudur for one, so troubled by this event that they hasten to Penrhyn to comfort Piers's wife, Margaret Griffith and her daughters then immediately put pen to paper, mourning such a widespread tragedy.

For Piers, who is only too familiar with this dark Jacobean world, tragedy and anguish are to persist, searingly and ruinously. The death of his only son and heir marks the inevitable end of his estate, of his inheritance still hanging by a thread, signalling the beginning of his descent into a desperate spiral of loss, both economic and personal.

And his marriage is on the rocks.

❧

Piers's own private sphere has always been troubled. It may be said that he escapes or is sent away to a life on the high seas in an obsessive quest for riches, after being married off at 14, reluctantly perhaps but it seems it has to be done in such times. This wedlock of children is a property-driven deal sealed in with the double-fix marriage of his parents, as we have seen. Margaret Mostyn is a catch, a virginal heiress of the aristocratic recusant Catholic Mostyn family (on the noble side) and of the rich Goodmans, Tudor Merchants of Chester (on the trade side.) She has her uses. Now she steps forward from the shadows as a real person. The Pirate's Wife begins complaining to confidant/confessor and priest

Sir Huw Roberts, of Piers's frequent absences at sea, as shown in *Ode to the South Wind*. This mood back home peaks around the 1590s, at the very time Captain Griffith is away albeit in the service of the Queen, until, beset by mounting debts, greedy in-laws and the tragic deaths of infant sons Rhys and Robert, Margaret almost despairs. Then there is the premature loss in 1610 of heir William and further obstacles like Piers's feud with Sir Edward Herbert, Earl of Powys, in a tenuous, indeed illegal claim on Penrhyn lands through Herbert's wife, a Griffith kinswoman. There follows the Duelling Episode of 1612 (see later.) One way or another, all these tortuous pathways of Piers's life will lead to prison, debt and exile.

By 1616 the seemingly abandoned Pirate's Wife separates from Piers on the orders of her father, Sir Thomas Mostyn on pain of losing her allowance by the terms of his Will of that year, on condition she separates from *"Piers Griffith and all his troubles"*. Now in his dotage, Sir Thomas Mostyn has long been separated from Lady Catherine, and grumbling for years that his wife's son, the Pirate, quite puts him off his food, *"so that he can scarce take time to eat his meat quietly."* (Manuscript NLW 9054/584)

Around 1616-18 Margaret Griffith removes herself from draughty old Penrhyn Castle, bag and baggage with her five remaining daughters, Dorothy Edwards, Ursula Lloyd, Elizabeth Humphreys, Jane Salusbury and Grace Bromhall. These surviving girls are now settled in marriage to young men of the prosperous gentry in the Welsh Border Country between Chester, Wrexham and Shrewsbury, where the sisters and their mother will live on as neighbours until after the Civil War.

Author Dr Dafydd Wyn Wiliam of Bangor University and an expert on Welsh manuscripts comments as to why, after the deaths of Piers's patrons, Drake, Leicester and the Queen – and especially after the death of his son William in June 1610 and the execution of Raleigh by King James I on October 29, 1618 – "life was never the same again for Piers. In my view, he squandered his estate, relinquished his inherited traditions, and abandoned his wife and family, yet he was a unique individual, a true Renaissance man."

The key to the adventurer's mysterious, elusive life may lie in the secret files of Sir Francis Walsingham and Sir Robert Cecil, not to mention the Vatican, or in endless Muster Books. It is Cecil who, influenced by James I and his good friend the Spanish Ambassador, Don Diego Sarmiento de Acuña, Count of Gondomar, outlaws piracy as a treasonable capital offence, relentlessly pursuing the likes of Piers Griffith in an effort to keep peace in Europe, raise legitimate port taxes and heavily fine offenders or worse – with all the horrors of the age: Tower, rack and thumbscrew. Indeed, had it not been for the probable string-pulling of Piers's rich, ambitious Machiavellian cousin (later Archbishop) John Williams, Lord Keeper of the Privy Seal and manipulative close companion of King James I, Piers too might well have lost his head in Palace Yard that day.

Safer by far, cousin Thomas Prys advises in his unfinished memoir, *'The History of the World in My Time'* and in his poem, *'Counsel to my son'* (bearing a subversive similarity to Raleigh's work), is the wisdom of abandoning the sea and living a gentleman's life in the country, no more to experience that sinking feeling of *"Farewell England, and dry sand"*. It is curious how the fate of Piers Griffith mirrors that of their joint mentor, Sir Walter Raleigh who is executed in 1618 partly for treason, partly for attacking Spaniards in South America, after his failed mission to find El Dorado, which is the reason greedy King James released him from the Tower on parole two years previously. Meanwhile Raleigh too has lost his son, Wat, on the same expedition. Piers's heir, William Griffith never gets that far. Did Captain Griffith accompany Raleigh at this point? The hefty mortgages recorded in the Penrhyn Papers at this period, 1612-1616, are plainly for some desperate purpose, possibly for keeping in the King's good books by funding and investing in another such venture.

Both Piers and Raleigh fall foul of royal favour in the new Stuart Age. Both, inevitably, have experienced long absences from their wives, but Bess Raleigh, businesswoman and supportively impassioned letter-writer, seems to fare better as a 'woman alone', before her path is to cross with Piers's, this time through that enigmatic money-lender and courtier, the Earl of Pembroke, kinsman of our pirate's old duelling rival for Penrhyn lands, Sir Edward Herbert of Powys Castle, Welsh-speaking magnate and diplomat abroad, thus sealing the fate of Piers's inheritance for ever.

Is it possible that Herbert, a shrewd and calculating man, is starting to eye Piers Griffith as a useful sort of intelligencer, a vulnerably 'stoney-broke' ex-privateer, yet with good contacts in Ireland, the Netherlands, Portugal and France, countries Griffith still probably trades with, from Porth Penrhyn to Hamburg, La Rochelle, Galicia and Lisbon? The evidence of Sir Huw Roberts suggests that Piers is an

> *Ambassador of southern courts.*

Thomas Prys says his friend

> *served as an eloquent ambassador for his country,*

but several times warns him that

> *the day will come when you are sure to get arrested as a spy.*

1603 ... 1610 ... 1612 ... 1616 ... 1623 ...
A LITANY OF LAWSUITS

Inexplicably, Piers disappears from the records from time to time, leaving a mysterious trail of clues, intrigues and bad debts: family feuds and lawsuits, the Fleet prison, Ludlow Castle, Ireland, The Netherlands, the Port of London. Is he falling prey to human weakness and changing times, or is he so heavily enmeshed in the Robert Cecil espionage web that he is forced to sell useful information for money? Secret intelligence that has since been shredded … Now a note of desperation creeps into his miserable litany of lawsuits and he starts using various aliases:

Peter Griffith, Perys Griffith, Pierce Gruffydd, Peers Gruffyth.

Who was the real man?

Is someone else signing on his behalf? His lawyer, his brother or his wife perhaps.

The pressure mounts from a continuing list of debtors:

15 December 1598
Deed of mortgage by Piers Griffith of Penrhyn to Richard Gwynn Archdeacon of Bangor upon lands in Maenol and Gwyrhyddion; a consideration of £100; final term of redemption …

1 August, 1610
… Coed Howell Isa and Gweirglodd Newydd in Cororion to Robert and William Bateman of London.

30 December, 1612
… Cariadog, … Moelyci [and again the two properties above] *… to Robert and William Bateman of London.*

12 September, 1614
Moelyci [as above] *and Bodfeurig in Cororion … to Henry Rowlands Bishop of Bangor.*

5 August, 1616
[Five properties mortgaged] *… to Henry Pierce of Dublin.*

15 August, 1600
… to Thomas Middleton of London upon Coed y Parc in Cororion … a consideration of £400 … to be redeemed by 24 August, 1601.

> **29 October, 1601**
> *… Piers Griffith of Kyllgerraint in Cororion … to Piers Mostyn of Talacre* [his maternal kinsman acting as surety for him with three others] *… a deed of mortgage to Thomas Middleton for a consideration of £800 …*

Piers is now relentlessly pursued in lawsuits by grand families like the Bagnalls of Plasnewydd and Ireland, and by the Herberts of Powys Castle, cases he deftly overturns:

> **1609-1610**
> *Proceedings … in the Council in the Marches of Wales between Sir Edward Herbert of Montgomery, Knight, Dame Marie Herbert his wife, and Sir Arthur Bagnall of Plas Newyth, in the county of Anglesey, plaintiffs and Pieres Gruffiths, esquire …*

On and on it all goes, again and again, at head-spinning speed:

> **18 June, 1610**
> *INFORMATION by Peeres Griffith against Sir Edward Harbert, Knight, Dame Mary his wife, Arthur Bagnall esquire, Sir John Savadge, Sir Richard Trevor, Knight, Richard Predderch, Hugh Lewis, esquire, and other in the Court of Wards and Liveries …*

⁕

Piers's pressured life, his melancholy mood on a cold winter's day just before Christmas, are implicit in his letter from Ludlow Lawcourt, probably dating from this troubled period of litigation and looming penury:

LETTER BY PIERS GRIFFITH TO AN UNKNOWN PATRON

Ludlow Castle

20 December [year?]

Worthy Sir,

… Your good entertainment was like to cost me my life, I was never well, hence I have kept to my chamber this month, sick, and surgery hath cost me twenty nobles … It shall be a warning to me all the days of my life …

I must entreat you to give commandment that my poor horse may be taken up and put in the stable for three weeks that he may be able to carry me to Ludlow again … being over bold to trouble your worship.

I crave pardon with remembrance of my duty and services to yourself and with hopes of happiness and all good fortune may happen unto you and so I rest ever

Yours if not his own

Piers Gruffyth

(PFA/1/556/Penrhyn Castle Further Additional MSS./ Bangor University.)

Who can he be, this *"Worthy Sir"*? Someone Griffith wants to placate, keep on the right side of, we suppose. Cousin John Williams perhaps, a man who soon becomes Lord Keeper of the Privy Seal, the future Archbishop of Lincoln then of York, and Dean of Westminster. Or possibly a high-placed judge of the court like Sir William Jones of Castellmarch, of smuggling fame. Lord Bulkeley of Baron Hill might be another contender, or even the Earl of Pembroke, but wild guesses lead nowhere. Still surviving amongst the Penrhyn papers, the Pirate's Letter may well have been meant for John Williams, the new powerful owner-to-be of the Penrhyn Estate.

Around 1616, documents in the Powys, Baron Hill and Penrhyn Papers record Piers as living at his sister Alys's house, Cilgeraint near Tregarth on the outlying lands of the Penrhyn Estate, but it is not clear whether she is still alive. He is troubled too by simmering conflicts with his brother William and other relatives – those disagreeable Tudor monarchy dogsbodies like the Pulestons, the social climbing Bagnalls, not to mention the omnipresent Mostyns in clashes with his father-in-law, the overbearing Sir Thomas.

Yet Piers has the loyalty of his friends. These include his London Griffith family and soldiers-of-fortune/poets Ifan Llwyd Sieffre and Hugh Middleton who, on scrutiny, are both seen to witness several documents on Piers's behalf. This time, it is Hugh who supports him in court, as the Penrhyn Papers record:

COURT OF CHANCERY, LONDON

22nd of October 1616
Sir Thomas Mostyn, Plaintiff.
Piers Griffith and Hugh Myddleton, defendants

Piers Griffith is brought to court in charge of the warden of the Fleet Prison; difficulties over payment of his daughters' marriage portions, seeing that most of his lands are either sold or are under mortgage; he is ordered to perform his accredited agreements to pay them, Sir Thomas Mostyn being grandfather to the aforesaid daughters.

Piers now suffers the ultimate humiliation of imprisonment for debt. The malice and persecution of his step-father know no bounds, even from beyond the grave. For it is Sir Thomas Mostyn who puts Piers in prison, who brings the case against him for non-payment of his seven daughters' dowries, for failing to reach the correct marriage settlements due to young ladies of their class. This lawsuit, slapped down on Piers just before Sir Thomas's death in 1616, smacks typically of a disagreeable someone determined to blacken a victim's name. The Mostyns are a wealthy family and

Margaret is an heiress in her own right with the means to bail out her husband from time to time. There is no evidence that Piers is *never* going to fail his beloved daughters (to the contrary, as far as the surviving ones are concerned) nor to blacken his own name in the process. Viewed from a modern perspective, why make the relationship with his wife any worse than it already is, or than Sir Thomas would like to make it seem in the eyes of their acquaintance?

So lawyer son-and-heir Roger Mostyn, Piers's brother-in-law, is now sent to Penrhyn to sort it all out: a man who has himself incurred his father's displeasure by marrying Mari Wyn of Gwydir against Sir Thomas's wishes, thus daring to link the heraldic lion of Mostyn with the eagle of the Conwy valley. As a lawyer, Roger is a man well used to untying his father's legal entanglements and fractious quarrels with others all over North Wales; his surviving elder brother Thomas has by now been largely disinherited and is mysteriously treated as "*incompetent*".

⁏❧⁏

Eventually, Widow Margaret's later Lawsuit of 1643 and her Will of 1648 are to show that there is money still owing to herself and her remaining three daughters, payment that has still not been honoured by her two Mostyn brothers. So Piers cannot be blamed for everything.

Or may we infer from this that up to Piers's death in London in 1628, Margaret and/or at least one of her daughters has broken the ban on a reconciliation with Piers, as laid down in Sir Thomas Mostyn's proven Will of 1618?

Scanning the Penrhyn and Mostyn Papers, also the Welsh Port Books from 1568 to 1623 when Piers Griffith finally sells out, it is clear that many of his financial dealings are with ships' traders in Conwy, Beaumaris, Caernarfon, Chester, Dublin and London.

> *Three hogsheads of beer,*
> *twenty four hundredweight of bisket bread,*
> *four barrels of hardware,*
> *five hundredweight of iron, two half-barrels of salt.*

But the biggest debts of all are to those great merchants of the City of London who bankroll the Captain, led by the Lord Mayor, the Welsh–speaking Thomas Middleton, Director of the East India Company and himself heavily into privateering, ironically one of Piers's rich friends, operating from Westcheape, the financial heart of the City, as several bonds reveal, for example to the well-known financiers, the Batemans.

Other mortgages raised to clear debts are on Penrhyn estate property fallen into decay through rent arrears, more by the odd troublesome cleric of Bangor Diocese than the poorer tenants whose future Piers secures even when he winds up his affairs. Other crippling costs seem to be a relentless array of family feuds with distant relatives by marriage like the rapaciously rich Sir Edward Herbert of Powys Castle, his deadly enemy with whose servant Griffith fights a duel outside the court-house inn '*of Dafydd ap Cadwaladr*' in Caernarfon in 1612. Ex-pirate he may be, but one who is still smarting from the death of his son and heir in "*hellish London*" only two years before.

The last straw, some say, is when Piers (in debt this time to Sir John Conway, Richard Bulkeley of Porthamel and four others) has to sell his horses, a fine stable of the best breeds of the time, fleet-footed and glossy-coated.

Does Piers have a gambling problem? Privateering is essentially a gamble, a risk, and Thomas Prys more than once records their days together at the London gaming tables with "*dice … and the wheel of fortune*". Gambling can be addictive, like treasure-hunting, the obsession of a driven man. He is not the only one. This is an age of adventure when gambling is rife, whether aboard ship, in manor-houses or taverns, in Wales or at the *Flask* or the *Spaniards* in Highgate, key-points on journeys to and from the country.

By 1618, the Pirate's Wife, Margaret Griffith is nowhere to be seen within the accursed environs of Penrhyn Castle. Three sons from amongst their ten children are dead: William, Robert and Rhys. Daughters Margaret and Catherine survive long enough to marry after 1616; but five remaining daughters, Dorothy Edwards, Elizabeth Humphreys, Jane Salusbury, Ursula Lloyd and Grace Bromhall live on, marry well and produce for Piers and Margaret several surviving grandchildren between them. Margaret will spend her remaining years first at Northwood Hall, near Wem in Shropshire, the home of her daughter Grace and husband William, the squire of the estate and commander of the guard at the Court of King Charles I and Queen Henrietta. Margaret the Pirate's Wife will end her days at Erbistock, possibly at the home of astute business-woman daughter Dorothy, prosperous widow of William Edwards; both are rich merchants and property owners of Wrexham and Chester.

Margaret Mostyn Griffith's proven Will of 1648 suggests that she too is left comfortably off, cared for by her loyal Welsh cousins Jane and Thomas Ellis and by her maidservant Mary Bently, leaving generous legacies to her daughters and grandchildren at today's reckoning, in money and silverware (perhaps once part of the splendid Mostyn Silver Collection now on display at the National Museum of Wales in Cardiff.) By the Restoration of Charles II in 1660, both Dorothy (dies 1670) and Grace (dies 1680) are prosperous enough to leave plentiful sums of money and gifts to their daughters, sons-in-law and grandchildren like *"Magdalen ... for her education"*, as seen in Grace Bromhall's Will and in her remarkable list of goods and chattels from Northwood Hall, providing a fascinating insight into the domestic and agricultural life of a seventeenth century woman.

Jane marries into the Salusbury family of Denbighshire gentry fame; Elizabeth marries a John Humphreys, possibly a cleric or a lawyer; and Ursula marries into the Lloyds, prosperous lawyers, landowners, merchants and industrial investors in North Wales. Elder brother William, the last male heir of Penrhyn has died of 'the plague' in 1610 and their two small brothers, Robert and Rhys do not survive beyond childhood, but the daughters remain. Three of them survive the Civil War, like their mother.

⁕

Released from the Fleet Prison by 1617, Piers meanwhile has had time to think. Realistically he will cut his losses. Will he stash something away before his debtors pounce?

"He would be mad not to", is a suggestion from the business world. Why not launder money while he is about it for the benefit of his daughters, with the possibility of grandchildren, if not for his estranged wife's sake and his own?

His poetic friends testify to his *"good heart"*, and *"generous spirit,"* his *"entrepreneurial skills"* and *"happy, laughing face"*. Why believe ill of him?

In retrospect could it be that many of Piers's debts, on closer scrutiny, are not all for "pirate fines" as has been noted, but rather to raise ready cash in the manner of most people of the era, and to equip his expensive expeditions, like Raleigh, who has also lost his fortune by now, not to mention his head? In Tudor and Stuart times it cost at least £250,000 in today's money to equip, crew and provision a ship, often with disappointing return profits.

Is Piers actually bankrupt?

Clearly unwilling to name his brother William and his offspring as the next male heirs thereby inheriting everything 'for free', he becomes in documents *"Piers Griffith of London"*. The once rich domain of Penrhyn, land of poets and princes, is now signed away from his grasp. He sells out to his rich cousin, the future Archbishop John Williams, a personal favourite of King James and Lord Keeper of the Privy Seal, in a curious deal financed by the Earl of Pembroke, busy-body money-lender and patron of Shakespeare.

The deed is done:

> **Indenture, March 1, 1623,**
> *Lord Keeper of the Privy Seal Dr John Williams an additional £1,000 (after the consideration of £9,000) for Penrhyn and all its appurtenances.*

1620 – 1628
"Piers Griffith of London"

In London, he is leading a gentleman's life amongst good companions – other ageing adventurer poets like Hugh Middleton and Ifan Llwyd Sieffre certainly, if not literary celebrities like dramatists Ben Jonson and John Chapman who are of the same social circle as John Williams and the Earl of Pembroke. Piers and his friends are doubtless frequenting taverns and theatres; he is visiting his Griffith family, even John Williams in his Deansgate cloisters; as an ex-privateer, Piers is possibly still *"serving as an eloquent ambassador for his country … respected at home and abroad"*, according to Thomas Prys.

Piers Griffith, high-living privateer, spy, gun-runner, lover, duellist, adventurer, the bane of the Spanish fleet, dies on August 18, 1628 aged fifty-nine and is buried on the twenty-first, a month before his sixtieth birthday on September 25. Retirement age certainly for a pirate, especially one of the old freebooting, outdated kind.

It is more likely than not that Piers *does* continue to see at least some of his daughters during his last years, if not his wife; it is possible that the family somehow finds a way around the ban imposed by Sir Thomas's Will. 'Blood is thicker than water' and the clues linked to Grace, one of his youngest daughters born about 1600 and the namesake of his ship, are interesting, knowing that her husband John, heir to a Shropshire estate, commands the guard at the Royal Court in London.

Young King Charles I has by now succeeded his father James who dies on March 27, 1625. As Grace and John Bromhall probably marry around 1620, it is not impossible for this particular daughter to have attended Court too, thereby being in a position to see her father in London before he dies in 1628. Her aunt, her mother's elder Mostyn sister, Lady Catherine Hanmer is lady-in-waiting to Queen Henrietta Maria while husband Sir Thomas Hanmer is a courtier at the royal palaces. Grace's husband dies intestate in 1643 but there is a *"John Bromhall gent.,"* possibly a relative, who leaves *"estates in Barbados"* amongst other riches in 1653, a prosperous London merchant with a country estate in Northwich, Cheshire (which is near Wem in Shropshire where Grace and John have lived at Northwood Hall.) Is there a connection? There is also a *"John Bromhall gent.,"* agent of a London Trading Company who bequeathes houses in Venice and Zante including *"many gold coins"*, which he leaves to his *"Blackamoor"* slave-girl in 1680.

May we also speculate that Piers Griffith, in company with other Merchant Adventurers on raids in foreign parts, has already secretly staked out land abroad for investment, with entitlement to deeds which he may have passed on to Grace and John Bromhall, together with a few pearls? In 1643 she certainly signs her name using a wax seal clearly embossed with a galleon, as do her mother Margaret, sister Elizabeth and elder sister Dorothy, in their claim against cousins Roger and Thomas Mostyn, as recorded in the Mostyn Papers. Is this Piers's ring lovingly retained as a keepsake?

This also begs the question whether Captain Griffith ever returns again to Penrhyn. It would take a brave man indeed to grit his teeth and revisit his old lands, his people and lost heritage, under the changed ownership of John Williams to whom he has by now entrusted the security of his tenants. It is to Piers's credit that all these individuals are meticulously listed with their farms and cottages, all named at length in the Penrhyn Rent Rolls but the new owner might have insisted on this. It has long been Piers's custom to keep rents low; he may or may not have taken a proportion of produce but there was little profit to be had in agriculture except for exported wool and cattle, as John Williams famously bemoans later.

Piers's lawcase with Sir Edward Herbert also reflects his concern for his tenants whose loyalty he seems confident he can keep. He insists for instance, on keeping the Ogwen river rights and the Menai Strait fishing weir at Gorad-y-Gyt (still well-known locally today) for the use of 'the people', according to ancient custom; his brother William's Cororion Estate is safeguarded too, together with the remains of Piers's own hideaway at Abercegin Farm still detectable amongst later renovations in Porth Penrhyn, perhaps as a foothold for himself in the new era of maritime merchant trading rather than as an illegal pirate's power-base. The allied practice of smuggling is to persist for about another two hundred years around his uncle Hugh Griffith's cove at Porth Ysgaden on the Cefnamwlch estate, where Piers's sea-faring career once began under the aegis of East India Company foundations, established in the golden age of Queen Elizabeth.

There is a record of a ship called *Grace* sold at auction in company with other vessels in the 1650s for a new Holyhead passenger-ferry service to Ireland. Old ships conjure up old mysteries …

One local poet crystallises the bereft feelings of those left behind after Piers Griffith's departure, in a manuscript found amongst the papers of W. Williams, Llandegai, author and land-agent to Lord Penrhyn; the writer's identity is a mystery, but the verse is also quoted in English in the travel-guide of Richard Fenton:

Cold and bare he saw the Penrhyn
The foreshore and Abercegin
Ever since the Captain Gruffydd
Went overseas to plunder countries.

The verse of Thomas Prys also describes the loss of his dearest friend, in a tone of personal melancholy and longing/*hiraeth* for Piers, and for all the adventures of their youth:

We two risked death in the salty searoads of the South
Never doubting we would return here to land.

⁕

The Penrhyn estate now passes into unexpected hands, via administrators or trustees, who hold the entire property, castle and lands. Debtors are dealt with and dismissed. When examined, this may seem a complex deal. Is there a whiff of money-laundering here? The Earl of Pembroke, of the antagonistic Powys family and a notorious money-lender, takes centre stage as a mutual friend of both King James I and Archbishop John Williams, Keeper of the Privy Seal,Dean of Westminster until he falls from favour after Charles I succeeds to the throne in 1625. One suspects it is the Earl who lends Piers's cousin John Williams the initial deposit of £1,000 for the future purchase of the Penrhyn estate when funds allow, as Piers's inheritance has been valued at £10,000 by 1620, a sum equal to billions today. So Penrhyn passes for a time to the Earl of Pembroke, in name only, and it seems that John Williams is soon able to find the remaining balance of £9,000 in order to buy the entire estate in 1622/23 for "*Penrhyn and all its appurtenances*".

Perhaps Williams's close companion, King James himself has had a hand in some of this.

By 1628 Piers Griffith is dead, buried in Westminster Abbey courtesy of the Dean, his rich cousin, a younger son of the lesser estate of Cochwillan and now the new master of the Pirate's ancient domain.

As the sun sets on the Age of Piracy, Piers has been lucky to hang on to his secret hideaway at Abercegin Creek, a quay-side farmhouse where his name is still rumoured to be faintly seen carved in stone dated 1589, a fading signature that continues to fascinate, like those evocative names highlighting his lost adventures ...

Cadiz, Santiago de Leon, Hispaniola, La Rochelle, The Azores, St Jean de Luz ...

❧

The legend of Piers Griffith has lived long after him around the coves, creeks and harbours of North Wales, persisting to the present day.

He sailed with Raleigh and Drake ... and Cavendish too, despite the hardships and perils of the voyage ... records the memoir of his old friend Thomas Prys, whose superb Elegy to Piers Griffith seems to be the last word on the Pirate of Penrhyn:

Icy and leaden in life
I feel a sharp cold pain like steel in my heart,
A wound ...

Rich cousin John Williams, who possibly officiates at that sombre cathedral service in London, may after all, have reluctantly admired if not envied his spendthrift, daring kinsman. Add to this the open hero-worship by Piers's London nephew, William Griffith, bodyguard to James I and Charles I, and Piers's loyal follower who arranged to be buried near his *"valiant uncle"* in 1637. Nephew William's own wife, Margaret, Piers's niece-by-marriage, is also buried there, at nearby St Margaret's in 1634 as recorded in Henry Keepe's 1683 book on the Abbey Inscriptions. The Pirate's Wife, Margaret Mostyn Griffith is probably buried at Erbistock, Flintshire; their daughter, Dorothy Edwards at Wrexham Parish Church; their son and heir William Griffith at St Giles-in-the-Fields with Ellis, the eldest son of Thomas Prys.

The quest for Piers Griffith, Pirate of Penrhyn has been a unique journey. A rogue perhaps? *"Tipyn o dderyn"* was a suggestion, *"a bit of a bird"*, a charming one nevertheless. Those close to him remember him as a swashbuckling hero, a wit, a poet, a generous master of noble blood. We may recall his passionate affinity with the sea, his courage and daring in company with the finest merchant adventurers of the land, a free spirit who always manages to elude his enemies.

He leaves behind his manuscript signatures and personal seals, his verse and his letter, his castle turret with its winding staircase, his pirate's creek and exotic sea-chest.

He now lies in honour at Westminster Abbey, in good company at Poets' Corner and near to Henry Tudor's Chapel, a special place his forefathers would surely have known. The mind muses impossibly on the horrors of excavating Piers Griffith. "His bones are under there all right," says Archivist Christine Reynolds. The exact situation is the broad aisle on the South side of the Nave near the door to the West Cloister, within a whisker of contemporaries like Ben Jonson (died 1637) who had several Welsh friends. Sadly someone thought fit to remove Piers Griffith's engraved memorial stone some time after Henry Keepe described it in such lamenting detail in 1683, three years after the death of Piers's daughter Grace.

Piers did not die alone. He would have been buried with his London Griffith family in attendance amidst the candle-lit choral

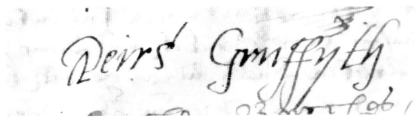

Signature of Piers Griffith, aged 14.

Personal Seal of Piers Griffith of Penrhyn.

William Griffith I (Fychan c.1420-83) and his first wife, Alice Dalton. Sir Roland de Velville (died 1535) and his wife, Lady Alys née Griffith may also be buried here, at Llandegai Church.

© Royal Commission for Ancient Monuments in Wales.

The Field of the Cloth of Gold, June 7, 1520, after Hans Holbein the Elder (1460/5 – 1524) by Friedrick Bouterwek (1806-67). Versailles/Giraudon. Bridgeman.

The Engagement between the English Fleet and the Spanish Armada in Crescent Formation off the Start Point near Plymouth 1588 (engraving), English School, Brown University Library, Rhode Island, USA. Bridgeman.

Armada 1588, The Battle of Gravelines, possibly by Nicholas Hilliard (1547-1619), showing the Spanish leading vessel, the Reale.

Queen Elizabeth I (1533-1603), the Armada portrait c.1588, English School.

Arms of Sir Francis Drake aboard the *Revenge*. Wikimedia Commons.

The launching of the English fireships on the Spanish fleet off Calais, on the night of August 7, 1588, Flemish School c.1605.

Portrait of Sir Francis Drake c.1583, Anglo-French School.

Private Collection.
Photo: Philip Mould Ltd, London.

Sir Walter Raleigh (1554-1618) 1588, English School.

Private Collection.

Robert Dudley, Earl of Leicester c.1560-65. Attributed to Steven van der Meulen.

© Wallace Collection, London. Bridgeman.

Sir Richard Hawkins (c.1562-1622) in armour, 1588.

© National Maritime Museum, Greenwich.

The Golden Hind in the Pacific Ocean, an imaginative view by Jean-Leon Huens (1921-82).

Piers Griffith's Pirate Chest, attributed to Spanish/South American provenance of the 16th century.

The family of Henry VIII : An allegory of the Tudor Succession by Lucas de Heere (c.1570)

Sir Francis Walsingham (c.1532-90) from Lodge's British Portraits 1823, engraving. English School, 19th century.

John Owen, private secretary to Walsingham and possibly to Robert Cecil, *"a keeper of secrets"*, kinsman of Piers.

Smugglers' cove at Porth Ysgaden near Cefnamwlch, Llŷn Peninsula.

Pirate islands, Ynys yr Wylan Fawr & Ynys yr Wylan Fach off Aberdaron, near Ynys Enlli.

© Photo: Marian Griffith.

Thomas Prys, pirate-poet (c.1565-1632). Artist Unknown c.1605.

Signature of Thomas Prys on the manuscript of his poem, *Cywydd i yrru y Llamhidydd / To a Dolphin*.

MS HR 142 Cefn Coch MS. A. The National Archives.

Robert Devereux, 2nd Earl of Essex (1566-1601), favourite of Queen Elizabeth I, by William Segar, 1590.

splendour of the Abbey with its aura of ethereal valediction and ceremony:

> *Here lyeth the body of Peeres Gruffith Esquire, sonne &*
> *heire to Sr. Ree. Gruffyth & grandchild to Sir William*
> *Gruffyth chamberlaine of North-wales, who dyed the 18*
> *of Aug. 1628.*

The Griffith family crest once headed this fine inscription on the now lost gravestone with all its heraldic symbols of ancestry and tradition.

> *Gules, a chevron ermine between three old mens heads*
> *coped proper, their periwigs or"* which was quartered
> with eight other coats-of-arms ...

Finally, if you care to embark on such quests, you may still hurry down to the Pirate's lair in Porth Penrhyn to catch a glimpse of that elusive hero haunting the misty quayside, only to find that once again, he has slipped away mysteriously on the evening tide.

II

A Pirate's Life
in Poetry

Highlighted scenes from
Welsh poems in translation,
dedicated to Piers Griffith
and his family

1400 – 1628

Note

Here, every poem tells a story. Without any attempt to establish a scholarly text, the paraphrase translations of verse in this work are meant only to convey the essence of meaning. The rich metrical and allusive complexity of the original verse is impossible to convey accurately. Any errors here and elsewhere in the narrative are entirely my own.

Part I gives only the broad outline of Piers Griffith's story. Part II provides more specific details, mainly from the poetry of the sixteenth and seventeenth centuries.

Chapter 1

From the Age of Chivalry
to the Age of Piracy

THE LION OF GWYNEDD AND THE WOLF OF BRITTANY

C.1500 Old Penrhyn Castle

The bright flags of two jousting knights blaze with the heraldry of two dynasties in the summer sunlight. They charge at each other with their lances as their horses gallop and snort over the grassy turf, their chivalric top-coats embroidered with armorial symbols shifting like turbulent beasts under the muscular movements of each fearless steed. The colours of Penrhyn are displayed in red, green, yellow, blue, white and gold to emphasise the *"blood-red clawed lions"* of Sir William Griffith, the Pirate's ancestor on one side, and the stark military black and white background of the Wolf of Brittany on the opposing side for Sir Roland de Velville, Sir William's brother-in-law and reputedly the 'natural' son of Henry Tudor before he became King Henry VII.

The crowds at the lists gasp and wonder at this high-point of the summer, the clashing of Titans as two noble knights, accoutred in the steely cruelty of their armour with their swords biting into their jewelled scabbards loudly jangling at their sides from their fearsomely buckled belts, remind the onlookers of the daring deeds of each opponent: Sir William's *"bloody red sword"* fresh from the French Wars and Sir Roland's crafted blade that has recently seen service, like his lance, toppling the *"virtuous Prince"* Henry in a fair fight and in good, raucous fun it is said, to general acclaim at the Royal Lists.

Here at Old Penrhyn, both knights have reputations to live up to and they are brothers-in-law. The scene is set on an expanse of green pasture skirting the glittering Menai Strait and the Celtic sea across to the Isle of Anglesey in the north. To the south is the magnificent back-drop of craggy mountains and cloud-edged Snowdonia peaks, as the two riders charge and re-charge each other in a battery of blows that send shudders through the spectators, startling the deer in the distance.

Today, *"all Gwynedd "* high and low, as poet Dafydd Alaw reports, are attending this festival of jousting, to see in the flesh the new challenger, the Wolf of Brittany who once trounced their young prince Henry, son of Henry Tudor, whose Anglesey kinsmen are amongst the most eager in the crowd. Lady Agnes de Velville shudders too, both for her husband and her brother, as she sits next to her sister-in-law Lady Jane Griffith with their guests and attendants, both ladies decoratively positioned to display their richly exquisite gowns and head-dresses beneath the shade of their private pavilion, decked in colourful tassels and flowers of the field.

There is feasting to follow, food for all in plenty, with great outpourings of wine and milk and light beer or cider for the children, sword-fighting with wooden weapons and make-do sticks, some in velvet and fine Irish linen, others in coarse cloth, tenants' children or schoolboy sons of Bangor and Beaumaris merchants and sea-captains, ragamuffins and rat-bitten guttersnipes rescued from the stinking slums of nearby towns or the abysmal flea-infested poverty of country hovels with collapsing thatched roofs and mouldering walls. Today everyone is outdoors and thankful for the beneficence of the *"chivalrous"* Sir William and his *"fine lady"*.

꧁꧂

Who wins? We never learn the outcome of this Penrhyn joust but perhaps a gamely balance of power is sustained and soon there will be a new challenge from across the Menai Strait, over there on the green fields around Beaumaris Castle before the summer is out, only a boat-ride away.

Lady Agnes de Velville of Penrhyn and Beaumaris, will be pleased to welcome *"all Gwynedd"* and doubtless *"all Mona"* too, for more sport in the *"genial presence"* of her husband. Sir Roland is *"Constable of Beaumaris Castle"*, as he will be recorded in documents like his Will of 1533 and with more personal detail in his 1535 Elegy by Dafydd Alaw, probably the best, indeed the only poetic obituary the *"Wolf of Brittany"* and his *"grieving, superbly black-and-gold-dressed"* lady could leave to us.

In this rare manuscript source, the same poet describes in realistic detail how the corpse of Sir Roland de Velville is taken from Beaumaris Castle to *"the funeral bier of the Breton knight ... house of St. Francis ... of the good brothers"* at Llanfaes. Meanwhile his youngish widow, Lady Agnes (Piers's great-aunt) is observed wearing that superb *"black and gold braided gown"* and *"it is sad"* for her companions seeing her join

> *the funeral procession almost fainting*
> *As we see them all pass by under their black hooded*
> *cloaks.*
> [Lines 63-66]

Dafydd Alaw reports on how Anglesey is bereft of *"its most generous lord ..."*, with his *"triumphant trumpet-calls"* and *"chronicle"*, with his *"Arthurian power"* and famous *"battle-cry ... against the fortresses of France"* .

[lines 74–78, Ms. A-B 3106, 230b]

Sir Roland is buried in Llanfaes in the same grave as Lady Agnes's Penrhyn kinsman, Gwilym Gruffydd "Fychan" c. 1420-83 and his wife, Lady Alice Dalton, or even possibly Gwenllian, Gwilym's mistress, later his second wife, daughter of the nobleman Iorwerth ap Dafydd. Agnes died some years after her husband, Sir Roland de Velville and it is now thought that she also may be buried within the tomb of this 'double sarcophagus' that was moved sometime in the past over the water to the Penrhyn Parish Church of Llandegai, where it now lies for all to see on the right of the main door at the rear of the nave.

Originally Roland and Agnes were both buried, he preceding her, at the Monastery Church of Llanfaes, near Beaumaris. They were in good and bad company, status-wise. The Black Book of Basingwerk Abbey, according to the erudite Victorian feminist, Angharad Llwyd, recorded that "in 1280, the Princess Eleanor was buried here *'yn anrhydeddis iawn'* with royal pomp and honours. Here too were interred 'several of King Edward's leading warriors slaine in the action of Menai', also … Gryffydd Grûg, the bard … 1330 to 1370 … an able opponent of Dafydd ap Gwilym …" Buried too, the Llwyd source says tantalisingly, was "The Lord Clifford."

The Will of Sir Roland de Velville, proved by Archbishop Cranmer in 1533, leaves £8 to the friars of Llanfaes to celebrate mass for his soul. He was *"squire of the bodye to Henry VIII"*, implying he was a close friend of the king. Also the poetic evidence that in youth he once toppled Henry at the jousts, does not suggest that the *"virtuous prince"* did anything but take such triumph in good part, but another view is that, as King, he later suffered some of his notorious health problems as a result of this early sports injury. And there remains that fascinating rumour about Sir Roland being the illegitimate son of a French lady and the young Henry Tudor, later King Henry VII, and therefore the king's half-brother.

"I Sir Roland Velville, constable of Beaumaris Castle, Knighte & c. My wille is to bee buried in the monastery of Llanvaes …". He also left money for *"the Chapel of the blessed Mary att Beaumaris"*, the Monastery of Friars at Bangor, *"the Church of St. Eistyn"* at

Llanddona, "… *6s. 8d.*" to the *"fabric of the Bangor Cathedralle, 6s. 8d. the same to the Church of St. Tegvan"* at Llandegfan, *"and to Agnes, my wife, all the lands, burgages, fines, houses, & c. lying in Beaumaris. The residue of my goodes I leave to my wife Agnes Gryffydd, alias Velville, who, I alsoe appointe sole executrix. Dated to the place of my habitation, the Castel of Beaumares …"*

Lady Agnes, a daughter of Penrhyn, great-aunt of Piers, was thus left with the grand town-house of Cwrt Mawr just off the main street of Beaumaris. Another property amongst the *"lands, burgages, fines, houses"* left to Lady Agnes was probably the de Velville summer residence at Hafoty, set in the picturesque landscape of Llanddona, now restored and open to the public with its superbly carved and crested stone fireplace, after being excavated by the Commission for Ancient Monuments when my children, nephews and I were shown the remains of a delightful walled garden and the curiosity of a newly discovered rat's skull, which pleased them.

So now Sir Roland and probably his wife Lady Agnes rest in magnificent, cool tranquillity at the Parish Church of Llandegai in a marble tomb together with Sir William Griffith and his wife. But which wife? The remarkably life-like stone figures of the Griffith couple seem transfixed in some timeless moment. Surrounding them, poignantly etched around the bed-like structure on which they lie and chiselled by the best craftsmen from their Age of Chivalry, are enchanting little carvings of their many children, all angelically posed in devout prayer.

Interestingly, one of the surviving de Velville children grew up to be the mother of the celebrated beauty, Catrin of Berain near Denbigh (died 1591), kinswoman to Queen Elizabeth I and recognised as such, a guest at her Coronation in 1558. If one may fast-forward again on two more points here: first, Catrin's favourite husband was Sir Richard Clough, a rich Merchant of London and the Low Countries working within the trading and espionage network of Thomas Gresham, the English financier. Gresham proposed currency reforms in 1558 founded on the principle of 'Gresham's Law', that 'bad money' drives 'good money' out of circulation, a trading assumption Piers Griffith must have been aware of, yet pressed on regardless forty years later in the 1590s. Second, another shadow cast here across the Griffith story is the link in Piers's ancestry back to Lady Agnes, a trail leading again to her grand-daughter Catrin whose first husband – she was widowed three times – was Thomas Salusbury of Llewenni. It was their tragic son, Piers's cousin who was executed for his supposed role in the Babington Plot of 1586, uncovered by the Queen's secretary Sir Francis Walsingham, head of the security services.

Back in the chivalric days of the Breton Wolf (Velville) and the Lion of Gwynedd (Griffith) during the reigns of King Henry VII and King Henry VIII, the inter-marrying gentry of Gwynedd would have included not only ruling families linked to Penrhyn in the old 'two Gwynedds', east and west of the river Conwy, but also the cream of Anglesey high society: the related Bagnalls of Plasnewydd and Ireland, the Bulkeleys of Porthamal and Baron Hill, and the Hamptons of Henllys. If we look ahead to the time of Henry's son, the boy-king Edward VI, these ruling families of North Wales would have been represented by their sheriffs from amongst other factions like the Lewises of Presaddfed, originally a medieval manor estate, and the family of nobleman Dafydd ap Rhys ap Dafydd ap Gwilym of Llwydiarth, both groups being traditionally the patrons of poets. Then, progressing into the Elizabethan Age of Piers Griffith, we see other dominant families becoming well-established in North Wales through land and maritime trade, socially linked to Piers's circle, like the Old Faenol family and the gentry of Anglesey who were marrying in from their manor-farms at Bodeon, Bodlew, Trefarthen, Maes-y-Porth, Cichle and Penmynydd, as the Penrhyn Papers and other documents attest. Others pursued bitter feuds amongst themselves and more relevantly here, with Piers, the pirate/privateer: the Bagnalls, the

Mostyns and finally the Herberts, who were constantly stretching their resentful hands over to Penrhyn lands from Mid-Wales and Pembrokeshire, by way of a mixed bag of heiresses in a hotch-potch of claims with not a legal leg to stand on, which is why Piers's hotly defended law-suits eventually end in that dramatic Duel of 1612 in a Caernarfon back-street.

This élite of powerful and wealth-driven families owe their promotion to the success of their hero and kinsman Henry Tudor at the Battle of Bosworth Field in 1485. They were duly rewarded for supporting him. This event was to be the springboard to eminence for Piers Griffith and his family.

ARTHURIAN LEGEND

The Battle of Bosworth, 1485, was given legendary status by the spin and PR image-makers of Henry Tudor, Earl of Richmond, when he became king and keen to establish his own dynasty. Bosworth has rich associations of visual imagery, with symbols of heraldry, dragons, white and red roses, and the political theme of valiant knights fighting for the good King Henry against the 'evil' Richard III, usurper and murderer of the little Princes in the Tower. The same year, the chivalrous world of King Arthur and the Knights of the Round Table (as popularised by Sir Thomas Malory's "*Morte d'Arthur*" and published by Caxton in 1485), was again brought to life by firing the popular imagination with the strategic pageantry of the Tudor Court in London. In Wales this also signified rewarding Henry's loyal supporters. In the Border Country at Ludlow Castle there was the spectacle of the complete re-enactment of Camelot in 1501/2. This was a romantic occasion when Henry VII made sure that his heir to the throne, Prince Arthur, the Prince of Wales (now married to another teenager, Catherine of Aragon in a political marriage with Spain), established his mini-court' providing more career opportunities for Welshmen at this administrative and legal centre in the Marches or Border Country.

These carefully orchestrated events by a monarch anxious to legislate, establish his position, spread culture, bring peace to the war-torn kingdom, expand trade and fund voyages of exploration also included wisely marrying Elizabeth, daughter of Edward IV, thus uniting the Yorkists and Lancastrians; and yes, Henry VII announced, 'wicked uncle' Richard III *did* murder the little Princes in the Tower after all. On September 19, 1486 Henry's heir Arthur was born and created Duke of Cornwall. In 1487 Henry established the Court of the Star Chamber. His daughter Margaret (destined to marry, again politically, King James IV of Scotland in 1502 at the age of 13) was born in 1489 and Arthur was made Prince of Wales. In 1491, amidst troubles in Scotland, Ireland, France and Spain, not to mention the treacherous upstart claimants so feared by King Henry VII (the impostors Lambert Simnel and Perkin Warbeck), the future Henry VIII was born at Greenwich Palace. In 1496, when Margaret's sister Mary Tudor was born (a girl later forced to marry old King Louis XII of France although she was in love with Charles Brandon, Duke of Suffolk), the King founded Jesus College. Significantly, Oxford became the destiny of so many Welsh students including Piers Griffith, Thomas Prys and their sons.

Henry VII was also patron of John Cabot in one of the first official voyages of discovery leading to the development of the Newfoundland Fisheries, where ships from Bangor, Port of Beaumaris, even possibly Piers himself, were later to trade. Henry VII's reign, besides his encouraging of the wool trade in the Netherlands and the awarding of a new charter in 1505 to the Merchant Adventurers in a monopoly of English cloth, also saw a blossoming of patronage for music and the arts, particularly verse, with Welsh poets eager to comment on the current scene and entertain at Court, a dynastic sponsorship which King Henry VIII and King Henry VII's grand-daughter Queen Elizabeth I continued after him, from the Age of Chivalry to the Age of Piracy.

In 1501 there were hopes of securing diplomatic links with Spain by Prince Arthur's teenage marriage to Catherine of Aragon (both partners were about seventeen years old), daughter of the powerful 'Catholic Kings' Ferdinand and Isabella of Castile; but Henry Tudor's hopes for the strategically planned marriages of all his children were dashed at the death in 1502 of Prince Arthur (1486-1502.) The court poet Rhys Nanmor wrote a haunting elegy on this occasion to comfort King Henry VII who understood and possibly spoke some Welsh from his boyhood days in hiding at Raglan Castle under the protection of his uncle, Jasper Tudor. Something of a control-freak given to temper and depression, Henry VII then had Arthur's eleven year old brother Prince Henry moved forward like a chess figure into the board-game of Royal marriages, in an alliance to the same vulnerable foreign princess who was so far from home, Catherine of Aragon; but the engagement was broken off in 1505 only to be set up again later and formalised into marriage in June 1509 following Henry Tudor's death in April, with fateful consequences when Henry VIII was later to find excuses for breaking with Rome. But now his youthful marriage to his dead brother's widow was being outrageously celebrated by the seventeen year old new King Henry VIII and Queen Catherine "with feasting, dancing and general rejoicing". Then followed a magnificent Coronation at Westminster a fortnight later "to sullen, quiet crowds", wrote David Starkey, an occasion when the grandparents of Piers Griffith may have been present, Sir William Griffith III and his wife, Lady Jane née Stradling.)

Following Henry Tudor's well-laid dynastic plans for his children, his heir King Henry VIII was never to find the one perfect loving marriage that David Starkey says he sought; Catholic Catherine was eventually rejected and divorced in her middle age having failed to give him a son, only a daughter: 'Bloody' Mary, a Catholic whose marriage to Philip II of Spain later brought all hell to pay with the Armada. Henry VIII's four-year passionate courtship of Anne Boleyn, overshadowed by religious controversy, wars in Ireland and Scotland and Haley's Comet in 1531 caused universal panic and reached the point of a secret low-key marriage in Whitehall in 1533 when Anne was already pregnant with Elizabeth I. Henry VIII's 1534 Act of Supremacy asserted his control over the English Church, cutting age-old ties with Rome. His first Act of Succession secured the Throne for the heirs of King Henry and his Queen. Henry had Anne Boleyn's head cut off three years later for adultery (on more or less trumped-up charges concocted in less than a month, mindful of her tendency to indiscretion and her unwise crossing of swords with Thomas Cromwell.) Such talk would have reached Penrhyn of course and interestingly, an anonymous Welsh poem of the era does suggest that Henry became tortured by post-execution guilt and remorse. Their small daughter Elizabeth was only three years old at the time, labelled a bastard unfit for the throne, forbidden to speak of her mother thereafter and did not dare do so until well after her father's death. Yet she was to become the great Queen of the Golden Age in the time of Piers Griffith, the Age of Piracy. Before that however, there were more violent dramas to come: the young 'Lady' Elizabeth got on endearingly with Protestant boy-king brother Edward VI, but was ruthlessly imprisoned in the Tower by her big sister, the Catholic Queen Mary ('Bloody Mary') who specialised in bonfiring her victims; one of the few things the sisters had in common was that they had seen their father's uneasy marriages come and go. Then there was the tragedy of Lady Jane Grey, a distant cousin and barely more than a child when she was beheaded only two weeks after a power-hungry faction led by the Duke of Northumberland declared her Queen (i.e. their puppet figure-head.)

Once on the throne at last in 1558, "our girl … our Elspeth" as the Welsh poets called her, could be sure of the support of families like the Griffiths of Penrhyn, the Mostyns and the Bulkeleys who all visited her Court and held offices there from time to time, as she changed from girl to woman to old lady through the lives of Sir William, Sir Rhys and Piers. She had long surpassed the day when she must have come to terms with the true facts of her tyrant father's reign. No wonder she wanted to make amends, the 'woman's way'; but Julia Fox is of the view that Elizabeth "could not care less about the dying Armada sailors. She was indecisive. She drove her ministers mad. She had the language of a fish-wife. She boxed people's ears and threw her shoes." Here was the telling reality beneath the pomp and glittering splendour of all those jewel-encrusted costumes. At Court, there were observant foreign ambassadors, the entertainment of musicians, dancers and singers, a Queen suspicious of romantic intrigues around her, threats of treachery and assassination by poison or dagger, amidst the spectacular glamour of Gloriana.

This was the Elizabethan milieu of Shakespeare's generation with which Piers Griffith was familiar, a young man keen to gain the Queen's favour when she herself was as excited by the New Learning and the adventurous international explorations of her glorious reign as she was by the boldness of privateering, of risking and gambling money, lives and ships.

This was Piers Griffith's piratical Tudor inheritance derived from the tumult of his chivalric Bosworth ancestors.

BRAVE LORD OF THE BLOOD RED SWORD

Yet back in the fifteenth century, when the poet Rhys Goch Eryri wrote that tongue-in-cheek, opening tribute to Sir William Griffith II, great-grandfather of Piers, quoted in the Prologue, he was writing for a captive audience who already knew the score, and who shared satirical jokes, praise and contemporary references alike. So it was not all boot-licking. Intended for party performance at Penrhyn during and after the lifetime of the subject (Sir William) this poem would have been, literally, music to the ears of an invited cross-section of society, a cultured but not élitist audience, well-used not only to the social function of Welsh poetic traditions, even to the point of criticising the lord, but also to the sounds of richly intricate alliterative and allusive verse. What kind of people would have enjoyed this? Lawyers, poets, shopkeepers, ladies of the house, children, farmers, even the poor at the door; soldiers, sailors, craftsmen, gentry and nobility would all have absorbed this kind of entertainment in their own way over a good dinner (or the scraps) and plenty to drink. The poem may be said to represent one of the last echoes of a mead-hall community:

> *There is opposite Anglesey*
> *A fortress of oak that favours minstrels,*
> *a house, …*
> *Of white stone-work the colour of a swan,*
> *A dwelling-place that is a hundred times better as regards*
> *The wood and the excellence of its construction,*
> *… than the sad*
> *Greystone Tower of the Eagle, seat of anger.*
>
> *… for the sake of God's Son do not hide*
> *Its ambry and its chapel*
> *Smoking incense within its walls*
> *Fine, great, sweet frankincense, myrrh and wax,*
> *Which strangers or wandering minstrels can smell,*
> *On its pavement from every chimney.*
>
> *Better by far*
> *Is the proud white court, …*
> *Of Gwilym, …*
> *The Golden, than the Eagle Tower.*
> *The* (Penrhyn) *bastion, built within three hours,*
> *Many-sided, thick-walled, turreted and huge,*

Which was built by plumbline,
A wrathful attempt to confine a man
And to subdue with intent
The hearts and napes of men.
The impressive thick-walled great house
Of the son of Gruffudd, brave lord of the red sword,
Brings happiness every hour.
And dignity to every minstrel.
If one dared ...
... to compare
The court of God on high ...
... with an earthly court.
The appearance of Gwilym's court ...
Is more like ...
The cloister of God than the court of man.

(Trans. W. Williams & R. Davies, Bangor MS Uncatalogued 1211;

NLW 19075E, 1769.)

An array of poets also celebrated the Griffith family in verse from the 1400s to the early 1500s and in another link to Tudor royalty, Cynwrig ap Dafydd wrote to Sir William,

Thou art a shield upon the Castle of Harry
Thou art the Sovereign's hand ...
... the golden eagle of Snowdon.

c.1500

Owain ap Llywelyn ab y Moel praised Sir William for his hospitality,

Below stairs from the hall-table is the spacious cellar,
whose fair capacious floor could
admit wine-trading ships.

White wine in plenty is brought …
The three upper rooms
Are fit for an earl to live in.

c.1450

At the same time Gwilym ap Sefnyn compared Penrhyn to

the Courts of King Arthur and Charlemagne.

Lewis Môn reported poetically:

There is a room warm and spacious; the velvet is broader than the floor. There are a hundred beds. Under its wall is the fume of wax and red wine. Your kitchen is equal to that of an earl. There is a large dish of the colour of gold. There are cups and caps of ancient gold. I am permitted to pour my wine into a golden cup … Penrhyn, situated on a hill, owns the wood within the enclosed park. Thy seat is palisaded on each side of the eminence. One park is for bucks and does, causing stags to be put in the other park. Thou hast fish, if they could be got out. Thou hast a right to fish in every pool. Game of every sort thou supplied us with at thy dinner.

(Paraphrase translation by Williams and Davies.)

Dafydd Pennant wrote in praise of Sir William Griffith III and Jane Stradling, the grandparents of Piers Griffith:

The lady is *"a consort meek"*, with *"brightness of Morgannwg," "of princely aspect"*. She is *"an additional star to our Country. Jane has grace, and the sense of ages. She is fair of the blood-line of Stradling…"*

Tudur Aled referred to *"the winding curve of the river"* flowing into the sea at the Ogwen and Abercegin Creeks near Penrhyn Castle.

Robin Ddu described the fine robe of Sir William Griffith and his *"spurs of gold"* adding that *"Thy children should be ennobled,"* in a form of ironic prophecy.

"You who hold the Golden Chain of Gwynedd", wrote Lewis Môn; *"you who have also an eye to England"*, boldly wrote Dafydd Pennant, possibly in mock deference to William III and his wife, Lady Jane née Stradling, an heiress from the influential Glamorgan family with a good deal of clout at the English royal court.

The Elegy to Gwilym ap Gruffydd (William II) by Rhys Goch Eryri remembered his *"sharp spur, before the sons of the Dragon,"* beating France at the Jousts – *"the betterer of France ... In his day there was no one more respected ..."*

Tudur Penllyn said of Gwilym Fychan (William I):

gold is had for giving an oration,

thus relaying the message to contemporary court poets and half-decent troubadours roaming the countryside reporting news, that the Penrhyn lord is so generous with rewards, that it is worthwhile visiting him at the castle and the word is, 'be as eloquent as possible for the entertainment of dinner-guests'. This ancient tradition of the lordly patron rewarding his poets and retainers lasted longer in Wales than in England where the parallel Anglo-Saxon poetic *comitatus* culture of alliterative and allusive verse-readings aloud dispersed with the Norman conquest after 1066. Indeed as late as 1829, Gwynedd poet Gutun Peris published a praise-poem to 'his' Lord Penrhyn in a local North Wales newspaper.

Gwilym ap Sefnyn praised Gwilym ap Gruffydd's military prowess, *"an assailer of fortresses"*, as a hero like Arthur *"who wore a coat of mail with all his forces,"* possibly referring to the elaborately expensive games with life-like models of castles and sieges that so delighted the young sovereign Henry VIII, noting also the real campaigns which Gwilym/William fought for his King.

Hywel Dafi addressed his poem to William Fychan of Penrhyn, as *"the blameless hero of the race of Ednyfed Fychan"*.

> *He shall enjoy quietness (peace) to crush outlaws*
> *Who will be put to … death in Wales*
> *… On New Year's day was never seen such a banquet …*
>   *a hundred fat*
> *bullocks hasten thither: a hundred butchers every day*
> *receive them a hundred hogs … There is white bread, and*
> *the choicest juice of the grape. There are a hundred beds,*
> *a hundred apartments, a hundred fires, a hundred feasts*
> *for us, during the life of William Fychan. Goblets serve …*
> *men look into them … No good bard is degraded. Every*
> *good poem is closely woven … Every land is traversed to*
> *seek for outlaws who sleep out of doors* (in the wild) *…*
>
>   (Williams and Davies.)

THE COURT AT COCHWILLAN

What did Old Penrhyn Castle really look like in the days of Piers Griffith's ancestors? Perhaps the nearest we can get today to its past splendour is the restored Old Hall of Cochwillan, set in a nearby valley, but Penrhyn would have been far grander, with turrets.

Lewys Môn (c.1465 – c.1527) wrote many superb *cywyddau/* poems to the Pirate's ancestor, Sir William Griffith of Penrhyn, and also several poems in praise of the comforts of the neighbouring court of Cochwillan and its lord, Wiliam Gruffydd ap Robin. Both kindred houses excelled in hospitality for wine, feasting and warm firelight incomparable in Snowdonia:

> *…mwg i'r nen yn magu'r nos*
> *Oedd fwg i'r Wyddfa agos.*

Poet Iolo Goch however, scorned such new-fangled coal fires at Penrhyn and Cochwillan, doubtless from fuel imported from the Mostyn mines, preferring the old cosy, crackling glow of peat to *"the silent nothingness of sea-coal"*:

> *Tân mawn a gawn neu gynnyd*
> *Ni bydd yno'r morlo mud.*

A century later the famous well-travelled soldier-poet, Guto'r Glyn certainly preferred the luxury of coal/*"glo"* at Cochwillan, appreciating the comforts of its two grand new stone-built chimneys and inglenook fireplaces, *"crackling with logs from the grove mingled in with the coal"*. He describes vividly how one large fireplace is to be found in the Main Hall and the other smaller one in the stylish solar bed-chamber upstairs, where both rooms were hung with fine tapestries and lit with beautifully crafted bright candlesticks:

> *Gwely Arras, goleurym,*
> *A siambr deg sy'n barod im ...*
> *A gwych allor Gochwillan*
> *Ac aelwyd deg i gael tân.*
> *Y mae deuwres i'm diro,*
> *Ei goed o'r glyn gyda'r glo.*

There is a mysterious history to this atmospheric and now restored bedroom where I confess to having slept for a year until driven out by ghostly fears and imagination.

"The extremely curious little chamber (the solar) ... is immediately behind the division at the end of the hall ... occupying the space used as a stable, whereas it is immediately above it, and is now filled with hay," wrote E.L. Barnwell in *Archaeologia Cambrensis, Volume XII* in 1866, with several interesting speculations.

"The present stable was once probably the buttery. Near the left hand corner was formerly the staircase leading to the solar above, access to which would be through the buttery; which, however, may have been divided into two partitions, so that the room (above) might be reached without going among the servants ... Through the central door, still perfect, with its grotesque ornamentation, the more distinguished persons would enter the hall; while others, together with the servants, would use only the opposite side door. The solar, more properly the withdrawing-room than the parlour, was devoted to the use of the ladies of the household, and, with the hall, often constituted the whole dwelling, with the exception of kitchen and offices, which were usually detached."

Cosmopolitan gentleman Guto'r Glyn was given the privilege of this finely tapestried and fire-lit upper chamber. At "the opposite end of the hall," Victorian tourist Barnwell continues, "are ... two doors, fast approaching to ruin ... the space between them is at present filled with hay and boards; but there can be little doubt that here once existed the gallery for the minstrels."

Both accounts provide a fascinating glimpse into the medieval world of Penrhyn cousins William Gruffydd ap Robin and his family, with echoes of Ednyfed Fychan before them, Seneschal to Prince Llywelyn ab Iorwerth; echoes too of the lifestyle of heiress Eva in her long, elegant Plantagenet-style gown, fingering her rosary beads and pilgrim's reliquary; there would have been scurrying servants; roasts on the spit; "*beer and wine ... in waterfalls ... the wine of Africa lasts barely an hour*", wrote Guto. The Court of Cochwillan was a busy one: poets arriving to entertain; children being put to bed; cattle lowing, sheep bleating, geese squawking, dogs barking and the distant clatter of horses' hooves on the cobbles of the courtyard...

Later, in Tudor times, Piers Griffith would have been familiar with this place and its tales of past inhabitants in the house of his Cochwillan uncles and rather remarkable aunts, one of whom,

Annes, the year before he was born, was proud to be the mother of a new Renaissance writer and pioneering publisher of the Elizabeth Age, Wiliam Salesbury, translator into Welsh of the New Testament and of the Book of Common Prayer published in 1567 on the Queen's own authority. The Griffith and Salesbury/ Salusbury families continued to inter-marry, like Piers's daughter Jane Salusbury.

Other tourists give us glimpses and clues, travelling through Wales on their quests for legend and adventure. Richard Fenton's *Tour in Wales* (1804-13) refers to "the House of Penrhyn" standing on the coastline beside the "Styx of Menai to (the monastery at) Llanvaes," which was the final destination of the dead Princess Joan, daughter of King John of England, grand-daughter of Eleanor of Aquitaine, wife of Llywelyn the Great and a much revered lady whose coffin was rowed in her funeral barge across the water by the friars for burial.

Fenton was also fascinated by the story of Piers Griffith:

> *Over a Window in the pine end of a new House close to Penrhyn Pier on a stone the initials P.G. 1589, being the initials of Piers Griffith of Penrhyn, a naval commander in Queen Eliz. time,* (sic) *and used to refit his Vessels here.*

The inscription "P.G. 1589," the year after the Armada of 1588 and significantly, the publication date of William Morgan's full Welsh Bible, again under the encouragement of Elizabeth I, is now nowhere to be seen at what remains of Abercegin Farm Cottage retained by the Pirate in the big sell-out of 1620-23, but the detail was scrutinised on good authority in 1960 by Mr Idris Roberts, a respected local historian.

Fenton also visited Cochwillan and wrote that "through a hole in the end partition we saw sufficient to discover that it was open to the Roof, which was supported by wooden beams, as the roof of a Church, resting on pilasters of wood annexed to the side wall, carved and moulded, having escutcheons of Arms here and there … which indicated its having been a grand old room. The doors into it were cased with stone arched Fire place seemingly large; windows not in proportion, and only two tracery [sic] of stone."

Barnwell, writing in the 1860s and taking a tour of 'Antiquities' in North Wales, wrote that the "mansion itself has fallen to ruin, like many others." It was restored over a hundred years later by Lady Janet Douglas Pennant of Penrhyn Castle during the early 1970s, the heiress of the last Lord Penrhyn of Llandegai, who had inherited the estate from the same family line dotted with other interesting heiresses back to a great-niece of Archbishop John Williams, cousin of Piers and close friend of King James I and King Charles I.

Barnwell reminds us of the role this long line of strong women played in the lineage of both Penrhyn and Cochwillan:

"…by heirs female, the estate descended to the posterity of Ednyfed Fychan," [their mutual ancestor] "whose arms are, *gules*, a chevron *ermine* between three Saxons' heads, couped, proper."

"Gruffydd ap Gwilym of Penrhyn about 1360 gave Cochwillan to his second son Robert, known as Robin of Cochwillan. After this the succession runs in parallel streams by the designation of Griffithses of Penrhyn and Williamses of Cochwillan, with several intermarriages," wrote Barnwell.

In conclusion, the two Courts had seen the emergence of two great landed families, developing originally from ancient princes of Romano–British and Early Christian descent c.500-1066, with their traditional system of *cenedl*/(kinship) and close inter-relationship between lord and people, encoded in poetry and story-telling, of honour, protection, military prowess, gift-giving, bloodlines, marriage, heirs, welfare, land and property. These values were sustained throughout their medieval feudal years to the Elizabethan Age of Piers Griffith from 1568 to 1603; but such traditions were largely disbanded after 1620 by the ambiguous overlord-ship of the new owner, Archbishop John Williams who died childless and by the fragmentation of his heirs. Yet the renewed concerns of the present family of 'Lady Janet' as she was fondly called, do them credit and forge new links with the past history of Piers Griffith.

Having survived the Glyndŵr Rebellion of 1400-10, the tumultuous years of the Wars of the Roses leading up to the Battle of Bosworth in 1485 and the establishing of the Tudor Dynasty, the two branches of Ednyfed's descendants found themselves on opposing sides. The Penrhyn people were mainly Yorkists, but changed their allegiance when Henry Tudor, Earl of Richmond was crowned King Henry VII and married Elizabeth of York. Penrhyn cousins at nearby Cochwillan were Lancastrian but both were richly rewarded and thus in a position to improve their houses in early Tudor times between 1485 and 1580 up to the death of Sir Rhys Griffith, Piers's father. The Penrhyn family, like the Mostyns, continued in their patronage of the poets from the Age of Chivalry and throughout the Elizabethan Age of Piracy into the Stuart Age of James I, Charles I and Charles II.

Piers Griffith was part of the surviving legitimate family of Sir Rhys, courtier, soldier and Chamberlain of North Wales like his father and grandfather ("the two Sir Williams".) This established context was the one which the Pirate, his soldier brother William and their sister Alys were brought up to accept as part of their inheritance whilst they lived within the ancient Penrhyn domain, in the care of their redoubtable mother, Lady Catherine Griffith Mostyn.

ANCIENT ANCESTRY

To sum up, Piers Griffith was descended from one of the ancient noble families of Wales spanning the centuries back to the 'Dark Ages', from the time the Romans left about A.D. 400 to the Norman Conquest of England in 1066. The roots of the Griffith or Gruffydd family certainly pre-date the Edwardian conquest of Wales in 1282 when the lands of the slaughtered Prince Llywelyn were ravaged then allowed to remain within the same families under the jurisdiction of the English king, Edward I. Meanwhile Llywelyn's brother, Prince Dafydd was despatched at Shrewsbury by the same new-fangled method of hanging, drawing and quartering endured by Scotland's 'Braveheart', William Wallace.

King Edward I disinherited the Welsh Royal children, using kidnapping, incarceration, child abuse, terror and possibly the assassin's knife to rid himself of Llywelyn's direct heirs including the Prince in the Cage at Bristol Castle.

Who got their lands and riches? After the Crown and the new order swept away the ancient principalities, the remaining leading North Wales families, through deals and favours, managed broadly to retain their domains, geographically within the same area we see today; so the Old Penrhyn estate of Piers Griffith eventually swept up a large expanse of what was once the ancient kingdom of Gwynedd at the time of the Last Prince.

Piers's ancestor Ednyfed Fychan had once been a powerful landowning lord, Chief Minister and kinsman to Prince Llywelyn at his courts of Aber, Aberffraw and Nefyn. Together with the Tudors of Penmynydd, who were also descendants of Ednyfed as well as being ancestors of Queen Elizabeth, as she herself acknowledged, the two related Griffith families of the medieval courts at Penrhyn and Cochwillan form the main branch of the Pirate's ancestry. With their high rank, came their family's chivalric responsibilities towards their people, the inhabitants of their ancestral lands, according to Welsh sociological traditions in the Celtic style.

In the poetry dedicated to Piers Griffith and his family, elegies, praise-poems and messages-in-verse, a good deal is made of their cultured ancestry as far back as the legendary heroes of the much maligned 'Dark Ages', of Romano-British descent annotated in the Welsh Genealogies, variously edited by Lewis Dwnn, Peter Bartrum and J.E. Griffith, "the only ones but the best we've got", as one university archivist commented recently.

Ednyfed's extensive lands and rich bloodline were largely inherited by Piers Griffith. Afterwards, through Piers's cousin, Archbishop John Williams who bought the domain in 1623, the Penrhyn estate, give or take some new additions, has remained within the same family network to the present day. The eighteenth century Penrhyn map of the *"Demesne"* shows the same lands, properties and geographical features that are broadly as they were in Piers's time. John Speed's map of Bangor 1610 shows part of this location.

The family of Piers Griffith, spreading itself over the manor houses of Penrhyn, nearby Cochwillan and the seat of the Tudors at Penmynydd, have descendants today in the counties of Caernarfon, Anglesey and the Welsh Border Country, also in Ireland. Through intermarriage with rival families and a strong female line, the prominence of Old Penrhyn dominated the scene until the time of Piers Griffith, when it was already in decline. (See the heraldic illustration from Westminster Abbey.)

Where did it all start? "Before the Battle of Bosworth", comments Edmond Douglas Pennant of the present Penrhyn family. In his volume, *"The Welsh Families of Penrhyn"* he writes:

> *Prior to 1485, a great many Welsh families had not served, in any capacity, the Kings of England. The Griffith family are one of the few that did.* [sic] *After 1485 a great many of the royal officials and courtiers were Welsh. No less than three members of the Griffith*

*family were Chamberlains of North Wales and no less
than three were knighted between 1489 and 1547.*

The Griffith family of Penrhyn, c.500 – 1066, and their related
ap Gwilym family of Cochwillan (later anglicised to Williams)
descended from a common ancestor, the legendary and powerful
lord Marchudd ap Cynan, a warrior contemporary of Rhodri
the Great, King of Wales, the Lawmaker who engaged Viking
mercenaries to keep the Saxons at bay in the ninth century.
Marchudd's descendant was Ednyfed Fychan (Vychan) whose
private residence was at Cochwillan with its emblazoned shields
and hall-house atmosphere.

The ancestors of Piers Griffith were:

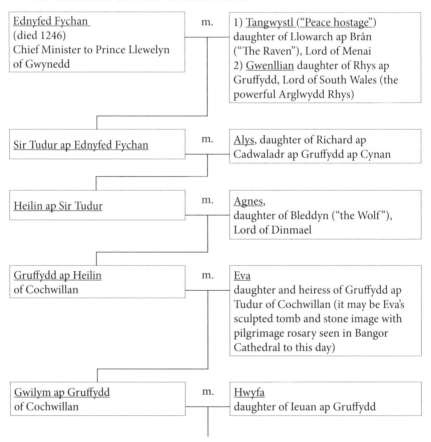

Ednyfed Fychan (died 1246) Chief Minister to Prince Llewelyn of Gwynedd	m.	1) Tangwystl ("Peace hostage") daughter of Llowarch ap Brân ("The Raven"), Lord of Menai 2) Gwenllian daughter of Rhys ap Gruffydd, Lord of South Wales (the powerful Arglwydd Rhys)
Sir Tudur ap Ednyfed Fychan	m.	Alys, daughter of Richard ap Cadwaladr ap Gruffydd ap Cynan
Heilin ap Sir Tudur	m.	Agnes, daughter of Bleddyn ("the Wolf"), Lord of Dinmael
Gruffydd ap Heilin of Cochwillan	m.	Eva daughter and heiress of Gruffydd ap Tudur of Cochwillan (it may be Eva's sculpted tomb and stone image with pilgrimage rosary seen in Bangor Cathedral to this day)
Gwilym ap Gruffydd of Cochwillan	m.	Hwyfa daughter of Ieuan ap Gruffydd

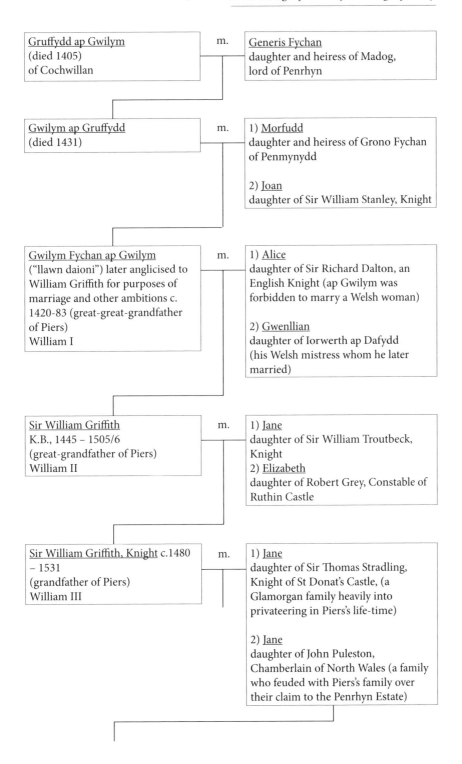

Gruffydd ap Gwilym
(died 1405)
of Cochwillan

m.

Generis Fychan
daughter and heiress of Madog,
lord of Penrhyn

Gwilym ap Gruffydd
(died 1431)

m.

1) Morfudd
daughter and heiress of Grono Fychan
of Penmynydd

2) Joan
daughter of Sir William Stanley, Knight

Gwilym Fychan ap Gwilym
("llawn daioni") later anglicised to
William Griffith for purposes of
marriage and other ambitions c.
1420-83 (great-great-grandfather
of Piers)
William I

m.

1) Alice
daughter of Sir Richard Dalton, an
English Knight (ap Gwilym was
forbidden to marry a Welsh woman)

2) Gwenllian
daughter of Iorwerth ap Dafydd
(his Welsh mistress whom he later
married)

Sir William Griffith
K.B., 1445 – 1505/6
(great-grandfather of Piers)
William II

m.

1) Jane
daughter of Sir William Troutbeck,
Knight
2) Elizabeth
daughter of Robert Grey, Constable of
Ruthin Castle

Sir William Griffith, Knight c.1480
– 1531
(grandfather of Piers)
William III

m.

1) Jane
daughter of Sir Thomas Stradling,
Knight of St Donat's Castle, (a
Glamorgan family heavily into
privateering in Piers's life-time)

2) Jane
daughter of John Puleston,
Chamberlain of North Wales (a family
who feuded with Piers's family over
their claim to the Penrhyn Estate)

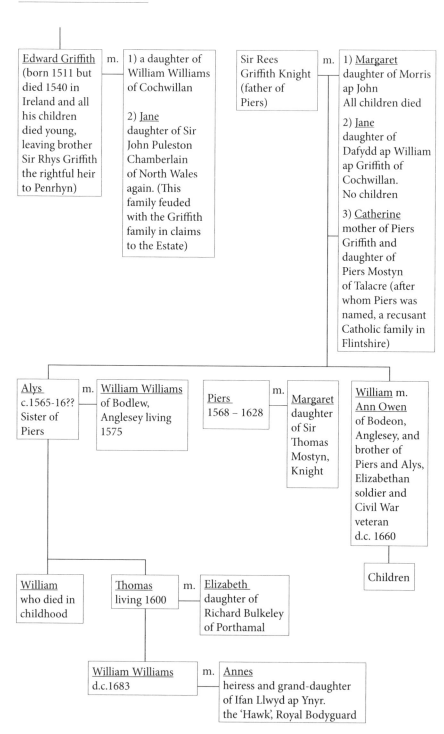

Edward Griffith (born 1511 but died 1540 in Ireland and all his children died young, leaving brother Sir Rhys Griffith the rightful heir to Penrhyn) m. 1) a daughter of William Williams of Cochwillan

2) Jane daughter of Sir John Puleston Chamberlain of North Wales again. (This family feuded with the Griffith family in claims to the Estate)

Sir Rees Griffith Knight (father of Piers) m. 1) Margaret daughter of Morris ap John All children died

2) Jane daughter of Dafydd ap William ap Griffith of Cochwillan. No children

3) Catherine mother of Piers Griffith and daughter of Piers Mostyn of Talacre (after whom Piers was named, a recusant Catholic family in Flintshire)

Alys c.1565-16?? Sister of Piers m. William Williams of Bodlew, Anglesey living 1575

Piers 1568 – 1628 m. Margaret daughter of Sir Thomas Mostyn, Knight

William m. Ann Owen of Bodeon, Anglesey, and brother of Piers and Alys, Elizabethan soldier and Civil War veteran d.c. 1660

Children

William who died in childhood

Thomas living 1600 m. Elizabeth daughter of Richard Bulkeley of Porthamal

William Williams d.c.1683 m. Annes heiress and grand-daughter of Ifan Llwyd ap Ynyr. the 'Hawk', Royal Bodyguard

[E. Douglas Pennant, Marian Griffith & G.L.]

Apart from Piers's early family connections to the English Crown, his people were not immune to disfavour for committing acts of rebellion. Yet they had the good fortune to acquire their property and land through heiresses like Eva of Cochwillan, Generis of Penrhyn and Morfudd of Penmynydd, seat of the Tudors. For a time, the court of Robin ap Griffith at Cochwillan, Grade I Listed and restored in all its late medieval splendour just off the main North Wales A55 express-way, seems to have almost eclipsed that of Penrhyn, despite the fact that one son, Thomas, was beheaded in 1466 at Conwy for attending Henry Tudor, Earl of Richmond to France.

The poet Gwilym ap Sefnyn wrote:

Streams have always impended me
To Robin, generous with wine, great his preparations,
To Cochwillan [I will go]
Where I could get used to wine
And mead with honour,
And a large room as white as the colour of snow high-roofed
Often drawing me there.

Menai the river of the mother island,
By Mary, keeps me from the court,
Brine mingled with seaweed
Is the girdle of Anglesey's narrow flank.
Mighty is the wave...
And rough where Ceris is.

(Williams and Davies.)

Host Robin's grandson, Wiliam ap Griffith of Cochwillan (not to be confused with William Griffith of Penrhyn) "led a troop of horse, for his own retinue, to the Battle of Bosworth on August 22, 1485 to assist Henry Tudor, Earl of Richmond, later

King Henry VII, against King Richard III. After Henry became King in 1485, he was appointed, by patent, Sheriff of Caernarvonshire for life." (E. Douglas Pennant, 1985.) Recent forensic evidence on the corpse of King Richard III has revealed that he was hacked to death by his enemies in a repeatedly ferocious attack, before his body was finally taken to the Franciscan monks at Greyfriars in Leicester for burial. Eye-witness soldier Guto'r Glyn, in a poem to Syr Rhys ap Tomas of Castell Dinefwr, active at Bosworth against the '*hunchback*' and the man who seems to have finally dispatched him, describes the butchery in hunting terms:

> *Lladd y baedd, eilliodd ei ben.*
> ("Killing the boar, he cleaved his head.")

The recent archaeological find of a boar symbol ornamented into a high-status sword hilt in the very place where Richard III is supposed to have fallen, adds interest here. Actually, "*eilliodd*" can mean "*shaved*" or even "*scalped*". Echoes of the medieval splendour of both courts, Penrhyn and Cochwillan, may be seen today in the window frames of the ruined chapel at Penrhyn and the skilfully restored windows at Cochwillan, still part of the Penrhyn estate. Confusingly, another descendant of Marchudd and Ednyfed at Cochwillan called William (later becoming the well-known Wynn-Williams family) married before 1557 his cousin Dorothy, daughter of Sir William Griffith, lord of Penrhyn, probably the namesake of Piers's daughter Dorothy Edwards.

Eventually, the Trustees of Piers Griffith on behalf of the (by then) established "Williamses" of Cochwillan sold this ancient court to the Earl of Pembroke in 1620, at the same time as cousin Piers was concluding his Penrhyn deal. So it would seem that the Archbishop, who had been born at Cochwillan in 1574, eventually bought the entire estate by 1623, thus having to pay for what could be deemed part of his own inheritance.

The first Griffith to be lord of Penrhyn was Griffith ap Gwilym of Cochwillan, acquiring Penrhyn by his marriage to heiress Generis, daughter of Madog, lord of Penrhyn in about 1370. They had three sons: Robin (or Robert) ap Griffith who inherited Cochwillan and entertained in grand style; Gwilym ap Griffith who became the first anglicised "William Griffith" succeeding to Penrhyn in 1405; and Rhys ap Griffith who inherited Nant, a property in Caernarvonshire. This first 'William Griffith' (alias Gwilym ap Gruffydd of Penmynydd in his Will) did well from his first marriage to Morfudd, by whom he inherited Penmynydd, "the seat of the Tudors before becoming the rulers of England" notes Douglas Pennant; then this William became "enmeshed in the Rebellion of Owain Glyndŵr between 1400 and 1410 to his cost."

Naturally for a Welshman with ancestral roots back to the Last Prince, William Griffith of Penrhyn first supported Glyndŵr, a descendant of at least two royal Welsh dynasties and a military-trained London barrister to boot, with a fine country estate near Oswestry that was later ravaged by the English. Glyndŵr recruited an excellent command of superbly schooled but disaffected officers and soldiers who had done military service in England and Europe.

"Then William changed sides, supported King Henry IV and had all his estates, which he lost, returned to him in the same year, at a cost of a hundred pounds, which he paid to the then Chamberlain of North Wales, the notorious Thomas Barnaby, who acquired great wealth by cheating others…"

Dafydd Johnston in *Llên yr Uchelwyr*, a scholarly analysis of Welsh poetry and its relation to the nobility during the Age of Chivalry, comments that Gwilym/William managed to acquire further lands in Anglesey forfeited by his cousins who remained loyal to Glyndŵr. When heiress Morfudd died, having borne him three sons, doubtless presiding at feasts in peace-time and driven panic-stricken to her chamber with her children and attendants during hostilities, he married Joan Stanley, an English heiress, daughter of Sir William Stanley, Knight, of Hooton in Cheshire, a family who later figured with their powerful private army at the Battle of Bosworth in 1485, famously turning up late to join the winning side of Henry Tudor.

Gwilym/William and Joan had one son, William, his heir, and two daughters: Elin who married William Bulkeley, Constable of Beaumaris Castle, and Elizabeth who married a Grey. "In about 1417, he built the nucleus of the present castle at Penrhyn. It consisted of the main part, which was the hall itself, which was entered at the north end," wrote Douglas Pennant and Roberts in the National Trust Guidebook.

Inside, the castle (eventually inherited by Piers Griffith) was enormous and "richly decorated", as recorded by the time of Wyatt's survey and Moses Griffith's drawings. "In the east side was a vast fireplace, with another entrance to the left of it. It was lighted by windows on the west side, two of them large and a third, smaller, because of the raised area at the south end of the hall. At the north and south ends were the solars, separated by half-timbered screens. Between the north solar and the hall was a tower which took one up to the upper north solar and down to the vaults below. The tower was built without sanction in circa 1417 and was made legal in 1438... The hall stood in a court which consisted of a gateway, through which it was entered, a chapel... and other outer buildings... built of a soft, white stone which originated from Cheshire... The hall and solars are now encased by Thomas Hopper's Neo-Norman structure that we see today." (Pennant and Roberts.)

Dafydd Johnston is one of several literary critics who note the satiric tone of poets like Rhys Goch Eryri in excessively praising

> *the fortress of oak that supports minstrels*
> *… a hundred times better*
> > *… than the sad*
> *Greystone tower of the Eagle, seat of anger,*

because the original Gwilym ap Gruffydd's Welsh contemporaries would have derided his name-change to the anglicised form of 'William Griffith' before his marriage to rich English heiress Joan Stanley. Such a go-getting move would have been regarded as sheer snobbery and obsequiousness which is why Rhys Goch Eryri boldly took his poetic licence to say so. This particular William also applied to be made an English citizen on the grounds that his son William was the son of an English lady, a move undermined again by poet Rhys who still went ahead reprovingly, but in a fashionable tone of tongue-in-cheek, to compose reams of seemingly flattering verse reminding his patron of William's pure Welsh listed ancestry. When William Griffith was succeeded by his son William in 1431, his widow Joan Stanley developed into a shrewd businesswoman after later marrying John Rykemere who died in 1443; her elegy records how this remarkable woman administered and expanded the Penrhyn estate for fifty years.

Gwilym/William and Joan together laid the foundations of Piers Griffith's Penrhyn. Their heir, to avoid confusion, we will now refer to as William Griffith I, possibly the same lord who was also known to his Welsh contemporaries as *"Gwilym Fychan llawn daioni/full of beneficence"*.

"About 1443 William Griffith I was made Chamberlain of North Wales and released from the restrictions of penal laws that Henry IV had imposed on Welshmen following Owain Glyndŵr's Rebellion, on the condition that he did not marry a Welshwoman," wrote Douglas Pennant. So in 1447 William Griffith I married rich English heiress Alice Dalton of Northamptonshire, thus acquiring her lands at Apethorpe. She was a lady with Stanley family connections, but his Welsh mistress meanwhile was Gwenllian, daughter of the nobleman Iorwerth ap Dafydd of Talybolion; after Alice's death, he legitimised his children with Gwenllian and 'married the mistress' (see previous family tree.)

The poet Tudur Penllyn wrote of William Griffith I, again with irony:

> *The man whose house is upon a rock*
> *And the wall of the house on the fine sea,*
> *He is the captain and the chieftain*
> *Of Arvon's town and Menai's bank.*
> *To keep Wales from harm,*
> *It is good to call on God and William.*

With Alice Dalton, William Griffith I had two children: his son and heir who became William Griffith II, great-grandfather of Piers, and his daughter Janet who married Sir Thomas Stradling, a family with notoriously piratical connections on the South Wales coast. It is now we find in the Penrhyn Papers a reference to their *"newe gardyn northward and the lytyll hey under the new berne,"* a garden later referred to in Piers's final sale, possibly to the dismay of the ladies of the house, Margaret, the Pirate's Wife and Lady Catherine; a garden which, archaeologically may be traced today to the north-west of the private estate.

Like his father, William II bought more lands in North Wales, extending the estate. Meanwhile, with his mistress Gwenllian, he had three 'natural sons', Robert, Edmund and William and four 'natural daughters' who were recognised under the name of Griffith, and indeed, after poor Alice's death, William I *did* marry the forbearing Gwenllian. In 1438 that particular William and his mother, the powerfully administrative Joan Stanley Griffith, (her male relatives held force between Cheshire and Wales), were granted a Royal Licence to build the famous tower at Penrhyn on to the main hall, a specially crenelated affair designed to display the Griffith status to neighbours, and to passing gentry and nobility. The satiric comments of visiting poets with their traditional licence to report, comment, criticise and advise, would have reminded him that this trendy make-over had not gone unremarked amongst the local inhabitants. But their *"Little William full of kindness,"* was a feudal lord who would have taken this fond jibe in good part, for he continued to bestow his patronage upon the poets and keep as close as ever to the people of his community/*'cenedl'* in the manner of Welsh noble families, a caring facet that can be traced back to earlier tribal roots in Ancient Britain.

When he died in 1483, William I was succeeded by Piers's great-grandfather, his only legitimate son, William Griffith II (1445–1505/6), who was appointed Chamberlain of North Wales by King Richard III in 1583. He married Jane Troutbeck, another kinswoman of the Stanleys. After her death he married Elizabeth, daughter of Robert Grey, Constable of Ruthin Castle.

On the eve of Bosworth in 1485, William Griffith II became embroiled in a dangerous intrigue. Richard III, recognising that Sir Thomas Stanley held the balance of power in military terms in England, tried to secure his allegiance by blackmail. The King imprisoned Stanley's son, George, Lord Strange, in Nottingham Castle in company with William Griffith II, his kinsman, great-grandfather of Piers. The men escaped, poets celebrated their heroic deeds and both the Stanley faction and the Griffith family joined Henry Tudor on the winning side at the Battle of Bosworth Field in 1485 when the valiant Henry apparently killed Richard III, and was proclaimed King Henry VII in his place, even as the tyrant's crown seems to have been conveniently found in a nearby thorn bush.

So ended the Wars of the Roses, but Henry Tudor still had a tough time ahead establishing his authority and maintaining stability throughout the land. For this he needed his Welsh friends like the Griffiths.

William Griffith II, like many other Welshmen, now received favours and lands from his grateful King and on November 29, 1489 he had the privilege of being made a Knight of the Bath. On the creation of the teenage Prince Arthur, Duke of Cornwall as Prince of Wales, William became Chamberlain of North Wales until his death in 1505-6.

He was succeeded by his eldest son, Piers's grandfather, William Griffith III, who was made an *Esquire of the Body of the King* in 1509 (Henry VIII) and like his father, appointed Chamberlain. During the English expedition to France in 1513 in company with the young King Henry VIII and serving under Charles Brandon, later Duke of Suffolk, Piers's grandfather distinguished himself at the Battle of Tournai and was knighted by the King on the field at 'The Battle of the Spurs', on September 25, 1513. Poet Tudur Aled wrote a praise-poem in the Welsh language celebrating William's chivalrous deeds:

> *Because your guard was as close*
> *As that of the Emperor upon the walls*
> *You encircled Therouanne with steel,*
> *And upon the wall of Tournai the second blow,*
> *You charged a hole through it…*

At the same action, and under Brandon's command was William's kinsman, Ifan the Hawk, Royal Bodyguard to Henry VIII and later to his three children, then in a favoured capacity to the King's surviving daughter, Queen Elizabeth I until his death in 1591. Like the stalwart Ifan, William Griffith III attended Henry VIII at Calais, and was present at the Field of the Cloth of Gold, so Piers's grandfather was in the unique position of being able to pull powerful strings at Court, for instance in securing a legal system for Wales not least to banish banditry and control crime. Being close to the throne also meant witnessing royal events which could then be relayed back to Penrhyn and elsewhere, briefing country folk with up-to-date, intimate details: the fashionable beauty of Boleyn and all the scandal; dazzling arrays of pavilions; fashionable parades of earls, dukes and popinjays to the blare of trumpets; show-off jousting challenges with thunderous horses, plumes, banners and great clashes of steel.

An esquire of the body was a kind of high-class companion, not exactly a servant, as he would have been of noble birth or of the gentry at least; in this respect, loyal Welsh Tudor kith and kin were deemed ideal for the purpose. An esquire would have been a member of the King's personal household, familiar with his private apartments, "upstairs" rather than "downstairs", commented Julia Fox. He would have had the ear of the King, thus wielding a measure of power, being in a key position to be a keeper of secrets, his eyes and ears, and to dole out patronage to the favoured few. Such a man was William Griffith, placed close to the Tudor monarch.

Yet this could also be a fatally dangerous occupation within the closed inner world of court intrigues, as in the case of attendant gentlemen like Norris and Brereton who were executed for alleged adultery with Anne Boleyn.

Another key factor in these Tudor connections now comes into focus. Piracy. When royal companion William Griffith III married Jane Stradling of St Donat's Castle, Glamorgan, he was linking himself with an influential family that was to be heavily into privateering, if not piracy, by the time Piers was pro-active. Jane was Piers Griffith's paternal grandmother, so perhaps it was in his blood. When she died, Sir William III married Jane Puleston, daughter of John Puleston, Chamberlain of North Wales. Sir Rhys became the legal heir to the Penrhyn Estate after his elder brother Edward (who had succeeded his father William III in 1531) died of dysentery in Dublin Castle in 1540 whilst serving as a professional soldier. He left a wife, Jane Puleston, three daughters, and his brother Rhys, Piers's father.

Yet another factor in our story is the disputed inheritance of Piers Griffith from his father Sir Rhys and his grand-father Sir William. The Pulestons and other Griffith in-laws will be the main challengers.

"After Edward's death, disputes arose as to his true heirs which led to court action. After two years the court made an award which, in effect, was to split up the medieval Penrhyn Estate. Most of the Anglesey lands were to be divided between Edward Griffith's three daughters, Jane, Katherine and Ellen, while the Caernarvonshire lands, including Penrhyn, were to go to Sir Rhys Griffith. Decades of litigation followed."

(E. Douglas Pennant & T. Roberts, The National Trust 2000.)

This mêlée was the spark that lit the fuse that later lit the gunpowder of enmity between Sir Edward Herbert of Powys Castle and Piers Griffith, culminating in their 'Devil's Lawcase' and the ensuing 'Caernarfon Duel' of 1612.

Sir Rhys Griffith, Knight, the father of Piers, was born in 1514. His marriages and offspring before Piers was born are crucial to understanding the Pirate's disputed inheritance (see family tree.) Sir Rhys was Sheriff of Caernarvonshire in 1566-7 following Sir William Herbert, Knight, husband of his niece Catherine Griffith, daughter of his dead brother Edward, yet another accursed element in Piers's future disputes.

The first wife of Piers's father, Sir Rhys, was Margaret, daughter of Morris ap John of Clenennau, a landed family who produced two shadowy but key characters standing on the fringe of the drama of Piers Griffith: kinsman John Owen, 'career' secretary to Walsingham, the Queen's Private Secretary at the time, and then Owen's son, Colonel John Owen who was to fight one of the last battles of the Civil War on Penrhyn fields. All seven children of Sir Rhys and this Lady Margaret were alive in 1553 but all died before their father did in 1580.

Sir Rhys's second wife was Jane, daughter of Dafydd, his cousin at Cochwillan, but he was to have no luck with heirs there either, when Jane died childless. His third wife was Catherine, daughter of Piers Mostyn of Talacre and mother of Piers Griffith (born 1568.)

Their second son was soldier William (c.1570-c.1660), married in 1604 to Jane Owen Lloyd, young widow of David Lloyd and daughter of Sir Hugh Owen, Knight, of Bodeon in Anglesey. Sir Rhys and Lady Catherine's daughter Alys, their eldest child (born c. 1566), married William Williams of Bodlew, producing two sons, William and Thomas.

When Piers inherited the Penrhyn Estate in 1580 held in trust for him until he was 21, he also inherited a backlog of legal disputes and dark memories that were to beleaguer him all his days.

"Piers has many crosses to bear," wrote Sir Huw Roberts in 1610 at the time of heir William's death in London, tragically timed to meet the contrary forces of the Herbert, Puleston and Bagnall inheritance challenges, not to mention pressing mortgage debts.

If the on-going feud with celebrated duellist Sir Edward Herbert was to be one problem, the tiresome Pulestons were the source of another; and they were all relatives of Piers Griffith through marriage. In any case, the aftermath refused to go away.

In 1540, soon after his Uncle Edward Griffith's death, but before the boy Piers was born, distant kinsman John Puleston raided and entered Sir Rhys's house at Penrhyn with sixteen men, *"by force of arms"* and stripped the place of its family heirlooms, tapestries, furniture and brass implements *"incased in wood which had seen more than two hundred winters."* Also removed were Edward Griffith's suit of armour and other battle arms, *"wine and food which were given to Lord Leonard in return for favours... these items were at Edward Griffith's house in Dublin"*, quotes Douglas Pennant in his vivid account.

On February 22, 1547, Sir Rhys Griffith, the Pirate's father was knighted at the coronation of the boy-king, Edward, brother to Elizabeth Tudor, and was thus a key-witness at one of the dazzling pageants of the Tudor Age. By 1575 when his growing new family of two boys and a girl were seen to be flourishing healthily before his eyes, Sir Rhys clearly had cause for celebration with his beautiful, gifted and much younger wife, Lady Catherine (or Katherine), mother of the boy-heir Piers, now seven years old. So they gave the place another makeover, *"repairing and ornamenting the house"* and having their initials lovingly carved together, above the fireplace in the great hall: R.G. and K.G., a last echo perhaps, of the Age of Chivalry at Old Penrhyn Castle.

Chapter 2

Tudor Favourites

When Piers's father, Sir Rhys Griffith was knighted on 22 February 1547, two days after the coronation of the Protestant boy-king Edward VI (see Shaws: *The Knights of England*, II, 60), he underwent the usual ritualistic ceremonies and parades that accompanied this role, with its chivalric code of honour, duty, dignity, responsibility to one's own people and absolute fealty to the crown. He is listed amongst the Justices of Caernarvonshire for 1574 and 1575 and on other commissioning bodies 1569-70. (Egerton 2345, 46; Flenley 60, 69, 75, 127, 135.) He was Member of Parliament for Caernarfon in 1555 and Sheriff 1566-7.)

Sir Rhys "… seems on the whole to have lived a quiet life between the too-generous largesse of his three predecessors and the too-adventurous career of his son Piers," (Dr. Thomas Richards, 1939.)

However, Dr Enid Roberts in her thesis on 'Poetry and the Nobility of North Wales' was of the opinion that Dr. Richards's view of Piers was unfair: "… he suggests it was Piers Griffith who began the process of impoverishing the estate; but I wonder if that is quite true?"

She continues by pointing to the "adventurous" deeds of the father too: "… it is well known that Sir Rhys had fought in the Irish Campaign during the Reign of Edward VI, 1547-53", quoting evidence from the alliterative verse of Siôn Brwynog, in Manuscript B 14901, f.10, about "that sad battle-field":

trist yw lle trewaist dy ôl
trwy Werddon (Ireland) *y tarw urddol*
trist oernad … (a sad cold grief-stricken keening.)

Dr. Roberts also notes that another contemporary of Sir Rhys at the court of King Edward VI, teenage half-brother to the young "Lady Elizabeth", was the poet Siôn Tudur, "in service" to Edward since his time as Prince of Wales during the Reign of King Henry VIII, an appointment the poet kept when Prince Edward became King. Tudur Aled also wrote poetry to King Henry. Sir Rhys and these three poets of his social circle were well qualified to report on some of the significant details of the Tudor Age. Other personal reports reaching Penrhyn from London about young King Edward's tragic death must have been harrowing indeed, with the manipulative Seymours hovering and Sir William Cecil trying to keep true to the last wishes of King Henry VIII, but of course one would have to be very careful in word and deed…

ODE ON A REQUEST FOR A NEW CLOAK FROM SIR RHYS GRIFFITH OF PENRHYN (father of Piers)
by Siôn Tudur, court poet to Queen Elizabeth I, c. 1570

This stylishly witty poem was probably performed at Penrhyn when Piers was about two years old, boldly providing an insight into his father's wild youth away from home, seen through the eyes of a contemporary 'troubadour', who is determined to use every ruse including blackmail to get what he wants.

Let us go straight to Penrhyn, on a journey
To see the fine landscape of our country
As we have the right to do, let us go without delay,
4 Go where we will gain great rewards.

Let us go, Poets, where we will be treated in a lordly manner,
To the house on the hill amidst green pastures.
An incomparable Court, famous for the awarding of great honours,
8 Penrhyn, set on a pleasant rising, where great gifts and privileges
are freely given,
The Court of Sir Rhys, traditionally the seat of patrons in ancient
times,
The most joyful of places for a good welcome, sustenance and
lodging…

Sir Rhys, of the same ancestral rib,
12 The same sparkling star-studded cut of cloth as old Sir William.
Always sharing out plenty of everything, what a wonderful sight is
this prosperous and cheerful way of life,
Dispensing graciousness everywhere, filling the streets with goods.
A rich be-ringed Knight in a responsible position governing people,
16 He is loved by everyone, his wife, children and humble folk.
Even in so remote a place in the country, he manages to organise
grand feasts,
I wish him a hundred life-times, with his Gwynedd ancestry.
The sanctuary he provides, as long as he lives, is an excellent place,
20 Sir Rhys pours a generous measure of cider and wine.

He was once a courtier in London, fond of taverns and wine-shops,
With their fashionably fine courses and mulled wine.
We used to understand each other very well he and I, you know, a
hundred times over,
24 In our quest for wine, we played hard and we worked hard.
He always went about town with an animated retinue of hangers-on
and tradesmen in his wake,
Did the Lion of Gwynedd, with many a band of wise-cracking
London street-urchins straggling along after him.
That was a place! And what good times we had there
28 In London, where there is a sophisticated life-style.
The place where a lot of excitement goes on day and night,
The place this gentleman frequented then.

We used to think the City streets were paved with gold
32 In the agreeable area around Westminster with all its wonderful
    buildings.
    I was in his service, we got into lots of amusing scrapes,
    I was this gentleman's messenger then;
    I accompanied him as his personal poet, he was easy to get on with,
                                  never finding fault with me,
36 I just joined in whatever he was doing, as his errand-boy performing
                                  many tasks.

    He used to go courting, besotted by love you know,
    By the golden love-knot of a young lady.
    He used to promise great things to a beautiful girl,
40 But only in jest, far more than he could give;
    And although he promised her favours,
    The girl knew they were dreams without hope of fulfilment.
    Merely the impulsive act of someone weak-willed enough to sin in
                                  a grassy grove,
44 Boasting of his love-life with girls.
    Yet he could, when he was determined to have his own way,
    Be very charming and courteous to fair ladies.
    But I am not telling you everything I know, at the moment,
48 If I were to announce all this publicly, assuming it is in people's
                                  interest,
    I would not want to upset his lovely wife of star quality,
    The beautiful, gentle, virtuous Lady
    Catherine, as she serves us superb wine with such dignity,
52 Of Mostyn, of ancient power, honour and grace.
    She has forgiven him all these misdemeanours
    Lovingly extending to him her favour and her pardon,
    As long as he agreed to reform the sort of life he used to live, his
                                  town-life
56 On condition he changed to suit her standards when she first
                          accepted him all in her own good time.
    If I was neglectful in my supervision of him
    When I was his go-between, or whatever, it was my fault entirely,
    But now I would not dream of doing such a thing today,

60 For a thousand gold coins.
By the Grace of God and Jesus,
May you forgive everyone concerned.
    Let us talk of something more agreeable, let us put our minds to
                       more serious matters,
64 I promise I will not refer to the subject ever again.

    Inevitably, I am growing old by now,
And very susceptible to catching cold.
My body shows signs of shaking in infirmity,
68 Blame the low-life of England for corrupting me.
My veins run cold, for my deeds,
My ribs are showing, I have observed it all in detail.
Beware my chest, the seat of my soul, the City over there affected
                       my health badly,
72 Giving me a hundred chills to poison me.
Wales is a cold country too, in spite of its beauty,
A man needs a robe about his ribcage.
That is the role of the bard, chiding his patron with poetic good
                       humour.
76 I am sure he will give me a cloak in exchange for a witty poem.
A robe from the generous Knight for Siôn, me,
Brand new, smart, of fine Irish woven wool
Like a beautiful casket to contain me and keep me cosy,
80 A bit of cloth to keep me in good health;
As I go up to bed at night I will feel no draughts
Inside that comfortable casket-like robe, with my goat's beard only
                       just in sight;

Like a hairy pony or monster,
84 Something to playfully frighten the children with;
That is what I am like, without hiding anything I am almost naked,
Just a boney, skeletal servant, like a fawning spaniel, begging.
I never saw such a poor robe as the one I am wearing at the moment,
second to none but a sack,
  88 I never saw a bear's claws more revolting than mine;
The legendary Shield of the Irish could come over

And attack me easily just like that, clamping me down.
What a superb mark of craftsmanship would be the hood of a fine
                        cloak that could enfold my whole body,
92 With generous proportions right down to the floor.
With fur-trimmed long sleeves, bear-like,
Edged along the hem.

It would be the best rug ever imported
96 From the land of the O'Neills out of Dublin harbour;
It will soon be coming into my possession, this bear-cloak,
Across the sea to Beaumaris.

I am a poet, now hoping I have a long life,
100 Reciting this poem in praise of a warm cloak, so you will get good
                        value from me for a long time yet.
A word to the wise, the best patron of poets in Arfon, *(Sir Rhys)*
I wish you a long life too, hundreds of lives indeed, as long as you
                        give me that cloak.

                        (G. L.)

LIFE-STYLE AT TUDOR PENRHYN

Tudor Wales is brought to life in the work of the Welsh poets of the gentry, illuminating for us the noble values and customs of their patrons: from their fine array of clothes to their carved furniture; their generosity to others and their care of the poor; their lavish hospitality to all classes of society and their scrumptious feasts to the point of keeping open house, all traditions going back to long before the Norman or Edwardian Conquests. To some, it was all part of the family image. To a great man or a great lady (or 'son of' and 'daughter of') their reputation mattered, both within their own house and in the *cenedl*/community outside, as well as in the wider public domain where word would be sure to reach London. Furthermore, in the capital city of England, the useful affinities with influential 'movers and shakers' was considered to be in everyone's interest. In the Tudor age, this was not for snob-value in the modern sense. It was more a form of survival. This is how Piers Griffith may have got on in life.

As to his family or domestic agenda, the last remains of the Pirate's fortified manor-house are to be seen in the cellar of the Victorian castle standing today on the same site, incorporating Samuel Wyatt's eighteenth century renovations which had also incorporated Piers's main hall position. The house Piers Griffith and his family lived in, after his grandparents' makeover in the early Tudor period, had the distinctive plan of a three-unit medieval house dating back to at least the 1400s. According to Dr Enid Roberts, early Welsh poetry refers to the historical figure Rhodri Molwynog, Prince of Wales building the first house here about the year 720, when poets of that era detailed the escapades of Meredydd ap Owen, a princeling from South Wales "who destroyed Penrhyn in 978 during his conquest of Gwynedd. A parallel house existed nearby at Cochwillan, which may not have escaped the mayhem, but little of this earlier house can be detected in archaeological terms."

An expert on assessing the value of life-style historical evidence in Welsh poetry, Dr Enid Roberts wrote of Old Penrhyn, "It seems to be accepted that the medieval house, of which remains can be seen today, was built either by Tudur Hen ap Goronwy (died 1331) or by his son, Goronwy ap Tudur (died 1331.) They were descended from Ednyfed Fychan (died 1246) seneschal to Llywelyn the Great (died 1240) who, with his sons, received grants of land, covering what is now the Penrhyn Estate.

"In due course the property passed to Gwilym ap Gruffydd (died 1431)... his descendants, Sir William Gruffydd (died 1531) and his son, Sir Rhys (died 1580) restored or extended the house...", the grandfather and father of Piers.

...During "the peace and prosperity that came with the Tudor era, many families rebuilt their ancestral homes on more 'modern' plans, but by the mid-sixteenth century, ready cash was possibly scarce at Penrhyn… The estate was entailed on the male heir… Edward Griffith, who died in 1540, had no son, and the dowries of his three daughters must have depleted the coffers of Penrhyn… Edward was succeeded by his brother Rhys, who may have fritted both time and money in London. His son and heir, Pyrs Griffith [sic], was generally blamed for impoverishing the estate, but the down-side may have started earlier." (E. Roberts, 1980.)

The travel-writer Thomas Pennant visited Penrhyn in the 1760s and saw a group of "buildings standing round a court and consisting of a courtway, chapel, Tower, Vast Hall and a few other apartments. By several ruins may be traced its former extent."

The young lord Piers would have been trained in estate management and he clearly studied the law, as shown in his superbly argued 'Devil's Lawcase' with Sir Edward Herbert, Earl of Powys.

"Twenty four accomplishments were expected of young noblemen," wrote Dr Roberts. "The first ones are concerned with developing bodily strength and agility: wrestling, running, leaping or jumping, and swimming. Then came fencing, horse-riding … war horses, shooting with the long-bow and the cross-bow."

There is plenty of poetic evidence that noblemen of Tudor times were fond of chess, dice and cards. Renaissance people like Piers, his brother William, their cousin Thomas Prys and Gwydir kinsmen like John Wynn loved reading the Classics, poetry and books about history and heraldry; they also loved music and were proficient at field sports – shooting, hunting and fishing, all important as pastimes and for the purpose of stocking up the larder and seeing there was food on the table. Thomas Prys was well-known for his fishing, hunting and hawking activities, while poet Dafydd Llwyd enjoyed savouring roast curlews, pheasants and bittern amply supplied by the hawks at Penrhyn, while court poet Tudur Aled praised Plas Isa, Llanrwst with *"its six score swans from a hundred meadows and a multitude of rabbits."*

Then came training in the use of essential arms for personal protection like daggers, poniards and swords, as some luckless poetic friends of Piers and Thomas were to find at Abergele. Aboard ship, men were armed with caliver guns slung over their shoulders, while pistols could always come in handy on land and sea. Sword-play and swashbuckling with rapiers was much in vogue after about 1610. As for gentlemanly fashions, between 1605 and 1628 during the later years of Piers Griffith, there was a trend for leather or velvet close-fitting jackets, attractive on a fit manly chest, as a raft of popular historical films have portrayed; and there were outfits that were trendily set off with falling collars in expensive transparent lace as marks of distinction, as seen on the front-cover, "*Portrait of an Unknown Man*", and in Steegman's reproduction of the handsome, dashing Ithel Felyn of Cors-y-Gedol.

When Piers Griffith loses his father, Sir Rhys at the age of twelve in 1580, he may have been spoiled by his mother well into his teens and beyond into manhood, a possible source of annoyance to his Mostyn step-brothers and to step-father Sir Thomas in a theme of conflict that runs relentlessly through the Mostyn Papers. This maternal indulgence is to last into the Pirate's maturity, until he loses his mother Catherine too. But for the moment, we get a vivid glimpse of Piers as a twelve year old boy in the next poem.

Here we also note that his elder sister Alys is conspicuous by her absence. The poets tended to strictly follow the official family list of mourners on such occasions as the burial of a great lord like Sir Rhys. Alys may meanwhile be married already and living amongst her troublesome Williams in-laws at Bodlew in Anglesey, too busy rearing her children to attend her father's funeral, or she may simply be indisposed; neither is she mentioned in Sir Rhys's second Will of 1580.

ELEGY UPON THE DEATH OF SIR RHYS GRIFFITH
by Lewis Menai 1580

The planet Saturn exerted its cruel influence yesterday,
The news came to us as sharply as an arrow and was the undoing
of many.
There were great cries of anguish, at the passing of this perfect
knight
4   Like the legendary Cynfarch, mourned by a thousand people in
this place of mourning.
Sir Rhys was a true Knight, magnificent, chivalrous, honourable,
Great crowds gnashed their teeth at his departing *(at his lying-in-
state.)*
His personal crested golden banner, embellished with the best
ancestral coat-of-arms
and his suit of armour are on display in *(Llandegai)* Church above
his coffin.
8   He was magnanimous to high and low, famously keeping an open
house and giving great feasts.
Black was that night for our nation and our language, the night
that stole away Sir Rhys.
Griffith, the ancestral vine of nine islands,
Descended like a gilded heraldic leaf from the two great Sir
Williams
12   Once celebrated at Penrhyn Court.
The grandson of the William I knew, lies in his coffin,

A sarcophagus no bigger than anyone else's but bearing such
unique greatness.
The best representative symbol of chivalry descended from old Sir
Tudor
16   Who has long been mourned with chilling pain.
A knight of the ancient blood of Marchudd,
An established supporter of men is to be buried in a crypt hidden
from us.
This news has spread like a wave of stormy destruction throughout
Gwynedd

20 Amidst grief-stricken cries at his graveside.
He was a Knight descended from the Stanleys,
A wealthy, important man of Troutbeck ancestry.
Woe betide us as we see him enclosed within his tomb *(we imagine*
him being sealed inside just as we feel his loss pressing upon us)

24 Both the weak and the strong, all ranks utter deeply painful sighs
of condolence,

And every wise man senses the tragedy, everyone
Feels the wound, everyone who knew him.
Our great community of Penrhyn and its domain in Gwynedd
share the bereavement we are all going through,

28 The sympathy of neighbours calling at the house is heard
repeatedly over and over.

Lady Catherine is of the same lineage
As her husband and just as generous in the giving of gold and
wine.
The beautiful daughter of Piers Mostyn, what a great tragedy this
is for her

32 For all her beloved family, to grieve the loss of her husband,
She wears deep mourning and is in tears
Completely overwhelmed with anguish like Iseult when Tristan's
tomb was sealed.

She is from the Talacre branch

36 Of the ancestral Mostyns, a family of powerful status,
However she does have two sons, better to be with her than those
two immortal Eagles of Legend
There they are, the nation's treasure remaining with her: Piers is
the heir *(aged twelve)* may he be blessed,
Handsome, able and intelligent, willing and helpful, original and
entertaining company.

40 He represents the best virtues of his wise and wonderful
grandfather;
Piers, please be mindful of the responsibility that goes with
inheriting great riches;
You have a well-proportioned physique, you are a fine, good esquire,

The rightful, true-blooded, suitable heir for Penrhyn.

44 Then there is the other son called William (*aged ten*)
Leading us in the hymn of praise, as if directing the family
      tradition of patronage onwards by respectfully supporting his
      mother on his arm, the Lady who will continue this tradition.
These two sons will follow in the adventurous footsteps
Of their good father and ancestors.

48 It is a very sad experience to stand at the graveside
Crying and sighing in anguish as Sir Rhys the Knight is lowered
                                 into his tomb.
His tearful burial is like the out-pouring of great waters
With the rising full flow of the choir in Llandegai Church.

52 Tonight, after the funeral, there will be the sad relating of memories
      throughout the land extending as far as two hundred islands,
A hundred counties will mourn for Sir Rhys.
A hundred great men will grieve greatly as they tend his grave,
Sir Rhys will be sealed and locked inside the Church Crypt
                    forever, a grievous wound for all Gwynedd.

56 May merciful Christ let him lie in peace,
We remember his contribution to society as we greet each other.
More than fifteen hundred people share their life-long memories
      of him and pay their respects at his tomb
In the Year of Our Lord Christ, 1580, the tributes are sincere,

60 Before us we see the golden chain of Penrhyn, crafted with the-
            deer symbol of his lineage,
And the upright oak tree image of valiant strength denoting his
            ancestral virtues.
We remember the constancy of his word, the warmth of his
      generosity, how gifted he was in the way he held office,
We recall his easy, calm, aristocratic manner.

64 Like dear Prince Cunedda, he bore his role appropriately
For one who dwells in such a powerful Court.
The privileged descendant of the talented nobility of all Gwynedd
Following in the same upright pathways of life once trodden by
      Prince Caswallon in ancient times.

68 In his day he maintained this Court as was fully expected of him.

With wandering minstrels and poets, with the giving and
                         receiving of gifts in praise and honour.
Following the strong military and political path of the Stanleys,
A good Christian, a man without evil.

72   He kept his word, even in the face of strong opposition,
Sir Rhys has been sealed for ever within his tomb, the flower of
                             Wales.

O God preserve his soul at once
So that he may soon take his seat in Heaven, the place Christ has
                             kept for him.
                             (G.L.)

THE BODYGUARD

Ifan Llwyd ap Ynyr, an older contemporary of Piers Griffith and also his kinsman, represents many members of the Welsh gentry fêted by poets, generations who went as young men into Royal Service to be soldiers and trusted security guards, some in their scarlet coats interfaced with black velvet and with the Queen's gold and silver escutcheon on their backs. This particular 'Lifeguard of Elizabeth' had a long and distinguished life-span.

ELEGY TO IFAN LLWYD AB YNYR

bodyguard to Queen Elizabeth I, her 'Hawk', by Huw Pennant 1591

Great is the grief throughout Wales after
The death of this true valiant Welshman,
Who was famous, handsome, fit and quick on the draw,
4   A cheerful, gallant, tall man as strong as a lion,
A prosperous and successful man of the gentry and compassionate
                             to others
As praiseworthy as the ancient soldiers who were his forebears, in
                           whose mould he was.
He has been known for many years as a man of honour and
                         respected as such,
8   Descended as he is from the same ancestral line as the legendary
                         leader Llywarch.

Here today was buried
Under the earth Ifan Llwyd
Son of Ynyr, once the picture of health, once the pearl
of all good families ...
...A family lineage that has been
Praised by the poet Rhys Goch Eryri
... there were eighteen hundred mourners at Ifan's funeral in
Anglesey
... descended from the legendary Cadwgan
... and benevolent Sir Tudor
... also from the ancient family of Cilmin
... God and Christ have chosen
To take unto themselves this man of the blood of Meredudd,

Cold is the soil and the grassy glade
That lies above the descendant of Llywarch, son of Brân the Raven,
ancient King of the Britons.

Ifan, of heroic blood
Was a remarkable man like his great grandfather
Syr Howel of the Brave Axe fame ...
... As for Ifan here, what a distinguished life-story!
32 Think of his eager, adventurous campaign experience in the French
Wars.

When he returned
He performed gallant deeds of valour,
As one of the Men of the Royal Guard proven and true
36 Well known for his absolute loyalty to his Prince.
Indeed he served
His country well guarding
Two Kings of pure lineage
40 And amazingly, two queens
Of ancient royal blood,
... Henry the Eighth, of blameless praise,
Ifan was also bodyguard to the boy King Edward

And afterwards Mary as we know,
Now retired and rewarded with a well-deserved, generous pension
                              after doing a highly-paid job well,
48   Serving and guarding Elizabeth, that dear honourable lady;
Intelligent, wise, sweet prince as she is
May Christ and God our Father long bless her and for that, let us
                              devoutly make the sign of the Cross.
If Ifan her faithful personal servant
52   Now dwells hidden beneath the earth of the Church of Saint
                              Ceinwen

No finer man ever went to meet God in the Kingdom of Heaven
Than he who once entered the Court of the Crown,
Nor was there anyone more courageous and strong since Moses,
56   There was no one anywhere in ancient England, to compare with
                              The Hawk, as he was called.
Within this grave, there lies
The man who won the Championship at the chief Games of the land:
He was once the strongest man at those events,
60   Deserving of the same praise as his great military ancestor
                              Cadwgan of the Britons.
...

64   There has never yet been such a powerful archer as he,
I know of no reliable witness
Living today who can disprove the fact that Ifan was the best shot
                              with his bow.
In every feat, I am telling you now without a false word,
68   Valiant Ifan was the best.
If he had to deal with any foreign
Army, he advanced into battle without retreating.
...
72   He used to take part in all the championships.
He was intelligent, gifted and of good family,
He was brave all the days of his life unto the grave,
Here lies the beloved, well-mannered, finely accoutred Welshman
Yielding himself to great Jesus,

76 In the Year of Our Lord,
    1591...

    The land of Anglesey is not a particularly happy and healthy
                           place to be at the moment
    Now that the beloved brave handsome head of the family is no
                      more, always so true to his word,
    How tragic is the widowing of Siân, Meredudd's daughter,
84 For her husband has come to the end of his days;
    The family stands around his coffin, without a painless moment,
    Siân's husband Ifan has been struck down by a cruel illness,
    Her family give her strong support
88 Devoutly ...
    The whole family have always been kind to the poor and to the
                      poets of Gwynedd,
    We will be woe-begone for a long time after his grave is sealed.
    ...

(*... The poem continues with an account of Ifan's soul being entrusted
to Christ in Heaven by the priest at the candle-lit religious service in
Llangeinwen Church where his children form the procession of mourners,
then receive the condolences of the poet with other onlookers):*

    ... After the death of Ifan's first son, Sir Meredudd,
96 Lewis is now his heir succeeding him,
    (*And the other children are*):
    Angharad, a refined, adorable, beautiful girl,
    Elin, Elliw, virtuous and gifted,
    And Annes, all descended from strong family roots,
100 With Sioned, a good-natured, stalwart lady generous in the giving
                      of gifts and charity;
    As I name them, these children are our comfort and compensation
    For the sad loss of Ifan Llwyd
    ... The Hawk ...

                                            (G.L.)

PIERS GRIFFITH AND THE ROYAL BODYGUARD

Alys, the elder sister of Piers Griffith and daughter of Sir Rhys Griffith, Knight, married William Williams of Bodlew, Anglesey, a kinsman of Sir Tudor, ancestor of Queen Elizabeth.

Their son Thomas Williams (1582/3 – 1623) married Elisabeth, the daughter of Sir Richard Bulkeley of the Porthamal estate on the Menai Strait, now Plas Coch.

Alys's eldest grandchild was William, who married Annes, the grand-daughter of bodyguard Ifan Llwyd ap Ynyr and daughter of his son Lewis who, with his brothers and sisters, must have had an interesting childhood brought up in staff family apartments at the Tower of London.

Alys's descendants live on today.

The Bodyguard's family home was the small country manor-house of Maes y Porth, Llangeinwen, Anglesey within view of the Menai Strait. The poem gives an insight into the reliance of the Tudor dynasty on loyal family retainers like Ifan, their kinsman, a man who must have witnessed many dramatic events surrounding the monarchy, both in their personal lives and on state occasions. Known fondly to Queen Elizabeth as 'The Hawk' until his death in 1591, he had guarded her since childhood, also her brother King Edward VI (who died of T.B. in 1553 at Greenwich Palace), and her sister Queen Mary I (of 'Bloody' fame, and who died in 1558 at St James's Palace.) The Hawk had formerly guarded King Henry VIII (who died in 1547 at Whitehall Palace) and his sister, Mary Tudor, daughter of Henry VII and formerly widowed young Queen of France, then Duchess of Suffolk as wife of the notorious Charles Brandon. When old King Louis died, Brandon had been sent by King Henry VIII to escort his sister home from France, the girl he had previously known as Princess Mary Tudor, his former teenage sweetheart. Now he had to see her safely back to England by Royal Command. Brandon quickly and secretly married her. Like Piers's grandfather Sir William, both Brandon and young Ifan the Hawk were present at the Field of the Cloth of Gold in 1520, and at Calais in 1523, then at Thérouanne and Tournai in 1513 during the French Wars, an adventurous experience of love, danger and intrigue that an Anglesey boy of good family was not likely to forget.

Within this social circle of North Wales gentry with Royal Tudor connections, William (the grandson of Piers Griffith's sister Alys) married Annes, grand-daughter of the trusted Hawk, some time after 1591.

Piers and the Bodyguard were kinsmen. Like many young men brought up in the same traditions, they were tough, loyal and educated, with civilised manners. They were up for a fight, thriving on military campaigns, voyages abroad, sword-play, dagger-tactics and tripping up their opponents. They had status. They were brave. They distinguished themselves at home and beyond, as heroes.

By 1588, as the great Hawk's life draws to a close and Piers is nineteen years old, the sceptred isle is seriously under threat of invasion from Catholic Spain. The Protestant Bible (translated into Welsh and published by order of the Queen) is on display and chained for safe-keeping in every Church in Wales. Like his kinsman, Queen Elizabeth's Hawk, Piers Griffith has just the kind of C.V. needed to qualify for a role in the Defence of the Realm.

Chapter 3

Armada

PLYMOUTH, JULY 19, 1588

People everywhere are rigid with dread. The Spanish fleet is on its way. The pinnace *Golden Hind* out patrolling to westward has just come running into harbour with the news that she has sighted the Spanish fleet off the Scillies.

Unless they can be prevented, the enemy will sail straight into Plymouth Sound, trap our ships, overwhelm us in a quick, brutal attack, land on our Protestant soil and slaughter us in our beds. Then they will advance on London, kill the Queen and take over the kingdom, in the name of King Philip II of Spain, vengeful husband of our late Catholic Sovereign, 'Bloody Mary'. Defence is weak, so there will be the added relish of scourging our women with special whips stockpiled aboard the advancing galleons, bearing foreign insignia the like of which in an invading force, will not be seen again until the Nazi aerial onslaught nearly four centuries later.

The fate of Western Europe hangs in the balance. Catholic Spain is already dominating the Western seas from the Azores to Portugal, frightening France and terrorising the Netherlands. Queen Elizabeth is in no doubt that England will be next. Her desperate last-minute attempts at peace with Spain through secret diplomatic channels have failed. Amongst her great naval commanders now busily preparing their battle-plans, is the man whose daring fireship tactics are to prove crucial in this great clash of oceanic powers.

DINING WITH DRAKE

Sir Francis Drake was a down-to-earth sailor of Devon farming stock around Plymouth, a man who would have been approachable enough for young Piers to present his credentials to him at the harbour as the Armada approached in 1588. The rich and eager young lord, arriving in good time, in good company and welcomed by Sir Henry Cavendish, must have impressed Drake sufficiently for the commander to accept him as a guest at his dinner-table aboard the *Revenge*. From contemporary portraits and Edmund Howes's description of Drake, we may imagine a short, stocky man "low of stature, of strong limbs, broad-breasted, round-headed, brown hair, full bearded, his eyes round, large and clear, well-favoured, fair, and of cheerful countenance."

He was born in 1541 with no hope of inheritance, but he was educated, as shown in the evidence of his wide reading and well-written reports. As a naval leader, he was equipped with excellent practical seamanship.

In the 1560s he went to sea with his kinsman John Hawkins and one year after Piers was born, 1569, Drake went to Court to meet the Queen in person when he brought the *Judith* safely back to Plymouth after escaping a brutal encounter with the Spanish off the coast of Mexico.

The highlight of his career was his circumnavigation of the world in 1577-80. After this, young gentlemen like Piers seeking their fortune on the high seas, were required aboard his ship *The Pelican* (later renamed *The Golden Hind*) to "haul and draw" like ordinary sailors. Drake would begin each ship's day with prayers for the justice of their Protestant cause, deal personally and severely with wrongdoers, and dine off silver dishes to the accompaniment of music. He was knighted by the Queen at Deptford after pouring vast amounts of treasure, gold and pearls before her, as both rejoiced in their investments. All London was astounded; and the news of riches and wonders of the world there for the taking, soon spread across the land. To Penrhyn. Drake was now rich enough to buy himself a fine estate, Buckland Abbey, to marry, and to retire early from the sea for a time, becoming a Member of Parliament; then he made one last bid for the Queen's favour after a slight contretemps had cooled her enthusiasm for his exploits, by setting out on his last great expedition of 1595. Piers Griffith was part of this secret mission of empire-building, scientific exploration, map-making and pearl-hunting. (MS LL.G.C. Br 4, 292, and J. Dyfrig Davies 1965.)

If Piers saw Drake die and be buried at sea, if he escorted Drake's drum back home to Plymouth, he might well have recalled all the experiences he had once shared with the famous commander over the previous seven years, dating from the events of the Armada.

༻✦༺

Sometime in May 1588 Piers Griffith sat down at Drake's dinner-table aboard the *Revenge* lying at anchor in Plymouth harbour.

> *Pierce Griffith of Penrhyn, Esq. a gentleman of considerable abilities in body and mind. When the Spanish Armada threatened the destruction of his queen and his country, he bought a ship, and providing himself with all manner of warlike stores, he sailed from Beaumaris the 20th of April, 1588, and arrived at Plymouth the 4th of May following; and upon his arrival there, Sir Henry Cavendish sent him an invitation to dine at Sir Francis Drake's ship, where he was treated honourably, and highly commended for his loyalty and public spirit. He followed the above-mentioned commanders till the Armada was defeated; and after that, he went with Drake and Raleigh to cruise upon*

the Spanish coast; he parted from Sir Francis Drake at
the mouth of the Gulph of Magellan, Sir Francis being
employed in making discoveries.

Source: *Observations on the Snowdon Mountains,* (1802) by
William Williams, of Llandegai together with *A Genealogical*
Account of the Families of Penrhyn and Cochwillan 1764 by the
Rev. John Thomas M.A. Headmaster of Beaumaris Grammar
School, published by E. Williams, No.11. Strand, London.

In Spring 1588 only 52 men and boys between 16 and 65 qualified for naval defence action in the Penrhyn area, so Piers's crew including 43 local recruits were also to be commended (NLW, MSS.585.) Who were they? Hardy local Bangor, Anglesey and Caernarfon lads (no one turned up for the muster at Conwy), interspersed with the kind of swarthy foreign cut-throats Thomas Prys refers to in his "Heldrin" poem, from their adventuring days together.

Piers Griffith was part of a whole generation of young lords eager to "sail with Drake and Raleigh", and he was not the only Welshman to distinguish himself at sea. There had been many heroic live-sparks around to inspire him into real action both in Wales and internationally, not to mention his schoolboy delving inside the richly bound adventure books of Classical legends like Ulysses, or of Tudor voyages of discovery that were available to him in the library at Penrhyn.

As the back-story to all this, far-seeing King Henry VII, Henry Tudor, a man closely allied to Piers's grandfather and great-grandfather, had wasted no time in investing in John Cabot's 1496 pioneering voyage to the Arctic with a royal patent for a shrewd trading syndicate to the Newfoundland fisheries in order to forge a route through the North West Passage to the riches of the East. By May 1502, after the tragic death of Prince Arthur at his Camelot court in Ludlow Castle, Christopher Columbus over in Spain was challenging Britain's nascent empire of the seas and representing the jointly ruling Catholic Kings, Ferdinand and Isabella, parents of Arthur's young widow Catherine of Aragon. Columbus had taken sail from the Canary Islands on a fair wind to the New World for a fourth time, aiming for the key power-bases of Hispaniola and Santo Domingo; but his enormous fleet of treasure-ships was sent away with several fleas in their ears, as Ferdinand and Isabella had warned. Nineteen ships were sunk and hundreds of sailors drowned. Such histories would eventually reach the Tudor Court at London and so to Penrhyn.

By the reign of Queen Elizabeth I (1558-1603) men brought up in the maritime traditions of the western seaboard of Britain, high and low from rebel Ireland down to Wales and Cornwall, had long been aware of their ancestors' defensive actions against Spanish and 'Turkish' pirates terrorising their coasts. In terms of adventurous seafaring, the people of Wales and south-west England "took a prominent part in naval expeditions and voyages of discovery which exasperated the Spaniards and finally goaded them into the disaster of the Armada," wrote G. Dyfnallt Owen in *Elizabethan Wales.* Boys like Piers were brought up in the principles and skills of navigation, of quadrant, astrolabe, hourglass, compass and maritime charts, especially if there was an expert in the family like Uncle Hugh Griffith of the East India Company, an ally of the Turks against the Spanish.

Miles Morgan of the famous Tredegar family for example, commanded one of the ships of Sir Humphrey Gilbert's 1578 quest to find the North West Passage. Here again there is a connection to Piers Griffith. Sir Humphrey was a friend of Sir Edward Stradling of St. Donat's Castle; his wife had nursed Gilbert through an illness (PRO State Papers Domestic 1547-1580.) The South Wales Stradlings were kinsmen of Piers through his grandmother Siân Stradling and he must have known of their association with privateering, legitimate maritime trading, mustering military forces, possibly organising piracy and smuggling too, features which continued around Wales throughout the Elizabethan Age and beyond.

SECRET INTELLIGENCE

In 1571, when Piers was but three years old and Sir Francis Walsingham's spy-game was effectively establishing itself, John Morgan, a gentleman of Carmarthen was instructed by the Government to venture on an intelligence mission to Vigo with two ships: spying on the Spaniards reported by trading vessels to be sending soldiers and secret agents to Ireland to stir up rebellion against the English rule but with little hard evidence. (PRO State Papers Domestic 1547-1580.)

The dramatic adventures of another intelligencer, David Gwyn, a boatswain on a merchant ship to Spain, challenge belief but may have been the actual experience of many an underdog historical records have ignored; however there does exist a lively picaresque Elizabethan 'novel' of the 'travels-of-a-gentleman' genre that is possibly inspired by his true-life story:

David Gwyn apparently docked in Spain in 1580 (when Piers was twelve years old) on a secret mission to gather as much useful information as he could about the Spanish fleet, and about reported assassination plots sourced to the Pope himself against the life of the Protestant Queen Elizabeth. Perhaps with a view to selling this information back in England, Gwyn was happy to report directly to Walsingham, or indirectly to one of his secret agents.

At Corunna, where many Spanish ships lay at anchor, Gwyn soon launched into his adventures, spying and being spied upon, this time by English traitors in the pay of the King of Spain. Dutifully Gwyn gave his confidential report to a Harwich sea-captain trading in the harbour, an unwise move, for the captain was a frightened man threatened by the traitors into betraying Gwyn who was then arrested and sent to the House of the Inquisition at the city of Santiago de Compostela in Galicia, "*where the lord knoweth his ende*," the State Papers record.

However the Elizabethan short novel with a parallel story has him escaping by the skin of his teeth after watching other victims horrifically burnt to death on bonfires by diabolical priests in the sinister back-streets of the Cathedral city; and eventually when Gwyn manages to take ship to England, he delivers the news to the delighted Queen Elizabeth personally, so grateful is she that he has foiled yet another assassination plot against her.

Meanwhile before and during the boyhood of Piers Griffith, the sea-ports of North and South Wales and the great sweep of ocean roads up to Newfoundland in the Americas and back down to the Bristol Channel, Brittany, France (La Rochelle specifically) and Spain, briskly expanded their coastal and overseas markets, with links to the Muscovy Company and the demand for rich furs. Piers Griffith traded both locally and on a wider spectrum with his coastal vessel *Elizabeth*, skippered by Captain Dobbe. Many sea-captains of the time traded in imports from Wales to Gloucester, for example, that included regular supplies of Welsh woollen cloth and best-selling fine friezes (colourful tapestries for bedding and interior walls), feathers, wool and skins; in return Wales imported their furniture, haberdashery, glassware and dry goods. The port of Barnstaple for instance sent calico and cloth, Bristol sent brass and pewter, the French sent salt, Gascon wines and cognac. Coal was shipped from Mostyn in the north on a grand scale and from Swansea and Neath in the south; Cardiff exported iron and coal, ordnance and munitions, wheat, butter, bacon, raw hides and tallow. There was a brisk trade too in good wine for the gentry and burgesses, also luxury goods of the kind Piers Griffith captured from the Spanish ship *Esperanza*: "…*silks, oil, spices, leathers*". Other port books record canvas, peaches, oranges, sugar and reams of paper.

As foreign merchant trade expanded in Wales, and as Beaumaris traders like Gabriel Roberts with son Lewis grew rapidly richer, there was always the added dimension of black market goods from smugglers and pirates who were in the know with good customers inland, like the Bulkeleys of Beaumaris and the Griffiths of Cefnamwlch, Lleyn.

The discovery and tolerance of gun-running at Cardiff may be seen within the context of a perpetual fear of invasion by the armoured cruelty of would-be Spanish Conquistadors. Tons of ordnance, guns and iron shot had already been shipped to Danzig, Amsterdam and Denmark, Protestant countries indeed, but one day the armaments might well fall into the wrong hands, the hands of the enemy; so there was a strict prohibition of weaponry exports even though every home-manufactured gun was needed to fortify the coast and supply the fleet before and after 1588. Piers Griffith managed to equip his ship *Grace* with "all manner of warlike stores" and the Bangor Port Books record his dealings in *"ordnance"* and *"iron"*.

Later, when Piers returned from Drake's Last Voyage of 1595, he would have been aware that the vessel *Pendragon*, a merchant ship owned by London businessman Thomas Hewett, was 'Westward Ho' along the English Channel carrying a cargo of iron, lead and tin. Hewett's plan was to slip into Plymouth on the outward bound journey to collect an illegal consignment of guns – "two minions, a scare, a falcon of brass and a demi-culverin", wrote Aled Eames, "with several hundredweight of iron shot". Arms-dealing with foreign powers was illegal of course, carrying the penalties of imprisonment or death. However, the profits were high, customs officials were lazy and detection could be overcome by tricks, bribery and lying low in remote coastal creeks. Clearly Hewett, mindful of the enormous demand for armaments in the world market, was prepared to take a calculated risk.

But who could accomplish such a task and bring off the deal? None other than Piers's uncle, Captain Hugh Griffith of Cefnamwlch, on the distant Llŷn Peninsula, mottled with secret coves, a man

Hewett now commissioned to captain his fine ship, the *Pendragon*. Meanwhile Hugh Griffith was already hand-in-glove with powerful local magnate Sir Richard Bulkeley of Beaumaris, a lord whose two brothers were well into a bold piratical-cum-trading network of their own extending to the Mediterranean; all were kinsmen and neighbours of Piers across the Strait; Hugh Griffith also had a clever lawyer for a son-in-law at Lincoln's Inn in London, just in case.

Uncle Hugh sailed the *Pendragon* from Plymouth to Toulon and Leghorn, with the Spaniards in hot pursuit but he managed to sell the guns and the ship to cover his tracks. Next he captained the *Phoenix* enjoying considerable success but it has been suggested that he was selling arms to 'both sides', indeed 'all sides'; in seven years' time Piers would be arrested at Cork, in 1603; and Thomas Prys may well have had hints of such skulduggery in mind when he wrote the warning poem *"To a Woodcock"*; or, by now, Piers may well have wanted to dissociate himself from his dishonourable kinsman Hugh. One of the *Phoenix*'s foreign crew members had once piloted a Spanish galleon in a fierce attack on Penzance in 1595. Captain Hugh Griffith and the *Phoenix* continued pirating and smuggling from the Breton Coast to the Rock of Gibraltar, not to mention recruiting some Turkish fire-power against the Spanish Armada, until he based himself nearer home on St Tudwal's Island, sharing the booty with his family and friends before sailing away to the Barbary Coast and dying of the plague in a rich Turk's house at Tunis in 1602 under the aegis of another potential power: the Islamic empire of the seas.

⁂

At the time of the Armada threat, on July 19, 1588, the first galleons of the Spanish Fleet were seen off the Lizard in Cornwall, sailing ominously eastwards in the direction of London and the Queen at Tilbury military fort. Drake's dinner-party was over, like his legendary game of bowls on Plymouth Hoe. Signalled from Plymouth by evening, warning beacons of fire were illuminating a chain of vantage points all over Britain, a highly organised system by hard-working locals determined to warn everyone of any danger to the Defence of the Realm. And at that point in Plymouth, Piers Griffith was probably preparing to lunge headlong into action aboard one of the famous warships safeguarding his country against the Armada.

The huge Spanish Fleet that sailed out of Lisbon on May 30, 1588 was a much more substantial force than it had been the previous February when the Marquis of Santa Cruz, "the Captain General of the Ocean Sea" died after a series of delays over the winter and some annoying prevarication by Philip II of Spain over the urgency of attack, until the King became aware firstly of Elizabeth's commitment by the Treaty of Nonsuch to help his rebellious subjects in the Netherlands and secondly, that every day was wasting Spain's resources in money, men, ships, arms and reputation, with the complexities of a delicate diplomatic and military balance neutralizing France and Turkey for the time being.

The new Spanish commander on this "Enterprise of England" was the seasick Duke of Medina Sidonia, albeit an experienced naval administrator. As we know, the Spanish plans would be destroyed by the English tactics of fireships, and by the vagaries of English weather. Going by the genuine ring of those precise dates of Piers's well-prepared departure from Penrhyn and Bangor, Port of Beaumaris "on the 20th April and his arrival at Plymouth on the 4th of May following", we know that Queen Elizabeth and her people were already vigorously informed by spies of the Spanish plan of attack. They also knew that they were up against a brutal, merciless and powerful enemy.

Dr Ian Thompson in *Royal Armada* wrote: "Between January 4 and May 28, nearly eight thousand Spanish soldiers and nearly three thousand of their sailors had been added to the basic fleet amassed by Santa Cruz. After September 30, 1587 the number of ships had been increased by 35 and the tonnage by 18,758. In the last three months, the guns on board had been increased by up to 200, and munitions supplies by 2,000 hundredweight of powder and about 50,000 shot (20 per gun.) Detained by contrary winds for two weeks off Cape St. Vincent and hit by a gale off Finisterre on June 19-20, Medina Sidonia was forced to put into Corunna in Galicia to refit and reassemble, and when he left again on July 22 he had lost 10 ships, 600 sailors and 1,500 soldiers…"

When Piers set off, like all the captains of the "little ships" converging on Plymouth from at least April, 1588, he was courageous, spirited and prepared to die for his country. Like others, he was a young man of action, doubtless fearing for his family, his people and his Queen, in the light of excellent naval intelligence and mindful of previous random murderous attacks on coastal villages in Wales and the West Country by Spanish, Portuguese and 'Turkish' pirates, peppered with Drake's and other mariners' tales about Spanish atrocities in the Netherlands and far-flung South America. It would be no exaggeration to say that the inhabitants of our island of Britain were as pulverised then by the real fear of invasion as people were in 1940 of a Nazi onslaught, when village halls throughout the land often staged morale-boosting lectures (for example Norman Tucker in North Wales) on the "valiant spirit" of Armada heroes, followed by cheering cups of tea and home-made suppers. There is a parallel. And today we have the threat of climate change, terrorism, invasive technological espionage, economic crises and other misfortunes.

STRATEGY

Imagine, like Piers, that during dinner aboard the *Revenge*, the commanders knew the reality of what lay before them. Yet the truth was much worse: "six front-line squadrons with a total of 63 or 64 fighting ships, plus four great, oared galleases from Naples, each carrying more than 600 men on board, and four light galleys.

They were headed by the two élite squadrons of royal galleons,... specialist warships... the flag squadron of the Crown of Portugal with nine of the largest galleons, and the Castilian Squadron, under Don Diego Flores de Valdés, consisting of the nine galleons of the Indies Guard completed in 1584, and five privately armed ships... [*at a*] ...cost estimated... a shade under two million ducats, 529,000 for the pay of the soldiers, 310,000 for the freightage of ships and seamen's wages and more than 1,000,000 for provisions. The cost of artillery and munitions was accounted separately." (Thompson, 1988.) These meticulous details given by the historian expose the incompetence that led to the defeat of the Armada. The crescent formation seemed invincible, but it was said that "Not all the gold of the Indies nor all the excellence of Spanish seamanship could bring England to its knees."

Dr Nicholas Rodger reminds us that Spain was "the most formidable military power of the age. The English, however, could never rely on wind and accident ... They had to find methods of defeating the threatened invasion, or at least of deterring it, and nobody was sure how to do it. In the first place there was disagreement between those who believed outright defeat was inevitable and outright victory possible, and those (including the Queen and her Chief Minister, Lord Burghley) who worked for a diplomatic compromise, were by no means sure that the Enterprise of England would ever materialize. If it did there was no single opinion about how to oppose it. Naval strategy was barely conceived, let alone born..."

One view was that the Lord Admiral, Lord Howard of Effingham, should guard the Strait of Dover opposite the Duke of Parma's ferocious army in the Netherlands.

We may visualise the scene and the table-talk aboard the *Revenge* under the stark black and white fluttering flag of Sir Francis Drake, or under the red and white Howard colours flying above the *Ark Royal* with all the attendant gentlemen present at dinner, doubtless more than once, thrashing out all their arguments, tactics, fears and enthusiasms: Sir William Wynter from the *Ark Royal*, Arctic veteran Sir Martin Frobisher with Lord Henry Seymour from the *Victory*, Sir John Hawkins, Sir Henry Palmer of the *Rainbow*, Lord Edmund Sheffield, young Richard Hawkins as Commander of the *Swallow*, Sir Henry Cavendish and his young guest Piers Griffith.

The majority of experienced naval officers were of the opinion that the English fleet should be stationed as far westward as possible, that is at their power-base of Plymouth. Then, in the prevailing westerly winds, they could intercept the Spanish invasion fleet before it reached the South Coast of England. From there, they would still be in a position to attack it elsewhere, up the Channel. This was Drake's view and it was shared by most of these senior commanders, all seasoned sea-dogs, who managed to persuade Lord Howard of Effingham, the Admiral of the Fleet, a sailor of some repute.

Word was sent to the Queen in London and at last the latest tactics were accepted by Her Majesty and her Government, who sent most of the official English naval fleet to Plymouth, leaving a brave little squadron to guard the South Downs. Meanwhile, soldier Thomas Prys was part of the land-army stationed at Tilbury under the command of his patron, the Earl of Leicester, and it was here that Queen Elizabeth inspected her troops, according to Thomas's reliable eye-witness account. As for Piers, we may assume he also shared the views of *his* mentor and idol, Sir Francis Drake.

There may also have been undercurrents at the dinner table, or indeed at several meetings aboard ship, murmurs and mutterings about why Drake, "the most famous admiral of his day, the terror and despair of Catholic Europe should not have been given command". But perhaps this is a modern viewpoint.

"In fact there were excellent reasons why not," wrote Dr Nicholas Rodger, "though Drake had more experience of commanding a large squadron than most of his famous contemporaries, he still had little more than Howard.

"Moreover, in an age of quarrelsome and touchy captains, he was one of the least tolerant of all. Chivalrous and polite to his enemies, he could be suspicious and overbearing to his immediate subordinates. On his last expedition in 1587, he had tried to repeat the precedent of his voyage round the world and hang his second-in-command, Thomas Doughty".

Drake was hardly the captain cryptically alluded to in the poem *"Pirates at Plymouth"*, the man nicknamed *The Rope* by Thomas Prys and Piers Griffith, but one does wonder and it may have been death-by-hanging to say so. Thomas at least, became disillusioned with 'pirating' and we get the impression that here in this poem is an example of a breed of such "quarrelsome and touchy sea-captains". Sir Huw Roberts also wrote that Piers himself was given to storms of temper which soon blew over into sunny spells. "What was needed was a man of equable temperament and unequalled rank, apt to take advice and able to give orders without offence, a man who could harness and employ the undoubted talents of his captains, not replace them," wrote Dr Rodger, "an Eisenhower rather than a Montgomery. Howard fitted this requirement exactly."

Howard was also the badge of authority representing Queen Elizabeth I and her Government. Hers was an impoverished and expensive navy, with an expenditure of 700,000 ducats a month during the preparations for attack. The previous year, 1587, the Queen spent only £44,000 on her official fleet, most of which went to pay for the small squadron, a policy possibly resulting from her characteristic penury, strict economies and her distaste for raising large loans or going into deficit finance. Yet because of the high competence of the Naval Board, the well-organised dockyards busy fitting out ships and stocking up on arms and victuals – just as Piers set to with his *Grace* just in time – the Queen was able to face the enemy of her people with a valiant heart.

The great Tudor Merchants of London contributed the biggest and best-armed ships. All England and Wales, dozens of ports, sent ships and men to fight, so Piers and his mainly local crew were part of this national emergency and duly commended.

Then there was the *Galleon Leicester*, the *Merchant Royal*, the *Edward Bonaventure* and the *Roebuck*, contributed by the great aristocratic ruling families of the land and by rich London traders; there was the stalwart *Edward* of Maldon, the *Crescent* of Dartmouth, and several manoeuvrable little pinnaces (including Piers Griffith's *Grace*, 40 tons) – the *Rat* of Cowes, the *Katherine* of Weymouth. The smallest ship apparently was the *Pippin*, of 20 tons with a crew of 8 men.

Howard, still convinced he could attack and overwhelm the Armada as it left Spain, made several attempts only to be driven back by contrary winds, until on July 7 he sailed from Plymouth for Spain and again was deterred.

The English fleet returned to Plymouth on July 12 and while they were eagerly refitting and re-victualling their ships, with Piers among them, he would have seen an amazing sight which proved to be the spur to all heroic action that summer.

On the afternoon of July 19 (July 29 old style according to the Spanish calendar) the messenger-ship pinnace *Golden Hind*, out patrolling the western sea-roads, came fast-running into Plymouth Sound. She brought the alarming news that she had just sighted a huge Armada of ships off the Scilly Isles advancing at an ominous pace.

INTO BATTLE

Whether Drake received full intelligence or not, King Philip of Spain had explicitly forbidden such a 'trap' strategy because his own espionage network was inadequate about the power and whereabouts of the English fleet. His commander, the Duke of Medina Sidonia had fully expected to meet Howard's main fleet along the way and out at sea but there was clearly another secret plan afoot.

English naval strategies, as we know them, were very different then; but such as they were in July 1588, together with other factors, they *did* save the day. Days. For this series of sea-battles was to go on and on here and there until late August at least.

That July evening, as twilight approached and when the ebb tide began to run, under cover of darkness, Drake's ships, with their boats and pinnaces in tow, gradually slipped out of the harbour into Plymouth Sound. By the next morning, Saturday July 20, most of the fleet was clear. By early afternoon Howard had sighted the advancing Armada of giant ships, far to windward.

That night the English ships, smaller and slicker than the Spanish galleons, positioned themselves to windward of the Enemy, that is facing the teeth of the wind yet well able to weather any stormy turns. They were brilliantly race-built; and their sailors, even the top commanders, had superb maritime skills compared to the Spaniards who were not all so experienced, albeit rigorously disciplined.

Lord Howard of Effingham, commanding the main fleet, was farthest out to sea with a smaller squadron which was the last to leave harbour, strategically left behind in order to sail between the Invaders and the shore. It is possible that Piers Griffith and some of his adroit, weather-beaten Welsh crew were amongst these men.

On Sunday morning, July 21 the two fleets came fully in sight of each other. It was now clear that the Enemy had lost the advantage of a surprise attack let alone the drama of close-up action, leaping aboard with thunderous blasts of fire-power and men screaming of victory or death.

Medina Sidonia and his Armada crews were amazed. How had 'the English' managed to escape from a potential trap? Get themselves to windward? And with the smallest of them (nothing but a tiny local squadron) dodging away to join their fleet when it was a foregone conclusion that these little targets were well within gunshot?

Yet as dawn broke on Monday, July 22, the captains and men of Elizabeth's ships saw what they were really up against: The Invincible Armada. This formidable enemy had the most astounding military procedures at sea, such as they had never seen before. The Spaniards were now busy enforcing a clearly long-practiced precise and defensive formation before the very eyes of their enemy, manoeuvring their huge armed ships ahead and on either quarter, while leaving their transport vessels in the centre of this ominous sea-army, then positioning their fighting squadrons on either side ready for the attack. Drake knew it was impossible to succeed without breaking up this deadly formation.

Defence concerns, after years of build-up to the Armada Real Event in 1588, were focussed on the "maritime counties" of the South of England, stretching from Cornwall eastwards along the Channel Coast, past Somerset, Hampshire and out to Cambridgeshire and Lincolnshire. Portsmouth and the Isle of Wight benefitted most from government expenditure on defences, with the Marquess of Winchester and the Earl of Sussex as Lords Lieutenant, in charge from the mid-1580s; but strangely, no royal cash reached westwards to Plymouth in Devon, possibly because the Queen was depending on the Hawkins and Drake custom of private finance. For example, £4,000 was spent by Plymouth on ordnance alone, on the advice of Sir Richard Grenville, and the only land-army at hand was a private militia of 300 men at Modbury over ten miles away. Raleigh managed to convince Elizabeth that the South-West too – from Cornwall to Wales, especially Milford Haven – was the danger-spot for a Spanish landing. In this context, Raleigh may have accepted Piers Griffith into some useful service while the knight of the cloak fame expanded his army and gunnery under the Queen's favour and authority.

BACK TO THE DRAWING BOARD

From July 22 to 31, after the initial shock, Howard and his Admirals were thrown into a cauldron of problems. They wasted days on brave ventures into random attempts to dislodge the Armada deadlock but to no avail. It was a case of re-thinking their tactics. Drake and the others set about their plans of attack. Perhaps young Captain Griffith was in attendance here, somewhere, somehow, awaiting further orders with his hardy men grimly busying themselves at mariners' tasks. Meanwhile supplies had to be delivered and men fed and watered on meagre rations.

Each opposing fleet believed in the justice and in the holiness of its cause: Catholic Spain and Protestant England, Wales and Scotland. 'God is on our side' was the theme pervading the atmosphere aboard every ship, the verbal thread running through the prayers of every man, from rank to rank, from ship to ship, from fleet to fleet, from friend to foe.

To reinforce morale-boosting, both sides had their maritime rituals, their country's naval traditions, their ancient codes of honour to carry them through and sustain them in the fight ahead.

The Duke of Medina Sidonia "hoisted his sacred banner to the maintop, and Howard sent his pinnace the *Disdain* to bear his challenge to the Spanish admiral, like a herald sent forth from a medieval army", Dr Nicholas Rodger wrote. This was a tradition Piers Griffith was well familiar with, from the classical and chivalrous tales of Penrhyn with their codes of honour whether at sea or on dry land, at jousts, battles, sieges and duels.

Lord Admiral Howard aboard the *Ark Royal* and leading the Fleet, attacked the Spanish ships on the northern side nearest the shore, while other smaller fleets attacked the other wing of the Armada. These were led by Drake, Hawkins and Arctic explorer Frobisher, three veterans of the sea, already legendary heroes of the Age of Voyaging and Discovery, once so inspiring to Piers Griffith from the security of his boyhood home, now playing key-roles in the defence of that very home of his, strategically yet vulnerably placed on the western seaboard of the Island of Britain, "Elspeth's" Realm.

As the first day of this great sea-battle ended, the one Piers had sailed all that way to join, 'his' side had achieved little more than blasting the Spaniards with rip-roaring cannon-fire from a safe range, and avoiding being lured into close action by several enemies, notably Martinez de Recalde on the seaward side, a daring captain who had hoped to waste no time launching a boarding-party but missed his chance. Howard and Company had to break the deadlock formation of armed ships, teeming with devoutly motivated Spanish officers, well-disciplined sailors, armoured soldiers and brutalised galley-slaves.

"We durst not put in among them, their fleet being so strong", Howard said.

THE QUEEN'S SEA-CAPTAINS
Yet at dinner that night, Howard with his captains, his admirals and their guests could take heart that they had done serious damage to the *Nuestra Senora del Rosario*, flagship of the Andalusian Squadron. "She lost her bowsprit in the collision, and the *San Salvador*, vice-flagship of the Guipozcoan Squadron was badly damaged by a powder explosion. Soon afterwards the *Rosario's* foremast went overboard, and having failed in an attempt to tow her, Medina Sidonia was obliged to leave her in the darkness," wrote Dr Rodger.

Meanwhile the English fleet was running dangerously low in ammunition, with a ration of about 30 rounds a gun. Desperate messages were despatched ashore in an urgent appeal for more powder, shot, cannon and guns. Piers Griffith and his men may well have played a useful role here, having brought along their own armaments from Wales.

That night aboard Drake's ship, the *Revenge,* the stern lantern cast its shadowy glow over the men of the guard, yet Howard's fleet was somehow unable to spot their vigilant light. As dawn broke on Tuesday, July 23, what had happened was plain to see. In the darkness Howard had cast too close for comfort astern of the Spaniards and was left dangerously vulnerable without most of his ships.

Meanwhile Drake and his men, possibly including Piers, had seized the *Rosario* and did not reappear until the afternoon, demonstrating Drake's irrepressible piratical instincts when opportunity arose. His daring nature in risking more conflict with the Spaniards for the sake of a prize of fortune, and causing disarray amongst the English commanders, surely tested the patience of chivalrous old Howard.

Did Drake extinguish his stern lantern on purpose? Was he planning to capture such a rich galleon as the *Rosario* under the very noses of both friend and foe? His admirers were amused and no one, apparently, blamed him. If Piers volunteered to go with him on this daring raid, it is feasible that the young ship-owning lord, his crew and his plentiful "manner of warlike stores" would never be short of a job under Drake's command.

Having served Drake from 1588 until 1595-7, Piers Griffith's later stunt in capturing the *Esperanza*, certainly places him in the highest rank of swashbuckling sea-captains brought up to believe that the rich prize of a Spanish galleon was the highest coup of all in warfare at sea. The tactics of how exactly to do this were probably learnt by Piers from Drake. It meant being adventurous enough to break the rules. 'The Queen's Sea-Captains' were synonymous with 'the Queen's Pirates', "*all honourable men*" – and all, like Piers, claiming at the High Admiralty Court in London that they qualified for Letters of Reprisal to regain their stolen goods, since the accepted attitude was that the enemy had attacked them first and stolen their booty. England was, after all, in a state of War with Spain.

On July 23 at the close of day, the *San Salvador* had also been taken, now a ghostly, waterlogged shipwreck empty of men. Yet the sailors of the English fleet were well aware that the enemy were now busying themselves re-grouping into another dreaded fight formation, schooled into the discipline of their huge ships so carefully prepared by the late Santa Cruz, who had not lived to see the actual onslaught ahead.

THE WINDS OF FORTUNE

The next morning, Wednesday July 24, as the two opposing fleets lay off Portland Bill in the English Channel, a strong wind blew in from the south-east as each enemy sought to grasp the wind's advantage, fire away at each other from a distance in a confusion of terrifying thunder-blasts, all the time avoiding close contact and missing out on forceful boarding-party attacks.

Then the wind changed back to westward as the Armada started to push its way gradually eastwards along the Channel to its final goal: the Crown on the head of Queen Elizabeth I, bastard Protestant half-sister-in-law of legitimate Catholic King Philip II of Spain, as they viewed things. Surely England was his and his people's by right?

By the time darkness fell, with the English fleet in relentless pursuit coursing their quarries, attacking and blasting them all the way to the point of yet again running out of ammunition, powder and shot, both sides were now suffering crippling destruction to some of their ships and men. Yet the Armada deadlock formation still remained unbroken. Howard's orders for more ammunition re-doubled. And so they continued eastwards for the next three days, July 25, 26 and 27, Thursday, Friday and Saturday up the Channel.

Secretly, during these three days, the Spaniards were sending despatches to their ally, the Duke of Parma over in the Spanish Netherlands, saying that their pre-arranged crucial rendezvous was imminent. Meanwhile the Queen's men and ships valiantly defended their South Coast from invasion and first thing on Thursday morning, July 25 saw them like bloodhounds surrounding a lone ship dawdling behind in the misty Channel, the *Gran Griffon*. This buccaneer-style assault tactic was also employed to fend off other Spanish galleons that came to her rescue. Thomas Prys refers to Piers as *"Griffon fierce in action"* in his *"Salmon"* poem; and with soldier Thomas as part of the action on land defending the south coast from Tilbury Fort with Leicester and the Queen herself, is it so far-fetched to imagine Piers as part of the *Gran Griffon* scenario?

On Wednesday afternoon, with the winds abated, Howard summoned his admirals for another battle-plan conference. What was on the agenda? The four split parts of the English fleet under Howard, Drake, Hawkins and Frobisher seemed to be fighting in perilous contrast to the unity and discipline of the Spanish fleet. The British were good at attacking in a line ahead so they could blast away at the enemy with their broadside guns. But it was to prove to their advantage also to avoid the solid block of unity favoured by the Spaniards. The Queen's ships accomplished this by keeping to these four brilliant squadrons with informal pinnace-style inter-coordination and communication between them, still ever watchful for any stray skulking Spanish ships. Perhaps this is where young Piers learnt his tactics and experience in message-taking, manoeuvring and intelligencing.

The Isle of Wight had already been earmarked by the Spaniards as a strategic landing-place for a full frontal attack on Spit-head. This was the scene of Thursday and Friday's actions, July 25 and 26 but light winds and a calm sea only further confused matters for both fleets. Drake aboard the *Revenge* saw his task as attacking the Armada on its seaward side, a risky strategy driving it further eastward and dangerously inshore. However this cunning move rammed the Duke of Medina Sidonia and his ships towards the Owers, stretching from Selsey Bill to Spit-head so that Sidonia was forced into a confusion between the devil and the deep blue sea. Would he battle his way up close to the English fleet and into Spithead, to establish a bridge-head on the Isle of Wight for a grand assault on Tilbury and London? Or perhaps he would change course to seaward and continue along the Channel to rendezvous with the Duke of Parma as ordered …

For Drake's part, he considered whether Medina Sidonia, a commander not given to recklessness, would risk such a disobedient rapid-raid of the type Drake himself favoured. Here Sir Francis may have calculated that the Spaniard would not. Not with the English fleet still at his back. The Armada was now positioned further out to sea mid-Channel south eastward, leaving the Isle of Wight and the vulnerable English coast behind them. This time, the dogged labours and seamanship of ordinary English and Welsh sailors, amongst others, with their varied commanders, were bringing them hopefully to the possibility of victory. Howard was well pleased, having succeeded *"so to course the enemy as that they shall have no leisure to land."*

DESPERATE STRAITS

On Friday morning, July 26, Howard knighted Hawkins, Frobisher and other captains to loud acclaim, but the fleet still had that ominous Sword of Damocles hanging over them: the imminent rendezvous of Sidonia with his ally Parma.

Still part of the action – he would never live it down if he opted out – Piers Griffith would have known, like everyone else, that 'Elizabeth's Men' faced a fearsome two-fold enemy with whom they had already *"exchanged certain bullets"*: Spain and the most powerful fleet in Europe combined with the greatest army. Howard's fleet had still not defeated the Armada; and the army of a war-weary, post-Netherlands Leicester at Tilbury, was now having to face yet again a military force notorious for its atrocities in Europe.

Perhaps as Howard and his colleagues took stock of the over-all battle, they may well have listed their own vantage points: the geography of their country and its variable summer weather. Could the enemy really land an army of over 17,000 men with Parma and even more from aboard the Armada? How practical was this on English soil? And was Leicester capable of defending the land? Also, could the gallant Sir Edward Seymour and his squadron guarding the Strait of Dover save the day?

Over amongst the Spaniards, even as they spoke together and despatched messages amongst themselves, Medina Sidonia was getting into difficulties near the coast of Flanders, an ally of Elizabeth and a land naturally protected by its treacherous and little-known sand-banks, with the help of the defensive action of Dutch rebels along the coast in what was to be called "The Battle of Gravelines". Medina Sidonia sent his communications to the Duke of Parma and so far he had received none in reply. Army and Navy simply could not reach each other to re-align and attack Elizabeth's Protestant Realm, where that ghastly English weather was now brewing an ugly storm.

On Saturday, July 27 the Spaniards docked off Calais and the English anchored nearby to windward, now thankful for the welcome arrival at last of Sir Edward Seymour's squadron, making a total of about 140 ships for Elizabeth's Fleet.

By Sunday morning, July 28 they were also awaiting the arrival of those crucial fireships planned some days previously. Howard and his commanders crowded around the outlay of maps on his cabin tables. This was an urgent meeting. Intelligence had arrived that the Armada was only 30 miles from the dreaded army of Parma encamped at Dunkirk, a harbour reported to be secretly in cahoots with Spain but purporting to be neutral, as far as English eyes and ears were concerned. And the fireships had still not arrived, even though their expert inventor was actually in England at the time.

DRAGONS BREATHING FIRE

As the night winds freshened and tidal currents ran in their favour, Drake, Hawkins and the others mustered together some of their own smaller vessels, set them alight with dazzling audacity and pressed them head first into the Spanish ships. Daredevil Piers Griffith may well be placed in this kind of action; Thomas Prys refers to him "*leaping from burning galleons*". But Medina Sidonia had guessed Drake's trick and was ready for the smoking fireships.

He had positioned a cover of pinnaces to grapple with or fend off "the beastly things" with the back-up of other ships ordered to break from their close formation but to be sure to return to their positions as soon as possible by morning. Nevertheless the Duke was tense with fear. Panic soon spread amongst his ships, not least because his ally Parma had once narrowly escaped such devices set up by the Dutch in Antwerp.

Now, as Drake's fireships advanced on them closer and closer, the Spaniards in their large, unwieldy galleons completely panicked as their carefully practised discipline disintegrated into uncertainty, then confusion and finally destruction. They managed to grapple two fireships and tow them aside. Another six flaming vessels were spotted heading for more ships lying at anchor. The Duke's discipline and chivalrous code of honour held him fast but some vessels cut their cables and escaped in terror, unfortunately for them, towards the treacherous Sealand Sandbanks out in the Channel.

As dawn broke on Monday, July 29, Drake, Hawkins and others knew they had succeeded at last in breaking up the Spanish fleet into a dispersal of demoralised units which they could now hunt down and destroy. If Piers was a witness at this point, he would have seen only five Spanish galleons left and a temptingly shipwrecked galleas, "driven ashore under the guns of Calais", a luckless remnant which Lord Admiral Howard seized for himself, boarding and looting and wasting several hours, so that foolishly, it took him until that afternoon to reach the great sea-battle that was now raging between the enemy and Drake and the four main English divisions who meanwhile had never let the Spanish ships of the Armada out of their sight.

The Duke of Medina Sidonia, predictably, fought a valiant rear-guard action allowing time for his scattered ships to re-group around him; but he was fast running out of ammunition and was now aware of the severe damage to his ships and the painful suffering of his poor men. The rising British storm was swirling all around and developing into unremitting, harrowing full-force winds with darkening visibility. Yet Medina Sidonia and his officers still courageously tried to regroup their men into their familiar discipline and formation, until by Monday afternoon they had managed to form a battle-line to challenge the English fleet. Nor were the Spaniards afraid of close-range combat; but by now they had almost exhausted their weapons and ordnance, were running short of food, water and supplies, completely out of round shot and had only small arms. They were forced, by a combination of unfavourable weather and complicated geography, into a defensive position when the English at last were able to unleash some terrifying destruction against them. As a result, two galleons were sunk, and two were driven on the sandbanks to be captured by Elizabeth's allies, the Dutch.

Relentlessly throughout the night, her ships pursued the Spaniards onto the shallows of the Channel until at dawn on Tuesday July 30, the wind unexpectedly changed to the south driving the Spaniards northward into the North Sea, with the Defenders not far behind, running short of ammunition again. Was the battle lost or won?

SHIPWRECKED AND SLAUGHTERED

Howard's words were, *"their force is wonderful great and strong, and yet we pluck their feathers little by little."* The stragglers lasted until August here and there around all the Islands of Britain. Howard knew, as did Drake, the Queen, Piers and everyone else, that the enemy galleons were now in a sorry state and at the mercy of the sea, wind and rain. They also knew that the Armada would have to be incapacitated to the extent that there was no danger of the Spaniards ever landing and attacking England, Wales and Scotland, nor Ireland indeed, where rebels were suspected of harbouring allies.

"If the wind should hold", wrote Dr Rodger, "there was nothing to do but attempt to return by a voyage north about Scotland and so home to Spain – a voyage for which they were in no condition. The wind held. On 2 August by their reckoning, past the latitude of the Forth, the English turned away in search of victuals and ammunition, leaving the Spaniards to hold on northwards."

The admiral of the Biscayan squadron recorded in his journal that the entire enterprise was lost because the English still retained command of their Channel, when the Spaniards were unable to rendezvous with Parma. Worse still, while retreating for home, their ships were sunk. It was a dismal retreat. A captain was hanged by order of Medina Sidonia for disobeying orders and at least twenty officers were arrested for similar offences.

About a half or three-quarters of the Armada ships were eventually lost, but not all as victims of English cannon-fire. Queen Elizabeth's Protestant Realm had been saved; the people and the government gave thanks and there was great rejoicing throughout the land, permeated with a sense of God being on their side, or at least the weather: "*...the wind blew and they were scattered*", said Elizabeth, referring to her intelligencers' last sightings of her enemies off the coast of Ireland, where many of them were so infamously cast, rescued or slaughtered.

Shipwrecks encrusted in sea-creatures, entangled in sea-weed have since been discovered by deep-sea divers to the present day, claiming golden salamanders, crushed shoes, broken pots and rusty armaments from the watery depths. Some desperate survivors, it is said, were washed half-naked on to the westerly rocks and sands of Wales, Cornwall and Brittany, with descendants to the present day. Some, a few, limped pitifully back to Spain and their sorrowful King.

As for Piers Griffith, Armada hero, when he had finished harrying the stragglers long enough, with Drake or Raleigh, Cavendish or Sir John Perrot, he surely turned the *Grace* about to windward and triumphantly sailed with the remnants of his battle-scarred crew for home.

His appetite for adventure had been whetted. It would not be long before he set off again along the Menai Strait, *"across the Foryd and over the bar,"* westward on his travels.

Chapter 4

Pirates at Plymouth c. 1590

A Poetic Debate between Mr Piers Griffith and Mr Thomas Prys in Plymouth concerning the sea

This unique double-edged poem, a swashbuckling duel of words between two pirate-poets aboard one of Sir Francis Drake's ships at anchor in Plymouth, may be found, with variations in at least five old Welsh manuscripts. Here in this paraphrase translation, the two adventurers share a witty dialogue on the pros and cons of privateering/ piracy: robbery with violence on the high seas. Is it 'a mug's game', they ask each other, this dangerous quest for fame and fortune?

Thomas Prys: You and your ship *Grace* have got us into a whole lot of trouble haven't you, Piers Griffith! The risks you have taken have cost you dearly. Now you are running out of luck. This relentless fortune-seeking only leads to misfortune. You have been battling against the sea for years but now the tide of your triumph is turning.

Piers Griffith: As for you, my friend, you would be better advised to stay at home farming your estate; and as for carrying on with girls, out to rowdy taverns every night, enjoying yourself dancing to the tune of harps, there is no excuse for it, chasing a girl in every port, just to indulge some wild passion for a mistress's eyebrow.
It is shocking the way you set about satisfying your own desires.

Thomas Prys: Well, you would fare much better chasing girls on
shore than following Lady Fortune on the high seas.
You too would be well advised to stay here and sort out
this crisis in your life. Frankly, my own misadventures,
consumed as I am by the flames of passion romancing
girls in hedgerows, are infinitely preferable to the sort of
predicaments you get yourself into, like jumping
off burning galleons.

Piers Griffith: And what about you? You keep searching everywhere we
land for the most beautiful girl in the world, on some vain
quest for the ideal image of beauty. But for myself, my
dear friend, I love riding high on the ocean wave, playing
the wheel of fortune. I love seafaring, the great surges of
the sea, the unique beauty and
light of the ocean in all its changing moods.

Thomas Prys: This riding of the great sea-roads, this heroic wandering
has never been a problem for you, has it? It has always
been a clear decision for you. You have always had this
determination to go to sea, seeking fame and treasure in
your azure-painted *Grace.*
Your Estate at Penrhyn, now that is where your true riches
lie. There is no point in all this talk about seafaring, this
quest for yet more treasure. Surely you have got what you
want already, in your own back yard?

Piers Griffith: What difference does that make? What if I *am* in
possession of wealth and privilege? Who knows what
kind of riches are best? The thrill of seafaring, or the
excitement of making love to a lady in the dark? A
difficult choice. Here are two quite different experiences
of the senses.
And this is my dilemma. To risk drowning at sea and
being burned alive in a flaming ship, or drowning and
burning in the flames of love.

Thomas Prys: Do not make excuses, not for being a pirate, a privateer
rather. Listen here, you are very likely to get caught soon.
The day will come when you are sure to get arrested
as a spy. You are not likely to be able to go on trading
profitably for much longer you know, not even as a
privateer, risking everything to follow the
call of the sea.

Piers Griffith: One may fail once but one often succeeds the next time
on the ocean wave, twofold. I thrive on it! In spite of the
freezing cold and the arduous nature of the voyage as I am
hurled about the ship in stormy weather.
Like me, you are only too well aware of the risks involved
in treasure-hunting – tell that to my bodyguards too.
It is a kind of trap, I know, this life of piracy, but one that
has its own unbeatable thrill.
You watch out, Tom Prys. You yourself have a taste for
other kinds of dangers, perils that may well entrap you
too, and trip you up!

Thomas Prys: Ah Captain! *(Greeting the Commander of the ship.)*
… Er … This is only a foolish, hotly disputed matter we
are discussing here, Captain. *(Who is he? Surely not Drake
himself?)*
(Muttering aside) What a stupid, ill-tempered man is
this we see before us, yelling drunkenly at the sailors. No
wonder the crew call him 'Rheffyn' (Rope.)
(Then, getting on with his duties as ship's officer)
"Aloft! Up the mains'l, you puffard.
Do not waste time talking nonsense, brace the yard and
trim the sails!"

Piers Griffith: Look here, *(Tom Prys)* you cannot write poetry for
tuppence. You are always flattering someone but you are
really only ridiculing them. *(There follows a sudden dark
mood-change where Piers now strikes below the belt, but*

these next words will one day prove ironic, considering the anguish-to-be of Tom's Elegy to their two sons and finally to Piers himself.)

Your verse is never created from the depths of your true being. It is not spontaneous, not freely spoken, not when you get yourself into a tight spot, like that time in the Ludlow Law-court.

(Both have faced charges there, Thomas for rape and assault, Piers for several family feuds and debt.)

<u>Thomas Prys</u>: *(Changing the subject with a new kind of cut and thrust)*:
To repeat an old saying, if the lady is cold towards you, your love-suit is frozen too. It is hard work trying to please a cold-hearted girl even on a romantic moonlit night. Like the chill wind of winter, so your words to me are cold and cruel. Which is the coldest, tell me, a frozen romance, the wintry wind or an unkind word?
I will tell you, the coldest thing of all is to go short of money.

<u>Piers Griffith</u>: The very coldest. You are a weak-willed man, certainly. So it stands to reason you will be shivering cold and poverty-stricken if you go on wasting time like this, hanging about in the chilliest snows of winter just to chase some girl. But I agree, the most miserable thing in the world is to have no money.

<u>Thomas Prys</u>: *(Having the last word)*:
Well I for one do not intend going seafaring ever again, riding high on the ocean wave. I dare not risk it. If I do, all my good humour and civility will desert me wherever I go. I will never succeed in reaching a safe haven that way. I must seek another, more secure way of life so that I can have ready money in my pocket to spend and keep me in high spirits!

(G.L.)

Popular in Elizabethan times, the hey-day of Piers Griffith and currently enjoying a new airing amongst Welsh poets, students and American researchers, these verses are based on the Classical convention of a formal debate, yet they have an authentic, conversational ring set in a realistic context.

There is a sense of drama here, possibly inspired by the fondness of Piers and Thomas for the London theatres. In Plymouth harbour, as young officers in Drake's fleet, or possibly around the time of Drake's proposed Last Voyage in 1595, Piers Griffith and Thomas Prys speak in turn, reciting the lines each has composed in order to counter the other's arguments, witty in tone until the unpredictable, mysterious mood-change towards the end.

We can almost hear the wind in the rigging, the creak of the ship's timbers and their ill-tempered captain yelling at his crew scurrying about the deck, up the ropes or down below.

We have the impression that the two adventurers have either just returned from another disastrous raid defending the island fortress of Britain, or else are on the eve of some hazardous new expedition. Their usual haunts are the coastlines of Western France and Galicia in Northern Spain, then past the Canaries and the Azores across the Atlantic to the Caribbean, attacking Spanish galleons laden with gold from South America.

The two pirates/privateers are clearly familiar with Plymouth and its maritime community. It may also be assumed that they are rather infamous characters along the waterfront, not a stone's throw from the legendary Plymouth Hoe where Drake is said to be fond of playing bowls. This is the setting for the poem, a busy natural harbour with rocky coves and sandy creeks ideal for 'pirating' and strategically situated on the wave-lashed seaboard of England's West Country, one of the main naval bases for repelling the Spanish Armada only a few years before in 1588.

Here Plymouth represents the heart of England, steadfastly serving as its guardian, its pilot through the risky tides of fortune.

From here, generations of hardy sea-dogs, men and boys, have voyaged in and out of its harbour lights. From here too, the Pilgrim Fathers will later set sail for North America.

Now, possibly in the late 1580s or even into the 1590s, in the last days of Queen Elizabeth's Golden Age, we may imagine the port bustling with its buoyant trading atmosphere, rowdy taverns, trundling wagons, attractive girls hanging about selling bread or fruit from their laden baskets, ragged messenger-boys racing along the dockside with the cries of seagulls swooping over the shoreline, as a multitude of ships lie safely at anchor: galleons, pinnaces like Captain Piers Griffith's *Grace*, schooner-rigged; fly-boats like his little *Elizabeth*; speedy single-masted balingers; brigantines and merchantmen; perhaps a huge warlike galleass or carrack from foreign parts, captured vessels, small fishing boats, rowing craft and so on.

In the poem, we get the impression that the two pirates know each other very well. Each seems long familiar with the strengths and weaknesses of the other. Both have shared boyhood dreams on their remote country estates in North Wales and during their student days at Oxford of voyaging and adventure overseas.

But are they still committed to following Drake's flag, sailing with Letters of Reprisal authorised by the Virgin Queen herself who takes a hefty percentage of the profits? Or should they, as the poem suggests, cut their losses and get out now? There may be a hint of anti-climax here after all the excitement of those former Armada days.

While the dauntless Piers remains fired with the spirit of adventure, Thomas Prys, in contrast, seems bitterly disillusioned. He is the first to throw down the gauntlet, challenging his friend to defend his arguments for continuing their piratical life together, obliged as they are to finance their own privateering ventures. Or they may even be reduced temporarily to hiring themselves out as ship's officers. And although Piers valiantly defends his own position, he manages to find holes in his cousin's arguments. He may be trying to persuade Tom to go with him on Drake's 1595 Expedition, which might date the poem more precisely. The tension grows between the two men until the final thrust, when their conflict explodes into a blazing row. Harsh words are spoken, shouted possibly. Home-truths emerge.

Poems in this format are still meant to be performed aloud before an appreciative audience in taverns, societies or eisteddfodau in Wales. In Elizabethan times such verses (like William Middleton's Caribbean poems and hymns, Lieutenant Peilin's 'Pelican' ballad and the soldier-songs of Ifan Llwyd Sieffre) served as entertainment aboard ships, often with music, pipe and drum. Here in this poetic battle of wits between Piers and Thomas, each duellist deals the other the next blow, and the next, as their quarrel grows more and more cutting and accusing.

The truth is, Thomas confesses ruefully, he for one simply cannot afford to risk any more financial losses at sea, let alone keep an armed band like Piers does.

No, Thomas must face the bleak reality of earning his own living. He must now return to his neglected country estate – small fry, his tone suggests, compared to the privileged lot of such rich young gentlemen adventurers as Piers and his wealthy aristocratic friends, the daring, spendthrift sort who follow in the wake of the maverick Earl of Cumberland perhaps, as Professor John Guy has suggested; and we may recall the Armada link with Sir Henry Cavendish, Bess of Hardwicke's son, her "bad boy".

Is there a note of resentment on Thomas's part, we wonder, in these concise verses where complex shades of meaning are inevitably lost and the rich, poetic subtleties of Welsh *cynghanedd/ alliteration*, versification, and clever word-play are dispersed in translation?

Frankly, he insists to the young heir of the Penrhyn dynasty, why bother? With a huge inherited fortune like that – something

Piers seems to be taking entirely for granted – why bother sailing out to seek more gold elsewhere only to risk losing everything *"on the wheel of fortune"*?

Only a close friend like Thomas Prys of Plas Iolyn, would dare speak out as boldly as this to Piers Griffith of Penrhyn, a much grander domain than the barren moorland where Thomas's ragged sheep may barely chew on a blade of grass. As such, he is in a position to advise Piers as no tough-guy sailor from amongst the young lord's bodyguards ever can, a position that can claim the traditional poetic role of critic-cum-supporter. After all, Tom is on Piers's side.

Dramatically speaking, this Plymouth duel of words between two pirates has a contemporary immediacy. Together these verses may be viewed as a realistic scenario, with Piers's ever-ready crew of Bangor lads and foreign brigands hovering in the background concealed amongst the shadows of the ship, sharpening their swords and daggers.

⁂

Chapter 5

Drake's Last Voyage, 1595

To Mr Piers Griffith by Ifan Llwyd Sieffre

This soldier of fortune, young lord of the manor of Palau ('Palé') in Mid-Wales, an Oxford man, was a distinguished poet and personal friend of Piers Griffith. "A dragon with Drake notoriously hunting the seas."

(Manuscript Brogyntyn 4, 292, 1595, see Sources)

If Fortune or a famous career are by this venture to follow him, let
                us praise this quick-witted
  Remarkable gentleman who is my friend, the person we all love,
I hope that soon we shall see you elevated to an earldom
4 Piers Griffith, I wish him a long life.

Go off on your violent adventures once more, to win
Fame again as the man we associate with conquering remote oceans,
Do not drop anchor in vain in any desert place,
8 He is a dragon with Drake notoriously hunting the seas in fierce
                pursuit of their enemies.

Armed men aboard their fleet, soldiers with a high reputation at
                stake, may live
Long after people have tried to besmirch them with false evidence,
And as for Drake's ships known for their fine craftmanship, no fault
                lies with them,
12 The heir of Penrhyn has seen fit to invest in them.

When he returns home from his expedition, I can vouch for this,
I hope he will not be deceived by Fate,
So may he return unharmed to the place he wishes most to be,
16   To the domain of his ancestors, the inheritance established by his
great-grandfather.

(G.L.)

DRAKE'S LAST VOYAGE 1595

Piers Griffith accompanied Sir Francis Drake on the final Expedition of 1595-7 to the New World, a journey from which Drake never returned. That legendary heirloom, Drake's Drum in Buckland Abbey near Plymouth, still seems somehow to be awaiting the magical re-appearance of its owner as a long-lost hero who just might hasten back in an emergency,.

Sir Francis was regarded amongst his own people as the rich local supremo and lord of the manor, public-spirited and genial, a role-model indeed for Piers Griffith.

Drake may have been planning this last voyage from 1591, during the years of his early retirement from the sea at his grand home in Devon, a place that today seems dense with the atmosphere and imprint of his presence; a place one may fancy to be only a horse-ride away from the strategic anchorage of Plymouth. Eager to sustain the Queen's good favour and to apply his abilities to the common good, Drake (at that point a Member of Parliament and a married man) set about planning the latest water system for the town, long troubled by the dangerously polluted River Plym.

With the gentlemen of the Borough and ever the entrepreneur, Drake made an agreement for the "bringing of the River Meve to the towne" and was paid the sum of £98. As in many villages and towns, people had to travel miles to reach safe wells and water supplies, unpolluted by animals, sewerage and human settlement. Ships anchored in the harbour could also fall victim to disease and the inconvenience of sporadic water supplies. So the scheme clearly fascinated him; and work began on the stone-lined channel from the River Meavy on Dartmoor to a reservoir above the town.

Was a similar, if not more primitive improvement ever planned at Penrhyn amongst *"the weirs, mills... gardens of Penrhyn and all its appurtenances"*? Certainly the territory in Devon was no less wild than North Wales, for the channel or 'leat' had to travel 25 miles through "valleys, wastes and bogs, and what was most troublesome of all, a mighty rock, thought to be impenetrable." (Norman, 2004.)

In any case, the clean water system or "Drake's leat" was completed "with great care and diligence" in four months by April 1592, when Drake with the mayor and corporation, "mounted trumpeters amidst the firing of salutes" and witnessed a dramatic free-flow of crystal water into the town. Drake was acclaimed as great a hero on dry land as he had been at sea.

On national and international levels, Drake was largely motivated by self-interest, like other adventurers of his day: Raleigh, Hawkins, Cavendish and others, so perhaps Piers Griffith followed suit. As entrepreneurs with investors and bankers ever breathing down their necks, these great merchant adventurers considered it good business to help others whilst at the same time benefitting themselves and pleasing Queen Elizabeth I. Drake the local hero was also keen on developing the usefulness of his community, for example building mills visible across the landscape, drawing on wind-power for six *'greast milles'* around Plymouth, with other rented mills at Millbay on Plymouth Sound above the turbulent sea, that would forever link him to his place as a national hero, not to mention the necessity he saw for the continuation of traditional ship-building yards around Bideford.

In 1592, when Drake was thus occupied, give or take the general alarm over a Spanish raid or two on places like Mousehole in Cornwall, Piers Griffith may have been drawn to the on-going plotting and planning of his other mentor, Sir Walter Raleigh, who was known to be now investing £34,000 in equipping a splendid new merchant fleet gaining notoriety throughout the land. Raleigh's already glamorous reputation was further enhanced by news of his successful raid in the Azores against the famous *Madre de Dios*, a huge, fiercely armed Spanish carrack, *en route* from the East Indies and bound for home, laden with treasure. In much the same way as Piers was to take the *Esperanza* eight years later, Raleigh captured the lot: a cargo of jewels, spices, ivory and silks to the value of £150,000. With high hopes for regaining the Queen's favour, which Piers probably did later with his 1600 prize, Raleigh now hoped to erase all shame for his disastrous Roanoke expedition to North America. A rescue attempt in 1589 found no trace of the colonists previously abandoned there, but recent archaeological evidence suggests they died of starvation, disease or murder by the native inhabitants.

It is possible that Piers, perhaps in a supply ship and with other daring companions, ventured to Roanoke initially, led by Raleigh only to return on a subsequent rescue bid. Such events could well have been added to the long catalogue of futile escapades which so disillusioned Thomas Prys in his dialogue with Piers in their poetic collaboration, *Pirates at Plymouth*.

Now Raleigh was to endure a metaphorical wrist-slap from an ageing Queen jealous of his secret love-affair with a 27 year old beauty, Elizabeth Throgmorton, one of her ladies-in-waiting, already pregnant by him. The Queen was livid, cried hysterically and hurled her shoes about the room. Raleigh and his Bess were then despatched to the Tower separately to cool down. They were released two months later, banished from Court to Raleigh's leased estate and castle of Sherborne in Dorset, where they married and had children. The eldest son, Wat, was to lose his life on Raleigh's final doomed expedition of 1616 in the reign of the anti-piratical King James I (albeit an avaricious patron of land piracy.) Again, it is possible that Piers *did* join such an expedition at that point, for both Piers and Raleigh were in London by 1618 when Raleigh lost his head and Piers spent time in the Fleet prison for failure to provide dowries for his seven daughters, by order of his stepfather-in-law, Sir Thomas Mostyn. Piers's troubles are so akin to those of Raleigh, and Piers's exploits so much in keeping with those of Drake, that one is tempted to see parallels between them in their personal lives and in their sea-going adventures, for good or ill. In seeking to emulate the great Merchant Adventurers, or follow in their wake, the Pirate of Penrhyn drew not only himself, but his family and his estate within their sphere.

All three liked to live life dangerously and small wonder, for they were not like other men. Raleigh, on land, was given to associating with religious sceptics like Thomas Harriot who went to Roanoke, North America in 1585. He was also friends with the subversive dramatist Christopher Marlowe and with Walter's brother, Cardew Raleigh, so much so that Thomas Howard, Viscount Bindon "was directed to examine Raleigh and his associates concerning their alleged heresies." (Norman, 2004.)

❧

By 1593, Piers's mentor, Drake who was not an Oxford man like the young captain but clearly an educated and well-read one, was busy representing Plymouth as its MP and still fuming with anti-Spanish feeling. He promptly set about strengthening the fortifications of the town which had been attacked and burnt by French, Breton and Spanish pirates periodically, like the coasts of Wales so dear to his protégé. In Plymouth, a fort was built to protect the entrance to the harbour, with Drake contributing £100. The fortifications at St Nicholas Island where Drake is said to have hid with his family after the brutally violent Catholic uprising of 1549 – now known as Drake's Island – were improved and a garrison guard installed.

Similarly, knowing Piers's close connection with the Foryd and the Caernarfon Bar separating its ancient castle ramparts from the open sea, it is reasonable to suppose that men such as Piers and his

99

influential, rich merchant uncle, Sir William Griffith of Caernarfon would share the coastal concerns of Drake and Raleigh. Sir William was a local magnate owning a manor-farm estate with a large slipway down to the sea, in the ancient parish of Llanfaglan that prominently borders this vulnerable western coastline. With Piers and others, he may have attempted improvements in the spirit of Drake but on a lesser scale across the water of the Foryd. There is further evidence of Welsh worries about invasion, from the still visible clues of other stone coastal defences around farmhouses and old settlements along the great sweep of sea-shore, northwards from Lundy to Holyhead. For centuries, Wales had been well used to random attacks by bloodthirsty pirates – Spanish, Portuguese, Irish and 'Turkish', even gangs of British thugs and escaped jailbirds, capturing amongst others, a boy from Nefyn and some ladies of Holyhead.

The pressure was still on, in the last golden days of Elizabeth's reign, to adventure for gold, conquest, discovery and empire. King James I from 1603 onwards, was not so impressed by the glamour of it all and was suspicious of Raleigh who, like Piers and Drake and the young men who followed them for fame and fortune, was obsessed by the legend of El Dorado: the famed City of Manoa, South America. Raleigh, falling in and out of favour with the King, who was himself greedy for riches and inclined to extravagance, first sent a servant on a mission to explore the Orinoco River, now in Venezuela, sailing on to Trinidad where he captured and befriended the governor, Antonio de Berrio, who confirmed the gold legend. In 1612, having desperately persuaded the King that this was a worthy expedition, Raleigh sailed off 'up the Orinoco' for 450 miles without ever discovering the glittering city, but still convinced there was gold there somewhere and pathetically clutching a lump of quartz speckled with small grains of gold and the first imported cargo of mahogany.

If we follow the reliable contemporary evidence of poet Sion Mawddwy and of Oxford-educated country gentlemen like Ifan

Llwyd Sieffre, Sir Huw Roberts and Thomas Prys of Plas Iolyn, together with that of Henry Keepe in 1683 and the later convincing Thomas-and-Williams source, Piers Griffith not only knew Drake and Raleigh around Plymouth, Devon, Dorset and London but sailed with them "upon the Spanish Coast", that is Spain itself and "the Spanish Main," areas of South America and the Caribbean dominated by Spain. Our sea-captain was clearly influenced by this fashionable in-crowd, to the point of obsession.

Furthermore Piers would have had wind of any impending expedition, and so would other friends, adventurers and soldiers-of-fortune who probably sailed with him, like the poet-witness Ifan Llwyd Sieffre (Evan Lloyd Jeffrey in documents), Hugh Middleton or Piers's servant "*Darby Bach, the Irish boy*", a consummate duellist and sailor.

In 1594, a year before he set sail with Drake for the Caribbean, Piers and his men were again raring to go. With salt in his blood and chivalry in his soul, he simply "must go down to the seas again…" It would all depend on keeping in the Queen's good books but Time was marching on. Who would succeed her?

There was one more daring deed to perform, before "our Elspeth's" demise. Late in 1594, the news Captain Griffith was waiting for came to Penrhyn. Sir Francis Drake had been commissioned by the Queen to sail with a brand new fleet to the West Indies. The planning stage was long and protracted, with Drake as Admiral aboard the *Defiance*, 500 tons with 46 guns and a lion-figurehead. Ex-slaver Sir John Hawkins as Vice-Admiral, commanded the *Garland*. Mustered were 2,500 soldiers armed to the teeth under the command of Sir Thomas Baskerville. Drake's fleet of 26 ships and pinnaces, like Piers's *Grace*, including six royal vessels provided by the Queen, one of the chief investors, finally left Plymouth on September 7, 1595.

Unfortunately by this time, Drake's carefully laid plans were facing obstacles. After sailing triumphantly from Penrhyn to Devon, Piers Griffith may be imagined again "on arrival at Plymouth" as part of the Ship's Company, trawling over rolled-out maps across tables with compasses and astrolabes.

However, news of this awesome expedition had been reported back to the King of Spain by a network of spies with links right along the south-westerly harbours of Britain and Europe. One culprit was Don Pedro de Valdes, amongst others, Drake's Armada ex-prisoner from aboard the *Rosario*, now turned and metamorphosed by the likes of Robert Cecil into a scared-to-death double-agent, then released into the dark, sleazy underworld of espionage and skulduggery. At once the Spaniards responded by strengthening their navy, reinforcing their port defences and making rapid-revenge raids à la Drake in reprisal attacks on Cornwall and Wales, burning Penzance and other towns and villages where they performed, it was said, unspeakable atrocities against men, women and children.

What lay ahead for Piers and his companions? On October 6, 1595 Drake's fleet arrived at Gran Canaria to a surprised and explosive response from the ferocious gunners along the fortifications defending the shore. In SAS commando-style, a party of Drake's armed men crept ashore the following day when they were surprised again by a group of wild shepherds who killed some of them and brutally took the rest prisoner. Amongst those enslaved was the surgeon of the *Solomon,* who was tortured mercilessly until the Spaniards dragged strategic information out of him. Details of the purpose of the expedition were spilled; military, scientific, geographic and piratical plans were revealed; and inevitably the Spaniards were able to send ships ahead to the Indies to forewarn their associates.

By October 26, Drake aged 56 and Hawkins aged 63, both now seriously ill, had reached the West Indies islands of the Lesser Antilles, then Guadeloupe by October 29. The *Delight* and the

Francis fell behind the grand wake of the other larger ships, and sailed disastrously towards another Spanish fleet commanded by the fearful Don Pedro Tello de Guzman. On first sight, the terror and shock of the ill-prepared crews aboard the little *Delight* and the vulnerable *Francis* may only be imagined; and if Piers and his companions were anywhere near, aboard the *Grace* or some other vessel, they would have witnessed the Spaniards giving chase, thunderously attacking the *Francis* with all their gunnery, leaping aboard with drawn swords, capturing the unfortunate crew and abandoning the ship to a ghostly, barnacled fate in the devouring depths of the sea.

However, the trusty *Delight*, slipping away and speeding ahead, was thankfully able to report this catastrophe to Drake. Meanwhile his great enemy, Don Pedro Tello de Guzman, calculating that the English were aiming for Puerto Rico, took a series of fast sea-roads and deviations to confront them there. Did Drake calculate this? As his fleet lay at anchor off Puerto Rico, another catastrophe befell the Commander aboard the *Defiance*: the death of his kinsman Sir John Hawkins on November 21, aged sixty-three, his vice-admiral, the mentor who had inspired him and others since their boyhood to lead an adventurous life at sea.

Later that evening Drake sat in melancholy mood at dinner with his officers in his lamp-lit quarters – possibly including Piers as courier aboard a pinnace, or even as captain of his own messenger–ship *Grace*, for such small ships were well able to be carried aboard a larger vessel to far-flung foreign destinations.

Then they came under yet another surprise attack. Thunderous explosions suddenly started blasting from the Puerto Rican fortifications out across the harbour waters to Drake's unsuspecting fleet. Dinner-guests were shuddered out of their seats as deadly shots penetrated the *Defiance*. Drake's friend, Brutus Brown was one of the first victims, shot dead as a bloody gash of flesh seared open his spurting veins. Sir Nicholas Clifford was so severely wounded, he died in agony later that night. Legend has it that Drake's stool at table was shot from under him as he was drinking his beer.

The Admiral immediately ordered his ships out of port, via his busy network of slick, manouverable messenger-pinnaces. Then the fleet anchored in safer conditions along the coast, only to return stealthily later that night and attack the Spanish warships anchored there with five devastating, flaming incendiaries.

This tactic seems to have been a fatal error on Drake's part. The whole harbour was now illuminated by leaping tongues of crimson flames, spewing smoke and the burning stench of flesh, wood and metal, as the English ships were revealed in full focus of the flare-path; easy targets for the ferocious gunners on the castle ramparts above.

Again Drake's fleet was lambasted with all the force of the enemy, a vicious bombardment that drove Drake out of Puerto Rico and into the open sea beyond.

There was tragic and heavy loss of life but Drake never lost his vision of success and still remained buoyant if not optimistic. He confided to Sir Thomas Baskerville, *"I will bringe thee to twenty places foure more wealthye and easier to bee gotten."*

Again the services of a reliable, speedy, Spanish and Portuguese speaking messenger of courage like Piers was required, when Drake sent word to the Governor of Puerto Rico, Don Pedro Xuarez, pointing out that Drake's men had previously shown mercy mid-battle to some Spaniards by rescuing them from their burning ships, according to the ancient chivalric code of honour amongst mariners. Now in return, Drake begged for the lives and safe delivery of the 25 or so subjects of Queen Elizabeth, taken captive by Guzman when the Spaniard captured the *Francis*.

Drake's fleet arrived a week later at Rio de la Hacha on the Spanish Main, having buried Hawkins at sea with full military honours aboard the *Defiance* in November, 1595 near Porto Rico. In the more agreeable atmosphere of the wide river with its friendly natural inhabitants, the Pearl Fishers, and its busy little ports and creeks, Drake's men were able to rest, and his ships were at long last able to be refitted. Yet when the people offered Drake a small ransom in pearls, he was insulted and ordered the town to be burnt, perhaps an indication of his ill-temper and advancing sickness.

Drake's party ruthlessly looted and put to flames other villages at Rancheria and Santa Marta on December 20 then sailed over to Nombre de Dios by December 27, but again the place was deplete of booty except for one bar of gold and the odd piece of silver. Two days later the party split when Baskerville took 900 men by road to the town of Panama to prepare for a rendezvous with Drake and his reinforcements who would meanwhile sail along the River Chagres.

But on the rough mountainous Pass of Capira, Baskerville's men got bogged down in muddy, slippery slopes that were treacherous and impossible to negotiate, when suddenly they were ambushed by Spanish soldiers. Baskerville had to retreat to Nombre de Dios, which Drake also burnt in revenge.

※

On January 5, 1596, Drake sailed to the west, telling the army captain Thomas Maynarde, who left his memoir, *"God hath many things in store for us, and I know many meanes to do her maiestie good serveice, and to make us rich"*.

Maynarde's comment about his commander at the end of this disastrous voyage was that *"he never carried mirth nor joy in his face,"* suggesting Drake's weary and heart-broken state of health.

Drake gave orders for two of their pinnaces to be destroyed because they were damaged – may we assume neither of these was the *Grace*? – and he organised efforts for the construction of four more.

Meanwhile a fever epidemic was surging its way ominously

through the brave sailors of the fleet and Drake himself was suffering the severe symptoms of bloody dysentery. They set sail again on January 24 but made poor progress without fair winds to take them. Drake and many of his crew became worse. Eventually, he had to sink into his bed, exhausted, ill and helpless.

Like all well-organised mariners – except Piers whose Will has not been found to date, a deliberate ploy perhaps – Sir Francis had already made his Will, leaving his manor and his mills to his wife, Lady Elizabeth, with some Plymouth properties to his heir, brother Thomas, £100 to his sea-captain nephew Jonas of the *Adventure*, between £340 and £100 to his servants and £40 to the poor of Plymouth, large sums in today's money.

Knowing he was about to die, Drake generously gave his officers parting gifts in the manner of honourable admirals. He handed plate and jewels to his servant Whitelocke, bidding him to dress him in his armour, in order to die "*like a soldier*". Then he made a supreme effort to rise from his bed and "*made some speeches, but being brought to bed again, within one hour dyed*" and "*yielded up his spirit like a Christian to his Creator, quietly in his cabin,*" about 4 a.m. on January 28, 1596.

Baskerville, now commanding the fleet, supervised Drake's burial. His body was sealed in a lead coffin. Cannon thundered from the bows and trumpets blared, proclaiming the sad departure of one of the men who had saved Elizabeth's Realm, benefitted his local community and forged new paths into the New World. The coffin slid down into the clear but alien waters off Porto Bello, "*a league out to sea*". Drake and Hawkins had failed in their ambition to wrench Panama from the grip of the Spanish.

If Piers witnessed this event in 1596, we may speculate on his deeply grieving response. His loss. His mentor was dead. He and his companions, all probably sick, weary and penniless, must now return home. Did this signal for him the end of an era? If the *Grace* was scuppered by Drake at Nombre de Dios, this would explain the subsequent five to six year absence from Penrhyn of Piers and presumably his crew from 1595 onwards, until he was next seen in 1600 bringing the *Esperanza* into Abercegin Creek. By 1603, his own captured ship at Cork was called a *"flyboat"*, not a pinnace; and he confessed to Captain Plessington that she had been *"three years at sea"*. A mystery indeed.

Where did Piers go between 1596 and 1600? Or between 1600 and 1603?

Or did he – needs must when the Devil drives – fall in with Raleigh who is known to be going off on another expedition around this time? Both men, after the anti-climax of Drake's death, would have been unable to resist yet another fortune-hunting challenge, perhaps fatally so, as Thomas Prys suggests in his poem, *To a Dolphin*. Or quite simply, our man may have been seriously wounded or he may have fallen ill, most likely of dysentery along with the others, from malaria or yellow fever, seriously weakening his health for years to come.

Meanwhile someone brought Sir Francis's belongings back to Plymouth, to Lady Elizabeth Drake at Buckland Abbey, along with all the messages and news that were needed to explain to his wife, his Queen and his country about what had gone wrong on this final, tragic voyage of discovery, plunder and revenge. In any case, a trusted someone bore these precious objects back: Drake's Bible, his sword, his navigational instruments, his maps, his drum.

Plymouth's *Black Book* records,

> *Sr Fraunces Drake and Sr John Hawkyns went to the West Indias with XXXVI sayles of shippes and pinnaces and both dyed in the Jurney and Sr Nicholas Clyfford slayne.*

That was how the voyage ended, the hoped-for daring deed.

Ironically, the next poem provides new evidence for Piers Griffith's role on this perilous expedition which began in such a mood of adventurous and reckless optimism, seen here through remarkable insights into his character, his private life at Penrhyn with his wife and children, his mother, his crew and their local families. The wise words of Siôn Mawddwy, a poet of some distinction, will prove to be prophetic.

PRAISE-POEM TO PIERS GRIFFITH OF PENRHYN, THE POET, AND MARGARET HIS WIFE, 1595

Upon his departure to the West Indies with Sir Francis Drake
by Siôn Mawddwy

Drake's famous Last Voyage

You are the lord of a great court that extends its welcome to all,
        you hold open house,
You are the powerful heir to such a domain, a credit to Christendom,
Your eternal destiny is clear before you, Piers Griffith,
4   There is no one to be compared to you for generosity, stag of the
        herd at Penrhyn,
On you go, keeping to the singular path you are determined to
        plough before you,
You are superior to other heirs of estates, for your father was a
        Knight of the Realm, gilded with honours,
Sir Rhys Griffith was a dearly beloved man,
8   The best of his kindred, highly respected as far as London,
The son of a knight who was himself the son of a knight,
Powerful at leading an army, a superb horseman,
The finest lord of chivalry, with celebrated ancestry,
12 Pure of character was this knight, from the lineage of Marchudd ap
        Cynan.
I refer to your grandfather, I remember him well,
Piers, you have the finest blood running through your veins, you
        command so much respect.
Who else is as praiseworthy as you, as fine as you, on such a high
        pinnacle,
16 As dignified and authoritative a lord as you, handsome young
        man?

Everyone respects you for your nobility and greets you as such
with formal manners,
The foremost earl of all Gwynedd with your own personal armed
bodyguard,
Is that who you are, a prophet of wise, perceptive words?

20 Even the fish in the sea and the village fool
have heard of your gilded reputation,
You are the heir to Penrhyn, a clear mirror of excellence.
The finest God-given gift

24 Your mother ever had was to give birth to you, may she be praised.
Dear God, your mother here is seriously worried about you,
Dear Lady, you are like a golden-gowned goddess with your gold-
braided head-dress,
Descended from Mostyn lineage, stately and powerful.

28 Piers, you are a leader who is charming both in personality and
appearance,
A name that is sure to endure throughout Gwynedd.
You are like the eagle, the king of the air; you should be knighted
with a golden sword,
Gilded twice over, doubly intelligent and wise as you are humane
and gentle.
You are the touchstone which men depend upon, the focal point
around which love and friendship gather,

32 Shrewd in strategy when planning a military campaign, you are
the sort of man who has to win.
Valiant and extraordinarily gifted, this is the essence of your being,
You are like an oak tree amongst lesser thorns.
You are quite fearless just like your father; resolute in a crisis

36 You are like a dragon cutting your way through the might of the
enemy with your sword.
There is no one here as gifted as you, as sturdy as a golden knot on
a rich robe,
No one is as clever an entrepreneur in sea-trading as you are, nor
as generous in the sharing of profits.
You are a strong leader, decent to the core,

40 For you have married into noble blood,

Margaret, a great lady dressed in a superb gown of cloth-of-gold,
Of the honoured Mostyn family, well-accustomed to wealth and
position.
A fine heiress in her own right, cheerful on all occasions,
44   With the same purpose in life as she, you may intercede with
Christ, the Lamb of God,
That you may enjoy a long and happy life together, may you depart
in worship,
Both of you, blue-blooded as you are.

Strong, kind lord, Piers, generous to a fault, with the power of
Solomon,
Within your country's bounds, you are an excellent gift to the
people,
The hearsay is, great and worthy lord,
That you are to depart from your great home and estate
52   For the West Indies, a great land far away.
You are voyaging overseas, dear lord,
Over the mighty waves, which makes us sad,
For the journey is long and arduous, three years,
56   And for that length of time, we will be without you, our leader, a
son with the best possible upbringing.
After you have gone we will miss our ruler of lands and feasts,
The people of Gwynedd will be without their very soul.
Your home is as righteous as a temple, it is so wonderful here,
60   Your delightful way of life, your good fortune, you have everything
And your family; yet no one can be sure what the outcome of your
adventure will be,
You are very much in our thoughts, all of us, we your friends,
Golden prince, you are such a fine handsome young man
64   Your people would deny you nothing; they would do anything for
you.
They adore you, fearless lord,
Yet despite all this, here you are setting out on your quest
Across the ocean, a heroic captain of men on a pioneering voyage
of discovery to the very ends of our great globe.

68   In the Year of Our Lord, the soul of Christendom,
One thousand, five hundred and ninety five,
You are flying away like a wonderful golden bird, let us bid you
                    Godspeed, therefore,
Piers, blessed as you are with your good looks and generous nature,
72   If this is what you really want.

    Therefore go, I am now speaking to you most solemnly,
Venturing as you are with the blessing of Elizabeth, that slender,
                    elegant lady,
You are a man of special gifts descended from fine ancestry,
76   You are going with Drake, and if you venture there
Your mother will need to pray for you daily for ever,
You are so dear to us and strong in mind and body, that I pray you
                    will return safely to us.
Your wife is praying for you, like the symbolic hind drinking from
                    a pure stream,
80   She is devout and faithful, only the power of her prayers can keep
                    you from danger and in good health,
Like Ulysses no one can ignore you,
She is your Penelope waiting virtuously for you to return home
                    again.
The prayers of your children, will bring good blessings to assist you,
84   As long as you are as watchful as an eagle, to safeguard your golden
                    body.
For your own sake, do cling on masterfully to your ship like Ifor
                    the Legendary Voyager,
The lands you journey to are in a sorry state, my generous lord
                    deer [*hind, to be precise, a play on words*].
We beseech God for you, on our knees,
88   We know your whole being is very agile and healthy, yet we are
                    still praying intensely to God on your behalf.
We are all in tears, praying incessantly for the length of two
                    lifetimes,

May the true God protect you,
And the lives of everyone you are employing

92   To go on this expedition with you.
      God in Heaven will hear our cry,
      God will be gracious to every man here amongst the crew in the
                                                          face of danger.
      May the Fate that Almighty God grants them be a happy one,
96   Let us hope it will be so, let us pray to God
      That you will achieve the wish of your heart,
      Golden riches fairly won, for the benefit of this country and
                            thereby your safe return home to your own land.
      God in Heaven, despite his suffering on the Cross,
100   By His own Grace, will bring you safely back here
      Navigating you in all magnificence, with great skill,
      Back home to Penrhyn once more.

                                                                    (G.L.)

NOTE:

TIMELINE FOR THE VOYAGES OF SIR FRANCIS DRAKE

1558-66   First voyage as a boy with older cousin John Hawkins.

1568-9   Slaving voyage with John Hawkins to Guinea and the
          New World. The Spaniards attack at San Juan de Ulua,
          Mexico.

1572-3   Voyage to the Americas.

1577-80   Voyage around the world in the *Pelican,* later re-named
          the *Golden Hind.*

1581   Drake's return to England when he is knighted by Queen
          Elizabeth I as Sir Francis Drake.

1585   Drake marries the beautiful Elizabeth Sydenham, his
          second wife.

1588   The Armada is defeated, with Drake's help.

1589   The disastrous expedition to Lisbon.

1590   Drake retires from the sea and serves as Member of
          Parliament for Plymouth.

1595/6/7 Drake's last voyage and death at sea.

Chapter 6

Spirit of the Age

Pirate Song of the Caribbean / Carol yr India / Bagad o Gymru / Cerdd y Pelican

A song composed upon our expedition to the West Indies aboard the Pelican by Richard Peilin and Lieutenant William Peilin c. 1570 – c.1590

THE POET
"In truth, as I went
Seafaring in the West Indies
In deep thought yearning for my homeland,
4   God only knows,

I saw a bird overhead
Perched on the branch of a tree
Piercing its own breast with its beak
8   So that the blood flowed over its crested feathers into the mouths
                                             of its chicks.

Good day to you, Pelican,
You beautiful bird with fine long wings,
How kind you are
12   To feed your tiny young on the blood of your own breast."

THE PELICAN
"Good day to you, where do you think you are going?
What are you doing in this country?
Where have you journeyed from in order to arrive at this place?
16   You are, as far as I can see, a Christian man."

THE POET

"I am, a man from Britain, a Christian indeed,
There are more of us here,
Not one of my friends has the faintest idea
20   What kind of a lost world we find ourselves in."

THE PELICAN

"As you have travelled so far away from your own country
I will serve as your ambassador
To tell your friends in Christendom
24   How you are faring on your adventures to distant lands.

I can survive quite happily at sea
Catching shoals of fish, truly,
I can swim, and fly great distances across the world,
28   There is no better messenger.

But I do not know one step of the way,
What direction to take whether north or east,
Nor how many miles there are by sea or land,
32   From here to Britain."

THE POET

"In miles, seven hundred
By sea to Britain,
And the set-course by Platt's Rule
36   Is directly to the east.

Fly there, Bird, and when you reach land,
Hasten to the Royal Court, with our latest news,
To a lovely princess virginal and kind,
40   Our righteous Queen.

There you may also greet
The celebrated Sir Roger Williams,
Distinguished in battle, loved by all,
44   A most excellent courtier, and incomparable Knight of the realm.

Say that we have not yet made one discovery
Nor territory, nor city, not even an entire island
Without conquering in every violent chase
48 All the enemies who threaten Her Grace.

Our first mission cost Spain dearly,
The country where spies lurk against us,
We hotly pursued their galleons
52 Like hawks after crows and their cursed chicks.

Sailing from there to Porto Santo
Their rocky peaked power-base on the coast of Madeira,
We burnt their towns and laid waste their land,
56 So brutally I doubt Spain will ever recover by Judgement Day.

From there, it was but a short distance
Southwards to Tenerife
Where we were not favoured by the wind, I have to say,
60 Thus preventing us from inflicting as much serious damage as we
should have liked.

From thence we sailed far off without incident
The wind behind us, dead aft;
At the end of one month's voyaging we sighted land
64 After many trials and tribulations.

Before we arrived here in Domenica
There came towards us, in boats, a tribe
Of naked savages with painted faces and tattoos all over their
bodies,
68 Armed with arrows in their grasp like devils.

Accursed fiends, with fierce primitive faces,
Their patterned skins like the kindred of Satan,
With metal rings pierced through their nostrils like wild boars
hoofing into the earth
72 And with bloated cheeks foaming furiously at the mouth.

In truth they were the most awesome of nations,
Those cruel cannibals.
They are not so much humans as creatures resembling crazed bears
76   Devouring the living flesh of Christians.

Because they were great in number
And of terrifying aspect
We did not tarry there long, for sure,
Even to seek water supplies to slake our thirst.

We therefore departed thence in haste
And landed on the Island of Coche
Where we knew there were pearls and precious stones for the
                                                        taking,
84   Once one had first conquered the inhabitants.

From there we sailed a considerable journey's distance
Directly to Cumaná in Venezuela
And captured all the enemy's ships
88   That lay at anchor along the river.

After a week's time we sailed close into
The lee of the desolate coastline of Caracas, the utmost end of the
                                                        earth,
Captured a fortress on the waterfront
92   And kidnapped the governor to boot.

We pressed on through this land
Despite hoards of enemies challenging us at every turn,
Through a jungle of the highest trees we have ever seen
96   Where no Christians have ventured before us.

We marched night and day
Over a high mountain, higher than that peak in the distance,
Without resting anywhere even for an hour
100   Until we arrived at the town of Santiago de Leon de Caracas.

We entered that great city,
Bombarded it to destruction and burnt it,
And laid to rest upon the ground
104 All the corpses of the men who had once lived there.

We did not stay long attacking this city
In the face of such a ruthless army for more than a week
For we were but three hundred, outnumbered,
108 It was not a place to hang about.

There were precious metals and gold everywhere in plenty,
We failed to plunder them all, to be sure;
But we dared not delay there any longer
112 For we were in sore need of reinforcements.

We sailed on to Coros, their lair on the coast of Venezuela,
And razed the town to the ground by fire and fighting,
We *did* conquer four fortresses, certainly,
116 All their fortifications between the city and the sea.

And on our long journey back
Again towards our ships,
The enemy, ten to one,
120 Attacked us.

Some to our rear and some facing us,
And some with a trained band surrounding us;
We were engaged in a fearsome battle
124 For over four hours on one front.

They shot at us menacingly
With their poisoned arrows,
We in retort despatched our lead bullets into their bare bodies
128 Driving them on with the purpose of our revenge.

We accomplished all that for two long leagues
Seizing land by armed force along the way,

Before we were able to pluck out their arrows from the flesh
132 Of our own wounded men.

In truth, although we numbered as land-soldiers
But a hundred and fifty men,
We killed far more of the enemy
136 Despite being so heavily outnumbered.

Go, Bird, and boldly tell this story
Of how some Welsh soldiers acquitted themselves splendidly,
As for the English, a third of them were killed,
140 Or wounded, or died of their wounds.

Captain Billings, with armoured breastplate like Hector
Is our Military Commander on land,
In every onslaught he has the strategies to overcome danger,
144 He alone leads us into battle.

Captain Roberts is second-in-command
Advancing heroically like Jason,
Or like Theseus with his deadly club
148 Bludgeoning down our enemies.

And Hugh Middleton who seems to be everywhere
Plays his part courageously to the utmost,
And those two lieutenants, so often part of every trained band:
152 Salesbury and Peilin.

Robert Billings, Sarjeant Hughes:
Never would either of them ever make a truce with the dark enemy,
Will Thomas, Will Jones and Hugh,
156 That was our gang of Welshmen.

Give them news, Bird, that we have gone to Newfoundland
Through the gulf with its perilous current,
And from thence we will return to Christendom
160 To visit our nearest and dearest once again.

And if we press on Northwards
Failing to keep exactly to the familiar sea-roads,
We may then glimpse Cape Clear,
164 And land there on the Irish coast.

When our mothers used to delight in
Bringing us up, mischievous boys that we once were,
Little did they fondly realise
172 That we would one day voyage along such pathways.

Farewell, Godspeed to you fair Bird,
Depart for Britain on our behalf,
Greet all our friends there,
176 And tell them how we fare in this far-flung world where we have
ventured."

(Signed) Richard Peilin
Lieutenant William Peilin
(Translated by G.L.)

❦

Queen Elizabeth engaged in several secret conversations with Drake and others amongst her sea-captains before they set sail on their adventures. The '*Pelican*' poem and its variations may have concerned one of Drake's mysterious diversionary missions using another ship of the fleet re-named the '*Pelican*'. Such a ship registered under a Captain Billings *did* exist, or else the ballad may date from an earlier voyage of the '*Pelican*'. The events correspond with some naval reports but not entirely. Drake's 1595 '*Pelican*', we know, was renamed the *Golden Hind* during the course of his last adventure, as a tribute to one of his main investors, Sir Christopher Hatton, whose personal crest was the golden hind, newly carved at the prow of the refitted ship, which was then able to continue on its originally planned voyage, thus avoiding detection by the Spaniards.

The Plague and the Rebellion of the Earl of Tyrone, c. 1599 – c.1601

(A Soldier's Song) by Ifan Llwyd Sieffre, soldier-of-fortune

> *This fine poet, long overlooked, was a close friend of Piers Griffith. (See* Drake's Last Voyage 1595.) *Here he comments vehemently on the Irish Campaign against O'Neill, particularly the slaughter in Ulster near Dungannon; on the Essex Rebellion; and on the widespread unrest during the last days of Elizabeth's Reign.*

True nation of Britannia, the last remaining descendants of the
blood of Troy,
People throughout Cambria,
Sing together in good voice, listen willingly
4   And say your prayers thoughtfully,

May God give you eternal salvation,
Elizabeth our crowned Queen,
May she give her Grace to the Members of the Council in order to
help good people
8   By punishing notorious traitors.

May Christ be merciful and grant happiness and peace for the
Crown
And good health to men afterwards,
Grant plentiful fruit on the trees and corn in the meadows
12   To make sure we always have food.

Understand that it is our good Father who gives us every Blessing
And gifts that are productive in the creating of good things,
Do not let the Devil seize hold of you
16   And tempt you too far like Judas.

Christ is merciful and slow to chide
And just in His judgement when it is given at last
Before giving His verdict and spreading throughout the whole world
20   Signs indicating a change for a better life.

We have seen three signs already that Christ is very angry,
Woe are we if we do not know how to escape
Firstly Death then Poverty because of high prices
24 And thirdly alas, War.

Unfortunately the Pestilence has arisen in London,
Some planet from the sky was said to be the cause,
Many did not cross themselves so death befell them
28 As much as fifteen hundred in a week.

Then following this came Want to Wales and England,
Deprivation for many and widespread Hunger
Having to give as much as seven crowns was many a sorry tale
32 For a sackful of Ruthin corn.

Before God and the Trinity granted us to be relieved of all this
trouble
The Plague and our impoverished suffering caused thereby,
The Earl of Tyrone started
36 His uprising in Ireland.

Burning and despoiling the land,
Killing and murdering the English,
Recruiting the Spanish to their side
40 With the intention of driving the English out of Ireland.

Twenty three captains and a thousand men from Britain,
Long was the grieving caused by the slaughter
Battling at Black Water as it is known to many
44 Who fell together immediately as soon as their venture began.

The campaign was disastrous, bad for England, weakening the
kingdom,
Death befell many a proud, valiant man,
We the soldiers of Wales are all woe-begone
48 After the killing of Sir Harry Bagnall.

It is well-known that we did not gain victory in Ireland,
That our enemies were of enormous numbers
And that Britain never before
52   Not once had such a defeat.

This is what our Grace the Prince Elizabeth
Did for her faithful friends,
She sent such brave armed men over
56   To avenge the innocent blood of those who had perished.

Under the command of the merciless Earl of Essex in his suit of
                                       armour
Many went to meet the enemy full of fury,
Lords, Knights, cavalry, captains, magnificent soldiers,
60   Let us pray for them in their departure from this life.

Everyone according to your parish, never waver,
Pray devoutly and put aside your complaints
So that God may grant a free pathway
64   Through the places where Essex, the stag *(leader of the herd)*
                                       marches.

His father went there before him truly
As Governor of the land of Ireland
And may his son have the reponsibility
68   Of conquering O'Neill and his supporters.

It was in France that he began his career as a soldier,
In the islands he made his name,
To Ireland he went as praise for him grew
72   And God is freely on his side, the leading lord.

Children in their cradles and women in their chairs
And old men staying at home
And the priest from his pulpit, everyone must pray
76   For God to grant good health to Essex, the stag-leader.

It was because of our sins that the Plague nodules came upon us
And the scarcity of crops and the War,
So it would be good for us to be relieved of our hardship
80 By crying out to Christ to keep us safe.

The prayer of the poor man hidden in the shadow of his hearth,
A man who is worthy of God the Father in a hundred ordinary
homes
Can conquer the distant enemy
84 If God wishes it, more than swordplay.

The churl is nasty and reluctant more is the pity
To spare a coin in tax
For the payment of the soldier to fight brave battles so marvellously
88 While the careless enemy is sleeping.

If he could see the enemies in their shining armour
And their neighbours' houses burning,
In his heart he would still fester the disease
92 Of not contributing any more taxes.

The Bible testifies that the people of Sodom perished
And also those of Gomorrah because of their sins,
Men of Britain, consider the danger of following this example,
96 Do not be long in deciding the matter.

There never was such contentment
Nor a better world for a Welshman
After seeing the Scripture in his own language
100 And the country gaining by that.

It is forty-one years for me to remember
Since she, Elizabeth came to the throne
May she live for another hundred and one years in good old
England and Wales,
104 As Queen over men.

The year she brought salvation to us
Was when the Stag Essex went to Ireland
In the year 1599
108 And that was when these verses were written.

Long live Elizabeth and all the country in her service
Good health and food without want,
She is the sweet Monarch we are indebted to for this
112 And to Essex the lively leading hart of England.

(G.L.)

Professor Glanmor Williams wrote in his book *Recovery* that during the last years of Elizabeth's Reign, "2.9% of the Welsh population fought in the Irish Wars of 1594 and 1602". They "fought doggedly and died bravely in the bogs of Ireland, the sand dunes of the Low Countries, under the walls of French and Breton towns and in the harbours of Spain and Portugal." Thomas Prys, and Piers's brother William, as well as poet Ifan Llwyd Sieffre were among these well-travelled soldiers-of-fortune, loyal to Queen Elizabeth I, *"our girl"*, *"our Elspeth"*.

Thomas Prys, who also served *"harshly"* in Scotland *"more than once"*, wrote graphically of how he and other Welsh soldiers hated the eternal rain, chill damp and gnawing hunger of Ireland, a blood-stained land savaged and depleted of resources during the military campaigns of Leicester, then later of Essex. Many of Piers's contemporaries shared part of Thomas's experiences, and the poet Rhys Wyn seems to have been their eye-witness companion,

(There was) *"Thomas Prys in his steel armoured breastplate, brave and straight"*.

At Cadiz in 1596 fought Captain Owen, John Salesbury, possibly Thomas Prys and the poet Richard Hughes, commented Dr Nesta

Lloyd, acknowledging Welsh poetry as a valid source of historical eye-witness accounts. Piers meanwhile sailed on Drake's Last Voyage 1595-7, as poetically reported by Siôn Mawddwy and the fighting-fit Ifan Llwyd Sieffre who may have ventured too. Young men from Wales of this generation were part of the adventurous Spirit of the Age, by choice or by compulsion.

As Elizabeth weakened and sickened towards her death by 1603, poet Richard Hughes said he could "*hardly write*", so worried and saddened was he, "*dreading the black day*". Like Piers and Thomas in these now dangerously changing times, he was familiar with the vulnerability of their privateers'/pirates' power-bases off the west coast of North Wales, describing the "*leap*" of the prow through the waves in the dangerous watery channel between Aberdaron and the rocky island fastness of *Ynys Enlli* set in the glimmering sea. Hughes also records, in verse, details of the Gunpowder Plot in 1605, "*The king and his heir rejoiced…*" Another contemporary poet, friend, Edmwnd Prys (1543/4–1623) celebrated the fashion for tobacco as a possible kill or cure; and Thomas Prys in his ode *To a Woodcock* likens the bird-image of Piers Griffith to a sharp-ended new-fangled "*tobacco pipe*", in 'metaphysical' mode.

The turbulent sea between the picturesque fishing village of Aberdaron and the holy island of Enlli/Bardsey, 'burial place of twenty thousand saints', marks the last stage of the famous medieval Pilgrims' Way. This westerly sea-road maps out the swirling currents of the Sound once navigated so skilfully by pirates Piers Griffith and Thomas Prys in retreat from their enemies. The strait, "*the overwhelming floods of Caswennan*" are referred to by three early manuscripts: Gruffudd Gryg who called them "*white foaming*"; by Hywel ab Einion Lygliw who described them as "*the turbulent boiling cauldron of Caswennan*"; and by an anonymous third poet, wittily warning of the difficulty of braving the deadly Caswennan currents in order to sail off to see his beautiful girlfriend waiting for him on the island where she lived amongst her fisher folk, "*to turn to windward"*, and the even greater ordeal of sailing back again to the mainland but clearly worth the effort.

Later in 1741 official hydrographer Lewis Morris was to write *"Ffrydau Caswenan … is one Mile westerly from Bardsey on which you have but 11 foot water…"* (British Library, Additional Manuscript 14910 t./p149 – "Celtic Remains".) In his *Plans of Harbours* 1748 Lewis records, *"There is a Bank of Sand about a mile W.S.W. of Bardsey, on which you have not two Fathom at Low Water…"*. Then he notes, sceptically enough, *"as is reported"*, a supposed connection with *"King Arthur"* having *"a ship called Gwenan cast away there."*

Whatever legendary associations this cluster of remote islands may possess, they have been well-known locally as the probable hideaways of Piers Griffith, Thomas Prys and others, especially after the death of their Sovereign Queen Elizabeth in 1603. From then on, this dare-devil band of pirates would have to convert to legitimate maritime trading.

Chapter 7

Coded Messages and Hidden Treachery

POEM TO THE SOUTH WIND, IMPLORING HIM TO ESCORT MR PIERS GRIFFITH OF PENRHYN HOME TO HIS WIFE, C.1590 – C. 1600
by Sir Huw Roberts

> *The poet, as family priest and friend, gives us vivid biographical details of the young lord, with references to the* Golden Hind *and to Piers's secret despatches abroad. He also demonstrates some rare psychological insights into the personality of the Pirate's Wife, Margaret Mostyn.*

THE POET:
Greetings to the Wind, Ambassador of southern courts,
Your face appears coldly out of the skies,
How strong and forceful you are, as you shriek through the sails
                          and the rigging.
4   You cause many a poor sailor to fall like a deer on the bank of a
                          clear, tumultuous stream,
Blowing and ever whistling overland
Causing bitter destruction to thousands of homes;
How fleet-footed you are, you wayward son of the elements,
8   Who can catch you, not even the most quick-witted;
You are brutish indeed and eager,

Driving angrily as you sweep across flat wastes,
Restless as you strike against mountainous regions, changing
                direction up hill and down dale,
12   If anyone tries to stand upright when you are around, you knock
                    them down with angry cries.
You are the enemy who invades
Our houses and ships along the coast causing widespread
                      devastation.
You are a creature of odd humours,
16   Today, you behave like a certain noble gentleman,
Who can be ferocious at times, but whose anger passes tomorrow
                      and who flies,
Out of his rage, then becomes his pleasant self again;
You follow the courses of the wind
20   Under sail causing the same sort of trouble as this noble gentleman
                      himself

Grumbling and blowing contrary
For a full hour in your ill-temper,
Then in another hour's time in the clear light of day with the dawn
                      chorus
24   You suddenly fall quiet as the grave.
Everyone knows you too have your moods,
You tend to be boastful, it is your nature,
Sometimes you travel the familiar sea-roads,
28   At other times across land.
Is there any place on earth if you so wish, you may not visit,
Is there any coastline that is not known to you?
Is there any place you have not been to yet?
If you can spot every injustice from your vantage point, or any
                      good for that matter,
32   How is it you know so much about everything that is going on
                      across the globe?

Tell me, Wind from the South,
For you are a magician like Merlin, tell me a thing or two,
Do you know of a certain rakish bird from a country estate
36   In the great kingdom of Gwynedd, a certain celebrity?

He sails the high seas, normally,
And in that sense only, he may be said to resemble the Apostle
                                                                    Paul.

THE WIND:
Who is this lord
40 From Gwynedd whose handsome face is so respected and famous?
There is no one between here and Spain,
Who is not known to me.

THE POET:
He is Piers, a nobleman of pure blood,
44 Piers the heir of old Sir Rhys,
Piers with no permanent base, a golden legendary hero like
                                                                    (*Prince*) Nudd,
Beloved, charismatic Piers Griffith.
He is a rare find, an incomparable one,
48 A remarkable man, the lord of Penrhyn,
Son of the magnanimous knight, Sir Rhys
The fleet-running deer of pure Talacre ancestry.

THE WIND:
Certainly, you are right,
52 I know this gentleman
Descended from the ribs of Idwal if he is the one I am thinking of,
The one who acts like a real son of Mars on the Spanish seas,
A man who excels in seamanship and navigation,
56 Our country regards him as a hero gaining us riches and power.

THE POET:
If you know him, Wind,
Like Ifor the Benevolent on his great adventures,
Piers was a man once bearing the badge of honour and respect,

60 He was so affectionate, sympathetic and just, that everyone was
                                                        keen to know him,
    If he ever had to utter a stern word to anyone
    He could cause a man to shiver in his shoes in fear of his anger.
    If there was a tyrannical, loud-mouthed man around
64 Oppressing the weak pleading for justice,
    Piers would deal with him, turn to the vulnerable ones to protect
                                                                  them,
    Striking a blow on behalf of the poor creatures.
    Like Solomon driving a herd of evil-doers away,
68 The sight of Piers protecting everyone was just like Solomon,
    He was wonderfully brave on land too,
    People hastened to him for help, as to the legendary hero Dyfnwal,
    He is the great Golden Hind of the sea in this day and age,
72 He is in the first ranks like Aeneas.
    It was a daring venture indeed for our beloved soul of Gwynedd,
    To sail the seas so often even to the death,
    And to gamble his life on dangerous expeditions,
76 Hurled from wave to wave on the deep ocean;
    And meanwhile seeing how fair each day dawns
    Over his beloved home set amongst trees,
    His court nestling high on a great rock
80 And his gilded towers,
    With beautiful views over the surrounding countryside,
    Cornfields, woodland, excellent pasture
    With every customary pleasure,
84 And splendid servants in attendance.
    Oh do come forth, magnificent Wind,
    You deserve praise for blowing here directly from the South,
    Will you, I implore you, for you are so brave,
88 For God in Heaven's sake, will you go forth and escort him back
                                                                  home?

THE WIND:
Who could refuse? Now that I understand the situation,
How can I refuse to go and fetch dear Piers without delay?

THE POET:

If you *are* going, please make haste,

92   Be gone at once to avoid disappointment,

Tell him how forlorn his wife is, how pained in her breast

Is the companion of his bed and his heart,

She is the daughter of a Knight of the Realm bearing helmet and

                                  arms,

96   A young lady nurtured in a grove of kindness and care,

Sir Thomas's lovely girl, of noble rank,

A distinguished branch of the Mostyn family, holding high office.

She is sad with longing for her husband,

100 And it is no wonder she wears a down-hearted expression, given

                                the circumstances!

Yearning so much has made her grow cold towards him,

And her predicament is making her ill

For she needs his advice and for him to leave the vast oceans,

104 To return home and if he did, she would gladly praise and

                          welcome him at their reunion.

Blow in his direction, you fine feature of Britain,

Bend, Fair Wind from the South,

Send the angel home from wherever you see him,

108 Send that gentleman here to tarry on land,

Send the Golden Hind to Arfon,

Send that charming seed of Penrhyn back here to stay.

Once he has returned home, from a mission to defend our two

                                lands,

112 When the Heir of Sir Rhys returns to his court and his country

Pray, do not let Piers cause any more suffering in our time,

For the Blessed Virgin Mary's sake, by being lured away again to

                              the sea.

                                (G.L.)

This classical poem, of which nine manuscript copies survive, is similar in purpose to Thomas Prys's "To a Dolphin". Both are messages urging Piers to return home to his long-suffering wife at Penrhyn after one of his mysterious absences. Both contain vivid images of the sea by poets with maritime backgrounds and both reveal unique insights into the Pirate's character. There are hints too of dangerous exploits and espionage. On a broader spectrum, there was treachery deep within the Court of Queen Elizabeth, with consequences for the future of her kingdom and for Europe.

Both poems assume that the audience is well aware of Piers as a high-ranking officer

> *"on an important mission*
> *to far-off lands*
> *for our Elizabeth"*

with Drake's great *Golden Hind*:

> *"Eurfawr Hydd"* …

On the other hand, Thomas Prys's poem seems to be in an altogether lighter vein, yet tinged with impatience, subtly suggesting clues about the crucial naval base of Lisbon and referring to the hidden creeks along the Galician coast as the most likely haunts of our elusive Pirate.

In this accomplished poem, '*Ode to the South Wind*' by Sir Huw Roberts, cleric, there is a deep concern for Piers's wife and family at home, the 'lady' Margaret bringing up at least eight of their ten children alone by now: William, the heir with seven sisters, Katherine, Jane, Dorothy, Ursula, Margaret, Elizabeth and Grace. The troubled private life of Piers Griffith (now well into the 1590s), on an estate slowly falling into ruin, contrasts sharply with his glamorous public image as a heroic adventurer eager to come to the notice of the Queen and be favoured by his Sovereign Elizabeth. She is regarded locally at the time as 'a good Tudor girl', gladly patronising Welsh poetry in the manner of her father and grandfather and who is given to asking after the well-being of her loyal Welsh contingents aboard the great ships of adventure and discovery in which she has personally invested, as reflected in the more vigorously militaristic *'Pirate Song of the Caribbean'* aboard the *'Pelican'*.

What is also brought into focus in the *Ode to the South Wind* is that Sir Huw seems to know Piers's character intimately. He has after all, known him since youth. The quixotic nature of the South Wind could well be a clue to the Pirate's true self. As a clergyman of Elizabeth's Protestant Established Church and a close family friend who was an older contemporary of Piers at Oxford, Sir Huw has opted out of the spirit of active exploration that has so gripped other students, deciding instead on a country clergyman's life and marriage to a rich young local heiress, Ann Pugh, a recusant Catholic like Piers's mother, Lady Catherine.

Sir Huw is ideally placed for being acutely aware of the terrible effect Piers's long absences abroad are having on his unhappy wife, who may naturally have taken the family chaplain into her confidence. Margaret has lost two children in infancy, Rhys and Robert; and as a young girl she may even have suffered a miscarriage or two. Piers was only fourteen in that property-motivated Double Wedding of 1582 and Margaret may well have been younger.

Meanwhile, Sir Huw's advice to Piers is clearly stated in this 'messenger poem', possibly despatched with a friendly sea-captain from Caernarfon or from Bangor, Port of Beaumaris, to the waterfronts of France, Portugal or Spain. These are troubled times at home and abroad. Piers's return to his wife and children should be his first priority, Sir Huw warns, in the typical gesture of family poets concerned for their patron's well-being. Futhermore, Huw can take the liberty of being frank, possibly because he is not financially dependent on patronage like some bards. Piers has been absent long enough, seems to be the consensus of opinion amongst everyone here at home on the estate.

But this is no angry rebuke. Implied in the poem is the priest's ready acknowledgement that Captain Piers Griffith has an established role to play as messenger aboard the *Golden Hind*, between Sir Francis Drake and other commanders of the fleet, possibly with his pinnace *Grace* in tow, as suggested in other poems like *'To a Blackbird'* by nephew William Griffith, by the soldier's song of Ifan Llwyd Sieffre, a fellow-adventurer, and by Siôn Mawddwy in his praise-poem to fellow-poet Piers Griffith and Margaret his wife.

'Ode to the South Wind' places the Captain within the Queen's secret network of trusted privateers, intelligencers, couriers or spies, reporting back to her on impending invasions by enemy shipping and on rumours of murderous Popish plots. He may even, as Thomas Prys suggests in *'To a Dolphin'*, be engaged on some secret diplomatic mission, say to Galicia or Portugal. Queen Elizabeth trusts few of her allies, having suffered at least fifteen attempts on her life, including the Babington plot of 1587, but in the main, she relies on the loyal Welsh who have followed 'their' Tudors to court for years; and according to the household staff lists of her faithful retainer Thomas Parry, she is happy to have several trusted Welsh servants and bodyguards around her, as her father King Henry VIII and grandfather King Henry VII had sometimes required.

Ruthlessly run by Sir Francis Walsingham until his death in 1590, then by Sir Robert Cecil, the Secret Service may well have employed an independent operator like Piers from time to time, with his Penrhyn pedigree of loyalty to the English Crown since the Age of Chivalry, thus slotting in conveniently as an intelligence-gatherer or propaganda-leaflet distributor in his *"superbly azure and gilded painted pinnace, Grace"*, as his nephew young William Griffith describes in his only extant poem, *'To a Blackbird'*.

During these dangerous war-games with Spain, it is not unknown to mail letters with ships like the *Dolphin,* the *Pelican* or the *Blackbird,* sometimes in code, often using a system of clever acrostics in poems, spelling out key-words in complex patterns, not to mention all the message trafficking of codebreaker Thomas Phelippes, agent to Walsingham (died 1590) and then to Essex. It is not impossible either for some secret messages to have been written in the Welsh language, a trick sometimes used to baffle others, as has been suggested, and a factor that will be the case, for example, in the 'scoop' World War II reports of Wynford Vaughan Thomas, and of correspondent Huw Wheldon famously telephoning his sister in Wales from South Africa, with instructions to pass on the news to the BBC.

From evidence in the poems, it is likely that an adventurous risk-taker like Piers is part of the Tudor espionage game, so crucial to Queen Elizabeth's well-being and the Defence of the Realm. After all, his uncle and associate Hugh Griffith of Cefnamwlch, fleet-owner, wealthy London businessman with useful contacts in Venice, Algiers and Tunis, has been a reliable and well-known example of '*spiery*' par excellence, and a recurring name in State Papers. Is he the mysterious *"Mr Griffith"*? This could be Piers, or someone else, one *"William Griffith"* perhaps, a treacherous suspect posing as a priest but playing a double game, referred to in *The Catholic Martyrs of Wales.* All three are entangled in the busy sea-traffic of the time, aboard the many vessels trading between Britain's shores and Europe.

This *"William Griffith"* (or someone else of the same name) wrote Walsingham a curious letter from Venice in the 1590s before he sets off to dinner with the *"Cardinal,"* then intending to go on to a Catholic college in Spain (perhaps the College of St Gregory at Seville.) There is also a reference to *"Parsons"* (Robert Persons, author of the biography of the Catholic Martyr, Edmund Campion.) The Venice letter, where terror and double-dealing leap from the page at every complex turn, suggests the duplicity and intrigue of both writer and recipient. This *"Griffith"* was in danger of his life. He 'comes over' as scared stiff. Who was he?

Welsh double-agent William Parry, the assassin, was at some point sprung from a Paris jail by Walsingham's agents so that he could come to London and give evidence about plots against Queen Elizabeth. Other disloyal Welshmen suspected of treachery but useful to Walsingham were the spies Walter Williams and Thomas Morgan, a man who mysteriously disappeared. There can be no doubt about Piers Griffith's loyalty to Queen Elizabeth but as the loving son of a recusant Catholic mother, he may have been able to place himself in Catholic circles with conviction, in order to report back to the Spymaster from these *"diplomatic missions abroad"*, mentioned by several reliable poet-reporters.

A certain Captain Dafydd Lloyd of Anglesey for example, as speculated by Aled Eames, would be an ideal candidate for delivering Sir Huw Roberts's poetic message to the Pirate of Penrhyn abroad, someone masquerading undercover as a *bona fide* trader like Piers himself, fluent in Welsh, English and Latin, with a smattering of other European languages at his disposal. A prosperous local merchant like Dafydd Lloyd must have been almost equally as cosmopolitan. Grammar school educated at least, in nearby Beaumaris, he too would have had the means to conduct his busy sea trade between Chester, Bangor, Caernarfon and Milford Haven, then on to Brittany, Hamburg and Antwerp, or down to St Jean de Luz and Lisbon as recorded in the Bangor Port Books.

If so, and within the poem's meaning, such a sea-captain would have been entrusted with a secret message, shared between the sender and the receiver. Implied here is an understanding that the South Wind, so vividly personified in the poem, always plays a key role in the perilous life of sailors, so it is crucial to secure its favours.

We may hazard a guess that once the Pirate has received his poetic message somewhere in foreign parts, he sets sail at once, hopefully, hurrying home northwards at the very next blowing of a summer gale.

Could an un-named sea-captain, entrusted with such a precious package, prove reliable? Highly likely, if we take the poem at face-value. Or we may interpret it merely as a literary convention of the late sixteenth century about message-sending, meant only for a gamely private performance in Penrhyn Old Castle after a welcoming supper with the lady Margaret as hostess and mistress of the house, and the servants and children creeping in at bedtime from the flickering fire-lit shadows, craning to listen to Sir Huw's poem, or that of Thomas Prys or of young poet/nephew William Griffith. All three would have made dramatic readings so beloved amongst such households at the time. This poet-priest with seafaring ancestors (living on the edge with a secretly Catholic wife linked to the family who had once smuggled Father Bennet abroad clearly aware of his illegal publishing activities) has skilfully evoked for us the atmosphere of a powerful and graphic poem of the sea. How could Piers resist?

ON SENDING A DOLPHIN AS MESSENGER TO PIERS GRIFFITH
C.1590 – C.1600 by Thomas Prys.

In this second poem, equally striking, the Dolphin-image portrays both the daring glamour of Piers in shining "gold-rimmed armour" riding the ocean wave, but also the dangers of his free-booting style of piracy: "These missions abroad... we cannot go back to the good old days... a perilous world that is out-of-joint is seen around us... your family is tormented by nightmares."

THE ADDRESS:

Beautiful, graceful Dolphin, with your sleek speed
Leaping lightly onward through the fair waves
Like a walrus-calf, with your shining eyebrows,
4   Your smooth pathway is clear-cut, your child-like cry a moaning
echo.
You are so happy swimming in your element,
Freely content and agile on the crest of the wave in your very own
environment near land,
You have a frowning face, a cold smooth skin,
8   Like a seal in the chill water.
You leap up in a circle, you shiver and shake like a palsy victim,
Hovering around there with your tail spinning,
Battling against the tidal water, like a black mushroom
12   (*It seems to me*) as I observe you while you snorkel and snort.
You plough through
The dispersing, fragile water of the waves;
The salty brine of the sea-fabric here is split apart as you plunge
through it,
16   You love being in your element, the powerful realm of the ocean
wave.
Brave creature, you are like a man eager to wear a spruce new
waistcoat (*uniform*),
At a naval training –school in a hideaway on the foreshore,
Or a sea-serpent, as you axe your way through the watery world,
20   Look at you rousing fearful wonder in everyone.

Your stomach is white, you are a remarkably tender creature,
Voyager of distant oceans dangerous to mortal man who may be
ensnared there,
Yet you are like a mole of the salty sea, your ambitions are not
controlled by it,
24 You quest and travel the sea, your journey there is clear, free and
limitless.
Throughout the summer, when the fine weather breaks,
You come to challenge the storm with your romping and roistering,
Like a wild boar, you whirl about in a hell-bent fury,
28 Vexed and full of mischievous feats swimming in the vanguard
force of the tidal wave before it crashes violently,
As if with a soldier's stave or pike and his gold-rimmed breast-plate,
Like a fish bound within an enclosed suit (*of armour*),
From the sea-tribe, gentle two-breasted one,
32 As you glide smoothly and hover there along the high, fine-edged
slope of the wave.

THE MESSAGE:
Like a bundle (*of letters*) in the saddle, with your foot in the
(*rider's*) stirrup hot-foot in the right direction,
You are keen to venture to any violent trouble-spot; over the sea-
salt water to the continuous whip-lashing groans of the wind;
Choose a messenger, on my behalf I beseech you
36 As an ambassador, a reliable man who can clearly remember the
message;
Take the word from Menai, you mischevious little monkey,
Towards Lisbon, on a certain appropriate journey,
And swim there awhile
40 To the coast of Spain, to where its land juts out breasting the sea.
You are an ideal swimmer sent from Heaven,
Swim as if on a chase, you are so full of vitality!
Ask after landing there,
44 With considerable praises, for a warrior, Piers Griffith (*is not
everyone missing him desperately?*)
He is a real pearl of a man believe me, of a pure, loving heart,

Respected lord of Penrhyn, a member of the leading family

hereabouts,

48   A tender-hearted gentleman, who is more cultivated and noble?

Six years (*oh how wearisome these long years of waiting are!*)

Aboard ship, since he departed for the sea

To oceans beyond the Foryd

52   Over the bar across the world.

But does it not go against the grain for him to have

These missions abroad considering there is so much salty sea in his

blood, notwithstanding his bravery and generosity,

For must he not return, safely in one piece,

56   To his own Court from the badlands,

And remain here, in the place we all love,

To the welcome and rejoicing of all his family and friends?

When you see him, (*if you do*), as you painfully seek him here and

there,

60   Aboard his ship a very heroic captain to all appearances,

Call out to him, in his shining armour,

Go and see him as my ambassador on request,

And address him, with the message of your mission,

64   (*That is*) this poem like so many others, sent from his companion

(*Thomas Prys*)

(*Who is now*) a better man than he was before

Off sailing on the same sort of troublesome adventures,

Until he (*Piers*) swore in truth,

68   That he would stand by everything his education, birth and

experience had trained him for, just at the moment when

he realised he was becoming impoverished,

And yet he went back on his word, promising one thing only to

subsequently break his vow

To give up the sea and all its involvements.

Be strong, and tell him plainly:

72   'You must change your mind again

And this time leave the ocean

To others from now on!'

It is difficult to succeed at merchant-adventuring when we face
>> dark declining days
76   At sea, it is cold to hang about waiting on shore,
     And if news of some opportunity arrives, it is bad news,
     (*Situations*) one could easily therefore dangerously be entrapped
>> within, in changing times today.
     It is fine for a happy, witty confident man to depart the foreshore
>> as you once did
80   On world voyages over land and sea far away
     (*As long as he can afford to finance them*) for good investment,
       fame and fortune, in spite of cold, harsh obstacles and difficulties,
     He may gain knowledge and experience by venturing thus
     But it is not a profitable and wise thing to do (*nowadays*),
     I am not giving religious advice but talking sense,
84   We cannot go back to the good old days,
     I shall not go on and on about it, (*having given it up myself so you
>> should do the same.*)

Explain to him, that there is sad, real cause for the downcast faces
>> back home,
     I have clear facts about this unprotected long-suffering family:
     Let us hope that when the wind blows, the word is that he (*Piers*)
>> looks very ill,
88   Blowing high over the hilly slopes,
     When such a crazy, dangerous world that is out-of-joint is seen
>> around us to a large extent,
     With everyone praying and complaining in a disgruntled manner
     In case an ill wind, blowing complex threatening events towards us,
92   Endangers his frail handsome body with his fine head of hair!
     Many men, and many people know him well
     Are complaining that he is a long time returning home
     So much so that they cannot sleep at night worrying about him
>> with hurt and disappointment in their breasts,
96   I know this, for they are tormented by nightmares.
     In vain it is only foolish men who go exploring

And none of these own one inch of foreign soil at the far ends of the
earth,

So he should return home again a wiser man

100 From amongst these Merchant Adventurers.

Let him come home, consider this carefully,

To lead his men back to his own excellent country:

Captain of the azure *Grace*, a merciful lord of grace,

104 A Captain with pure uncorrupted hands (*a sincere man never
doing anyone an injustice*)

May God of his Grace, wisdom and patience give (*Piers*) his own
reward of treasure,

Namely the *Grace* to depart from the sea!

(G.L.)

AN ODE

On sending a Blackbird to escort Piers Griffith home from the seas
c. 1590 – c.1600

By William Griffith

> *This third message-poem is the work of Piers's young nephew,*
> *the boy's only extant poem, providing graphic images of the*
> *natural world and of what the pinnace* Grace *really looked*
> *like, emblazoned with the Adventurer's colourful Penrhyn*
> *coat-of-arms. Here he manages to both hero-worship his uncle,*
> *Captain Griffith and reprimand him for his absences: "sailing*
> *a proud pinnace... with the most handsome face you have ever*
> *seen, an aristocrat of long and noble lineage... implore him to*
> *come out of his hideout and the troublesome adventures he has*
> *got himself into."*

THE POET:
Sweet Blackbird with your happy tuneful song,
Warbling a fine poem in the ashgrove,
What a neat little bagful of notes you are, a tiny chestful of vibrant
sounds,
4   This is your very own original composition released from your
bright beak and clever little head,
Gentle Jack, with your musical complexity of accented notes,
Why, you have a perfect shepherd's pipe of your own to keep
yourself entertained,
There you are,
8   Conducting your own harmonious choir, keeping it in perfect tune
amongst the leaves.
What a dear sweet little song you sing, such a pleasant tune
Pitched on the best melodies,
12   Go abroad, o chosen one, you treasure you,
Go to the most perilous of places beyond the seas.
Search there to see if you can find a certain gentleman, a hail-
fellow-well-met,

Someone who is likely to be in some sort of tricky situation,
sailing a proud pinnace,

Piers, with the most handsome face you have ever seen, an
aristocrat of long and noble lineage,

16   Griffith, the best leader of men,

The son of Sir Rhys, a perfect gentle knight,

The grandson of Sir William, a man of faultless reputation.

I beseech you, Blackbird, on behalf of his family,

20   Who are descended from the best ancestry,

To implore him to come out of his hideout and the troublesome
adventures he has got himself into

Like the most excellent gentleman he is, always sailing before the
wind,

Following the roaring call of the sea chilled to the bone,

24   Please persuade him to return home to Penrhyn, a peerless place,

Where his wife's suffering aches her heart and her anguish weighs
heavily

Upon her, such is her need for him to be there with her.

Where there was once fine verse delightfully performed,

28   Sweet, haunting music, harpsong and lute,

There are no longer any praise-poems performed over there, at
Penrhyn

Nor the splendours of rejoicing, nor mirth.

And where joyful flocks of birds once sang

32   If you take a look high up, Blackbird, you will see only ugly old
crows there,

And where nightingales used to linger amidst the pathways

And sing nightly near the banks of streams

36   There is no one now but the Owl, what a blind head from ancient
times he has on him,

The White Owl certainly, when he turns right round, going on and
on with his rambling old speeches.

THE BLACKBIRD:
O praiseworthy Poet, with your timely song,
You are such a craftsman in verse with passion and poetic accuracy,
Do not, without payment, describe in poetry
40   My garment and my beak, for I am accustomed to being like the
                              man dressed in black, the bearer of sad news.
Nor do I have the ability as the sailmast of a ship does,
To swim over the salty sea (*I can only fly.*)
But I know of another ambassador for you, a messenger who can
                              carry a cheerful letter,
44   Someone who is riding in the turmoil of the ocean wave already
And he will take your letter to this gentleman, in his face indeed,
He will carry the mail in all honesty, and promptly,
For he is none other than the wild seal with his rough, savage cries
48   And his custom is, this wild-headed creature
With the efficiency of a pannier loaded with mail carried on a
                              horse's haunches,
His custom is to swim over the waves, on the sort of unpleasant
                              journey I can do without,
But this wild seal can do it, leaping over the waves over and over
                              again.
52   The enemy of deep-sea fish with their swallowing jaws, that lurk in
                              fierce, powerful wave surges,
(*Huge monsters of the deep with enormous teeth and lunging,
                              sucking throats*)
Yet with instinctive delight the seal basks in the midst of it all,
                              dodging in and out,
For his body is as strong as the spine of a harp, if we may imagine
                              it used as a powerful kind of oar to stir up the sea,
May I present to you the seal, ashen-grey with his sleek form of
                              simple line and blubbery skin,

56   Born of the tribe that comes from the sea, the seal-people, who
                              swim in their watery element then are cast wet and naked
                              upon the shore.

THE POET:

At the stern of the pinnace

Above the rudder, most excellent and efficiently wrought

Is his coat-of-arms, designed by the most skilled craftsmen.

60   Specially made for the journey by ironsmiths into the shape of a
shield.

Three heads on complex heraldic arms

The best, in scarlet, is the one I am fond of,

A fine chevron in superb silver

64   Heritage of Ednyfed and an excellent appropriate gift,

The arms and distinction of Marchudd of ancient times

The Saracen's head in sanguin,

And descended from the same man I referred to

68   The lively clear azure set in green heraldry,

The best lineage in an upright golden chevron

We praise, between the three mullets,

The silver lion rampant, signifying the family coat-of-arms

72   And set in azure,

Where the symbols of his family crest merge within one shield.

Blackbird, from these distinguishing images

Descended as he is from Cadrod the Handsome, the best of
bloodlines

The black lion rampant, most finely wrought from a host of
possible lion designs,

76   In ermine, with blood-red claws

This is the sign of Rhiwallon as noted in the 'Chronicle of the
Princes' symbolising

A fearless man, of the best stock.

Three stags' heads, bright with a pale sheen,

80   A coat-of-arms that is golden and poem-like, with a silver chevron,

A stag set in silver, with superbly gilded horns,

A shield wrought like verse in a magnificent green hue.

Madoc, his ancestor was also famous for his good upright life,

84   Who can be compared to him in dignity? The descendant of
Iarddur too,

With the three harts' heads of this excellent lineage,
With a superb azure bend like a peacock's fine feathers
Silver-tinged, pure and praiseworthy,
88 What a remarkable symbol this is,
Set in silver on a bright blue bend,
These are the heraldic arms he bears on his armoured cuirass;
The three golden mullets of a soldier who is
92 Very accomplished – is there a more skilled man?
He wears the Stanleys' shining bright armour,
Everyone knows he has descended from a great Earl.
A White Lion with an intelligent face,
96 Beloved and fine, with blood-crimson claws,
The Lion rampant on the crosses of Christendom
On a blue background with fine craftsmanship
These arms Piers has inherited from the noble Daltons,
100 An added enrichment to the excellent land of Gwynedd.
Blackbird, depart, chirping so sweetly and purely,
Cheerful bird, take wing with all speed
To the margins of the sea, to the rugged coastline,
104 Today over there he will be easy to reach for there is a breeze to
carry you along.

And there you will find him, the roguish fellow,
Beautiful bird with your delightful tune,
With your unique harmonious poem of paradise,
108 Send the Seal, a fine specimen, with my message
Over the cold waves race towards the fine weather,
He will come through the salty sea,
Amen, bringing my uncle home to me.

(G.L.)

On Sending a Sea-Salmon as an Ambassador to Wales
c. 1600
by Thomas Prys

The poet may be writing whilst abroad, or away in London, or from a situation where he is confined in some way. Jail, possibly. He was sometime incarcerated in the Fleet Prison, London and at Ludlow Castle in the Welsh border country on trumped-up charges ranging from debt to rape and murder. The intensely personal image of the Salmon for Piers Griffith may be the key to the true meaning of the next poem, a warning about enemies now on Piers's trail. The poem is allusive in a subversive way, as understood only by a select coterie of friends and family. No one 'in the know' can doubt that it is Piers Griffith who is being directly addressed here, a vivid personification, in the same mode as To a Dolphin *and* To a Woodcock, *which could also be classed as 'pirate poems' in this context. Beneath the delightful Nature imagery of these works, there lurks the ever-present theme of danger born of dark deeds: "The wind is making music in the rigging and this wind-music drives me on… to attack a weak vessel, a likely victim and capture her in a tight corner."*

Splendid young Salmon, bright and sleek,
Of pure heart, ever faithful and true
A natural wonder so free,
4   Without breathing the air you are able to survive under water.
Without a care in the world, you are never ill,
Although you are cold-blooded, you are very healthy.
You challenge the waves, yet you can ignore their deafening roar.
8   And you have perfect eye-sight even to a second glance.
Your jaw may be compared
To a blacksmith's tongs, as I know,
And your gills are wide open,

12 Ever gaping, I love that,
    And under your breast, it is important to remember,
    Are two fins wonderfully fine,
    With two exquisitely formed fins on your back also
16 To steer your winged oars through the water,
    You fit superbly into your surroundings, and that goes for the
                                    movements of your rear fin too,
    Your colour is the same light hue as the long tail of a swallow.
    On your scaly skin are beautifully inlaid
20 Jewels shining like a coat of mail in perfect overlaps
    On a background glistening with azure blue,
    In fine form like a length of steel;
    If your body were to be laid to rest,
24   It would be like the beautifully crafted square frame cast by the
                                    shadow of a man in the water.

    Run to the flowing rivers
    Along the watery domain darting fast to and fro like a weaver's
                                    shuttle;
    Cutting zig-zag through each wave, then plunging underneath it,
28 You are the sharp-nosed mole of the waves,
    The traveller treading the crystal waters of the glade,
    Like the field-mouse with its long white breast close to the ground,
    Wisely keeping to the hidden shadowy depths unseen
32 Dispersing a black cloud as cover, the camel of the water.
    You have buried your eggs like a wild boar hoofing into the earth,
    You have shimmered and shaken the pebbled floor of the river,
    And by the willing means of shingle and stone
36 You can produce a harvest of thousands of tiny wheat-like grains
            dispersing through water, kernels and chaff through the air,
    You lay eggs by the thousand like pellets out of a gun, indeed I am
                                    enjoying writing this,
    For in every egg there is hope of life.

    Be my ambassador, delightful Salmon,
40 Lively, early and prompt,

Be my messenger and bear this in mind
To Wales without sleeping a wink,
Take a sign to a far frontier
44   Happily, lightning of the sea.
Go from here, sweet messenger,
To Caernarfon in a fair land,
And address everyone a hundred times
48   Within the town walls, that would be a useful mission.
If they ask, remember for a moment,
Wherever I am in the world, near or far,
Say that I am travelling
52   Across the sea without finding treasure,
Sailing, and soon getting into trouble,
The wind is making music in the rigging and this wind-music
                                            drives me on,
Waiting my opportunity like an intelligent man with his wits
                                            about him,
56   To attack a weak vessel, a likely victim and capture her in a tight
                                            corner,

And whether good luck is to follow or not
Yet I will still go after the crew in hot pursuit.
From there, on a good strong wave
60   Go along the Menai Strait past beautiful manor-houses
Opposite, where you will see, beloved kinsman,
Fine Porthamal, with its land down to the water's edge,
And there address passionately
64   Richard Bulkeley, a reasonable man.
Swim, you will not regret this,
Opposite picturesque Penrhyn,
Address Piers Griffith there
68   And if he is at home, call to see him.
Go then, so that you may gain more success,
And address some people I know in Conwy;
Choose the most favourable tide, then plunge down under the
                                            waves,
72   And swim along the River Conwy,

Keep silent and be happy,
And go to lovely Llanrwst:
A town with a church, set in a glade, a valley, and a meadow,
76   A gentle cheerful place lying in its domain,
A special meeting-place on market days, so good, so contented,
A place full of faithful, loyal companions,
Where there is romance, warm camaraderie, and interesting,
                        intelligent discussions,
80   Where everything is in abundance at fairs, houses and inns
Where there are no complaints and more than enough to go round,
A place where there are welcoming, genuine people,
An easeful place where there are no cares, an interesting,
                        entertaining bolt-hole,
84   A familiar place, in truth, to share a goblet of wine with a fellow,
A lovely situation on the banks of a river bringing fruitfulness,
A heavenly spot, full of wit and culture.
When you arrive here, without a worry or a scar
88   To take your chance on socialising in this town,
Please take my greetings, do not forget,
To every man without exception, to all the people,
Do remember me to that green glade,
92   If it is convenient,
If there is unity, take my blessings
Throughout the entire parish:
Do not let one special son nor daughter go by
96   Without greeting them, if they are at home.

Be wise, be cunning but truth-seeking and cautious,
Guard against deceivers, with evil intent;
Keep clear of the man with the cruel trap and net,
100 The malice of the seaweed-entangled creeks and fish-weirs,
Watch out for the treasure-hunters with nets
And guard against traitorous plots, or it will be the worse for you;
Avoid dangerous, tight places,
104 Escape into the dark mist from the flaming torches of the night-
                                fishers;

Be careful of nets across rivers, for they are bad places to go,
If you see a crow, take it as a sign that there is treachery about;
Do not venture too near land, because there you will be vulnerable,
108 Never go where there are fords for crossing;
Follow, directly without hesitating
The safety of the black watery depths;
Set off from a place where you can avoid
112 Fishermen and seemingly fair but false people.
Go, my beloved one, I am your true chosen friend,
May God go with you, if danger should befall you,
Be careful, be well-organised,
116 Hurry back to me with your reply in fine form to tell me where
you have been:

Good fortune and fond farewell to you,
May sweet Jesus go with you to your welcome there!

(G.L.)

On sending a Woodcock as Messenger to Piers Griffith
c.1600 by Thomas Prys

> *"You… cut a dash with your fine figure in London, a villainous, dangerous place… Beware the gallows… As you walk around your estate, be careful of chill-hearted envy and treachery… (Be) ready to do (your) duty through bloody deeds."*

> *This mysterious and enigmatic poem of warning hits hard to the heart of a sinister world plunged into fear and uncertainty at the end of Elizabeth's Golden Reign. By now there is no fine line between privateering and piracy. Piers must escape, go into hiding and in time, return home to face the consequences, do the honourable thing, albeit to "burn" in the flames of his wife's anger and love, just as "He has fled, when necessary, / Without acting dishonourably, away from a lady or two: / He has always escaped without getting hanged or drowned."*

> *She might forgive him this time but will the Law? Someone is out for his blood.*

Beautiful tawny bird over on the hill,
On the desolate summit, glimpsed from the valley,
Poor little bird, in fast flight,
4   Your beak is as sharp as a tobacco pipe,
You are so precious, you cut a dash with your fine figure
In London, a villainous, dangerous place.
If you are foolish, this is the belief,
8   You are like the woodcock.
Long is your jaw, of good breeding,
May you have a long life privateering!
Your dwelling lies in a land of meadows and groves
12   And you offer hospitality to high-born lords.
You rise early in your bedchamber with views through your trees
As you set about your work at the break of day.
Be careful, watch out for the prowling cat's paw

16   And for the crumbling, craggy false foothold (*being set up in*
                    deceiving situations), and beware the gallows,
      You risk, if you see fit to do so within your social circle,
      Being shut within the blackness of prison;
      As you walk around your estate, be careful of chill-hearted envy
                    and treachery,

20   You are in danger of being betrayed, deceived and robbed in your
                    own house.
      Like the Woodcock, you move your dwelling from place to place
                    into your hideout
      High up on the wild, comfortless moors and like him you will be
                    hard to find there in the hinterland,
      Dear Woodcock, in your perfect, protective cloak,
24   During the bird-hunting night-season, ice-bound over a hundred
                    winter nights, trying to find grain.
      Go, Bird, like an outlaw away from the traitor,
      Fly low under the wind to a certain man,
      Piers Griffith, with the pain of danger showing on his face,
28   Like a golden pillar fly in haste for this is a crucial moment,
      I do not know of a better messenger than you, you are as remarkable
                    as he,
      Nor (*is there*) any other better ambassador to faraway places than
                    you,
      Nor any other nearer here, I confess,
32   Who is intelligent enough, who knows him well enough to
                    understand this imminent threat of danger.
      Escape from this country, lie low, stay in hiding somewhere for a
                    short while,
      Be gone from here, Bird, when the leaves burst forth in Spring.
      And after you have left, I know,
36   Sadly to tell, I will not see you again until the next dark winter-
                    time.

      Therefore against my will
      Piers too must go away at once
      To journey far from here on a voyage

40   Across the ocean riding high on the vast adventuring sea-roads of
                                                              the world.
      Many such journeys, I would not be entirely surprised,
      He has already made indeed, unfortunately,
      Leaving me behind, it was easy for him to do so,
44   Leaving me to call longingly after him for a year
      And because he set off on his mission as usual in Spring on his fair
                                            voyage before winter,
      Someone complained about him, reported him and betrayed him
                                                              again.

      Even though some have been quick to blame him
48   During his life,
      His fault in actual fact is but small, merely
      A change of direction.
      Fighting, killing in cold blood, attacking a warship
52   Of enemies, a shipful of them,
      And despatching them, succeeding famously,
      I tell you truthfully, more than a hundred
      And losing through no treachery nor dishonour,
56   His own men speaking the best language (*Ancient British/Welsh*),
      Was it not right for him to kill the enemies of Wales and England
      Losing ten of his own men for one of them, showing that there was
                  no treachery in him does it not, that he fought loyally
                                            for his country?

      If the red blood
60   Of the British was shed, loyal decent men of honour,
      Without a doubt, even though they are no longer alive,
      There was no treason in this attack and they acquitted themselves
                                            well in this deed.
      It is better for a man to spill blood honourably
64   When fulfilling his duty to his country, than to murder for
                                            treachery and money;
      Piers, as captain, was ready if necessary to do his duty through
                                            bloody deeds,
      He knew the price that had to be paid.
      Go, Bird, far and wide,

68   Tell him to return to Penrhyn
And to stay there as head of his household
And go no more to the sea ever again.
Tell him he has adventured enough, not like a galley-slave or a poor sailor,
72   But by fighting against our mighty enemies, yet he has been away at sea quite enough,
He has developed into a valiant adventurer and yet he was never boastful,
Now it would be better for him to stay by the warm hearth of home, (*keep his home-fires burning and look after his wife, family and estate.*)
I would prefer, twice over a hundred times,
76   To see him burn than drown in the depths of the sea;
A fate second to drowning in this world is to be burned alive.
He has escaped, when necessary,
80   Without acting dishonourably, away from a lady or two:
He has always escaped without getting hanged or drowned.

               (G.L.)

"HELDRIN" / HASSLES
On revealing the troublous times that befell me when I was away at sea   by Thomas Prys

Here the poet recalls the swashbuckling drama of the privateering adventures of his youth, now that 'pirating' has been outlawed.

By 1600 it is clear that times are changing. The ageing Queen seems out-of-date and "our Elspeth", "our girl" somehow becomes "*the Lady that Time hath surprised* ", in the words of Sir Walter Raleigh. Piracy parading as privateering is going out of fashion.

In the *Woodcock* poem, written around 1600-1603, at the time of the Queen's approaching death and Piers's arrest at Cork, or perhaps even dating from about 1612 when Piers may still be associating with Raleigh, Thomas Prys is implying that Piers is now in danger of being hanged or imprisoned in the new reign of James I (1603-1625.) Is he not committing at *"great cost"* and *"sacrifice of blood"*, the same acts of *"honourable bravery for his country"* ... *"against England's enemies"*, as before, courageous deeds now defined by the new régime as murder and treason? *"Treachery"* and *"betrayal"* are referred to many times in this poem, possibly in the light of the latest Stuart foreign policy: King James and Sir Robert Cecil are keen to make peace with Spain, a deal that is clinched by 1616 when Don Diego Sarmiento de Acuña, Count of Gondomar is formally made Spanish Ambassador at the Court in London. Robert Cecil, son of the late Sir William Cecil, Lord Burghley, has long replaced Sir Francis Walsingham (died 1590) in the department of espionage and national security. And Gondomar, for years now, has been busy trying to hunt down the likes of *"Piers Griffithe, a notable pirate"*.

His friend *"was betrayed"*, Thomas Prys states in a suggestion that would have been little short of scurrilous at the time, warning against someone *"very close to home"*. Piracy and privateering are now banned, not to mention crimes nearer to embezzlement, as from 1603 when Grace O'Malley and Piers are both arrested at Cork on the Irish Coast. Piers is imprisoned and fined to the tune of at least £500,000 in today's money.

The allusive poem, *To a Woodcock* also centres on the Stuart change of direction, which, when applied to Piers, seems so unjust and hypocritical, the writer riskily suggests. Here we gain the impression of a secret shared at the time amongst Piers's friends in a sub-text where a kind of coded language is at play in this ambiguous message to Piers, warning him of life-threatening intrigues and deadly spies. In a similar vein, Shakespeare's enigmatic poem, *The Phoenix and the Turtle*, is dedicated to poet John Salusbury and his wife Ursula, daughter of Henry Stanley, the Earl of Derby; they married curiously and speedily three months after John's hapless brother, Thomas Salusbury was executed after the Babington Plot. Shakespeare's poem was performed as part of the celebratory wedding masque, but noting the bridegroom's *"doulfull mynde"*; and all the time, as the family still asserts, "dangerous spies were everywhere watching". In Prys's *To a Woodcock,* games of acrostics in verse may be implicit in the sending of covert messages, as with the discreet disguising of ladies' names in the love-poetry of Wyatt, Sidney and others; but it would perhaps take, not exactly an Enigma expert, but certainly someone fluent in the poetical complexity of the original Welsh to work them out.

Who is the *"cat's paw"*? There are references to a sinister *"false foothold"* and to the *"assassin who kills for treachery and money"*. Nearer home lurks the mysterious traitor who has betrayed Piers. The lord does have enemies, it is acknowledged. The list of suspects looms large. Who is the prime suspect, the mole under the mole-hill of intrigue?

First, there is his cousin John Owen of Clenennau, but he is no assassin surely, more a plodding clerk and keeper of secrets. A man still working for the government and once Secretary to Walsingham. Such men guarded cipher alphabets and kept phials of invisible ink to hand. Although Thomas does not directly say so, such a man may have once recruited Piers Griffith as a useful *"honourable, dutiful"* intelligencer during the Reign of Elizabeth, only to stab him in the back in changing times as an embarrassingly unwanted pirate/privateer now that King James is on the throne.

Secondly, Lord Keeper/Archbishop John Williams may not be above suspicion here, at least as a tell-tale. In 1603 he is already a handsome young favourite of the King, courtier, sycophant, close companion and confidant of His Majesty, and possibly already envious of his cousin Piers with his fine estate. Somehow, in changing times, the Lord Keeper of the Privy Seal, John Williams never seems far from focus.

Thirdly, the Mostyns: brother-in-law Sir Roger Mostyn or father-in-law Sir Thomas. Could they have reported Piers for piracy? Both quarrel with Lady Catherine at this point and both have shown their teeth against Piers, partly for his neglect of his wife Margaret and partly for non-payment of the Griffith daughters' dowries. A fourth possible suspect could be Sir John Wyn of Gwydir, that malicious old gossip with close ties to the Cecils, at the royal court. But would such people go so far?

The poem's reference to Piers's *"cutting a dash in London"*, keeping up with high society, may be an allusion to the lord's connections to high-ranking friends intimately familiar with the world of maritime adventuring and the *"well-known sea-roads"*, risk-taking men like Sir Henry Cavendish, or the Earl of Cumberland or Sir Walter Raleigh. Raleigh, in particular falls foul of King James around this time for criticising His Majesty and for other misdemeanors, and he is subsequently imprisoned for fourteen years. By 1612 Raleigh is persuading the extravagant, money-hungry James to let him out and support him on a last-ditch South American expedition for gold and pearls up the Orinoco River, not to mention colonisation in North America, the beginnings of Empire. Piers like Raleigh is now mortgaging heavily and he has barely survived the most traumatic event of his life: the loss of William, his son and heir, of the 'Plague' in London during the summer of 1610. There is also that unpleasantness at the house of Dafydd ap Cadwaladr in 1612 at Caernarfon, a duel with the dastardly lawyer of Sir Edward Herbert, Earl of Powys in the public street outside the Court House, with the valiant *"Darby Bach the Irish boy"* as part of Piers's street-gang. In the same dockside area, King Henry VIII's tax-collector, one of the dreaded Pulestons, had once been strung up and hanged by a mob in the upper room of a nearby tavern within living memory, possibly the same building.

In this clued-up poem, *To a Woodcock*, through the image of an elusive Bird Messenger, Piers is being warned by his friend that now he really is sailing close to the wind and rather too near the shadow of the gallows.

There is a real sense of danger here that is almost Marlowe-esque.

A tenor of conspiracy pervades the verse, the kind we associate with the dark Jacobean underworld of contemporary dramatists like John Webster and Thomas Kyd. The poem ends with the desperate hope that this time Piers will come home for good, perhaps hinting at a hideout in Snowdonia, *"a cottage"* or *"small farm"* ("tyddyn") in the hinterland. Somewhere like Cilgeraint perhaps, home of Piers's sister Alys and her two small boys, encased as it still is within a wild, hidden valley near Tregarth on the Penrhyn estate. There are also other houses nearby rumoured locally to this day, to be "the places where we were told as children Piers Griffith used to lie low", such as Cororion, home of soldier-brother William, whose own career brings to him just as many hair-raising adventures as Piers's illegal exploits, but who seems to pass by, almost unnoticed, untouched as he is by the fashionable in-crowds of Oxford and "hellish London".

In contrast to his friend, Thomas Prys made the decision to quit the sea while he was still in his thirties before the end of the 1590s, certainly by the time of the Captain's return from Drake's Last Voyage, possibly in 1597 or even in 1600. The poet seems to be speaking in the persona of Piers Griffith: *"I bought a ship and sailed the seas..."*. Thomas never did that – he could not afford it – perhaps suggesting that he is speaking for Piers too, as he later implies in his nightmarish Elegy to their two dead sons in 1610. The two voyagers have shared the same experiences. As a poet himself with the action-packed life of one of the Queen's sea-captains, the Pirate of Penrhyn clearly has little time to follow his friend's advice nor to write of his own escapades, still less to give up the *"dangers"* and *"folly"* of the sea (or else such memoirs have been lost.)

There is a strong theatrical ring to this *Heldrin* poem, conjuring up the maritime hey-day of the Elizabethan Age, when privateers, sailing under official Letters of Reprisal were legally granted by the High Court of the Admiralty and 'allowed' by the Queen and her Council (not always in agreement on this point.) The system of 'Reprisal' was accounted legal after vessels of the small British

Navy (swelled in numbers by privately-funded ships invested in by the great Merchant Adventurers and by the Queen herself) had already been attacked, it was claimed, by England's enemies, mainly Spanish galleons. Any counter-attack by Elizabeth's ships therefore, was considered justified.

⁂

In contrast to the *Woodcock* poem, the theatrical comedy of *Heldrin* (Hassles) on *"the troublous times"* of a pirate, manages to echo all the drama of action aboard a privateering vessel at sea: adventure that is graphically brought to life in a series of thrilling episodes, an amalgam of English and Welsh in the original manuscript. Doubtless these words would have been acted out aloud by the poet himself for the entertainment of his family and friends back home, or in places like the *Blue Boar* tavern in London and other dockside haunts of sea-dogs, actors, ne'er-do-wells and the likes of Shakespeare (died 1616), Marlowe (died 1598) or Webster, Kyd, Jonson, Chapman and others.

> *Full fathom five thy father lies;*
> The Tempest (I ii 49.)

In the following extract from *Heldrin* by Thomas Prys, we have a first-hand, reliable, autobiographical account spoken from the point of view of an Oxford man of the gentry with a ready wit and a family tradition of royal service, a well-known, popular and learned Elizabethan Adventurer and Renaissance man in early retirement, now heartily relieved that all the danger, expense and skulduggery is finally behind him.

Recklessly *"I believed I would discover all the treasure in the world"* and it was great fun while it lasted, he seems to say. Doubtless he wishes he could be speaking for Piers too, implicit in the bold use of nautical dialogue to conjure up the exciting scenes they once shared in youth, as part of the camaraderie he recalls aboard ship amongst his crew of swarthy thugs with *"Hellishly rough and hairy chests"*:

Weigh anchor, all you junkers!
... Where is Meurig...
Trim the ship ...
Bear hard ...
About again,
Farewell England and dry sand
And Scilly, fine sunny island;
Roll away with royal wings...
Here's Atkins, where is Woodcock?
...
Our course is to the Southern Cape.

Bring near the timber, Tom boy,
... A can of beer, lad!
Monson, hoist up the mainsail!
Be merry, I see a sail,
Give chase ...
Starboard ...
Port hard the helm, you bastard, ...
Keep the prize ...
He shot three ...
Shoot again, broadside gunner!
Fear not, shoot the wild fire now!
Now enter ...
We lost our men on a vessel amidst smoke.

We cry in the pain of our misfortune!
Ffoulk Harri ...
Was drowned ...
Brown Robin Austin withal

Is dead …
Wenforth, Rowland and Winfield,
William and Cobham, are killed;
Tom, Meurig, Dick …
Are hurt and so is Horton.
Our Ship is, as we struggle to right her,
Weak and full of leaks below
There will come
A storm …
Go to, with endless struggles, we must get to harbour,
We are thirsty, but the beer is sour.
This is the kind of trouble I had
For voyaging at my own expense;
It was a wonder that I, Thomas ever returned
Home safely from those translucent blue waters;
As for ships, by now I think I'd rather be a shepherd!

(G.L.)

NOTE:

A List of ships and men (mostly Welsh) under arrest for piracy on the high seas, including the name of "Pierce" Griffith 5/37, 213; 60/2:-

H.C.A.1, 1/5

H.C.A.1, 1/60

High Court of Admiralty: [1604-1616] Oyer and Terminer Records *(with reference to "Pierce Griffith" and "Thomas Price".)*

INDEX OF H.C.A.1 (Public Record Office)

" *John 4/77; 6/147; 148; 37/196; 45/114.*
" *John, ap Jevan ap Yeollyn 36/272.*
" *John, ap John 36/262.*
" *John, ap Llyn or ap John 36/364, 370, 387.*
" * *Pierce 5/37, 213; 60/2.* *
" *Rees 46/142.*
" *Richard 45/116; 49/156.*
" *Robert 6/18; 45/117; 47/42.*
" *Robert, ap David ap John 36/268.*
" *William 36/387.*
" *William, ap Jevan ap Bolkyn 36/293.*
" *William see also Griffin, William.*

Reference	Date	Document	Offence
H.C.A. 1 45	1604 May 23	Indictment of Thomas Price and others.	Piracy against L'Esperaunce of Rochelle.
H.C.A. 1 213	1608 May 13	Petition of pardon for Pierce Griffith.	

(P.R.O. 2007)

The kind of crimes others in the list are accused of are:

Piracy against the St Paul of Toulon

Piracy...

Piracy...

Killing Andrew Furnace in the Suzan of Wells.

Killing Jacques Faveres in the Serena or Mermaid of Olonne.

Killing William Androwes in the Hopewell.

Piracy against the Black Balbiana of Venice and Killing Francis Padalogus...

"The High Court of Admiralty was established to deal primarily with questions of piracy or spoil but later developed a jurisdiction in prize and a civil jurisdiction in such matters as salvage and collision, based on Roman or civil law. Actions could be taken against ships and goods as well as against persons. The criminal jurisdiction of the High Court of Admiralty was established by an act of Parliament in 1535; it lasted until 1834. Commissions of oyer and terminer (to hear and determine) and of gaol delivery were issued to the Admiralty or his deputy authorising them to try cases of piracy and other crimes committed on the high seas, according to the procedures of common law."

(P.R.O. 2007)

Queen Elizabeth I tolerated the system of Letters of Reprisal, which was how piracy worked during the war years with Spain, or at least amongst the privateering fraternity. But after the Queen's death in 1603, King James I (VI of Scotland), eager to make peace with Spain, would have none of it and made piracy a criminal offence for so-called 'adventuring', 'trading' or 'smuggling'. Piers Griffith fell foul of these new laws, as did Sir Walter Raleigh and others. Their poor, barely surviving, hard-working crews were now out of a job.

Chapter 8

The Earl of Essex visits Mostyn Hall

PRAISE-POEM TO SIR THOMAS MOSTYN UPON HIS KNIGHTHOOD IN 1599
By Siôn Tudur, poet at the Court of Queen Elizabeth I

Fine knight, you are highly praised,
Extend your lordly hand to represent the high rank of the Mostyn
family,
With this office comes great power, and a code of honour,
4   Sir Thomas, with lofty status.
You are now dubbed a knight with a golden sword and wearing a
gold chain, may you enjoy as long a life as the legendary deer
three times over.
That is my joyful wish for you.
As a poet, I rejoice in your knighthood
8   For I have already foretold of your success,
Composed a poem about my intimations,
Now you truly are a happy 'Sir', whereas before, your insignia was
of mere silver.
There was never another so gifted,
12   Nor at handling your own horses and men, noble Knight.
Next summer season, I will not need to go wandering throughout
the land in the manner of poets and troubadours
To delve into heraldry at the houses of strangers
For I am sure of a welcome at Mostyn
Nor will I have to research other people's ancestry as part of my
poetic craft.

16   Will I, when all I need to master now is the family history of Sir
                                                              Thomas.
      You are the best Sir, favoured with enduring grace,
      If everyone in the country were a Sir, it is you who would be the
                                                    best Sir of all.

       Your court excels at patronage and generosity,
20   Young and old congregate there.
      Mostyn Court, although it could hardly be so, is an even greater
                  domain than ever, now that it has become the court of a
                                                    knight of the realm.
      This very manor, so it is told far and wide
24   Has excelled in the past as the lodging of poets,
      Indeed it is known as a house where everybody in Wales is
                                                              welcome,
      You are also the host to earls,
      Those of high rank on their way to Ireland,
28   And no one passes by without visiting the house of Lady Catherine
                  who is as remarkable as Non, the mother of Saint David.
      Many more such celebrations for earls and lords will be arranged
                        here for those awaiting a fair wind for their voyage.
      Your guests are always doubly entertained, at your manor;
      Many delicious courses from your kitchen arrive at table for the
                                                    guests to enjoy
32   With the wine wildly overflowing from your casks;
      There never was such a feast since the legendary days of Lord
                                                              Cadell,
      Not a single earl here has ever seen a finer entertainment.
      The Earl of Essex is present, a gentleman accompanied by his
                                                    personal retinue,
      For him this feast will be engraved in his memory for ever.
36   Other earls accompany him, with all his officers
      In attendance, all his staff and soldiers,
      And other lords too, finely arrayed gentlemen,
      An enormous host of the best accoutred men following in his wake;
40   Cavalry, knights in loyal service, at least ten,

Superb, all around the place, and more besides.
Let us pray that God may bless him with good health
For bringing such a magnificent spectacle to Wales for everyone to
see.

44   And may God also bless you, Sir Thomas
For giving such a feast in honour of my lords,
For Her Grace has had word of this
And her Privy Council too, the Lady of Windsor, Queen
Elizabeth.

48   May I hope you will receive great thanks for receiving all these
guests and for the grandeur of the occasion.
This praiseworthy news about you has spread like wildfire through
her Court,
So that no one will be able to undermine your good name to the
end of their days, your grandchildren's that is.

52   There never was, in the whole history of the defence of the realm,
A royal mission whereby Her Majesty did not call upon you in her
service.
Everyone should congregate in the area where you are,
Lieutenant, the surrounding countryside is under your authority.

56   Sir Thomas, here you are with your splendid gilded helmet
And the heraldic lion on your golden cloak swathed over your suit
of armour,
Kitted out and suitably equipped for battle,
With the strongest of war horses.

60   Good knight, you are famous and your countenance is recognised
throughout the land,
Your Lady, a wonderful hostess at the feast
Is the virtuous and beautiful daughter of the Talacre family of
noble blood,
Catherine extends her generous welcome with bright charm.

64   You yourself, receive secret letters under the Royal Seal
For you have reached a high, privileged position of trust.
Powerful Knight, you bear your role with grace,
I am very happy for you in your elevation to the Knighthood.

68   There never was throughout Tegeingl, you handsome, proud
                                                                peacock,
        Anyone like you in soul and body,
        You are the only prominent knight in these parts, with a
                                                ceremonial gilded sword,
        For the past two hundred years or more.
72   As a leader, there has never been a word said against you,
        As a knight, you are top of the pile.
        Over there in Ireland the people are sure to obey your strong
                                                                commands,
        There are not two thousand amongst them who will rebel against
                                                        your wise judgement.

76   They will agree with your opinion, with whatever the Queen has
                                        instructed you in those sealed documents,
        The opinion is that the Rebels of the Red Tower must be crushed.

        May Christ give you long life
80   For all your days, because you are a famous son of His.
        You are our master and commander, who else will muster us?
        You are a distinguished politician representing the right and good
                                                                of the State:
        A prominent statesman leading his nation, true to his word,
                                                                respected,
84   The owner of the manor, honoured on your domain;
        Scrupulously fair, everyone knows this,
        A pillar of strength at Mostyn;
        You are the most upright and pure, everyone is of this opinion;
88   The head of the harvest crop descended from the strong blood of
                                                                royal Pengwern;
        You are the strong wooden post that bears the weight of two
                                                                counties
        The noble ruler of the fortress from the time of your father;
        A whole history of high praise for you has always been a tradition,
92   Through you the peak, the highest rank of honour has been gained
                                                                for Gwynedd.
                                                                (G.L.)

AT HOME WITH THE MOSTYNS AND THE GRIFFITHS

Several other invited poets (apart from the more prominent Siôn Tudur) also celebrate this grand occasion, soon to be viewed with ironic hindsight after the tragic Irish Campaign and the beheading of the doomed Essex. One of these poems to Sir Thomas, by Sir Huw Roberts, somewhat tongue-in-cheek, gives the date of this lavish entertainment at Mostyn Hall as 1599, on the eve of Elizabeth's army setting sail for Ireland. The poet describes the generous welcome extended by the local magnifico to

> *Earl Essex proudly valiant*
> *With his superb army and all the other earls besides.*

Army Captain Richard Gwyn of Anglesey seems to be included, himself a man of means and patron of poets, but here Gwyn is more concerned with cattle-breeding and securing the services of Sir Thomas Mostyn's prize bull. Another source refers to Essex and his entourage 'stopping over' at Baron Hill, Beaumaris, seat of the Bulkeleys, but this printed prose account from an eye-witness is unclear about whether the event is on the way *there* or on the way back. The vast host from the Irish Wars certainly lands again in Wales on its return, in the shadow of *The Plague and the Rebellion of the Earl of Tyrone*, but with far less appetite for feasting and strutting about.

The popular *Book of Etiquette* dating from 1557 advises on good table manners, the requirement of every gentleman and lady before they visit the Court or are invited out to dinner:

> *Thy mouth not too full when thou dost eate;*
> *Not smackynge thy lyppes, as commonly do hogges,*
> *Nor gnawynge the bones as it were dogges...*
> *Pyke not thy teethe at the table sythynge,*
> *Nor use at thy meate over muche spytynge...*

On Feast-Days, or Saints' Days like the Feast of St John the Baptist, after everyone has tucked into haunches of venison and roast game, or fillets of fish produced from ponds on estate farms by retinues of labourers and servants, there would be the serving of preserved fruits, cherries, blackberries and mountain whinberries. As an added luxury, there might also be the Subtleties, a stylish fashion observed at Court – marchpane baskets of sugar bowls, ginger, almonds, dates and sugar fruits decorated and often mounted into an elaborate assembly in a variety of shapes: ships, birds, animals, knights in armour, flowers like roses cast from moulds into molten sugar tinted with rosewater.

Lavish entertainments at the court of King Henry VIII would still be legendary forty years later: Sir Henry Guildford, as Master of Revels, organised it all, the below-stairs cooks of his steaming kitchens had fennel, aniseed, caraway and coriander spicing up the syrup for making such favourites as sugar hailstones. A special banqueting hall designed by Holbein had a ceiling that "was painted and gilded with the Constellations and Zodiac signs. The floor was covered in dark green silk embroidered with gold lilies. In the middle of the room was a white marble fountain," wrote Suzannah Dunn in *The Queen of Subtleties*, an original, entertaining book which historian Alison Weir called "a new way of telling an old story".

As for Lady Catherine Griffith Mostyn and Mistress Margaret Griffith, one of their cookery books might well have been Gervase Markham's *The English Hous-wife*, not published until 1615, going through several re-prints for the next fifty years; but the Mostyn and Penrhyn Ladies probably had access to earlier works that influenced her, by someone like the Duchess of Northampton for example. Gervase Markham (1568-1637) was their contemporary and the culinary expert may well have published earlier works, was the view of Dr Enid Roberts. Markham gives competent instruction on how to grow herbs and from them make medicines to look after the health of the family; other handy hints were given on cookery, producing different kinds of oil, organising feasts and dinners; brewing beers and creating perfume; dealing with wool, knitting, spinning, weaving cloth and dyeing it; dairy skills too were not neglected, especially the tricky art of 'separating', producing healthful buttermilk, cream cheese and butter, a traditional art that would have been practised by country women on the Penrhyn and Mostyn domains.

In Wales, several manuscripts on the art of cookery have survived, some based on the written recipes and remedies of Tudor and Stuart women, collected and shared amongst themselves. Some are linked to the Penrhyn family like the work of their kinswoman Merryell Williams of Ystumcolwyn in Powys. These were found amongst seven manuscripts inherited by Sir Robert Williams Vaughan, the antiquary of Hengwrt. Meryell Williams's collection has since been edited and published by Dr Roberts. Included with the manuscripts was a notebook by Meryell's kinswoman Catherine Nanney of Dolgellau, with recipes by Mrs Sidney Wynne of Melai and Lady Williams of Llanfarde. Also in this collection of papers was discovered the recipe book of James Smith, a *"cooke in Sallop"* (Shropshire) but containing much older recipes. Like portrait-painters, speciality cooks travelled far and wide; Smith was known to have hired out his services as chef to the great houses of North and Mid-Wales, and there is some evidence for such a man in Tudor Chester, cookery expert Eryl Hold told me.

This Hengwrt collection of domestic manuscripts 1650-1750 represents an elaborate style of entertaining much later than the lives of Sir Thomas Mostyn and Lady Catherine of course, and of Piers and Margaret Griffith at Penrhyn. But the women of the gentry and their hired chefs built on the tried and true recipes of the past, of their Tudor forebears, Dr Roberts noted. Many courses and dishes came from traditional recipes within the family or were filched from some celebrated best-selling cookery book by an aristocratic lady they sought to emulate. Merryell Williams, for example, may well have drawn on a whole range of these older sources. Her knowledge of herbalism was prolific, suggesting well-organised gardens at Ystumcolwyn and there is no reason to suppose that the Penrhyn gardens were any less; indeed they are described as once being "*fine*".

There is a professional, ambitious tone to her work as if she has drawn on only the best advice, according to Eryl Hold and top prize-winning chef, Hywel 'H' Griffith. Merryell also includes practical tips and diagrams with mathematical precision, for organising banquets and dinners in great style for large numbers of people. Lady Catherine and the other Penrhyn and Mostyn ladies were not to be daunted. They aimed high: you had to, then. Friends and neighbours traditionally were not only to be welcomed but impressed.

Chef Griffith, formerly at the Grosvenor Hotel in Chester (and interestingly a descendant of Piers Griffith's brother William) comments:

> "Preparing such feasts today without masses of servants behind-the-scenes would be almost impossible, even with our labour-saving devices and limitless selection of ingredients, so their creative skills must be acknowledged, considering the level of grandeur they managed to achieve with the resources they had then. Maybe such natural organic food was tastier! And of course they had great sauces."

The support-system for their menfolk provided by Tudor women of all ranks was considered important for the order and economy of home and community, but especially amongst the aristocracy and gentry, the merchants and farmers. The Essex feast would have been a huge drain on local resources. Anthony Fitzherbert's *Boke of Husbandry* published in 1523 gave advice to the farmer's wife about her duties from morning until night, whether or not she was a freeholder or tenant of places like Penrhyn or Mostyn; several such women are listed in the Rent Rolls of both estates, when a housewife would have been expected to supply *some* food at least for the 'Big House', as well as for her own family:

> *Set all good things in order within thy house: milk thy kyne, suckle thy calves, syc up thy milk, take up thy children and array them and provide for thy husband's breakfast, dinner and supper and for thy children and servants, and take thy part with them. And to ordain corn and malt to the mill, to bake and brew withal when need is.*

At the higher end of the social spectrum, there was the expected official function of provincial ladies going to Court. As a trusted courtier and royal envoy, and as a friend of Burghley, Sir Thomas Mostyn must at some time have been received by Queen Elizabeth; indeed he may have purchased his London property to that purpose. The wives of the three Sir William Griffiths and then Lady Catherine with her first husband Sir Rhys, may well have gone too. Possibly, they attended the coronations of the House of Tudor as their husbands certainly did. Yet the ladies of North Wales did not usually frequent the London Court in the normal run of things, with the possible exception of ladies-in-waiting later, like Piers's sister-in-law, Lady Catherine Hanmer in the 1620s; and a Catholic Lady of Powys Castle stayed close to the side of Mary Queen of Scots until the bitter end in 1587.

Queen Elizabeth's women were her companions. King James preferred men, as some of his passionate letters show and Archbishop/Keeper of the Privy Purse/Dean John Williams may have been a very close companion indeed. Certainly he was loyal to James 'unto death' as the King's religious adviser, confessor and friend, after others abandoned the horrors of the Royal sick-bed.

It was lucky therefore for Blanche Parry, a Welsh girl from Herefordshire, that her expertise in make-up and wiggery had kept her since childhood in the Queen's service without accidentally poisoning her mistress with arsenic. Blanche (a.k.a. Gwen?) is supposed to have written her own witty epitaph for her monument and she lies for all eternity in a quiet corner of a Herefordshire church:

> *I lived always as handmaid to a Queen*
> *In chamber chief my time did overpass...*
> *Preferring still the causes of each wight*
> *As far as I durst move her grace's ear*
> *For to reward deserts by course of right.*

Rowland Vaughan, a court official and a nephew of Blanche's, wrote later that although gentlewomen such as his aunt might prove useful contacts for their friends at Court, "*none of these (near and dear ladies) durst intermeddle so far in matters of commonwealth.*"

Whether Blanche was influential in any personal or political matters, it seems she had the ear of the Queen at times, but may have had her own ears boxed in return. These suitably connected ladies of the Court were well placed to gain access to the Sovereign or to seek patronage for someone dependent on a career, someone desperate for favours.

One aristocratic Tudor lady in England for instance, left precise and touching written instructions for her nursemaid to whom she had nervously entrusted her baby when she was required to go to the royal palace with her husband. The servant must take "*care with his little head*" whilst bathing him, and then must tenderly dress the child with "*gentle*" movements, to swaddle him in soft, folded cloth. Some mothers of the gentry in England and Wales employed foster-mothers for the early years of childhood; but more ladies than was thought previously, actually breast-fed their babies themselves. In childbirth they employed good, experienced midwives, in a dark, curtained room, with or without a doctor at hand, but otherwise men were not allowed near, nor wanted to be. Such women played their role in safely delivering heirs.

On the whole, ladies of the gentry in Wales did not spend much expensive time, if any, at court in the grand, seductive, dangerous style of some whose lives have been recorded in vivid narrative histories like Julia Fox's *The Infamous Lady Rochford*, who attended second wife Anne Boleyn and fifth wife, Katherine Howard, both of whom were beheaded – the condemned Rochford "did not flinch" – a blood-curdling price to pay. No wonder one foreign princess, Cristina of Milan, turned Henry VIII down flat with the spruce reply that she had too much respect for her own head.

After hearing of such gruesome court gossip reaching the Penrhyn or Mostyn ladies and their kinswomen at home, perhaps they found life more agreeable *chez nous*. And for this they were celebrated by poets at their manor-houses in the chivalrous manner of the *amour courtois*/courtly love tradition, purely and from afar. Their lives, their dynastic talents and achievements, the heirs they left behind them, all show the role women played from basic childbirth in generations of nurture and comfort, to being the inspiration of poets. Some *did* break the mould. At home in Denbighshire, Piers's great-aunt, the sophisticated and well-travelled Catrin of Berain, for example, (Denmark, Spain and the Low Countries), was a guest in her own right at the Coronation of her cousin Queen Elizabeth. Catrin was in possession of a

> *Fair dwelling with household organisation and good fine*
> > *furniture*
>
> *Crafted in wood and gold*
> *Engraved in pearls*
> *Exquisitely precious imported from overseas...*
> *Fit to welcome a prince for dinner,*
>
> > (G.L.)

wrote Siôn Phylip of his rich patroness. She had also lived in London and Antwerp with her even wealthier merchant-special agent-diplomat husband, Richard Clough (died 1570.) She died in 1591 aged 56, five years after her son from her first marriage, Thomas Salusbury, was executed.

During her life-time, she became the wife of one of the Wynns of Gwydir, then of the cultured magnate, Edward Thelwall of Plas-y-Ward, Llanynys, a manor associated with the trading family who so dogged Piers for debts; nevertheless, as mistress of the house, Catrin like others had a flair for designing gardens; her *"wonderful green garden, was a happy place to be,"* with *"well-tended lawns"* and *"swans on the lake".*

Plas Iolyn, at the time of Thomas Prys's father in 1534, was a welcoming, hearty place, white-washed and comfortable, with plentiful food and a fine cellar, *"a palace on a hill, fit for the pleasures of a king,"* doubtless due to the attentions of his wife, if not his mistress, but not in the same class as Mostyn Hall.

Tudur Aled, a well-travelled court poet at royal Windsor, praised the lovely Hanmer house of Yr Owredd in early Tudor times, the family home Catherine Mostyn married into, the Pirate's Wife's sister. The workmanship of its high-mounted, superbly timbered Tudor construction is equal to the fine houses the poet had seen in *"Paris or Venice".* The Hanmer *"white tower"* offered far-seeing views 'as picturesque as those of Calais', he wrote of this manor-house situated in the Welsh border country, similar to the oak-timbered Little Moreton Hall and other such gems.

Amidst *"a forest setting Gwydir stands,"* wrote Huw Machno about the Wynn home in the Conwy Valley where Roger Mostyn stole his bride away. Gwydir is described as a haven for poets with its *"wonderful labyrinth"* of hedges and chimneys. Court poet Siôn Phylip (who wrote a famous elegy to Queen Elizabeth) called it *"a good place to walk, a golden domain like the gateway to Rome",* but then he rather over-egged it with a comparison to the *"royal lawns of Ancient Troy".*

Perhaps one of Piers's coastal landmarks, medieval Cricieth castle is brought to life for us by the early descriptions of Iolo Goch:

A magnificent fortress high on the headland above the coast
[with] *busy serving-men* [and]
pretty maids and ladies of the house
… working skilfully at brilliantly coloured silk tapestries.
Reflected in the sunbeams of the fine mullioned windows…

The new style architecture of Siôn Llwyd's Faenol Fawr at Abergele, built in 1597 was admired for its magnificence, masonry and carpentry. Early medieval Cochwillan was praised by Guto'r Glyn for its "*delightful domestic comforts out of the cold*", its wine and flaming fires. Penrhyn, where gentry, tenants and townspeople had always freely mixed, had the "*kitchen of an Earl*," wrote Lewys Môn, and "*jugs and flagons of gleaming copper*," with golden and glass goblets – "*not one of silver, mind*".

None of this would have been possible "without the best co-ordination between Upstairs and Downstairs and a lot of hard work by droves of servants", comments Hywel the Chef; and we are now made aware of this wider picture by many fascinating social historians.

Tudor family portraits throughout Wales reveal rich costumes, head-dresses, hats and gloves, furs, dashing leather-gear and painted armour, belts, swords of honour, tournament ribbons and arm-bands, adding symbols of authority, coats of arms, books and skulls, not to mention secret signs and cryptic codes.

"Detailed descriptions of clothes are very few," Dr Enid Roberts has disclosed, "but we gather that expensive materials were not in short supply. Besides velvet, silk and damask, other expensive materials mentioned by the poets and in other documents are *pali*, French *paille*, a kind of silk brocade; *siamled* or chamlet, a beautiful and costly eastern fabric, made in the sixteenth century from the hair of the angora goat; *du o lir* or *blac o lir*, a rare and valuable broadcloth from Lier, in the Low Countries; *mwrai*, murray, cloth of mulberry colour, *mwtlai* or *medlai*, medley, cloth with threads of many colours; *ffris*, frieze, a kind of coarse woollen cloth with nap, usually on one side, generally made in Ireland, like the new cloak begged from Sir Rhys by poet Siôn Tudur. Outer garments were often decorated and lined with miniver, ermine or other fur, and garments were edged with *pwrffil*, purfle, an embroidered band, possibly the work of the ladies of the court."

Besides arranging for scraps at the back door to be supplied to the less fortunate, the ladies of Mostyn, Penrhyn, Cochwillan and elsewhere in England and Wales sewed clothes for the children of the poor; and like Catherine of Aragon, a lady would sometimes lovingly sew shirts for her husband, absent or not.

Siôn Tudur's poem praises the virtues of Piers's mother, Lady Catherine, when Lord Essex arrives at Mostyn Hall on his way to Ireland:

> *Your Lady, a wonderful hostess at the feast*
> *Is the virtuous and beautiful daughter of the Talacre family of*
> *noble blood,*
> *Catherine extends her generous welcome with bright charm.*

Yet this may have been a veneer to keep up appearances, an essential social duty. In actual fact it has never been clear whether Sir Thomas and Lady Catherine ever lived together at Mostyn Hall. By 1608, nine years after Essex's visit and several quarrels later, sometimes about Piers, they certainly seem to have been living apart (MS NLW 465/491.) She is recorded then as living at Gloddaith, the property Sir Thomas had granted her as his second wife at the time of their 'arranged' marriage back in 1582.

There were other inter-marriages within these two families. Indeed, the Mostyn and Griffith connection harks back to the Battle of Bosworth in 1485 when William Griffith and Richard ap Hywel of Mostyn both fought for Henry Tudor. At some point Richard ap Hywel was famously hiding the fugitive Jasper Tudor at Mostyn Hall, the second son of Owen Tudor of Penmynydd and his wife, the widowed Queen Catherine de Valois, grandparents of King Henry VII.

In an interwoven background-tapestry to the poem on the Essex visit, when Sir Thomas had to dig so deeply into his pockets, it is worth noting that in 1517, ap Hywel's son, Thomas ap Rhisiart ap Hywel of Mostyn had married Jane Griffith, daughter of Sir William Griffith of Penrhyn and after about 1540 the surname Mostyn was adopted by the family, their great hall dating from the 1450s with its traditional raised dais and minstrels' gallery, noted Dr Anthony Carr. Add to this their vast, industrially rich estate including the ancient *"Five Courts of Mostyn"* – Gloddaith, Tregarnedd, Trecastell, Pengwern and the splendid Feasting Hall itself, so vividly graced by Piers's step-father, the Queen's trusted emissary to Ireland and by her commander, Lord Essex, possibly wearing the Queen's ring for all to see, her personal gift to him against all danger. Some significance is given here to the new role of Sir Thomas Mostyn as knight and diplomat, entrusted with *"secret, sealed letters"* from her Majesty. But, as time is running out for her, is she now beginning to mistrust her favourite, Essex himself?

Chapter 9

The *Esperanza*

A Request for a Spanish Galleon from William Morris
of Clenennau, Admiral for the Coast of North Wales,
Lord Lieutenant of Caernarvonshire c.1600
by Thomas Prys

> *"Brave eagle powerful over men,*
> *How handsome you are, elevated to honours,*
> *Brave William, with your golden helmet,*
> 4   *He has bailed us out of many a conflict when necessary ..."*

After these striking opening lines about eagles, golden helmets
and tricky piratical situations, lines 5–22 then compliment
Lawyer Morris on his noble ancestry in an expansively humorous
tone. Some forebears like the Pulestons, the Stanleys and the
"Legendary Voyager Ifor" of ancient times are kindred, the likes
of whom Morris shares with Piers Griffith and Thomas Prys, so
the ironic implication here is that they are all jolly kinsmen in it
together. Morris is hailed as the respected representative of Her
Majesty's High Admiralty on the Coast of North Wales. He is also
Lord Lieutenant and Sheriff, a local big-wig, with military powers
in an emergency like the Armada or the threat of attack from
ferocious foreign marauders. He is praised for his wisdom and
politics as High Sheriff, highly valued in Wales *"and impressive in
England"*, Thomas Prys adds sardonically. He flatters the Admiral

by calling him a cheerful, magnanimous, richly-robed man with courteous manners and Morris knows this of course; surely, the poet suggests, he has the good humour to take this poem "*in good sport*".

The ship referred to here is probably the "*Esperanza of Ayamonte*", captured by Piers Griffith and his crew in 1600 and brought into Abercegin Creek at Bangor, Port of Beaumaris as a spectacular prize for all to marvel at her, with a cargo of silks, oils and spices. Legally, but annoyingly, these now belong to the Admiralty, like the ship herself.

The official record in the Penrhyn Papers implies that this great spectacle ought to be surrendered to Admiralty officials from London and not kept locally for all to see nor presumably, for Piers to trade her goods; still less to spirit them away amongst the smuggling fraternity, albeit gaining for himself an enormous scoop as far as his adventuring reputation goes:

20   Admiral, as officer for shipwrecks along the coast you keep the
                                                                    peace,
       You give work and offices to us in Gwynedd:
       No ship can approach our coast
       If it is armed with guns without you as Admiral giving your
                                                              permission;
       Lieutenant, you have great power ...

43   But I, Thomas, maintain that I
       Have often been in the thick of the fight
       In the defence of the realm
       Yet I have neither ship nor boat to call my own!

49   But you, Admiral have in your safekeeping, I have to say,
       A fully rigged ship set for summer sailing:
       If health permits, I should really love
52   To venture out into the water in her.

Thomas now takes up the poetic convention of addressing the ship in personalised terms:

53   Courtier of the water, pulling strongly on the face of the waves,
You are like a cradle for carrying and nurturing men, young and
old;
Your sides cut freely through the strong currents,
Your sails are lively, billowing out and bubbling like a cauldron pot;
Your oars are like spades for us to handle,
Low-lying in the water splashing away
White foaming spray dispersing, knitted into the wind,

60   Oarsmen can heave them along the backs of waves;
These men beat them, all in order, each man aligned in the motion
of effort,
Against the wind, what a great commotion
At other times with the wind in our favour

64   Great sport is to be had, her prow sailing on marvellously.
In a storm, in some seasons,
The Dolphin will be glimpsed in the water;
Leaping skilfully in all its natural beauty,

68   The ship is like a casket with tough hairy-chested
Able-bodied sailors, who lead us on,
In a vessel shaped, to our eyes, like a flour-barrel or a narrow cage;
We see, as we drive her on, a wave like the side of a hill

72   In our many-decked gallery sailing in salt water.
There is danger ahead, cold and tense is the sway of a ship in chase,
Like a parlour sailing on the topmost edge of pure green-blue
water.
The finely constructed form of the ship, goes on its adventurous
journey,

76   In mortal danger, clean and ship-shape,
Either riding the sea or landing by grazing its bottom on a shingle
beach
And then how noisily she rocks and scrapes!
Travellers are carried, scurrying hasty voyagers all in a hurry,

80   The prow is like a long-nosed mole seen out in the wild,

Restless here, staying in one place
Unpredictably moving up and down on the water;
This vessel is similar, with its narrow prow,
84   To a flea poised for action if it is forced to jump;
It is such a reluctant leaper,
Like the spring of a deer.
A coffin, is how a ship is sometimes regarded
88   Or as an eternal grave by men who hunt greedily for fortune,
For treasure on faraway seas, that is their dwelling-place,
We have to haul and work in our home at the mercy of the wind,
Angry, wild, and unsteady like a bad servant,
92   If we come close to land,
Her prow we will tie there, with a rope-knot on a ring or post;
But if we fail in rough seas to sail in close to land we have to cast
anchor
96   Hanging the ship itself as it were, lest we are all shipwrecked on the
rocks.

The poet then changes his tone of voice to address his patron, Admiral William Morris, in a witty, familiar vein, suggesting that as the three men know each other very well, it would be a good idea for the Admiral to grant Piers and Thomas a favour or two. Perhaps he already owes them one.

Please send me out for one happy hour
On a Spanish galleon with its special finely-pointed prow
To carry me smoothly, that would be so good,
100 In a ship full of joy;
I will then send you one passionate address after the other,
A praise-poem to you for ever like verses of admiration to a girl,
Like a poem of appreciation on a young lover's tongue
104 As long as you keep that ship lying at anchor near the town
harbour and its green bank.

(G.L.)

Chapter 10

Pirate's Sunset

*I love seafaring, the great surges of the sea, the unique
beauty and light of the ocean in all its changing moods.*

Piers Griffith, *Pirates at Plymouth*

The capture of the Spanish galleon *Esperanza* in 1600, places Piers in the vanguard of gentlemen adventurers during the days of Elizabeth Tudor. This is a rare prize indeed. Such men led the field.

Griffith's outward reputation amongst most of his contemporaries was as a *bona fide* merchant adventurer, an aristocratic captain of an armed pinnace in the service of Queen and country. With his fine education, intellectual gifts and wide network of contacts, he was also a scientific explorer and a reliable diplomat on missions abroad. Yet beneath this honourable veneer lay the dark, violent underworld of plots and espionage, in urgent defence of the realm and of the Queen's personal safety from the daggers and poisons of assassins. Viewed in this light, the *Esperanza* stunt would only add to his profile. The murderous deeds of his boarding-party to achieve this would be accepted as a necessary evil: kill or be killed. His spectacular coup, reported far and wide via the Admiralty, was the culmination of his glory days of the 1580s and 1590s.

During the 1590s, when we associate him mainly with Drake, Griffith was clearly mortgaging heavily, so he may well have gone on other expeditions and raids with other piratical superstars of his generation.

In 1591 for example, a squadron of ships including six of the ageing Queen's own, commanded by Sir Thomas Howard, a kinsman of the Lord Admiral of Armada fame, sailed from Plymouth to the Azores to intercept the Spanish fleet laden with treasure. Another Armada associate, Sir Richard Grenville was also part of this venture as vice-admiral commanding the *Revenge*, Drake's former flagship of 1588.

Howard was lying in wait off the Atlantic islands of the Azores (Flores) when he sighted the treasure-fleet, escorted by a squadron of warships. He kept clear but Grenville impulsively took the risk of attacking the Spaniards alone. The huge, lofty galleons of the enemy proved his undoing. The *Revenge*, as she drew close in, found herself too near to the galleon in the lee of the wind, and so was disastrously becalmed. The Spaniards fired and boarded her only to meet a valiant challenge aboard ship. Grenville was fatally wounded and taken prisoner on the Spanish Admiral's ship, the *San Pablo* where he soon died.

Piers's pinnace *Grace,* or possibly another ship he had acquired, "the flyboat", would be commandeered in 1603 by Captain Plessington of the Royal Navy at Cork. Even then, the "notable pirate" seems to have still held on to his small trading vessel the *Elizabeth*, operating locally out of Bangor, Port of Beaumaris. He may have followed in the wake of other prominent men, but some veterans were already suffering a downturn. Sir John Hawkins's *Victory* for instance managed to survive until 1608 and the late Queen's ship *Elizabeth Bonaventure* captained by George Raymond, was scuppered as useless in 1610 after a hardy fifty-year service. The Earl of Cumberland had run several vessels, sometimes wastefully like the *Samson*, recruiting the gentlemanly likes of Piers Griffith "*leading his men*".

But the glory days of the old sea-dogs were not over yet. After Drake's death in 1596, a fleet under the command of Sir Thomas Howard and the Earl of Essex sailed for Spain after the Queen's intelligencers brought news to new Spymaster Robert Cecil that Spain was planning another invasion attempt. Sir Walter Raleigh played a courageous role here, although he was seriously wounded commanding the *Warsprite* in another dramatic raid on Cadiz, where Piers may conceivably have been part of the action. The venture impressed the Queen and it did include several other Welsh contemporaries, like poets Richard Hughes and Piers's friend, Ifan Llwyd Sieffre.

In 1599 Spain made yet another plan for an Armada invasion after the death of King Philip II in 1598; but this fizzled out as times were changing. The Queen was growing old and Robert Cecil, her Chief Minister was making secret diplomatic communications with Spain to bring peace on land and sea. Also, he was already beginning covert negotiations with Scotland via his network of agents to set up James VI as Elizabeth's successor to the throne after her death. James had already written a shrewd letter to the Queen at the time of the Armada assuring her of his backing "*as your natural son and compatriot of your country*" which he called "*Britain*" and "*the Ile*", not "*England*", implying the concept of the ancient Island of Britain, of which he hoped to be the future King. His great-grandmother had been Henry VIII's sister, Margaret Tudor, who at the age of only thirteen had married the King of Scotland; this Tudor connection, together with his status as an anointed king, and his Protestantism, were his claims to the throne as Elizabeth's kinsman despite the infamy of his Catholic mother, Mary, Queen of Scots.

Lord Charles Howard was now appointed Lord Lieutenant General of 'all England' (i.e. the Island of Britain) in charge of, amongst other commissions and duties, the coastline of the country in preparation for James Stuart; and it was Howard who helped to negotiate peace with Spain in 1604 for the new King James I, VI of Scotland.

An elegy in Welsh upon the death of Queen Elizabeth, written by politically-minded palace guard, Siôn Phylip (a gentleman-farmer of Harlech), declared that,

> *Such a woman will never rule over you again*
> *As long as the sun shines.*

She is *"Defender of the Faith"* and

> *It was our holy God who took our Prince and Head,*
> *The star of all the Princes of Europe.*

As for the Islamic empire of the seas in North Africa and the Mediterranean, they feared *"Prince"* Elizabeth more than any other *"illustrious emperors"*, he reminded his audience:

> *Even the Turk feared the banner of her dynasty,*
> *The truthful and wise virgin.*

Her Reign

> *was a time of abundance and joy,*
> *Every day was a golden day of plenty.*
> (G.L.)

Her soul *"has gone to the God of Trinity to be crowned"* and *"her kingdom passed to her nephew James"*, he concluded in a bald statement, perhaps treading a fine line between treason and reportage.

❧

Meanwhile, Sir Walter Raleigh is faring rather worse. If Piers is associating with Raleigh at this time, he is heading for the sort of hot water suggested by ex-pirate Thomas Prys. Sir Walter

Raleigh already has several enemies at court including, before she dies, the Queen's new favourite, Robert Devereux, Earl of Essex, but his Rebellion in 1601 suddenly removes him from the scene, followed by his execution not long after the Mostyn Feast. In another contemporary context, Thomas Prys comments on *"these uncertain, dangerous times"*.

To be precise, Raleigh is indiscreet about letting it be known that he opposes the accession of the son of the beheaded Mary Queen of Scots, James, to the throne of England. As soon as Elizabeth dies on March 24, 1603 and is buried in Westminster Abbey, James slips over the border into England, committing acts of terror along the way, like having a heckler in one local crowd beheaded without trial. Raleigh is immediately stripped of his position as Captain of the Guard, has his wine licences suspended and is ordered out of his home at Durham House on the Strand.

He is first sent to the Tower on July 17, 1603 on account of his friendship with Lord Cobham, a diplomat who is in communication with Count Aremberg, a Spanish secret agent in London. At Raleigh's trial in November, he is found guilty of plotting the death of King James I and seeking to deliver his country into the hands of the enemy. It is the Tower again for the Defender of the South West, the great explorer, the once-favourite of Elizabeth Tudor and associate of Piers.

As the poet Ifan Llwyd Sieffre wrote subversively in *The Plague and the Rebellion of the Earl of Tyrone*, there is widespread famine after atrocious weather and failed crops, plague and revolt during the last years of Elizabeth's reign and a bitter, extended war with Ireland. The Wheel of Fate is turning for everyone in Griffith's once-adventurous time-zone.

By June 1617, Piers's mentor Raleigh has spent fourteen years in the Tower, writing his *History of the World* and venturing out on the walls, chatting to passers-by. Like Piers, Raleigh has finally exhausted the wealth of his estate on voyaging and privateering, this time on his last-ditch failed expedition up the Orinoco. Piers is again mortgaging heavily between 1612 and 1615, so it is possible he accompanies Raleigh at this point.

The unsympathetic King James has Raleigh tried, then executed in Old Palace Yard, on the south side of Westminster Hall. Piers Griffith and Thomas Prys, whose verse and memoir bear striking signs of inspiration from the works of Raleigh in theme and tone, possibly calling out to him from outside the Tower Walls as people did *en passant*. They may even have attended his trial, but perhaps the heavy atmosphere of melancholy weighing darkly over the small court-room is more than they can bear. Executed for treason? A national and respected hero, he of the gallant-cloak-and-puddle fame?

Raleigh is a man out of tune with the new Stuart Age, like Piers and Thomas and that stalwart group of subversive old fans of Queen Elizabeth back in Wales, retired heroes who sing of miserable times nowadays and villainous lawyers upsetting ordinary folk, all expressed in their fond nostalgia for past times,

> "*pan oedd Bess yn teyrnasu,*/ when Good Queen Bess reigned over us."

Thomas Prys also conveys this mood in his poem *To All My faithful Companions of Old* after 1628, carefully sub-texted with innuendo between the lines. Amongst these lost pals, he includes the deaths of his son Ellis, of Piers and William and other beloved travellers along the London Road, pale ghosts of riders journeying past his lonely manor-farm at Plas Iolyn in Snowdonia, a haven Piers once knew so well, one of his mountain hideouts perhaps.

It is Thomas who grasps the nettle of writing an elegy to his dearest friend in 1628. Someone has to. When the time comes he can hardly bear the agony of remembering and writing, as he himself admits in the poem (see later.)

The last literary works that Thomas Prys, pirate-poet leaves to us, are flooded with melancholy, nostalgia and allusive social comments on the Stuart Age, ironic asides that would have been mutually understood by this departed 'Hamlet generation' of companions, now living in the last twilight shadows of the Age of Piracy.

Thomas hopes there are still some people around who *do* understand. He leaves his Elegy to Piers Griffith, his unfinished memoir, his map, his survey of their Bardsey Island power-base teeming with the marvels of wildlife. His elegies, praise and message-poems all convey his sense of drama, his humanity and his worldly experience in a fusion of passion and intellect. His lively Renaissance-style Nature poems display his knowledge and fine wit, his original use of Classical conventions, his unique personal voice, his fashionable metaphysical mode of writing comparable to that of his contemporaries like Donne.

Some poems make tragic reading but his work in total is perhaps as near as we can get to the voice of Piers Griffith himself. Thomas Prys, pirate-poet retired, seems to speak for his friend and for the era in which they were both such dynamic forces, when "Elspeth's" motto had been *"Semper Eadem"*/*Always the Same*, her Tudor monogram.

The last works of Thomas Prys (he died in 1634, six years after Piers) and his elegy to his *"notable pirate"* cousin all seem to sum up the uncertainty and transition of King James's final years between 1620-25 and the even greater upheaval of King Charles's new reign from 1625 onwards, in worrying times that would eventually spiral into worse and lead to Civil War. After that, and partly as a result of Cromwellian and Restoration foreign policies in the Caribbean, the Age of Piracy would be re-born later in the new dawn of the Buccaneers: Captain Blood and others, including two more notable Welsh pirates, Black Bartholomew of Casnewydd Bach and Captain Harry Morgan.

BESS YN TEYRNASU

(In the Reign of Good Queen Bess)

A popular Welsh song of the early seventeenth century.

"In those days not many people were in need or went short of money, everyone knew everyone else, leaving each other in peace, on their own land; musicians and poets used to be welcomed every week.

Some would visit to entertain us over the summer, and others at Christmas, the Season of Festivals.

Chorus: How life has changed these days in Wales
           Since former times when Bess ruled over us!

           In those days there was hardly any talk of taxes
           Nor of Land Laws, nor of raising rents
           But there was a sense of community and kindness in every
                                        neighbourhood
           So now let Satan pay the Lawyers' wages.

Chorus: How life has changed these days in Wales
           Since former times when Bess ruled over us!"
           (Traditional)
                             (Trans. G.L.)

Of course other satiric verses were sometimes added. The original Welsh language musical source is by kind permission of Siân James, international harpist and singer, who still performs in this tradition. There is a later version by John Jones (Jac Glan-y-Gors), 1766-1821.

Chapter 11

Plague Years

ELEGY TO WILLIAM GRIFFITH OF PENRHYN AND ELLIS, SON OF THOMAS PRYS OF PLAS IOLYN, 1610, AGED 20
by Sir Huw Roberts, Cleric

> *"As for his father Piers, every night and day*
> *Into his breast he bows his head as he cries rivers of tears.*
> *As for the boy's mother, she does not care at all these days*
> *To see her daughters any more."*

A tragedy has befallen Gwynedd,
The people have lost two of their best young men, the talent store
of the land is now weakened,
The pain of grief is making us ill, as if there is a fever shuddering
through us.
4   Great tearful mourning is apparent everywhere in Wales.
There is sorrow in our time,
There is heavy cause for this sighing;
How strange that such a tragedy has stricken us
8   When there was already great suffering last year!
There have been cries of anguish again throughout the fine city of
London,
The cause of it was immense, and of not inconsiderable
consequence,
The days of two young men were shortened,
12   Fatal Plague was the reason for this.
They were two beloved cousins, good, gifted, unique,

Their loss is like the barbs of bitterly sharp arrows, three times

over.

These firm friends, fond companions went
16   To London as everyone in the country hereabouts knows,
Setting off together, in cheerful companionship, that is the shock

of the tragedy,

They died there, more is the pity.
Woe is Chance, what a cold, harsh event to happen on a journey
20   In the lives of men.
One by one, of good family,
The healthy, strong, beloved son of Master Piers Griffith,
And the special grandson of cultured knights of old,
24   Excellent knights and earls.
And the second boy, golden lion as he was,
The heir of Thomas Prys, as was well-known.
There was no hint of what might happen to those gilded youths
28   As everyone could see they were so fond of each other.
Being friends and beloved cousins neither would separate from the

other even for an hour

Nor go a step without his companion.
William would not go
32   To Saint Paul's without Ellis for an hour.
Ellis would not go the length of a little finger,
Without his beloved cousin; who was more upright and suited to

each other than these two?

For William the heir of Piers, of the pure golden helmet fame,
36   The two Counties of Gwynedd suffer the pain of mourning.
The people of all the country for the grandson of Sir Rhys
Have been encircled in an island of chill suffering and indisposition,
Woe to the local community and the people of Gwynedd
40   For fine, promising William has been enclosed fast within the

knot … of his own grave …

*The next fragmentary lines in the manuscript translate as "respect
… swan … why … completely floored us … heavenly … between*

pain … Sir Thomas Mostyn … the same time…", *before going on to discuss "the adventurous bloodline of the Stradlings and the Stanleys". The poem continues:*

      There is talk in every church and court
56   Of William and Ellis.
      Thomas is also here … his rib has struck ice.
      For Ellis his son he is crying … his heir
      The grandson of The Red Doctor, a prominent hero of old,
60   Ellis was like the second Sultan … a wound of our time,
      And of the heroic lineage of Rhys Amrhedudd.
      To Penrhyn all now go in cold distress,
      A crowd of people from Gwydir are rebellious with anger.
64   In the year of our Lord, Son of Mary, this is the truest word,
      Bitter was their journey in early summer,
      One thousand six hundred and ten, when the pair of them
                   cheerfully set out full of hope and ambition,
      When the two beloved companions left, they departed also from life
                                            itself.

Another fragment describes Ellis as

      cold … laid to rest
      … constant pain
      … the fine cedar tree
      … Cypress tree of Gwynedd
      In London with a pure rosary bead in his grave …

and again, possibly now referring to William

      … in his grave
      … like ice over him
      … bitterly cold it was
      … sprinkling him with earth at his burial
      … of high lineage …

The manuscript continues:

81   Greetings today here
       The welcoming wise deer, leader of good men
       For William there is mourning.

84   For everyone who knew him, all the family is mourning.
       As for his father Piers, every night and day
       Into his breast he bows his head as he cries rivers of tears.
       As for the boy's mother, she does not care at all these days

88   To see her daughters anymore.
       If it is bitter sorrow for those who are inconsolable,
       For his sisters, it is more bitter than ever.
       As for his Uncle William, alas, *(brother of Piers)*

92   Into the deepest marrow of his ribcage is shot the arrow of pain as
       William Griffith grieves for his nephew William, and my kind
                                    friend,
       His two cheeks covered in watery tears.
       The grandfather is an intelligent deep-feeling man, *(Sir Thomas*
                                   Mostyn)

96   The grandmother is almost dying with grief for the loss of her
                                   grandson,
       Cold is her breast, encrusted in jewels, robed in cloth-of-gold
                                   without warmth,
       Cold for knowing he is buried, my poor Lady Catherine.
       What planet now has affected the people of Gwynedd?

100 What cold shade? Who wears a normal face without any sign of
                                   sorrow?
       Everyone is in a horrified shivering state, there is a profound sense
                                   of regret,
       The chill of sudden fright has shuddered through all Penrhyn, that
                                   is the story which is being told.
       Master Piers in his life has carried many crosses,

104 It was God's will to take more than two children from him.
       Kidnapped they were, the dark night's plunder,
       His dear fruitful little trees so close to each other *(Robert and Rhys.)*
       Death came stealing by like a thief and robbed his family tree, age
                                     did not count for anything,

108   Three beloved spears, straight branches descended from Sir
                  Gwilym ap Gruffydd the ancestral head of the family.
     Three dear sweet trees have now been taken
     From his beautiful fine orchard by God.
     Although stealing one had to be insisted upon by our Lord,
112   Two sons were taken, descended from Ifor the Great.
     In spite of stealing two, lively little imps of the three that they were,
     One was for the good.
     Now that three sons have been taken, this is a paralysing,
                     oppressive experience,
116   Who would not cry for such pain of mourning?

The manuscript ends with more haunting extracts depicting in detail the personal suffering of Piers Griffith:

    … the youngest was
    … Heaven.
    … innocent to his grave
    … the rosy bloom of his cheeks.
    … Robert pretty and pure *(and Rhys?)*
    … more pain.
    … losing three sons,
124   … *(left?)* without one son.
    It was a mistake, the causing of such losses,
    … *(the anger of?)* God this loss.
    … three sons …
    … warmth to the very marrow of his wounded ribcage.

                                     (G.L.)

ELEGY TO WILLIAM GRIFFITH OF PENRHYN AND ELLIS PRYS OF PLAS IOLYN, 1610 by Robert ap Rhys Wyn

> *Another major poet who records these events is an educated man of good family, also given to adventure, if not disillusion and penury. He may be the bringer of bad tidings from the city to country ears, but here we have a dramatic eye-witness account of the "merciless circumstances" of the event itself and of the funeral:*

"In London… yesterday, the fall of many an excellent man."

SUMMER TIME AT PLAS IOLYN, THE HOME OF THOMAS PRYS

Once a lively and prosperous manor-farm estate grown rich by sheep-farming, Plas Iolyn near Betws-y-Coed is a remote and atmospheric place, as if standing still in a curious dimension of Time Past: a hidden retreat where it is easy to imagine hearing about the tragic events of Summer 1610, the arrival of shocking news from London, *"a bad place"*.

The long wide pathway leading up to the house is set amongst rich green pastures at the foot of the Snowdonia mountains. This was territory gifted to the Prys family by Henry VIII at the time of the Dissolution of the Monasteries, as a reward for the services of Thomas Prys's father, Dr Ellis Price, 'the Red Doctor' who was once jeered outside the courtroom in Bala for bringing his mistress along.

Nowadays, as in 1610 at the time of the London Plague, the well-trodden drive-way to the house is bordered by ancient, roughly hewn dry-stone walls edged in a sheen of moss, entangled in thickets and shaded by the deep roots of huge trees. A powerful spirit-of-place seems to draw you in. For this would have been the familiar riding-route of country squires like Thomas Prys, pirate-poet retired, of his family and friends like Piers Griffith with all their comings and goings, of his son to Oxford and London.

Think of two students setting off on horseback in the early summer of 1610, Ellis and William, a journey from which they would never return.

In this wild landscape, it is not difficult to grasp at the raw emotions imprinted in the manuscripts, conveyed in graphic words by four accredited poets. These four elegies to the lost boys are intensely personal. Everyone knew everyone else. One poet was an eye-witness, one a family friend and priest, another was the father of one of the victims and uncle of the other. Racking himself with grief, Thomas Prys, like Piers the other afflicted father, was no stranger to horror and death. We are given details of how the boys died and of how their families bore the tragedy. Only minutes before the news struck home, everyone would have been going about their daily lives: Margaret and her daughters at Penrhyn; Lady Catherine at Gloddaith or Penrhyn; Sir Thomas at Mostyn; and at Plas Iolyn, the family of student Ellis, then friends, tenants and neighbours. Where, we may wonder, was Piers and where was Thomas when this anguish first felled them?

Of one thing we may be certain, life for Piers Griffith would never have the same thrill of adventure ever again.

❧

Like "crowds of others" in town at the time and hearing of this gruesome event, the poet Robert ap Rhys Wyn says he turned out for the funeral in London,

[l.2] "in merciless circumstances … in
       The place which unfortunately corrupts the century …
       They were struck down by the poison of London."

The city is a place where, he says (knowing it so well and seeming to have fallen on hard times) you can visit in perfect health only to die within hours. This was the sudden fate that befell

These two ...

... Virtuous youths it seems to me who knew them,

The heir of Piers Griffith, a pleasant, handsome boy.

[l.12] The finest from amongst the young men of Gwynedd,

... in the flower of his days

From the Court of Penrhyn and its estate;

And Thomas Prys's heir, a bright gifted boy handsome as a
picture, ... of Plas Iolyn.

Two of the same kind, in breeding, dress and upright life

Two men outstanding in academic learning and eager to get on
in life

[l.20] Now in the grave like a bed together,

Two beloved ones lying there,

It is right that they are in the same grave.

Sadly it is the special ones who are taken ...

The call of the trumpet

Ended the lives of these two men...

Death "over there" in the far-away city is transformed into a worse agony, the poet declares:

[l.28] Too early was the taking of their lives,

Cutting them down, talented, promising, and good.

A strong flowering before the July harvest

Shearing the beauty before its time

[l.32] Was the end of these two fair beings.

Stealing away two young men, adventurous, free,

Leaving the older people behind as Death often takes the young,

Alas for London splendid and sophisticated to all appearances

With its towers and fair houses.

But woe is the place where they disappeared,

Bitter it is for me to tell and grievous the manner of it.

If poison was the food of life

[l.40] Let no good come to the person who gave it to them.

If it was an ungodly devil

Let him not live long after them.

Whatever he is, the curse is upon him.

[l.44] Their fate was to be touched by an invisible Evil.

[l.49] ... I cried when I saw the two coffins

And walked about amidst the enormous funeral procession,

With everyone gathering around, every dear friend they had

[l.52] In the Church of Saint Giles full of mourners, singing in good

voice

And me living in a tiny attic

Through poverty in an unhealthy city,

Fearing a fat-bellied bailiff

[l.56] Greedy for a profit on a loan

And so I was not in a position to be able to carry the coffins as I

should have liked, being gallant and mindful of custom

My heart was deeply sorrowful ...

And my senses were shocked

[l.64] At their sudden departure unto death the same way ...

[l.69] There is nowhere one can escape death, if you, God so wish it ...

A blessing on their two virtuous souls.

(G.L.)

ELEGY TO ELLIS PRYS, 1610
by his father, Thomas Prys of Plas Iolyn, pirate-poet retired

This harrowing and intensely personal elegy is considered to be amongst the poet's best work. Implied in the verse is the sense of his own guilt and that of Piers for time lost, "following Lady Fortune on the high seas". Judged even today and depleted of its original metrical complexity in translation, this is surely one of the finest laments ever written by a father to his son.

My family orchard has been severed three times
As one fruitful pure tree after the other,
Was cut down, thinned out, eliminated
4 Yet all were once living in the flower of their youth.
One of these fine trees has gone to earth
At the height of its flowering and branching.
It was impossible to escape the day of mourning,
8 We had to bend to the will of God who took him.
Yet he who gives, also has the right to take,
This was right, it was God's will,
But it was Christ's will too, sad was such a violent tragedy
12 He was taken too early, and I protested.
He lost his life, his precious vulnerable life,
Suffering the anguished groans of fright, before his life had really
begun,
My son was stolen from me, gifted, handsome and virtuous,
16 O bountiful God, what is this, why?
The sight of dull sober colours has utterly shaken me,
The hand of Jesus took my hopes away from me.
O Mary, I am sad after the loss of my fair heir
20 That you have not granted him more of a life-time!
Dear Ellis, his eager intelligence and high ambition
Were the cause of his being taken, God only knows why!
For me, time is now endless, one day is like one hundred ages,
24 Without one good night, life is dragging indeed;
I do not pass an hour, what a price to pay,

Without crying for the death of Ellis.
I imagine I can sense his presence when I call
28 Him over and over but I cannot hear him answer, there is no one
there,

And although I want to, in intense feelings of sorrow,
I imagine I can visualise him clearly before my sight.
Although I cannot see him in reality, I weep a gallon of tears,
32 I cannot see him even for an hour,
Alive for an hour, my dear lovely son.
Only his imprints, the belongings he left behind, the paths he trod.
Not one night passes when I do not see these visions before my
eyes, coming nearer and nearer.
36 Before slumber falls I think about him but I cannot really see him.
My white eagle, oh in the name of Mary, hidden in your grave,
Have your two blooming cheeks really been buried in earth?
Boasting is inappropriate, but you were once such a happy boy,
40 It is a nightmare for me to think of earth being sprinkled over your
smile.
I would give the world to have you back for one second, one word,
To have you back to speak one word with you;
Oh, oh, I remember the things I used to complain about to you
when I was bringing you up,
44 O woe is me for fathering you and your mother for giving birth to
you if you had to be stolen from us like this.
Why have you gone, young golden faun,
Before me, son, to torture me with pain for ever?
And leave me, if I live to grow old and weak,
48 Grief can weaken body and mind, I shall be longing for you all my
life.

Your age in the world was near to being twenty,
You are like a shining rosary bead,
And by the time you had reached that age, many people were
speaking highly of you,
52 At the height of your achievements with a promising future ahead.
It was a happy experience bringing you up, fulfilling and extended
for a time,

Whenever I cried, you caused my tears to disappear and my
happiness to be restored,
And you were very good interesting company, you are good, so
you are in Heaven,
56   Your past was like a short hour of entertainment.
I defended you against everything that came across your path,
To safeguard you, from the opinion of any man who went against
you;
I did not think this would happen, our father-son relationship was
so ideal,
60   I did not think there would be a condition to all that, of what was
to befall you.
Your death is a debt paid to God the Father,
I know it is a worthy payment, an oath,
You had intended to fulfill great deeds,
64   Working at your career was expected to lead to great things.
But you swam towards Heaven
Before me over there along the River of Death, to the point of my
exhaustion,
In truth dear brave son, I shall not be found
68   Living long on earth after you;
Before long, (you will not have to wait much) wherever your father
is known,
There will be no doubt that I will come to you one day,
You must light a candle to illuminate the way for me
72   To the Kingdom of Heaven to lead me there indeed,
To direct me, without getting lost,
To the right path that leads into the company of Abraham.
I remember the day, when every day was a pleasure,
76   When you hurried towards me busily playing.
You went to faraway London
Healthy and free at the beginning of summer,
Come back home from that distant domain,
80   Come and see me once again.
Take a short walk, come back into the world,
Back home here, Ellis my dearest one;

To cheer us up a little by talking,
84 Lifting the heavy beating ebb and flow of grief in your father's heart.
I will not be afraid, I believe I will cry to see you again like a ghost,
My soul will grieve again to see you,
My blessing and yours I wish for, like glistening dew in the meadow,
88 So that I may believe again in this glimpse of you, as a sign for me
to follow.

You departed as it were yesterday,
Pure white lamb, to follow your dear cousin,
William Griffith, golden and great, of commanding status,
92 Like the legendary Prince of an enchanted land with a bright
jewelled aim in life
The heir of Penrhyn, the fount of grace;
Of the same pure blood was your family relationship.
The two of you were staying in the same lodging the day before
yesterday
96 Face to face in the night,
Like two white angels from the same family
Lying in the same grave for ever.
You both went, in the early morning of your lives,
100 To Heaven, young men, in youth,
The same age, of faithful heart, full of optimism
To attend a festival together in each other's company.
Like Jesus the young son of Mary during his education, gaining
good words of recommendation and respect,
104 Deserving of praiseworthy words of address,
The year was one thousand six hundred and ten, a year to remember,
When you, our two sons were taken.
Oh may your bodies be given honour,
108 Fruitful berries of the world, in the same grave,
May your two souls have a superb spiritual journey,
To the same place in Heaven at the same time,
To tarry there for ever, after living an upright pure life,
112 To reach the Court of Heavenly Justice.

(G.L.)

ELEGY TO WILLIAM GRIFFITH OF PENRHYN AND ELLIS PRYS OF PLAS IOLYN, 1610 by Huw Machno

> "It happened not because of the anger of anyone against these two
> Nor through violence and duelling with weapons."

This Classical scholar-poet conveys the dark uncertainty of a Jacobean world out there, gloomy and bereft after better days have passed, a world in a state of shock after the news of sudden death by plague.

God rules the state of our health,
God also decides the length of our lives.
It is inevitable that everyone has his day
4   That has ended or will end.
A bitter and frightening experience is death, nightmarish,
The Spirit of Death is close at hand on one's very doorstep.
Not only do the old have their lives cut down but all ages, infants,
                          children, youths,
8   They are cut down at all stages in life.
These two were felled before they flourished
Leading virtuous lives like a tree, they were well-known for this;
Two branches, two sons of exceptional ability,
12   God was angry yesterday and so He took them,
Even men such as these *(from)* prosperous country estates, heirs …

21   The death of two heirs is like a storm at sea to the ordinary people,
The discordant planet spreading its influence wide over a
                          Christian country;
Black was the night, there was great destruction,
24   God only knows! For they have gone to earth.
The grave has closed over William, there is anguish.
Of the excellent Griffith family, he departed this life a very dearly
                          beloved boy;
Of good family from the start of its ancestral roots,
28   The heir of Penrhyn, who is there to compare with him?

The grandson of Sir Rhys Griffith; every time anyone was in need,
he responded,

A Knight dearly beloved;
Of the lineage of Ednyfed

32 And of Stradling, paying riches to provide everything.
The son William, if he was ruthless in sword-fighting
He was after all descended from the two famous Sir Williams he
was named after.

The heir of Piers, who is crying *(for his heir)* is going to the grave,

36 The great-grandson of Piers *(Mostyn of Talacre)*, cruel is the world.
A sudden horror causes painful sorrow,
It was a shock for his father to place the earth over the forehead of
his son;

Piers Griffith is in a tortured state of suffering,

40 Anguish for the lord to endure.
Yesterday the frightful news reached the boy's grandfather Sir
Thomas Mostyn,
The terror of having his golden grandson stolen away.
There is mourning here and crying,

44 As cold as ice in sorrow are his mother and his grandmother;
For his sisters the day passes heavily,

For his uncles *(William, Roger and Thomas)* this is an oppressing
experience.
A very chill shuddering blow has struck the Penrhyn family at
the moment,

48 It is cold and desolate over on the moors of Hiraethog as well;
Because of the death of Ellis, here they weep,
For a boy who was pure and upright all his life.
He left home setting off on his journey, that cheerful heir, but by
now he is cold and lifeless,

52 There is painful mourning at Plas Iolyn;
A delightful boy's life has been changed, gone to earth, the lowest
place,
A boy descended from the famous Doctor Ellis *(civil servant to
Henry VIII)*;

Also from the lineage of Rhys Amredydd, the celebrated hero of
>> the Battle of Rouen.

61   The world is cold and desolate from the loss of Ellis,
The world is full of pity for his father Thomas Prys.
Sad for his brother Thomas, from the same inherited privileged
>> position,
And sad for his sisters and beloved ones, family and friends.
The late Ellis and William
Shared the same family blood-line running through their mothers'
>> veins;

67   They were first cousins, handsome, healthy and charming …

72   … They shared the ways of their forefathers, the special
>> distinguished way in which they were nurtured;
As for their two grandfathers, it is sad to follow the pattern of how
>> people are related to each other,
They had been travel companions *(Sir William Griffith and The*
>> *Red Doctor)*
Likewise the two dear fathers, *(Piers and Thomas)*,

76   The good name of these men is well-known,
They have distinguished themselves both on land and on sea,
We are all in agreement, everyone knows that.
The sons too have inherited the same blessings, the same careful
>> upbringing,

80   Beautifully so since their birth,
They loved being together, two remarkable young deer,
They enjoyed the riches of just being together;
In Wales through their abilities, while they lived,

84   As in England, for they were highly praised there too, they earned
>> a good name for themselves
For being good company, and for being of decent gentlemanly
>> conduct, together as one
But alas there is now not one of them left alive …

The poet Huw Machno, a Classical scholar of some note, then compares William and Ellis to other mythical and historical friends.

They resembled, he says, Damon and Phithias "in their heroic feats"; *Pilades and Orestes* "without deceit"; *Scipio and Laelius* as "ideal images of two happy companions"; *Titus and Gresipius,* "of the same mind, the same interests"; *Euryalus and Nisus,* "of one face, of similar appearance" *like the two lost sons of Piers Griffith and Thomas Prys:*

> …Of the same lineage with great privileges.
> Two faithful vulnerable youths, equal in all things, of equal worth,
> 100 They were always true to their word, were William and Ellis.
> They lodged together, they were pursuing the same golden
>   opportunities and high ambitions for a role in life,
> They died together like brave leading deer of the herd.
> The place they went to, a revolting, cold-hearted place of eight lives,
> 104 England, where through chill misfortune things took an evil turn
>   for the worse;
> This tragedy has had a horrifying, devastating effect on the whole
>   of Wales,
> London took all our purity.
> The grave in the Church of Saint Giles, just talking about it sends
>   shivers down one's spine,
> 108 The grave hides the gifts endowed to these two young men
> And their best attributes graven on the best of faces,
> They have been laid to earth with valiant hearts.
> Of similar looks, the same virtues these two had,
> 112 One life, nearly twenty!
> Sharing the same tragic fate even unto death,
> One grave was the end for both of them.
> Two angels going up to the same bedchamber
> 116 Sharing the same doubly assured privilege of going to Heaven.
> The general complaint amongst people, as they sigh deeply is that
> The Year of our Lord, one thousand six hundred and ten
> Has been a nasty, unhealthy year, when
> 120 The summer took these two.
> Although they by misadventure,
> Died young, giving us the fright of nine lives,

No one will ever forget them, the shock will last for a long time.
124 It happened not because of the anger of anyone against these two
Nor through violence and duelling with weapons.
God saw two so excellent of one heart
To give his love to in this day and age,
That He brought them unto Himself because they were so
beautiful and brilliant,
He took them together, he did indeed, on the same day.
Their remarkable, special bodies were placed
Under the earth, amidst deep mourning that remained,
And yesterday God received them into Heaven,
132 When they died, God had selected their souls for Himself in
Heaven.
(G.L.)

1610 London. Another Plague Year

All "merry meetings are cut off … Playhouses stand … the doors
locked up … like houses lately infected, from whence the affrighted
dwellers are fled, in hope to live better in the country", wrote the
dramatist Thomas Dekker in 1609. A year later, Oxford students
William Griffith and Ellis Prys fell victims to another outbreak.
Both were twenty years old. There was no known cure.

Apothecaries in London kept their medicines in fine Italian
earthenware jars, or in plain pottery in the country, as did some
housewives. Doctors required to cause regular bleeding,
vomiting and the use of laxatives in an attempt to rid patients of
disease but these tactics only served to weaken the victims; young,
old and mad people were particularly vulnerable.

"Canst thou minister to a mind diseas'd?" Macbeth asked
the sleepwalking Lady Macbeth's doctor in 1606 before a Court
audience that included King James, already a sickly man.

Swellings or sores had poultices applied to them, or plasters
smeared with ointment but some ingredients were deadly. When

Archbishop John Williams, as his spiritual adviser, kindly kept poor King James company during his last, revolting illness in 1624/5, many people suspected that the King had been poisoned by such a plaster. It was Piers's cousin John who administered the Last Rites to their Sovereign.

Shakespeare's audiences laughed at Falstaff's alcoholic cure-all in *Henry IV, Part 2* in 1598, but other plays Piers Griffith and Thomas Prys may have seen, signify the real fears of the age:

> *Diseases desperate grown*
> *By desperate appliance are relieved,*
> *Or not at all...*
>
> Hamlet, Act 4, Scene 3 (1602-3)

In *Love's Labour's Lost*, we find these tragically prophetic lines indicating the terror people felt at the very mention of 'plague':

> *They are infected, in their hearts it lies,*
> *They have the plague, and caught it of your eyes:*
> *These lords are visited; you are not free,*
> *For the Lord's tokens in you do I see.*
>
> Act 5, Scene 2 (1594-5)

At home in Penrhyn, Piers's mother Lady Catherine, wife Margaret Griffith and sister Alys, like those who could afford it, probably had reference to health cures from books like *The English Housewife*, *The Castle of Health* or *The Accomplished Lady's Delight*, which also gave hot tips on beauty care, how to keep hands soft, skin white and hair blonde.

'Herbals' like John Gerard's popular book published in 1594 identified beneficent plants with delightful illustrations and notes on use. Remedies were often ancient, like comfrey or 'knitbone' for healing broken bones. The flowers of the marigold were good for treating children with cuts and sores; liquorice and senna were effective laxatives to purge the body. The antiseptic properties of sage were well-known, like lemon balm for tending fevers, often a critical point in any illness. Some were poisonous in the hands of the unskilled. The juice from foxgloves (*digitalis*) was used to treat heart problems, but some ladies used it on their eyes believing it to make them look bigger and more beautiful. Several Court scandals involved overdoses from plants and even Queen Elizabeth's own doctor was executed for supposedly trying to poison her.

The 'Sweating Sickness' (partly similar to sepsis which can still attack people today) had influenza-like symptoms of sore throat, breathing difficulties, fever, high temperatures, sudden chills, fast heart-beat, rapid breathing, dizziness, confusion, with nausea, diarrhoea and vomiting, quickly followed by death within six hours of first taking hold. Today, one known cause is the immune system going haywire, triggering a series of reactions that can lead to inflammation and blood-clotting, organ failure and death.

SAINT GILES

The present Verger at the Church of Saint Giles-in-the Fields, London, after careful scrutiny, has confirmed that in June, 1610 the accepted date of the tragedy, twelve people were buried there and their names entered in the Parish Register (which encompasses the years 1561 to 1610.) These entries for June are very indistinct and none seems to be for a "William" nor an "Ellis". However the July 1610 listing of Burials reads, as far as one can decipher:

> *"A child …*
>
> *…*
>
> *…*
>
> *William Gruff … (?) son of?*
> *Ellis Price (?) … Thomas? …*
> *William …*
>
> *…*
>
> *…*
>
> *William"*

while others are pitifully recorded as

> *"A man …*
> *A woman …"*

The original Parish Registers for 1611-1620 were also examined. The evidence of four reliable, major poet-witnesses/reporters-of-news, confirms the date of the tragedy as *"summer 1610"*; these four men, one of whom was the father, also state that the two boys were buried together *"in one grave"*.

There is no record of the burial of William Griffith at the Church of Saint Giles, Cripplegate, London. St Giles-in-the-Fields on the other hand, was an area well-known to travellers to and from Wales because it lay on the highway to the North via Highgate and Hampstead, villages sometimes referred to by Thomas Prys in other poems. Stow's *'Survay of London'* notes that in the area of St Giles there were *"lodgings for gentlemen, inns for travellers and such like almost … to St Giles"*. Only later in the eighteenth century did the place go down-market and sordid. In Tudor and early Stuart times there were grand houses there and an agreeable, healthy, fashionable ambience on the outskirts of London, *"in-the-fields"*.

Curiously, during my research in London, I received the following letter from Dr David Pearson of the Metropolitan Archives:

27 October 2011

"William Griffith (or Gruffythe) and Ellis Price (or Prys)

I began searching your names & variations in the parish of St. Giles Cripplegate (a composite register consisting of baptisms, marriages and burials [1606 – 1634] on Ancestry.) No matches appeared for either name. I then searched the Ancestry index for similar names wrongly transcribed, and then examined the relevant scanned pages in the register which also proved unsuccessful. I then opened up the search on Ancestry to parishes limited to the City of London, where I came across the following entry:

Ellie Price [sic]
Burial Date: 4 Jul 1612
Parish: St Stephen Coleman Street
County: London
Borough: City of London
Parent(s): Thomas
Record Type: Burial

St Stephen Coleman Street, Composite register, 1598 – 1636,
P69/STE1/A/01/Ms4449/1

Consulting the scanned image, the name is not 'Ellie' but Ellis son of Thomas Price. This is the only person who actually comes as a match, despite the two year discrepancy. I was not able to find any reference to William Griffith (or Gruffythe.)

As you might be aware we do not hold the original Parish registers for St Giles-in-the-Fields and only hold a microfilm copy X105/001. Unfortunately the pages relevant to your research were very faint and not very clear to read."

Dr Pearson concludes by recommending that I contact the Verger at St Giles-in-the-Fields, to request him to carry out a search on the originals (which I later did) and I am grateful to them both.

1609 had already been a Plague Year, as noted by Sir Huw Roberts in his elegy composed upon the deaths of the two boys, followed by another outbreak in 1610. However historian Julia Fox in an interview on BBC Radio in 2006 (*'Honourable Pirate'*) is firmly of the opinion that it was the fast-striking 'Sweating Sickness' which took the boys that summer, "when the death-rate was double what it was in 1609 and would be in 1611. You could be fine at ten in the morning and dead by four in the afternoon". Visiting overcrowded London, especially in summer, was risky. "You would be automatically prey to disease," she said.

Dr Nesta Lloyd suggests that poet Huw Machno's ambivalent image of *"cyrff nodedig"* (*"remarkable, special bodies"*) could mean the notorious "nodule" symptoms of the Plague known to appear in the arm-pits of the afflicted. Eye-witness Robert ap Rhys Wyn refers to the cause only as *"poison"*; and he curses, to the death, some unknown, *"ungodly"* carrier of *"an evil disease"*.

Why go to London at all, especially at the most dangerous and pestilential time of the year? It has been suggested that like their fathers before them, William and Ellis went to the city "for a good time". It was probably more than that, surely. Evidence in all four elegies repeatedly states that they went *"to get on in life"*, *"to realise high ambitions"*, *"full of promise"*, for they were both boys of *"remarkable academic abilities"*, *"leading virtuous, honourable lives"* with good looks, cultured style and personalities to match, gifts that were always useful in forging contacts in the City and at Court, *"highly recommended"*. Also stressed is the devastating effect the tragedy has on all members of the family and on local people, not only in personal terms but beyond into a wider sphere.

There is a hint that they were adept at swordplay, William Griffith especially, but *"small wonder for the grandson of two Sir Williams"*. But this is no Marlowe-esque scenario and Piers is still two years away from his swashbuckling duel with Sir Edward Herbert's lawyer. In all four poems, the Pirate's grief is emphasised, with bowed head *"weighing on his breast shedding tears of anguish"*. Is he blaming himself for pushing his son and heir too hard that particular summer as opportunities arose, in the direction of a well-paid Court or Diplomatic career in London and abroad, his nephew Ellis too, son of Thomas Prys? Torturing himself for all those lost years away at sea? But it is too late for remorse. Too late to regret the disastrous events of seven years previously in 1603, when the *"notable pirate"* got into King James's bad books. Small wonder Piers is now keen to pay up his reparations immediately, so that his family, possibly through the Court influence of cousin John Williams, may regain Royal favour, so essential for 'getting on in life'.

What is the *"festival"* referred to by Thomas Prys, that could have been so important in June and July 1610? A festivity so crucial as to attract these boys to *"Hellish London"* after excelling at their years of study in Jesus College then at 'Hart Hall', Oxford. Why go off to the city during the summer vacation away from the natural concerns of *"their careful, loving mothers"* and the promise of a good, festive harvest back home at Penrhyn and Plas Iolyn, wonder the poets and local people.

The London scene that summer is scintillating with opulent ceremonies and parades, as Neil MacGregor has illustrated. There are spectacular jousts, fireworks and mock sea-battles on the River Thames. In June 1610 Prince Henry, King James's eldest son is being proudly presented by his father to the Kingdom as Prince of Wales and Earl of Chester, a diplomatic compliment to Wales. Shakespeare, after producing his 'King Lear' of Ancient Britain in 1605/6 (*Y Brenin Llŷr* in Welsh Legend) is now producing *Cymbeline* with another Romano-British theme for the King's Players at Court. Ben Jonson, another man with several Welsh friends, is putting on *The Alchemist* (possibly a hint at the late Scientist Dr John Dee.) Actors are rehearsing; and Court Drama producer, the Earl of Pembroke is up to his eyes creating theatrical spectacles for the entertainment of fashionable and celebrated guests, lords and ladies, the in-crowd.

Prince James with his dazzling lordly retinue are due to go to Chester and be received by the Mayor and dignitaries on a grand summer progress around the country, a timely PR tactic by King James, mindful perhaps of the 'Cult of Elizabeth' in popular celebration, with her bells, bonfires, pageants and tours.

It is customary in Tudor and Stuart times for great families linked to the Court for several generations to be invited to such occasions, in the manner of the glamorous Catrin of Berain, not to mention Sir Rhys Griffith and Lady Catherine in their day, or the *"two Sir Williams"* and their Ladies back in the Age of Chivalry. All these are the dead boy William Griffith's ancestors mentioned in the poem. Also referred to several times is grand-father *"Doctor Ellis"*, the famous Red Doctor, former rigorous legal adviser to Henry VIII. And if the boys' fathers, Piers and Thomas once basked in the reflected glory of Drake, Raleigh and Leicester, the four poets now loyally recall *"their valiant deeds in the service of their country"* in the days of Good Queen Bess. At the same time everyone is aware that King James's new reign, bearing in mind the recent Gunpowder Plot of 1605, means many major changes, not all of them for the good. If the two boys *are* guests in 1610, perhaps on balance and in consultation with their families, they decide to accept their royal invitations, to their cost.

Furthermore, there are disturbing political undertones in Siôn Phylip's *Elegy to Prince Henry* (*"Harri"*), the Prince of Wales who also died in London, *"struck down"* with *"the plague"* in 1612, two years after the boys. The diplomat, a well-travelled Court poet who wrote such a powerful elegy to Queen Elizabeth herself as we have seen, Phylip illustrates how in matters of health, social rank spares no one. An experienced political commentator, he expresses sympathy for the Prince's mother, the discreet and wise Catholic Queen Anne, *"a cry is heard in Denmark, his mother's land ..."* for the Queen is suffering *"a grievous bruise"* ... *"a cold rib"* while King James *"grew sorrowful"*; the cause was *"A thick miasma of fog, like a roof covering the sky of London ...,".* The effect on European politics will be enormous, Phylip says, *"The mourning has reached the Mediterranean".*

Tragically for Wales, all hopes promised at the recent Induction Ceremony for Prince Henry have now been bitterly dashed, along with the ambitions of all the suitable young men who were to have gone with him on his travels to Europe, the poet adds. Were William and Ellis to have been among them on his 'Prince of Wales Tour', we may wonder, likewise their cousin, diplomat Siôn Wynn of Gwydir?

Phylip reminds us that the Prince of Wales was

Of the lineage of Anglesey ...
He resembled Henry Tudor ...
"His funeral" (was harrowing) *"... he was twenty years of age ..."*
(There was hope for him as a future king .)
"He was a Welshman, we had signs
That he held us in high regard, the dear boy ..." (G.L.)

A devout boy attending chapel twice a day, Prince Henry has for his personal Chaplain, Lewis Bayly, later Bishop of Bangor whose book '*The Practice of Piety*' is dedicated to the Prince; and Owain Wood of Anglesey is tutor to both Princes Henry and Charles, illustrating more possible connections with Piers Griffith's family.

People had yearned for the new Prince of Wales to *"protect and purify the Protestant faith"*; hope that is now invested in his brother Charles who will succeed him; and the poet compares the tragedy of Henry's sudden death to the manner of Prince Arthur's demise at Ludlow in 1502, its sad effect on Henry Tudor and on Wales itself; he also ranks the Prince of Wales with the heroic Edward, the Black Prince and concludes with a blessing for King James: *"May he keep us in peace ..."* / *"Harri will not be crowned but his soul will."*

Another source notes that,

"Just before 8.00 pm on November 6, 1612, Prince Henry breathed his last after a short but painful illness. The nation was stunned. Poets raced into print with their panegyrics." These are listed as, "Sir Edward Herbert, Sir John Davies, Joshua Sylvester, John Donne, George Herbert, John Webster, George Wither, Thomas Campion," with music by "Giovanni Coperario, *Lachrymae lachrymarum.*"

(Brian O'Farrell, 2011.)

When William and Ellis died two years previously in 1610, many people lived in fear of the 'Plague' being carried from

London during that summer season after the experience of the previous year, 1609; yet optimism and hope for the future may be urging events onwards inescapably. At such royal celebrations now energising the Stuart London of 1610 when William and Ellis are enjoying the "*festival*", it is customary for the monarch or his heir to give gracious presents in the form of miniature pictures of themselves to important guests. One such miniature, possibly by Isaac Oliver, has survived from the Plas Newydd Estate, Anglesey, once the seat of the Bagnall family at the time of Piers Griffith, who was sometimes in legal dispute with them. At twenty years of age, the new Prince of Wales, Prince Henry is an exact contemporary of the "*gifted*", "*civilised*", "*highly recommended*" William Griffith and Ellis Prys.

In this context, Sir Thomas Mostyn may well be imagined to be busy pulling strings for his step-grandson William at least, and for William's young cousin, son of "*the famous Dr Ellis*". Sir Thomas's useful contact at Court could be Sir Robert Cecil now that old friend Lord Burghley, Robert's father has died. The system of affinities, so useful to the Welsh, was at the time still deemed to be for the public good. Who else, in the well-established tradition of their fathers and grandfathers, would be better suited to represent the new Stuart generation of Lawgiving, Peace and Diplomacy in London and abroad, than these two admirable young men, William and Ellis?

Sadly it was the death of them both. Not only that, but any vain hopes for a fresh and ordered Age after the death of Queen Elizabeth were already being dispersed into the miserable "*miasma of fog*" pervading those early days in the Reign of King James I.

Chapter 12

The Pirate's Wife

1578 MOSTYN HALL

> Margaret, a lovely girl grown from a strong, noble ancestral tree
> …
> … the children have had a severe shock, the sorrow will last …
>
> Wiliam Cynwal: Elegy to Ursula.

This glimpse of Margaret as a child after the death of her mother Ursula in childbirth at Mostyn Hall, although haunting and shadowy, will develop into clearer scenes where she will grow into a formidable lady. Yet somehow she never loses that early vulnerability. Over twenty years later, on the eve of Drake's Last Voyage in 1595, we will see Margaret as a young wife and mother at Penrhyn Castle in the show-case poem by Siôn Mawddwy:

To Piers Griffith, the Poet and Margaret his Wife

Margaret, a great lady dressed in a superb gown of cloth-of-gold,
Of the honoured Mostyn family, well accustomed to wealth and
position.
A fine heiress in her own right, cheerful on all occasions ….
Your wife is praying for you, like the hind drinking from a pure
stream,
She is devout and faithful, only the power of her prayers can keep
you from danger and in good health …
The prayers of your children, will bring good blessings to assist
you …

Then in contrast, sometime during the 1590s, Sir Huw Roberts will write of Margaret and Piers in his Ode to the South Wind:

"The companion of his bed and his heart ...
A young lady, nurtured in a grove of kindness and care ...
She is sad with longing for her husband,
And it is no wonder she wears a downhearted expression, given
                                        the circumstances!
Yearning so much has made her grow cold towards him,
And her predicament is making her ill.
For she needs his advice and for him to leave the vast oceans,
To return home, and if he did, she would gladly praise and
                                welcome him at their reunion."

Now, at Mostyn Hall in 1578, the *"cosmic loss"* of Margaret's mother, Ursula is counterpointed with the image of *"happy children,/ Her little ones, here are five of Ursula's surviving offspring ..."*, William, Roger, Thomas, Margaret and Catherine ...

Death placed its cold hand on her newborn infant, and she departed this life the same time ...

She died too early, the poor people to whom she was so charitable will miss her acutely.

Elegy to Ursula by Wiliam Cynwal.

Ursula Mostyn, *"summoned away in her youth,"* was the sole heiress of her father Sir William Goodman, rich Tudor Merchant of Chester and Mayor of the city. By today's standards, she was a millionairess. Bountiful, maternal and stylish, she was the first wife of Thomas Mostyn. Their daughter Margaret was to marry Piers Griffith when she was scarcely more than a child herself.

Four years afterwards in 1582, widower Thomas Mostyn married the young widow of Sir Rhys Griffith at Penrhyn, Lady Catherine who already had three children: Alys, the eldest born before 1566, Piers born in 1568, and William born about 1570. After the relevant legal dealings had been settled between the Mostyn and Penrhyn estates, step-children Piers and Margaret (he was fourteen and she was possibly the same age) were also married on the same day "at the church door".

Ursula's second daughter, Catherine, later married courtier and kinsman Sir Thomas Hanmer of Hanmer and was said by John Steegman to be a lady-in-waiting to Queen Henrietta at the Court of King Charles I.

Roger (later Sir Roger Mostyn of Civil War fame) was Ursula's next son who became the heir after his elder brother William died; named sequentially in the elegy is brother Thomas but he seems to be brushed aside, the boy whom Dr Anthony Carr concluded was "incompetent". Later, Roger was sent by his dying father, Sir Thomas Mostyn in 1616/17 to sort out the legal and financial troubles of Captain Griffith at Penrhyn. Roger also provoked the anger of his father by defiantly marrying heiress Mari Wyn of Gwydir without his consent in about 1590.

ELEGY TO URSULA
by William Cynwal, 1578

> *"I know of no one now who is going to share out gold in Wales like she did. She supported so many people ..."*

The planets are creating troubled and unhappy times,
Shortening the lives of many good people;
The planet that has influenced us this year,
4   Has caused acute anguish, in opposition to us,
Casting its ill-fortune upon Mostyn, bringing the chill of Death to
    the family,
The sorrowful crying continues, that is what has been left in its
    wake.
The cutting short of life, this is the fate we have been subjected to,

8   Fair Ursula, with the lineage of dukes,
     The heiress of beneficent, gracious William,
     Who was always magnificently dressed with his gold chain of
                           office, the excellent William Goodman,
     Her kind father, he bore his powerful office with stalwart strength,
12   Did the Mayor of Chester, it must be said;
     This was a good sign, for Ursula's lineage was
     Of the Earls of England, and all her kindred,
     She was an honoured jewel for Wales,
16   Very prosperous, of the distinguished ancestry of the Marches.

     She died too early, the poor people to whom she was so charitable
                                will miss her acutely,
     Death placed its cold hand on her newborn infant, and she
                            departed this life at the same time.
     O alas, a far cry of woe is heard, for this is a cosmic loss,
20   A sighing cry for the living, to summon them to a better world,
     Old and young could be the victims at any time,
     Watery tears are shed for many a one,
     And there she is lying in her grave unable to give alms to anyone
                                  anymore,
24   Under the earth she cannot hear
     Anything, as if she were dumb, she had to take her leave,
     Despite all the pleading, calling after her for a long time, she was
                    but a beautiful painted image of perfection.
     That was a black day, it was God's will to take her, she was
                       vulnerable because she was young,
28   Her spiriting away thus was a loss for the land of Tegeingl.
     Her widowed husband looks very sad, as everyone knows,
     As every man knows who has lost his wife,
     Young Master Thomas, with his dignified noble way of life,
32   Of Mostyn, always so strong and confident in his step and gait,
     The heir of William the Elder, wearing the ancient authority of his
                  leading role in society generously and graciously.
     Bestowed with gold and diamonds, the grandson of the Elder
                                  Thomas,

May his family be honoured and respected, the givers of ceremonial
feasts,
36   Who has such magnificence? – The most prominent man in
Gwynedd.
This sad pain came unexpectedly, why?
Why were the Five Courts of Mostyn afflicted by such an
accidental tragedy?
The death of his good wife, woe is Wales bound fast in such a loss,
stunned,
40   O alas, it is terrible having to sigh and be unable to function
because of this.
Yet there are five offspring here encircled as if on a safe island
Here to heal the wounds and make the Five Courts (of Mostyn)
flourish again.

Her children live still, descended from excellent ancestry,
44   To fill Tegeingl is the purpose of their fair, good lives.
Honourable and happy children,
Her little ones, here are five of Ursula's surviving offspring:
William, the eldest, descended from fine lineage,
48   Is there a man who commands so much respect? At Mostyn forever,
The best heir yet, true to his word,
A clear mirror, a role-model, honest and transparent in his strong
representation of Wales;
Roger, he too excels in strength and grace
52   As he works hard at his studies to get through life, and Thomas;
Margaret, a lovely girl grown from a strong, noble ancestral tree as
strong as an oak.
Catherine, she helps to serve the wine;
All our people including the children have had a severe shock, the
sorrow will last for eight lives,
56   The gracious jewel, their mother Ursula once living has now died
young;
Mistress Margaret, hear our faithful supplication,
The lady of a distinguished Knight of the best ancestry,
Sir William Goodman, valiant, cheerful, kind and magnificent,

60   Descended from the fine blood of ancient Earls, of the Broughton
                         dynasty.

     The day she departed, good faultless Ursula,
     This one girl, into the supporting arms of Anna *(of Apocryphal*
                         fame),
     It was the year of our Lord Jesus, who died for us,
64   Fifteen hundred and seventy eight, amidst deep sorrowful cries,
     And widespread mourning plain to see.

     Great anguish seared through the breast of everyone as she was
                         laid in earth,
68   No one is glad that she has died; who will now give us sustenance?
     I know not, I cannot answer for we have lost one who has always
                         helped us,
     I know of no one else who is going to share out gold in Wales like
                         she did.
     She supported so many people, we are so sad,
72   The Marches are struck down into a grievous state with the loss of
                         lovely pure Ursula.
     In our time, as the star of the counties
     The Mostyn family has represented expansion and prosperity for
                         us all;
     Because of her death, I know of no one who is happy about dying,
76   Her family are now oppressed by heavy sorrows.
     How excellent she was!
     Is there a worse pain than this suffering at her departure? It would
            have been wonderful if she could have lived a long life.

     If she had lived, she would have distributed her gold generously,
80   She would have been a Lady dressed in a fine gown of cloth-of-gold.
     After she was summoned away, in her youth without wasting a day,
     She is now a noble Lady in eternal Heaven,
     It is God's Will, elevating her nearer
84   To his Sanctuary, our Lady Saint.

MARGARET MOSTYN, WIFE OF PIERS GRIFFITH 1568? – 1648

Margaret was the daughter of Sir Thomas Mostyn, the Flintshire magnate. When she was about ten years old in 1578, her mother Ursula died young giving birth to a child who also died. There were four other children: an older (or younger) sister, Catherine, and three brothers. William was the eldest, heir to the Mostyn Estate but he died fairly young when his brother Roger succeeded to the title and the estate, a privilege which bore with it all the attendant responsibilities for farm tenants, agriculture, industrial development and dynastic status. Another brother, Thomas, was considered unsuitable for such a role but he was respected enough to be mentioned in several documents, in cahoots with his clever lawyer brother, Sir Roger Mostyn, particularly in their dealings with Margaret's financial affairs, not always helpfully from the point of view of her husband Piers Griffith, nor later in 1643 after Piers's death when Margaret and her three surviving daughters had to press Roger and Thomas for full payment of her allowance owing. This rather suggests their mean, bullying attitude to her for years after she had already been forced by her father, virtually on his death-bed in 1616/17, to separate from Piers and possibly to stop giving him any more of her Mostyn money. Like most Tudor women, she was brought up having to accept that her life would always be ruled by men.

Ironically when Margaret's father, a handsome, dashing, vain thirty-five year old lord carried off Piers's attractive young widowed mother, Lady Catherine Griffith "at the church door" in 1582 and laid out all the prenuptial property-motivated marriage plans between the two of them, he also included daughter Margaret in his arrangements. As a virtuous, naïve teenage girl, and an heiress on her late mother's side (Ursula herself had been a young beauty with the wealth of the Tudor Merchants of Chester behind her) Margaret was conveniently slotted into her father's double-wedding scheme that also roped in fourteen year old rebel Piers Griffith, heir to the rival Penrhyn domain.

At the same time, widow Lady Catherine had her son Piers made a Ward of the Queen under the supervision of a member of the Court and of the Court of Wards, directing the boy's education and seeing that he was suitably married. In this case, the person chosen (always advisedly from within the family) was none other than her new husband, Mr Thomas Mostyn as the future Knight was then; doubtless it was his proposal, a typically lucrative move. At thirty-five years old with his new, younger bride, Lady Catherine, Thomas may well have hoped for another heir (but she was having none of it and the two lived separate lives) at an age when "*the lives of the young*" were "*especially vulnerable*", as the poets wrote; and very soon after that, the teenage Piers was sailing away "in peril on the sea". He may have disliked his step-father Thomas, Hamlet-style, and Sir Thomas *was* known to have been querulous and authoritarian with his own rebellious son Roger from time to time. In any case, Piers was probably raring to go off adventuring anyway, in the spirit of the age.

The first we hear of Margaret is in Wiliam Cynwal's *Elegy to Ursula* where the five young motherless children are described as "*well-beloved and happy offspring*", and where the child is observed as

> "*Margaret, a lovely girl grown from a strong, noble ancestral tree …*"

implying that her dignified behaviour and well-brought up manners at her mother's funeral clearly demonstrate her good breeding. More realistically, she is probably still in shock: deeply staring and thoughtful, suppressing her natural feelings beneath the expected control of outward ritual in Tudor times.

From a child, she is to grow accustomed to painful grief and to the absence of the loving, guiding hand of her mother. Who else is there for her? Grandmother Lady Margaret Goodman of

Chester is mentioned in Huw's *Elegy to Ursula* as someone who may intercede spiritually (posthumously) at least with the Virgin Mary on behalf of this little girl, her sister and her three brothers. Margaret is sadly in need of care and attention when her widowed father soon turns to kinswoman Lady Catherine Griffith for help. Yet the brutal reality that lies ahead for Margaret the teenage bride, is knowledge she already has: childbirth can be a serious danger to health.

Customs and conditions may have changed but a child's experience of its mother's funeral is sadly part of the human condition, rich or poor, transcending all eras, however it is recorded at the time, whether in the bald listing of a genealogy with dates or in an expressive poem by a sympathetic family poet such as Wiliam Cynwal at Mostyn Hall.

Because no elegy to Margaret Mostyn Griffith is extant, there comes a point when one may have to read between the lines and include this little clue about her seen in her mother Ursula's elegy, with all the fascinating glimpses we are given of her in other documents and in poetry dedicated to others, with the exception of the poem dedicated to Piers and herself as a married couple in 1595 hosting the Last Voyage ceremony.

Given the etiquette of poets on such occasions as family funerals or celebrations and given that Cynwal may have been singing for his supper in the Elegy to Ursula, this seems rather unremarkable evidence about the Mostyn heiress. The boys are given more attention: William "*is the best heir ever ... the ideal role model for the whole of Wales*", while Roger is "*working hard at his studies necessary to climb the steps of life.*" As an afterthought perhaps, "*And Thomas*" is added; only then does the poet single out Margaret. Catherine is noted last of all, clearly old enough to be helping to serve the wine but probably younger than her sister, because the poet would be strictly observing the customs of funeral listing and protocol at the Mostyn procession and reception, unless he places

Margaret's name before Catherine's because it fits better into his poetic patterns.

By 1582 Margaret is being married off without much choice to a fourteen year old boy she barely knows as part of a property deal, but she is surely pleased to see him as 'a good catch', judging by all accounts of Piers's attributes. He looks good; but is she convinced he feels the same about her, self-conscious and shy as she probably is? Huw Machno's *Praise-Poem to Thomas Mostyn on the occasion of his marriage*, flatters not only the parents but their teenage children too. The poet *"cannot wait to get back to Mostyn and its Five Courts"* after such *"long tarrying"* at Penrhyn, although *"moving back will be a mad house"*; but perhaps he feels for his poetic licence now that *"Master Thomas"* has changed his married status. The teenage pair are complimented on their noble breeding and good manners with attractive healthy looks and natural talents, emphasised by the poet who wishes both married couples *"happy love-making"* and *"good, fruitful offspring"* in this double-fix insurance scheme of securing family finances, if not true romance. They are *"thus twice ensuring a strong bloodline,"* reports the poet, who is the nearest thing we have to a high-society gossip columnist.

By the time Margaret's father eventually dies in 1618, with Lady Catherine surviving him and incidentally wasting no time in challenging his Will, the thirty-six year marriages of both couples have almost spanned a vintage wedding range peppered with various separations, quarrels and absences. So perhaps Margaret is well used to managing her own matrimonial concerns, unless circumstances are acutely adverse as they sometimes are to be for her. We are made aware of this factor in Huw Roberts's *Ode to the South Wind* recalling Piers home from the sea for the sake of his wife *"who is very ill without you and growing cold towards you"*. Until this turning-point, since almost everyone else seems to love and admire Piers, we assume she does too. She will bear him ten children after all, with the possibility of an early miscarriage

("Pierce" according to J.E. Griffith's *Genealogy*), so they will spend some quality time together. She may even have signed documents for him while he was away from time to time, since his signatures vary amongst the Penrhyn papers, as already noted in this quest to track him down.

One feels she is more capable than she is given credit for. Margaret's legacy from her father's Will for instance, is relegated to her only via her brother Thomas but some of it manages to turn up in her own Will later in 1648, if one is tempted to trace the circuitous route of the 'Mostyn Silver', from the sumptuously laden oak dining-table in the fire-glow reflections of polished wood at Mostyn Hall and of the vividly coloured, family-crested, mullioned windows, all the way down the pathways of time to the modern spotlit glass encasement where the remnants of this treasure now lie resplendent at the National Museum in Cardiff.

"*To my son Thomas,*" wrote or dictated her father, the dying old Sir Thomas in 1616/17, "*towards the maintenance of the said Margaret [wife of Piers Griffith of Penrhyn Esquire] 6 white silver bowles which lately I bought at Chester whereof three be great bowles and three little bowles, one silver white double silver salt which ordinarily I use, and one dozen of silver spoons.*"

He apparently dies on February 27 but mysteriously, is not recorded as being buried until a month later. So on that dark, shivering March night in 1618, Palm Sunday at Whitford Parish Church, after a torch-lit procession of bearers and mourners, Margaret's all-powerful father is finally put to rest. She surely knows from then on that her two brothers would inevitably feud together, quarrel with others, set themselves against Piers more than ever and try to obstruct her whenever the opportunity arises .

The funeral certificate of Sir Thomas Mostyn (Harl. MS 2180, f.8) lists his son, 'Young Thomas' (at that point his heir until considered to be "*incompetent*") as being married to Ann, the daughter and sole heiress of the Bishop of St Asaph, with their six children. These six are probably included in the Mostyn group of grandchildren old Sir Thomas is said to be fond of, sending for them all "*often*". Listed next is "*Margaret the eldest daughter of Sir Thomas maryed Peers Gruffith of Penthwyn* (sic) *in the County of Caernarvon Esq the [y] have yssu Kathern eldest daught, Jane, Dorothy, Margrett, Urselaw, Grase, and Elizabeth Gruffith* …", proof that the seven daughters are living then. Margaret Griffith's sister Catherine, Lady Hanmer is fortunate to be left £220 in gold coins by their father but Margaret fares differently: her "*incompetent*" brother Thomas is to retain £300 for her, about £200,000 in today's money, "*for the maintenance of Margaret Griffith*" on condition she "*lives apart from Piers*". After her death, what is left of it is to be divided amongst her children; brother Thomas must also set aside "*twelve cows, one hundred sheep*", a large amount of "*bed-linen*", and the famous silver heirlooms for her upkeep.

Otherwise it is the men of the family, including cousins and in-laws who fare best in this division of Mostyn wealth and legacies. While her brother Roger is admitted to Brasenose College, Oxford in 1584 at the age of 16 and as a student to Lincoln's Inn in 1588, Margaret would have had a very different kind of education, except perhaps to share an early basic tutoring at home with her three brothers, learning to read, write and do arithmetic. She would also have learnt to sew, embroider and later deal with household management, childcare and herbalism.

Typically in Tudor times, Margaret's marriage jointure is settled on her by her family. Rarely in such times are girls left large sums of real money, the exceptions being her sister, Lady Catherine Hanmer and their mother, heiress Ursula.

We may now reflect on what Margaret thinks her marriage has brought her. As a teenager, like other girls of the era, she already knows that she can expect nothing from Penrhyn if her young husband Piers dies before her. His estate would automatically pass back to his original family. Margaret has to have her own resources to rely on for herself and her children; but it seems that these are plundered from time to time, one way or another, perhaps by her adventurous husband and certainly by her parsimonious brothers, who are in any case given to so much conflict amongst themselves that lawyers refuse to act for them unless they are reconciled.

To his credit, it is her father Sir Thomas Mostyn, ill though he is in 1616/17, who lays down the law with kinsman-stepson-in-law Piers to provide his seven daughters with decent marriage portions. Somehow or other these settlements seem to be legally enmeshed in the financial dealings of their father Piers Griffith at the time of his Big Sell-Out, that circuitously runs from 1618 to 1623, as noted in Part I.

Margaret's Will of 1648, with the Penrhyn and Mostyn documents relating to her, provide a new dimension on the life of a woman of the nobility in the sixteenth and seventeenth centuries. At the same time, Margaret Griffith's life sheds new light on the *"notable pirate"* or privateer. Yet she apparently adheres to the expected role of any other woman in Tudor and Stuart times. Coping. We might well doff our caps to Margaret Griffith, Lady of the Manor of Penrhyn. Like many others, she loved her husband well and kept the home fires burning. She was almost constantly pregnant. She lost at least two infants, Robert and Rhys, probably when she was little more than a child herself. *"Kidnapped they were, the dark night's plunder."* We know of her inconsolable grief at the loss of her eldest son William and of her keeping to her room in Penrhyn when she *"would not see her daughters"*, whose own grief was therefore *"worse and more bitter"*.

The loss of a boy fortunate enough to survive infancy and live healthily for twenty years, when one third of all Tudor children failed to live older than the age of ten and most babies died before reaching their first birthday, was possibly the wedge that drove the anguished pair, Margaret and Piers finally apart, a tragic feature of bereaved marriage in any era. She had once been *"the companion of his bed and his heart*", as Sir Huw Roberts wrote. In their case, if the tragedy of William meant the end of their family life, it also meant the end of the Penrhyn Estate long before Piers became 'bankrupt'.

For Margaret, perhaps it also signalled the last time she would be celebrated within the Welsh poetic tradition, even as an afterthought. Yet she soldiered on, during Piers's many absences; elegantly dressed and proud even as she had been at the grand send-off at Penrhyn in 1595 when she saw her husband sailing away to join Drake, "*waiting like Penelope for Ulysses*"; attending carefully to her children, their education and discipline; helping poor and sick people in need; possibly trying to manage the estate, "*and all its appurtenances*"; seeing that repairs were done, rents paid, tenants and their families looked after; organising the domestic arrangements with the servants of the house from kitchen to solar to hearth-hall to bedroom; walking with her surviving daughters around the famous "*pleasant pathways*" and Herb Garden; for at Penrhyn she would be expected to know all the traditional and herbal cures and infusions to heal her family's ills, guarding against rickets, impetigo, head lice, accidents, bone injuries, coughs, colds and deadly infections. Domestically, she was all things for all people. Duty first.

If she had a friend at all it was surely Sir Huw Roberts, poet-priest. He may have been accompanied on his visits to Penrhyn by his Catholic wife, Ann of Creuddyn near Gloddaith, a Mostyn summer residence, so the two ladies may have known each other before marriage in a closely shared recusant Catholic upbringing. Margaret's only known woman friend had died, her cousin Siân, first wife of Thomas Prys of Plas Iolyn, near Betws-y-Coed, not too far away, a day's ride on the dangerous London Road where neighbour Ellis Vaughan was once robbed, "*brutally killed*" and "*left lying on the stone track*", as Thomas Prys wrote in an elegy on the subject, to spread the news.

It is quite possible for the Pirate's Wife to have stayed in touch with her sister Lady Catherine Hanmer, even though Catherine may have been absent at Court now and again from about 1625, serving King Charles I's Queen Henrietta, a devout Catholic. The Hanmer children, nephews and nieces, are mentioned in Margaret Griffith's Will of 1648/9.

There were other family links to kinswomen: sister-in-law Alys Griffith for instance, a young widow living nearby at Cilgeraint Farm on the Penrhyn Estate with her two little sons William and Thomas, in a place where her brother Piers himself sometimes took refuge. Alys was a girl with troubles of her own, but Margaret's step-mother-cum-mother-in-law was surely at hand, Lady Catherine Griffith Mostyn "*dressed in cloth-of-gold and encrusted in jewels*", an adept hostess "*at feasts and wine-serving*", doing all she could to help supervise the children and the domestic arrangements of Margaret's household, with her more mature "*wisdom, knowledge and intelligence*". Perhaps she passed on to her kinswoman-step-daughter-in-law some diplomatic advice about Piers to boot. Another bond between Lady Catherine and Margaret must have been their devout recusant Catholic faith, a deep-rooted Mostyn family tradition.

One has the impression that Margaret Griffith, the Pirate's wife became adept at being alone, "needs must", despite some lapses of grief and longing for her husband and three dead sons: that self-contained little girl at her mother's funeral, that devastated mother shutting herself away to be alone with the memory of her son William. She may appear to be in Piers's shadow but this was no shrinking violet. Could a young woman who had borne ten children before the age of forty be lacking in physical and emotional inner strength? She certainly kept her daughters close to her all her life and passed on to them her shrewd handling of finance and possessions, her dignity, self-reliance and womanly values, on the evidence we have from her Will and from the Wills of daughters

Dorothy and Grace, not to mention the inclusion of Elizabeth in their 1643 claim to moneys owing from the Mostyn men.

Margaret did not abuse the privileges of her birth, learned from the guiding hand of her mother Ursula, heiress of those great Tudor Merchants of Chester. The Pirate's Wife used these privileges to stand on her own two feet, remarkably so in the age in which she lived. She was a dutiful girl and had seen how it had all been done before her. Properly. She was wife, mother, sister, daughter, peace-maker, educator of her children, carer of the poor, herbalist and cookery adviser, like other traditional Penrhyn women: step-mother Lady Catherine; sister-in-law Alys of Cilgeraint; and long ago in the Age of Chivalry, those two redoubtable wives of Sir William Griffith, grandmothers-in-law Siân Puleston and Siân Stradling, fêted by poets.

Margaret was maturing into a devout church-going matriarch and lady bountiful as far as she could afford. The Will illustrates her careful planning, her sharing of everything out fairly, her clear-minded economies and 'going after every penny owing', in a woman not given to excess; a woman of religious faith; of family responsibility and love, courage and acceptance. It demonstrates too her methodical attention to detail in all things, from her care for her children, grandchildren, sons-in-law, kith and kin, old friends and loyal servants. This is the Margaret who comes to life here in this last testament of her unique life, these personal details: the silver; the carefully computed sums of money; the implied sense of loving, close family relationships built on over the years, her years away from Piers. There is no mention of any of the Griffiths, we note, as if she cut off all ties with Penrhyn and its people. No mention either of her brothers' offspring nor of Mostyn. Margaret had moved on.

Sir Huw Roberts and others have graphically described the suffering her Pirate put her through. But just as Bess Raleigh busied herself with the jugglings of *"business"* to help bail out her absent

Sir Walter, and just as the Dowager Duchess of Norfolk, in letters to her family, gave advice on how to cook good food and cure all ills, Margaret fulfilled her duties at Penrhyn. Whether other Tudor/Stuart wives were expected to endure their husbands' long absences at sea or not, away on business or at Court in London from time to time, or else inspecting the farthest borders of their estates, or extricating themselves from liaisons with *"a lady or two"*, so Margaret Griffith was not found wanting as the loyal wife and attentive mother who remained close to the family she had created. Here was a lady who had endured the pain of losing three sons and then four daughters during her middle years, possibly in childbirth: Katherine, Jane, Margaret and Ursula, leaving behind young children and husbands. The religious tone of this Will, with its fortitude and practicality, suggests she probably overcame her sense of disappointment in her menfolk, in her two brothers and in the notorious husband her father had chosen for her.

If the mysterious "Portrait of an Unknown Young Woman at Gloddaith" *is* Margaret the Pirate's wife, she appears before us in her early twenties, somewhere between about 1590 and 1600.

The artist has brought her vividly to life in all her youthful beauty, fingering her fabulous margarita pearls, wearing a devout gold cross and an exquisite heraldic emblem set in rich gems on the left sleeve of her fashionable jewel-encrusted costume of opulent material, with the accessories of a fine lace collar, pearl bracelets on each wrist, a stunning necklace of garnets, rubies and pearls, not to mention her immaculate, be-jewelled hairstyle.

Here is a lavish display of wealth worth millions today. Yet she gives the impression of someone modest, unworldly and agreeable, of a pretty young lady happy to be a stay-at-home wife, in contrast to the more court-orientated Bess Raleigh, whose portrait in the National Gallery of Ireland bears just a hint of lasciviousness, according to some.

The provenance of the Mostyn portrait may provide a significant clue to the identity of the sitter. The manor of Gloddaith was once Margaret's home and that of her mother, Ursula. By the 1590s, it became the home of her step-mother/mother-in-law, Lady Catherine Griffith Mostyn, the mother of Piers Griffith.

The extravagant image of the margarita pearls may illustrate the deep regard Piers had for Margaret (if this is she), decking her out in jewels, proudly determined that his wife must outshine all other women, with the possible exception of his own mother and of "our lady", Queen Elizabeth I.

Her pearls and other jewels on the other hand, may have once belonged to Margaret's dead mother, Ursula, rich heiress-daughter of those two great Chester worthies, Sir Thomas and Lady Margaret Goodman, perhaps indicating that Margaret, although wearing a wedding ring here, is still an independent heiress in her own right. Her husband and brothers will soon take advantage of this wealth. Could she be dressed up to the nines for the Essex banquet at Mostyn Hall in 1599, for the knighthood of her father, Sir Thomas Mostyn? Or for Piers's big send-off at Penrhyn Castle in 1595 for the Last Voyage of Sir Francis Drake? In any case, this is how such a lady would have looked at the time.

Margaret Griffith died at Erbistock, east Flintshire in 1648 and was probably buried there at the parish church with the Civil War raging all around her (the nearby Battles of Wem and of Rowton Moor, in a key area galvanised by other local atrocities.) Piers Griffith's wife had lived a remarkable life through changing times, the reigns of Queen Elizabeth I, King James I and King Charles I, and through all the violent conflicts that ended soon after her death at the age of eighty or so. As her long life drew to a close, we can be sure that most of her surviving daughters' families were in attendance. No poet wrote her an elegy, it seems, but the legacies of her spirited daughters, Dorothy Edwards, Elizabeth Humphreys, Grace Bromhall and their surviving children – the educated Magdalen amongst them – illustrate the true essence of Margaret Griffith, the Pirate's Wife.

Chapter 13

Alys, the Pirate's Sister

This girl, or rather the predicament she finds herself in, sheds new light on Piers Griffith's character.

Alys Griffith Williams, a young widow, lived with her two sons, schoolboy William and Thomas, *"an infant of tender years"*, at Cilgeraint, a farmhouse on her brother's estate of Penrhyn from 1587 until the end of her short life, most likely before Piers left for London in 1622/3.

The rugged stone-cast dwelling with remnants of Tudor chimneys, still stands on a wooded hillside near the village of Tregarth, inland from Bangor. A winding lane leads past the entrance above the green, mossy banks of the river Ogwen, cascading down rocky chasms bordered by luxuriant fronded ferns from moorland heights, atmospheric with legends, ancient pathways and traditional skirmish points.

Alys was born about 1566, at least two years before Piers, because she was married while her father Sir Rhys was still alive in 1580 when she must have been at least the legal age of twelve, or more probably at the 'practical' age of fourteen.

Alys Griffith and William Williams of the ancient Bodlew Estate in Anglesey married at Llandegai Church. Their first son William, born in 1582/3, is known to have died in the 1590s; it is not known exactly what year his brother Thomas faded from the scene, but he lived long enough to marry and have children.

Alys's young husband, William Williams, died early in the

marriage, after the death of his father John Williams. Bodlew manor-house (Lion's Dwelling-Place) was where Alys's little family was probably living at the time, albeit amongst his Williams relations who seem to have been a disagreeable lot: Grandmother Williams and her two surviving sons. Already we can see the possibility of tensions rising.

After the early death of Alys's young husband, her in-laws set about a series of law-suits against her and her two heirs, *"infant"* Thomas aged under four, and five year old William. The Bodlew clan seems to have been trying to disinherit Alys and her boys for years, drive them out and take possession of the house where her late husband's two younger brothers, their offspring, Grandmother Williams and possibly the brothers' wives and children, were now determined to live and draw rents from the whole estate, at least until Alys's two sons came of age *"by computation of whose age there will be sixteen years before the elder and seventeen years before the younger will be twenty one …"*. (Indenture of January 20, 1587-8 Cardiff Free Library.)

We can see their point of view, the Bodlew in-laws. They too had to survive. Alys and her sons had rich relations after all and the last thing the Bodlew family would have wanted would be the possibility of their home eventually ending up within the domain of Piers Griffith's extensive Penrhyn estate. Yet Alys clearly wanted to secure the future of her sons and their rightful inheritance from their father, the legal heir of Bodlew. This sort of difficulty, usual amongst such families, may well have been pre-discussed with Sir Rhys at the time of his daughter Alys's marriage agreement, for there is no mention of her in her father's Will of 1580 and Sir Rhys would not have left her unprovided for. The poets do not refer to her either. Cilgeraint Farm near Penrhyn, where she eventually came to live, may have been ear-marked for her as part of her dowry or marriage portion; but there was no possibility of her in-laws claiming that property in 1588, with big brother Piers standing guard over the proceedings now that his eagle-eyed law-student days at Oxford were behind him and what with the Armada known to be looming dangerously ahead …

Alys's two little boys, William and Thomas may have been perceived by their resentful Bodlew uncles as somewhat sickly in infancy. Yet they had survived the first year of life which only one in three Elizabethan children managed to do, with the immediate hope of living beyond the age of ten which not every little soul managed. Alys, seen in her persistence at the Law-court, and in her clear-minded forward-planning, cheerfully took the view that her sons would live to a ripe old age.

One may wildly imagine the tightly-knit Williams brood at medieval Bodlew trying to 'psych' her out, darkly plotting and whispering in corners or shadowy farm-buildings, possibly even willing each childish illness to take a turn for the worst while Alys herself, hardly daring to sleep a wink, would be hanging on for dear life through every fever and fight, every chill and danger to which her boys might daily fall victims.

She was made of sterner stuff than perhaps her dead husband's clan gave her credit for. She conducted her own lawcase against them. Educated at least as well as her cultured, intelligent mother Lady Catherine must have lovingly directed for her, and probably as well as her brothers by the best private tutors, Alys is described unusually in the Indenture documents as *tutorix* to William and Thomas. She took up the wardship of her own boys. All this was rare for a woman of her time. Like her mother, Lady Catherine, she may even have had recusant Catholic leanings and the farmhouse of Cilgeraint was an ideal hideaway. Then there was the legal involvement of her brother Piers that reflects well on his youthful character in standing by her in the middle of knowing the Armada was already a threat whilst preparing his ship *Grace* down on the Menai Strait to sail off as soon as possible to defend his family, his estate and the realm of Queen Elizabeth.

When matters were not absolutely settled in the first instance, Alys persisted in her second retaliatory lawcase. She refused to be downtrodden, or else she was being propelled by an even more determined Piers. Why would he want to quarrel with minor Anglesey gentry? His actions seem more defensive and protective than invasive or aggressive. Piers and Alys, as lively, undaunted young people, were scarcely more than teenagers themselves: a brother engaging in a tricky court action against disagreeable adults and powerful lawyers, on behalf of a sister whose personal and legal position has been made untenable. Yet still they fought on. Piers and Alys lost the case.

An imagined scenario over in Anglesey at Bodlew, might include two dastardly brothers-in-law (yet with deprived wives and children of their own) and their bitter hag of a mother, all long since immersed in farming feuds, born of sheer hard labour perhaps, foul weather, harsh conditions, rivalry, jealousy, injustice and impoverishment. Perhaps the Bodlew family had already done well financially out of Alys's dowry under the accredited magnanimity of her late father Sir Rhys and saw the possibility of further gold-digging in the time of Piers as heir. Or perhaps the problematic farming brothers were merely lazy yokels, unwilling to carve out their own careers like others amongst the lesser gentry were compelled to do, through a decent grammar school education for entry into the Law, the Church or the Army.

With good looks running in the Penrhyn family, it is unlikely that Alys was too unattractive to facilitate her own marriage without the enforced arrangements of parents; in any case this is not how people would have thought then. It would have been salt on the wounds of the farming brothers and their dominating mother having to endure the girl as mistress of what they saw as *their* house, a girl with all the finery provided for her within her own aristocratic advantages of class, the mortification of the resentful, possibly ruffianly Bodlew family would have been equally nail-biting.

Who knows what tactics of intimidation were brought to bear on Alys and her tiny tots? If not actual bodily harm, one may speculate as to what other accumulated unpleasantries were slyly and slowly being aimed in their direction, as sharp as any silent dagger in the dark: bullying; stalking; coercion; cowardly threats shouted from a distance; letting cattle out; stealing gates; manure on the front doorstep. All these were common country tricks.

Whatever one may surmise from the 'Alys Indentures', it would be going to extremes to sense the whiff of a wicked uncle syndrome here, times two, from her children's point of view, with a difficult grandmother-in-law thrown in, as the Williamses try to wrest the property "*and all its appurtenances*" from a small schoolboy and a toddler, who is still "*an infant of tender years*", not to mention a vulnerable young mother some distance away from her privileged castle home. Spymaster Walsingham's two young stepsons had, within living memory, been suspiciously blown up playing with gunpowder in an outhouse on his rich young widow-wife's estate.

Did Alys marry beneath her? The match seems a curious one. For love? When they met, William Williams was a young cleric or tutor or Oxbridge student, nevertheless in possession of a small country estate. Did they marry in haste, 'had to' in other words? The uncertainties are endless in this fragment of history which (like other documents sifted through along this quest) spark alight with fascinating stories of real people in real places still visible today: an old house viewed from a gateway through trees where passers-by might hesitate to venture past the 'Private' sign … a portrait of an unknown girl of the Tudor Age glimpsed through a door ajar in a remote manor house …

This is Alys's story, such as it is. As she steps into the limelight, her brother Piers is waiting in the wings. He supports her case (possibly egged on by their mother, Lady Catherine, or else she may have thought the case ill-advised. Why does she keep out of things in this instance, when she is perfectly capable of taking court action against her own husband, Sir Thomas Mostyn?) In 1587/8 Piers has still not strictly come of age. He is aided by "*Rees Gronow [Rhys Goronwy] of Llanvair vechan, co. Carnarvon, as friends of the said infant and also on behalf of William ap William ap John Wyn, second son of the said Ales Gruffith ...*"

The arbitrating judge is one Thomas Williams of Y Faenol, Caernarvonshire "*elected to settle disputes*". The witnesses are:

> *Henry Moston/Mostyn; Thomas Fletcher, notary public; Gruffith Fletcher; Gruffith Price, William Griffithe; John Morys ap Robert; Robert ap William Vaughan; Morgan ap Ieuan ap Meredydd.*

Another legal Indenture in this case includes the detail, "*Richard Matthew, notary public; Thomas Fletcher, notary public;*"

Both Matthew and the Fletchers were notorious throughout North Wales for taking bribes, a fact gleaned on good authority and another ingredient in this narrative brew.

Not everyone got to be the sister of a pirate. In her brief, unique life, and in the brief lives of her children, Alys achieved both her own independent identity as a woman of her era and as the daughter of Sir Rhys and Lady Catherine Griffith, with all the obligations that accompanied the dutiful role of a privileged, educated girl of her class: kindness, maternal tenderness and strength, religion, care for servants, the poor, the downtrodden, and loyalty to kith and kin.

Having lost her case, but mercifully getting rescued from her predicament, she made Cilgeraint her own haven and that of her boys as *meistres yr aelwyd*/mistress of hearth and home, all in view of her home base at Old Penrhyn where her little family were possibly frequent visitors. She was also only a walk across the fields away from her brother William's small estate of Cororion.

By 1587 Piers Griffith has prepared Cilgeraint farm on his estate and rescued his sister and young nephews from the threatening atmosphere at Bodlew. A quick get-away perhaps, or a proud, determined exit by Alys, aloft the carrier's cart with her belongings and her snuggling, subdued little boys, under the protective wing of young Uncle Piers, riding out on one of his superb horses with his bodyguards bringing up the rear. Alys, a country girl, is probably a good rider herself, likewise her boys, trained in horsemanship from infancy.

So here is the departing scene and in this context, it is tempting to be fanciful: their well-accoutred line of riders moving steadily against the dramatic coastal skyline of Anglesey, towards the boat that awaits them lying at anchor on the Menai Strait. The nearest point from Bodlew would be the main Abermenai Ferry Crossing to Caernarfon. After that and the excitement of travel, perhaps they receive a warm welcome at Penrhyn from Aunt Margaret, the Pirate's wife and their cousins (one or two would have been born by now.) Their grandmother, Lady Catherine Griffith Mostyn, would not be far from the scene, not to mention an array of curious servants bustling around them. Whether they stay the night or not, we may muse at only in fiction, but we do know the little group is soon installed at Cilgeraint with a household of its own, hopefully free at last from fear and intimidation. Alys maintained an independent household of her own. Or could it be that she was not welcome at Penrhyn? Her farm was solid enough, but not grand. Apart from the care Sir Rhys and Piers took of her, she does seem to have been treated rather like a poor relation.

Later, Piers is to use the farm *"of Cilgeraint"* as recorded in documents, suggesting he may have taken refuge there himself from time to time, with his sister and surviving nephew, Thomas. Piers loses his own two tiny sons, Robert and Rhys, Thomas's cousins and possible playmates at some point before 1610, when they also lose student William who never returns from that ghastly trip to plague-infested London, an admirable young man who has surely been an object of affection and hero-worship. Yet Alys and her surviving offspring are not mentioned as mourners by the four bards who wrote of the London event. Perhaps she was ill at the time, or simply passed over by male reporter-poets and scarcely noticed. Or was there conflict between herself and Margaret the Pirate's Wife (or Lady Catherine), serious enough to keep her away from formal rituals? Alys may even have been dead by 1610. Her son Thomas lived on however, became a lawyer, a judge indeed, and married into the family of the bodyguard who had once been Queen Elizabeth's vigilant Hawk.

One final thought remains about the gaps in recorded details about Alys. Could she have been the illegitimate daughter of Sir Rhys Griffith and a mistress, previous to his marriage to Lady Catherine? All the children of his first marriage died; his second wife, a Cochwillan cousin, soon died childless; and his third wife, Lady Catherine, mother of Piers his legal heir, was much younger than Sir Rhys, who was known to have become entangled with "a lady or two", like his pirate son later. Yet without more evidence pointing to the contrary, we may assume that Alys was the elder sister of Piers and William and that she was the daughter, born first, of Sir Rhys and Lady Catherine, as recorded by J.E. Griffith's genealogy. Alys may have been later legitimised, as ancestor Sir William had once done with his children by his mistress Gwenllian, making Alys the possible *step*-daughter of Lady Catherine, a girl she may have been forced to accept as her own, gladly or otherwise. Alys is not mentioned in either of the two extant elegies to Lady Catherine. It is as if this 'lost girl' never existed, apart from her appearance as *tutorix* to her two sons in the 1588 lawcase, with Piers.

Life for the ordinary women of the Penrhyn estate living in farms and cottages, an experience shared with Alys, would have been geared to survival through the four seasons. Foraging in hedgerows for berries and nuts was common practice. Root vegetables were grown in the gardens, within and beyond the estate. By the 1580s and 1590s potatoes were cultivated and stored over the winter, as were apples. Orchards too were part of life around Penrhyn and most farms like Alys's Cilgeraint had fruit-trees (possibly cherry, pear and quince) with wild strawberries, rosehips and plums; lettuce and radishes were also grown. Honey was used as a sweetener and bee-keeping was widespread. Sugar was expensive and available in large lumps from beet, or imported. At the royal court in London, too much sugar for putting in ale and in meat and fish dishes resulted in people's teeth growing rotten, as the fashion for sweetness spread to the countryside.

Poor cottages and modest farmhouses were lit with rush tapers dipped in fat by the women of the house, leading harsh, laborious lives day and night, occasionally with the aid of some poor skivvy, outcast or down-trodden daughter or two. Middle-class town traders, gentry and nobility employed a range of servants, but had the luxury of waxed candles at least. If the family had a good fire going, an iron spit was used for roasting meat, venison, chicken and lamb, basted by the mistress of the house or her servants at places like the estate farms of Penrhyn and Cochwillan, and at Alys's Cilgeraint, until the meat was deliciously cooked all over. Fires were smoky especially from hearths in the middle of the room. But the same smell of rush tapers would have pervaded the houses of poor and prosperous alike: salty, acrid and stale. In Wales, cow-horns have been found used as cups, also for keeping powder dry in battles.

Shoes have been discovered hidden in the crevices of farmhouse chimneys to remember the dead and pray for the living, denoting a lingering of ancient Celtic superstition, like iron chains cast into wells in the Caernarfon area, witch signs carved into house-timbers at Cochwillan and boar's teeth embedded in a wall at Old Faenol manor near Felinheli. The home front was the means of survival. Tough, yet fraught with risk, disease, birth and death. Natural phenomena like deformed animal births, cattle disease, meteors and eclipses still held their own terrors for unenlightened people, as did rumours of exorcisms, demons and witches. These poor wretches witnessed untold brutality by the law, hangings, torturings, drownings and incarcerations of all manner of miserable folk. At sea, the superstitions of sailors were rife: birds, sudden screens of mist, the distant cries of seals, on *"Ceris waters"*, dolphins and maelstroms all had significance, together with water spouts like the huge spiral that rose ominously from the sea below Harlech Castle just before the Armada crisis, and the tidal wave that hit the Atlantic coastline of Wales in 1607.

The Penrhyn Rent Rolls for 1593 (MS, Penrhyn 1628) record one *"ap Heilin"* living at *"Cae Cornchwiglan"* (Cochwillan.) Other tenants were:

> *"Elizabeth Griffith"* with *"a tenement in Cororion"* at a half-yearly rent of *"30 shillings"*.

> *"Rhys Griffith Llandegai"* on the *"land of Ieuan Delynor"* (Ieuan the Harpist) at *"11 shillings"*.

> Meanwhile his son *"John ap Ieuan Delynor"* is the tenant in *"Perthi Corniog"* at *"6 shillings and 8 pence"*.

> Then there is *"John Dafydd ap Huw"* occupying *"Tyddyn Mab y Saer"* (the Carpenter's son's smallholding) at *"10 shillings"*.

> MS Penrhyn 1623 for the year 1589 records tenants at the poetic sounding dwellings of *"Gwaun y Gog"* and *"Blaen y Nant"*, when the half-yearly rent for *"Cilgeraint"* (without mentioning Alys) is recorded as *"xiv s ii c"*.

> Rents at Llandegai are *"to be gathered at May Anno Domini 1589"*.

This was the year after the Armada when more glorious adventures were beckoning to Piers, promising wealth, enterprise and knowledge almost in Faustian terms, with an entrée into that famous Elizabethan élite who dared the Fates by risking their private fortunes at sea in the process and the personal happiness of those they left behind at home on dry land.

Chapter 14

Travels of a Gentleman

THE EARL OF CUMBERLAND 1558-1605

For good or ill, Piers Griffith may have sailed in the wake of someone like the Earl of Cumberland, a maverick amongst the privateering fraternity of the Elizabethan Age, as Professor John Guy has speculated. Both had a taste for dangerous escapades and both had certain characteristics in common:

> "For George Clifford, third Earl of Cumberland, to be afloat provided a thrilling relief from gambling at court and from this experience he was able to embark on a successful career as a privateer, happily combining both these vocations," wrote Neville Williams in *The Sea Dogs: Plunder and Piracy in the Elizabethan Age*, 1975.

At twelve years old "he had succeeded his father in 1570 … and on coming of age wasted his inheritance. As a symbol of chivalry he always wore in his hat a glove which the Queen had once dropped, having emblazoned it with diamonds. (The portrait that Hilliard painted of him shows Cumberland wearing fancy dress over full armour, ready for the tilt, but the glove is there.)"

Lady Anne Clifford, his daughter who had Stradling blood like Piers, later wrote of him "applying himself to the sea and to navigate, especially towards the West Indies and those new found lands, wherein he became the most knowing and eminent man of a lord in his time".

His first expedition, 1586-7, took him, as Piers's did, through the Strait of Magellan, but the plunder was "negligible – a Portuguese craft with negro women, friars and Catholic devotional wares, and ... a little sugar taken from the coast of Brazil."

If one may also speculate that Piers was drawn to other heady escapades straight after the Armada, he was of the same mind as the profligate Cumberland who, "two months after the Armada campaign ... set out in the *Golden Lion*, lent by the Queen but fitted out at his own expense," Williams recounted. "The loss of his mainmast in a gale prevented him from exploiting his captures, but he was eager to try again the next year with a larger expedition in the *Victory*" ...

There is some evidence that Cumberland recruited compatriots of Piers but certainly Welshman Captain William Monson "who came as his vice-admiral and his crew mustered 400. After ten days at sea they met with some of the scattered English fleet returning from the Portugal expedition who were desperately short of provisions so Cumberland relieved them and then made for the coast of Spain to seize ... sixty-three small Hanseatic craft carrying spices. Then he stood over towards the Azores and at St Michael's captured vessels by a bold ruse; at night he went out in the ship's boat to cut the cables of each in turn, and tow them away. Later on luck turned against him, for though a richly laden ship from the West Indies was taken and placed under Captain Lister with an English crew she foundered near to home, in Mount's Bay, Cornwall, and all aboard her were drowned. Before then Cumberland had the worst of an engagement with a Spanish vessel anchored under the castle at St Mary's in the Azores, when he again went out in boats to drag it away. Most of his men were killed, the rest wounded including Cumberland himself who had a shot in his left side, his head badly cut and his legs scorched by grenades ..."

They almost ran out of fresh water so Cumberland rationed each man to a few spoonfulls each of vinegar mixed with rain water whilst desperately trying to stop the even more desperate men from drinking sea water, which would have meant certain death.

Before he sailed off in the *Garland* in 1591, the Queen, a keen investor, wrote to him, in terms suggesting she knew his nature only too well and delighted in it. If this is the sort of colourful company Piers kept, he was amongst kindred spirits:

> *Right trusty and well-beloved cousin, we greet you well. It may seem strange to you that we should once vouchsafe to trouble our thoughts with any person of roguish condition ... but such is our pleasure at this time as we are well content to take occasion by our letters to express our great desire to learn of your well-being ... hoping well of good success in the action now you have in hand.*

She asked him "playfully not to let the Knight Marshal of the royal household know of her solicitations or he would think she favoured men whose misdemeanours ought to be firmly corrected. This was something of a private joke, because the Knight Marshal was not only the disciplinary officer at court but also the individual who recorded wagers and would know exactly what sums the gambling earl owed to different courtiers. Elizabeth assured him of her concern for his safety at the seas and looked forward to his return, '*whereof we shall be right-glad as any friend you have*'. That particular trip, however, was an unrewarding one, for Captain Monson was taken prisoner by the Spanish."

The following year, more skirmishes occurred, where Piers may well have been involved, possibly to his cost; and his Armada associate Cavendish is not far from the scene either:

At the end of a profitable voyage, "some of the earl's ships took part in the attack on the *Madre de Dios*. The Queen now regularly took shares in his expeditions, but prohibited him from laying any vessel alongside the enemy for fear of her being fired. In 1593

Cumberland in the *Golden Lion* became separated from the rest of his squadron and met with twelve Spanish hulks off the Peninsula. When they refused his order to lower their flags in respect of the Queen's ensign he took on all twelve, made them submit and secured a great quantity of ammunition from them. The earl was not himself present at the fight in 1594 when two large carracks, bigger, men said, than the *Madre* (de Dios), were attacked for a whole day by three of Cavendish's ships – 'like three good English mastiffs upon the Spanish wild bull'. They fired the *Five Wounds of Christ*, but her captain refused to surrender and all aboard, including a number of women, jumped into the sea. Nor would the *San Felipe* surrender a fortnight later, as her captain explained: 'I was at the taking and burning of the *Revenge*, the Queen of England's. Let him [the English admiral] do so much for his Queen; I will do as much as I can for my King.'

"After dark the brave Spaniard succeeded in making off. Reports of the failure to capture the two great carracks persuaded Cumberland to build an enormous man-of-war of his own. At 900 tons it was the largest vessel by far ever built by a subject and the Queen was so delighted that she asked the owner to name her the *Scourge of Malice*, later sold to the East India Company." (Neville Williams.)

In 1595 we know Piers Griffith accompanied Drake on his last voyage. We then hear nothing until he captured the *Esperanza* in 1600 after an absence of five or six years. Drake died of dysentery in 1595/6, along with many of his men; and the survivors, Piers amongst them, were in a sorry state by the time they returned in 1597. Thomas Prys and others have referred to Piers's long absences from home. Reports reached Penrhyn that he "*looks ill*". At last Captain Griffith astounded everyone with the captured Spanish galleon in 1600, then he fell foul of King James's regime by 1603.

If he *had* joined in with daring men like Cumberland and Cavendish in the meantime, or sought to emulate them, we can now see signs of the disasters which Thomas Prys and others tried to warn him of, particularly during the last dark days of Elizabeth's reign.

"Cumberland led his last and largest expedition in his new vessel in 1598, but though he laid waste Lancerota in the Canaries and took Puerto Rico," wrote Williams, "there was little to show for the expenses of the voyage. Its merit lay in preventing the sailing of the treasure ships from the New World. The earl was not a professional mariner of the calibre of a Drake or a Frobisher, yet he was very far from being 'a courtly seaman', that term of abuse that the sea dogs used for rank amateurs."

In any case, here was a multifarious influence on Piers Griffith possibly, in "*Ventures he hath squandered abroad.*"

SIR RICHARD HAWKINS 1562-1622

Another expedition Piers may have joined was the voyage of the *Dainty* to the Bay of Atacama and the Strait of Magellan with another young contemporary and Armada hero, Richard Hawkins, Commander of the *Swallow* and son of Sir John Hawkins, the veteran explorer and wealthy shipping magnate.

Sensible and disciplined, Richard "had been bred to the seas and had commanded the *Swallow* in the hectic summer of 1588. A thorough professional, there was little worth knowing about ships and the men who sailed them that he did not know and he imparted this specialist knowledge in his *Observations*, a wonderfully practical manual, that was published as he was dying in 1622. In this, for example, he discussed the pest of sea worms 'no bigger than a small Spanish needle' that could eat their way into the planking of a hull and eventually destroy a vessel unless his father's patent method of sheathing the hull (which he described) was used. Richard was a man of ingenuity and when in the Pacific he had to repair broken anchors, he succeeded in 'making coals', as he put it; at another time, when they ran out of drinking water aboard, 'with an invention I had in my ship, I easily drew out of the water of the sea a sufficient quantity of fresh water to sustain my people, with little expense of fuel. The water so distilled we found to be wholesome and nourishing.' One would be fascinated to learn the details of his method," wrote Williams.

"In June 1593 Richard Hawkins sailed in the *Dainty* with two vessels in company for the Pacific. One was a victualling ship which was unloaded and abandoned off Brazil, following a gale; the other, the *Fancy*, deserted him in the region of Rio de la Plata. So like Drake in the *Pelican*, Hawkins entered the Strait of Magellan alone. He entered the Pacific on 29 March 1594 and sailed north, taking prizes at Valparaiso, Coquimbo and Arica. The Spanish authorities were much more alert than during Drake's voyage and had improved communications between the various harbours. The viceroy of Peru in Lima ordered six men-of-war to go after him, and Hawkins not only eluded them but cheekily took another prize. At length three of the Spaniards caught up with the *Dainty* in the Bay of Atacama."

This sort of escapade lay at the heart of the daredevil world of privateering throughout the 1570s, 1580s and 1590s, when it reached its zenith of glory with territories claimed and mapped, scientific knowledge discovered by *bona fide* voyagers like Preston and Somers, trade routes forged, treasure seized. It was a free-for-all, to the delight of Elizabeth and the alarm of her Ministers who rightly feared all-out reprisals from Spain with its rival trading empire. Also dreaded was the holy vengeance of the Pope, head of the Catholic world and overlord of its terrifying Inquisition. These factors held no fear for the likes of young Richard Hawkins who revelled in brave deeds as a thrilling game of chivalry on the high seas, equally challenging to both sides, Spain and England. Good fun. Tales to recount and boast of back home amongst the rest of the free-booting fraternity: Drake, Raleigh, Cumberland, Grenville, Cavendish, Monson, Griffith.

"'We hailed first with our trumpets, then with our waits and after with our artillery, which they answer ... two for one; for they had double the ordnance we had and men almost ten for one', the fight lasted for three days and three nights before the battered *Dainty* was boarded and Hawkins felt he must surrender. There had been many casualties and Hawkins himself received six wounds, becoming very weak from loss of blood. His sailing master persuaded him they must put up a flag of truce and discuss terms of surrender. All lives were to be spared and the captains treated honourably. The admiral, Don Beltram de Castro, gave Hawkins his glove as an earnest that his word would be kept. Sent to Lima as prisoners of war, Hawkins and the others escaped interrogation by the Inquisition." (Williams)

SIR WALTER RALEIGH 1552-1618

In several aspects of their lives, both Piers Griffith and Thomas Prys sought to emulate that dazzling figure of the Renaissance, Sir Walter Raleigh, Thomas in his literary aspirations, Piers in his maritime quests.

Neville Williams gives a vivid and authoritative account of Sir Walter's expedition to Guiana in 1595, "prompted by his urgent need to win his way back to royal favour, but ever since the failure of the Roanoke colony he had been restlessly considering afresh the new World and had recently concentrated on the northern stretches of the River Amazon and the Orinoco basin. In part this was an explorer's genuine desire to investigate the unknown, yet in the way he promoted his design it was primarily a quest for gold."

Extant Welsh manuscript poetic sources make no mention of Raleigh by name, whereas Drake is mentioned many times. The Thomas Prys memoir, together with the Westminster records and the Thomas and Williams sources, certainly link Piers to Sir Walter. It is feasible that Piers, at the tail-end of Drake's 1595-7 expedition, joined up with Raleigh in some way, or even earlier, at the time of the Armada.

Raleigh noted that it was the King of Spain's *"Indian gold that endangereth and disturbeth all the nations of Europe as it purchaseth intelligence, creepeth into councils and setteth … loyalty and liberty in the greatest monarchies of Europe."*

To subdue Spain, "England needed her own source of precious metals," wrote Williams, "and Guiana seemed to offer the surest hope. For two generations there had been sporadic searches by Spanish adventurers for another Inca civilization in that region and strange legends had been woven from Indians' tales about the treasure of a great ruler, El Dorado, 'the gilded one', who powdered himself with gold-dust. His capital had been named as Manoa, a city by the shores of Lake Parma, hidden in the mountainous region of Guiana that travellers had found inaccessible."

These were accounts gleaned from "a Spaniard, Don Pedro Sarmiento, who had been brought to England as a prisoner by Captain Whiddon in 1586," two years before the Armada. The man had considerable knowledge of South America, all doubtless revealed under heavy interrogation, and he had once been instructed to found a colony in Patagonia. He was guarded in what he told Raleigh about the Orinoco region however, but Sarmiento's enthusiasm made a distinct impression on Raleigh.

Ten years later Raleigh wrote, "*many years since, I had knowledge by relation of that mighty rich and beautiful Empire of Guiana and of that great and golden city which the Spaniards call El Dorado, and the naturals Minoa.*"

In 1594, his wife Bess Raleigh was sufficiently alarmed by his conversation to write to Robert Cecil, begging him to change her husband's direction that "*you will rather draw Sir Walter towards the east, than help him forward towards the sunset,*" a sentiment which the distressed and lonely Margaret Griffith might well have shared, applied to her own husband, Piers.

When Raleigh was told off for not plundering and sacking towns, he defended himself by saying that such short-sighted tactics would have destroyed "the future hope of so many millions and the great, good and rich trade which England may be possessed thereby". Besides, he had by then established such excellent relations with the Indians that must ensure success, he pleaded.

But his "specimen rocks, including marcasite, were laughed at, for men remembered Frobisher's black ore". Yet Raleigh was adamant he was on the right track, "*... this dolt and that gull must be satisfied, or else all is nothing*", he commented, fully aware that many could not believe he had been all the way to Guiana and back.

As for Piers's exploits, they too have met with scepticism. Professor Laughton of Bangor University in the early 1900s, practically exploded the myth completely. Doubting whether a local hero at nineteen years old could venture so far and mix with Drake, Raleigh and Cavendish, let alone fight against the Armada, Laughton then set about scrutinising Muster Books only to find nothing. However the Penrhyn Papers and other documents were not available to him then, still less the kind of access to Welsh poetry made available in recent times.

Sir Walter Raleigh's ambition was colonisation and the expansion of World Trade. It is likely that Piers Griffith shared his vision. Raleigh's *Discoveries of the Large Rich and Bewtiful Empyre of Guiana* reads like a hyped-up company prospectus for business investment:

> *... the common soldier shall here fight for gold, and pay himself, instead of pence, with plates of half a foot broad ... Guiana is a country that hath yet not been torn ... the graves have not been opened for gold, the mines not broken with sledges, nor their images pulled down out of their temples.*

Raleigh needed "to dazzle readers with this alluring prospect, yet his real goal was to put the entire area under English control before the Spaniards moved in," concluded Williams.

At court Lord Burghley and his son contributed to the rescue mission by Ambassador Laurence Keymis, sent out in 1596 to sail "by the coast from the mouth of the Amazon to the Orinoco and find a passage that would lead to the mountain region where El Dorado was thought to be. They returned six months later without gold but with news that a great lake was to be found which one could reach from the Essequido. By then Raleigh had other employment at Cadiz, yet the mirage of El Dorado never left him and so he was to bargain with King James I for his life in 1617 to find the lost city … an ageing sea dog, 'fleshed in Spanish blood and ruin …'."

Piers Griffith, impelled by "vaulting ambition" also dreamed of El Dorado, again to the point of obsession.

⸙

The mysterious comings and goings of Captain Griffith in and out of his hidden creek and harbour at Penrhyn may not be reliably cross-referenced with his signatures in documents of the Penrhyn Papers, because others may have signed for him from time to time, although we can match up his genuine signature occasionally. Neither can the births of his children be calculated with precision apart from the J.E.Griffith genealogical source, because parish records have been lost and none may be detected so far amongst the Mostyn and Penrhyn Papers. We can only conclude that from about 1584/5 when Piers first went to sea, then from the Armada of 1588 and throughout the 1590s until 1603 when piracy was outlawed, he seems to have been vigorously involved in as many escapades and ventures as he dared. He was not the only one.

Another possible mentor, Sir Henry Norris had commanded

the forces at the unfortunate event of Lisbon in 1589 for example, another fateful mission where Piers and his friends may have been engaged in danger points.

Then there was the link with the vainglorious Essex, to whom Queen Elizabeth wrote upon his departure for Cadiz in 1596:

> *God cover you under his safest wings and let all peril go without your compass.*

On this venture, with several notable Welsh officers and sailors aboard, Lord High Admiral Howard and Lord Essex were said to have "quarrelled as joint commanders over who took the honours this time at Cadiz" and "Raleigh was often mistrusted for being too clever," commented Williams.

Raleigh's possible quest for an ideal society beyond England, a European colony founded on plans like Gonzalo's for colonising the ocean island seized from its natural inhabitant Caliban ("cannibal") in Shakespeare's *The Tempest* (1597), sets him apart from mere fortune-hunters and land-pirates. Perhaps Piers Griffith and Thomas Prys, in company with Raleigh, were prone to such musings too, except that Thomas gave up and went home:

> *No kind of traffic*
> *Would I admit, no name of magistrate; ...*
> *No occupation, all men idle, all;*
> *And women too – but innocent and pure;*
> *No sovereignty ...*
> *All things in common nature should produce*
> *Without sweat or endeavour. Treason, felony,*
> *Sword, pike, knife, gun, or need of any engine.*
> *The Tempest*, Act II, Scene (i)

The adventurous highlights of Elizabethan privateering and voyages of discovery may have drawn Piers and others to many exciting destinations, but also to many a perilous downfall. Such were the picaresque adventures of a gentleman in the Age of Piracy. Back home by now, there was an eager readership for such memoirs and for semi-fictional accounts like the works of Robert Greene and of Thomas Nashe, who published *The Unfortunate Traveller* in 1594.

Chapter 15

The Devil's Lawcase

A LITANY OF LAWSUITS

> *... after the death of said Edward Gruffyth and that afterwards the said Sir Rees Gruffyth and the said daughters fell to great controversy touching the title and possession of the premises and that suited in law did continue between them divers years for the same ...*

The tenor of these catalogued Penrhyn documents conjures up the unrelenting conflicts at Ludlow Law-Court and elsewhere surrounding Piers Griffith, particularly in middle age. His arch-enemy was Sir Edward Herbert, Earl of Powys. After much *"bickering"* and litigation, the *contretemps* would end with the duel in Caernarfon:

> *Powis Castle 9602 [p.204 in Catalogue]*
> *1611, Sept. 30*
> *DEPOSITIONS by virtue of a commission from the Court of Wards and Liveries for the examination of witnesses between James Ley, kt, attorney of the Court of Wards and Liveries by information, plaintiff, and **Pierce Gruffyth, esq., defendant**, touching the devolution of the estate of Sir William Griffith of Penrhyn, co. Ang., and the rival claims of defendant and Sir Edward Herbert and Mary, his wife, and others to the same. See Nos 9196, 9555, 9195, 9293-4, 16191. [A3, 234 ff.]*

> *Powis Castle 11140 [p.190, Catalogue]*
> *1609-10*

PROCEEDINGS in the suit in the Council in the Marches of Wales between Sir Edward Herbert of Montgomery, kt, Dame Marie Herbert, his wife, and Arthur Bagnall of Plaes Newyth, co. Ang., esq., plaintiffs, and **Pieros Gruffiths** *[of Penrhyn, co. Caern.], esq., Hugh ap Hugh and Anne, his wife, and others (tenants), defendants, including bill of complaint, orders (1609-10), answer of defendant* **Pieres Griffith** *(17 March 1609/10), and counsel's opinons as to trying the case in the Council in the Marches of Wales, concerning title to part of the estate of Sir William Griffith, dec., which was in dispute between the heir male and heirs general (see also Nos. 91, 95-6, ets., belonging to this period), particularly title to m's and lands called Tuthine Rhos y bol in Amlough and Tuthine y ty hen in Amlough ... Arriannell in cmt. Llyvon, Tythyn Sysyllt in Llysdualas ...*

[There follows another long list of anglicised, mis-spelt Welsh place-names].
Vouchee: William Davy.
Latin [English!]
Copy. [About A4 20 pages]

Powis Castle 12006-7 [p.210]
1612, Oct 31
BILL OF COMPLAINT in the Court of Wards of John Puleston, esq., deputy in the office of Escheator of co. Caern., to David Holland, escheator, against Rees Gruffith, brother of Edward Gruffith of Penryn, co. Caern., esq., and the said David Holland, defendants, who it is alleged had wrongfully confederated to deprive the daughter of the said Edward Gruffith of the interests in the Penryn estate in cos Ang. And Caern., and ousted Jane, late wife of Edward Gruffith and daughter of plaintiff, from the capital house of Penryn, and arranged the panel of jurors at the inquest on the death of Edward Gruffith, to the loss of the Crown; with the answer of Rise Griffith.
[A3, 16 ff., 23ff.]

To cut a long story short and with this kind of harassing detail beating about his head, Piers claims back as many as he can of his father's 'lost' properties, quickly persuading the tenants that they would be better off with the cheaper rents he is clearly offering them. *"The people all loved him"*, is the comment of several poets.

Nevertheless, storm-clouds are never far from his horizon but he acquits himself well, apparently conducting his own lawcase and getting to the bottom of things like rooting out suspiciously burnt documents, until he finally establishes himself as the legal heir to his father's estate, something that should not have been called into question in the first place. [See also Powys 12003 c. February 15, 1610]

"Interrogatories ministered by Pierce Gruffyth Esq. Defendant to examine his witness against Sir Edward Herbert kt Dame Mary his wife and Arthur Bagnall Esq. by examination plaintiffs":

Imprimis Do you know both plaintiffs and did you know Edward Gruffyth Esquire and Sir Rees Gruffyth kt his late brother …

2 Item Do you [.?.] that was and is generally reputed and taken for an undoubted truth within the several counties of Anglesey and Carnarvon that the said Sir Rees Gruffyth had good and lawful right and title to the premises and to all other the late lands and tenements of the said Sir William Gruffyth within the said several counties of Anglesey and Carnarvon as cousin and heir male of the body of Sir William Gruffyth kt deceased and do you know the said Pierce Gruffyth was next heir male of the body of the said Sir Rees Gruffyth son and heir male of the said Sir William Gruffyth and of the body of Jane his wife

3 Item Do you know that …

4 Item Do you know or have you heard that the said deed of entail came to the hands of Sir John Puleston kt Rees Thomas Esquire who married Jane the supposed widow of the said Edward Gruffyth or unto the hands of one Sergeant William Glyn or of some of them and that upon consideration between them the said Deed of entail was burned by the said Sergeant Glyn with purpose to obscure the title of the said Sir Rees Gruffyth in and to the premises and to give way to the pretenced title of the supposed daughter of Edward Gruffyth in and to the premises and was that in all the time of your remembrance by general voice and reputation of all the country where the premises do lie that the said Deed of entail was done away and burned as aforesaid and did you hear any person or persons say or confess that he had seen the burning thereof and that he or they could now be quiet in conscience till he or they had disclosed the same ...

'7 Item Do you know or have you credibly heard that the said Sir Rees Gruffyth often did say and affirm that he would now have referred the matter to the arbitration of any noblemen that he had supported ...

There is then a reference to a forced entry by Piers, doubtless with his armed men into "*the premises*":

And so on.

> *Witnesses included:*
> *'Evan ap John Owen of Llandrugarn*
> *Edmond Rowland*
> *Hughe ap Williams ap Hughe*
> *Cadwaladr Rowland of the parish of Llansadwrn*
> *David Lloyd ap Richard*
> *William Griffith of Bangor*
> *Rowland David Lloyd'*

"Pyrs Griffith had not come into his inheritance until 1591", (Douglas Pennant and Roberts, The National Trust 1991.) "He mortgaged the first part of the Penrhyn estate in 1592. There followed mortgage after mortgage until 1616. During this period he was also involved in much litigation concerning encroachments and illegal possession of his lands suggesting that he spent much time at sea and was not in a position to supervise his estate."

> *May God of his grace give him as a treasure*
> *Grace to depart from the sea,*

wrote Thomas Prys in his poem *To a Dolphin*, a defining moment. (For alternative text and translation see F. Fisher, ed., The Cefn Coch MSS, Liverpool, 1899, pp. 122-15.)

⁂

Inheritance at Penrhyn was no easy matter. There was the precariousness of birth, infancy and youth. Around 1568 when Piers was born, two-thirds of babies born failed to reach their first birthday, as previously stated and a third of all children did not live to see their tenth birthday. As one heir died, another had to take his place often leading to confusion and conflict, sometimes for years.

After the marriages of the Penrhyn children (Piers Griffith with Margaret Mostyn, Alys Griffith with William Williams, and William Griffith with Jane Owen Lloyd) and as *their* children were born, appropriate and careful preparations had to be made for the forthcoming births to ensure survival. A midwife with attendants accompanied the expectant mother to her confinement room a few weeks before the birth, with all the conceivable comforts a privileged lady could hope for.

Afterwards the father was presented with his offspring by the midwife often with words like,

> 'Father, see there is your child. God give you much joy with it, or take it speedily to His bliss.'

Baptism took place as soon as possible, within three days of birth or at least by the following Sunday and failure to do so could lead to imprisonment for parents, with enforced baptism for the child. Godparents chose the name, sometimes that of a grandparent or ancestor. Mothers of the gentry had longer to recover at their lying-in. The Welsh translation of the Book of Common Prayer was in use by then and at Penrhyn, babies would have been christened at Llandegai Church or in the family chapel (a ruin of which may still be found in the woods) followed by joyful celebration amongst family, friends, servants and tenants, as was sometimes recorded by the lady of the house.

Such a community on an estate like this would have depended for its well-being (or as much as could be expected at that time) on the rightful inheritance of its heirs and on the just administration of its tenancies, not to mention help for the weak. All this had always been the accepted tradition at Penrhyn. Now Piers Griffith was making doubly sure that he held on to that inheritance, out of the clutches of Sir Edward Herbert. Never again would the likes of the Puleston family or others raid and enter Penrhyn "by force of arms and remove all of the contents … suit(s) of armour and other implements for use in the battlefield ".

Chapter 16

Swordplay in the Backstreets

There is more trouble to come, with swashbuckling and dark deeds in back streets, as Piers Griffith and his bodyguard, *'Darby Bach the Irish Boy'* challenge the lawyer of Sir Edward Herbert, Earl of Powys, himself an infamous duellist.

July 18, 1612. Court-room at Caernarfon,

"At the house of Kadwallader ap Humphrey".

> *The Examination of Owen ap Owen* [servant/lawyer to Piers Griffith] *upon interrogation for wounding Rowland Owen* [servant/lawyer to Edward, Lord Herbert].
>
> MS Powis 11139

> Those present are:
> the Lawyer for Piers Griffith
> the Lawyer for Edward Herbert, Earl of Powys
> the interrogating Judge
> and
> the Clerk of the Court

Each witness or deponent must answer three questions and make their statements or depositions in answer to the Judge. In this scenario Piers Griffith must still be suffering the nightmare-haunted memories of his son's death only two years previously. On perusal of this document which is tantalisingly incomplete, we may be tempted to conclude that after the passing of several months, there was much fudging of evidence, string-pulling amongst colourful characters and money-bags on the table:

Owen ap Owen [aged 28], *servant unto Piers Griffith esquire … sworn and examined.*

To the first examination he sayeth that there was a commission awarded out of this court unto Sir Hugh Owen Knight, Thomas Holland esquire and others between the said Sir Edward Herbert Kt [and] *others and Piers Gruffith* [sic]. *And sayeth that the same Commission was executed at Caernarvon in or about the eighth day of April last and that Piers Gruffith, John Owen Treveilir, this deponent* [witness Owen ap Owen], *Morris Owen and Darby Bach were then at Caernarvon aforesaid.*

To the second interrogation he sayeth that he the deponent [Owen ap Owen] *and the said Morris Owen do now serve the said Piers Gruffith and the said Darby Bach did heretofore serve the said Piers Gruffith but doth not now serve him; and further sayeth that he* [Owen ap Owen] *doth now know the said Rowland Owen named in this interrogation but did see him at Caernarfon that day the said Commission was executed whether the said Rowland Owen, servant unto the said Sir Edward Herbert or whether he was the said Sir Edward Herbert's solicitor in the said commission or no, he knoweth not otherwise, then that he hath since heard so by the report of others.*

To the third interrogation he sayeth that he does not know or hath heard that the said Piers Gruffith did at the [inn] *of the said Kadwallader ap Humphrey named in this interrogation or elsewhere at Caernarvon aforesaid during the said commission threaten the said Rowland Owen or use any menacing speeches towards him or command him to go out of the said* [inn] *but sayeth that he hath heard and doth believe the said Commission was executed at the said* [inn].

To the fourth interrogation he sayeth that the said Rowland Owen gave him ill language in the foresaid [inn] *at that time when the said Commission was in execution and afterwards this deponent* [witness Owen ap Owen] *going into the town and returning toward the said house again, the said Darby Bach being with him, met the said Rowland Owen and his son coming in the street from the said houses he thinketh and so soon as they did see this deponent/witness* [Owen ap Owen] *they, both of them,* [father and son] *drew their swords upon him, this examinant and thereupon he, this deponent* [Owen ap Owen] *drew his sword to defend himself against them and that at the first bickering between them, the said Rowland Owen's sword fell out of his hand and then he ran away, this deponent* [Owen ap Owen] *took up his sword and so went into the* [court-house inn] *but whether he this deponent* [Owen ap Owen] *did wound or hurt the said Rowland Owen or not he knoweth not for that he ran away and this deponent* [Owen ap Owen] *never saw him since and sayeth there was none of the said Piers Gruffith's servants or any other person with this deponent* [Owen ap Owen] *at the said bickering or present as partaken therein but only the said Irish boy* [Darby Bach] *and he had no manner of weapon about him ...*

And so on.

The whole conflict seems to have turned into something of a damp squib.

Chapter 17

Another Stab-Wound

ELEGY TO THE LADY CATHERINE GRIFFITH MOSTYN C.1618
mother of Piers Griffith
by Siôn Cain

> *"The finest God-given gift*
> *Your mother ever had was to give birth to you, may she be praised.*
> *... your mother here is seriously worried about you,*
> *Dear Lady, you are like a golden-gowned goddess with your gold-*
> *braided head-dress.."*
>
> *"Catherine the great hostess at wine-filled feasts."*

Death never strikes without bringing deep anguish to the
bereaved,
    The mighty hand of God smiting the whole world!
    Heavy is the pain for everyone enduring their sadness,
4   A sad, chill lament extends across all Gwynedd.
    There is great mourning around me clearly visible
    For this one lady, so deep is the sighing!
    A planet of ill-fortune has brought to us
8   A great loss having to bury my Lady.
    We feel a hundred agonies for her, virtuous and gracious,
    For the Lady Catherine of noble birth
    Grieving after her, long will be my penance,
12   There is mournful crying in every room through all Penrhyn.
    The Castle has become desolate and chill, once a place of superb
                           beneficence

For want of her face, her wisdom and her presence sadly missed,
A place which once supported a hundred men's lives in patronage,
retainers and people of all ranks.
16 The place has become icy like sleet falling with cold lamenting
moans.

After her days, beloved is her name,
We will never have such sumptuous feasts in these parts again.
She was magnanimous in her gifts, never reluctant to bestow
favours,
20 Vintage wine, once so generously poured amongst ourselves by
Catherine herself,
Was shared with free-flowing outpourings, such as you never saw
before or since,
Her hospitality was wonderful like her father's;
As head of the family, as everyone knows,
24 Piers Mostyn once kept an established manorial household of a
hundred retainers.
The agonising news of her grievous death has spread
Over the turrets of Talacre and the surrounding estate.
Her superb lineage, the purity of her ancestry,
28 Descended as she was from the true blood of Adam and the
legendary Iorwerth,
A lovely delightful lady, a mirror showing a fine example to
everyone throughout the land,
She was of the lineage of the Earl of Hereford
There was no better blood-line and none more blue to declare
32 Than the four fine ancestral roots of the late Catherine.

She was a good person all the days of her life,
She had two good husbands,
And both of them were truly excellent, magnanimous men of
honour and authority
36 Were these two knights holding high office with considerable
power:

Sir Rhys Griffith, the representative of many
Descended from the ancestry of earls

273

A leader of people, a dignified nobleman, and a skilful

administrator

40   Honoured by many, the golden heir of beautiful gilded Penrhyn.
Her second husband, also good, we loved him too, was
Sir Thomas, kind and gracious was he,
A Knight of the Realm, steel-armoured and valiant,

44   Mostyn was the leading stag of the herd powerful and courageous
And when these two husbands died, even with pure healthy blood

flowing freely through their veins,

Bitter were the tears she shed in her loss.
And so eventually she was deprived of both, a terrible experience,

48   God also took her, indeed the worst plague of all for them would

have been to lose such a wife.

Cold was the funeral, seeing her stolen away in the grim grip of

Death,

The Lament lingers long as she is sealed into her grave.
God took her from us last night,

52   That is what has killed our spirit so completely!
Catherine the great hostess at wine-filled feasts
Followed her husbands to merciful Heaven,
Yet her offspring still live, they are good children,

56   Hundreds loved her, the people of her first husband's estate,
God has ordained that some are destined to rule and protect their

people with honour and justice

That is, two sons, good men who are neither vain nor boastful,
The first heir is strong, who can compare with him?

60   Piers Griffith, always vigilant like a hawk, a knight or a soldier

considering and measuring matters with keen intelligence,

A pearl, upright and valiant, he can be both tough and tender as

occasion demands,

He is the true-blooded ancestral heir, lord of Penrhyn.
The second son is William, generous in sharing,

64   The lands, his heritage, he is ruling and managing well,
A man who has achieved a high ambition,
Civilised and educated, wise, taking after his father.
These are the descendants of a gifted family indeed,

68   A brave dynasty of the body of Catherine, the lost lady,
     They are like pure shining devout rosary beads, serviceable, fine
                                   and true,
     Woe has befallen nine thousand people mourning for the loss of
                                 their mother.
     If my lady departed, for the blessing of many souls,
72   From her earthly dwellings into the heavenly Court of Jesus,
     May eight long lives be granted to these two wise lions
               (Lady Catherine's two sons, Piers and William)
     So that a well-deserved respect for them may flourish
     Until they are ranked as lords one day.

                            (G.L.)

ELEGY TO LADY CATHERINE GRIFFITH MOSTYN C. 1618
mother of Piers Griffith
by Sir Huw Roberts

Manuscript Peniarth 104, 11, is in such a fragile, fragmentary condition that it is difficult to read, making a full translation here virtually impossible. Like the better known and more metrically complex *Elegy* by Siôn Cain to the same lady, this lament does not give the date of the subject's death either, an essential detail that would traditionally be woven into the verse-pattern at some point. The circumstances of her death seem shrouded in mystery.

The poet, Sir Huw Roberts, is an enigma. He is also a close friend of Piers Griffith, probably from youth. Both poems provide some of the best biographical evidence extant about the Pirate's mother, a significant influence. Her Will has not yet come to light.

There is a reference to Lady Catherine, *"widow"*, last living on March 2, 1618 (Bangor/Mostyn Papers 129) when she was prevented from moving the contents from Gloddaith after her husband, Sir Thomas died. It is assumed she did not die until after Piers's 'troubles' beset her son. The death of his mother is another blow for him. Later that year, by September 2, 1618 she was clearly dead as she is referred to as "*late wife of Sir Thomas Mostyn, late of Mostyn, Kt., dec.*" (Bangor/Mostyn Papers 131.)

In this elegy, Lady Catherine is described by one of the people who knew her best, Sir Huw Roberts, curate of Llandwrog in Caernarfonshire and of Aberffraw in Anglesey, a family friend who has been a frequent visitor at Penrhyn since boyhood. He is linked to her through his marriage to the recusant Catholic heiress Ann Pugh of Creuddyn near Gloddaith, Llandudno, the former home of Lady Catherine herself. Now in the role of family priest, confessor and confidant, Huw is well placed to write this original, curiously 'modern' personal elegy to Piers's mother, a lady whose grace and favour he has long experienced at first hand; a lady who had once kept the Catholic priest Father Bennet hidden in her beautifully situated manor house of Gloddaith about 1582 at her own risk.

Referred to only obliquely by the poet as a "*sainted noble lady*" without revealing any family secrets, it seems that Piers's mother was a courageous and daring woman who ran a Catholic escape-line with the help of a bale-out bribe by her second husband Thomas Mostyn and the probable assistance of Huw's future in-laws living nearby, it has been suggested. Not only did they manage to fob off the skulking officers of the law for a time but after various disasters recounted in "*The Catholic Martyrs of Wales*", they succeeded in getting the priest sprung from the grim misery of Flint Jail, until they finally managed to spirit him away to bivouac for a bit in the Catholic hideaway Cave of Rhiwaedog above the sea at Craig-y-Don (once toughly tested out on television by Neil Oliver on "*Coast* ", quoting from the Welsh manuscript poem *Ogof Rhiwaedog.*) Then the Mostyns got the hapless priest lowered down a rope to a waiting ship for Ireland and from there on to a Catholic retreat in Spain.

Sir Huw Roberts is also the author of *Ode to the South Wind* summoning his friend Piers home from his voyages for the sake of his wife and children, and like Piers, he is familiar with sea-routes. This poet-priest too is surrounded by an aura of mystery. Very little is known about him except that he was an Oxford man, a historian and theologian, a brilliantly experimental poet with a style that is at once Homeric and original. Significantly he is a contemporary of Piers; he was husband to the recusant Catholic Ann Pugh, possibly childless and as curate of Aberffraw and of Llandwrog, he would have been a frequenter of several North Wales manor-houses, some with private chapels. Extant manuscript copies of his unique poems are rare and until now, all remain unpublished. They have been transcribed and edited by Dr Wiliam of Bangor University. All are in a decayed state from *"llygod a lleithder"/"the mice and the damp"*.

Like Siôn Cain, Huw addresses Catherine on her funeral cortège as it were, *"my Lady"*, perhaps indicating that as a priest, he was as close to her in her Penrhyn days as he was to Margaret the Pirate's Wife. Curiously, Margaret was Catherine's distant cousin, step-daughter *and* daughter-in-law at the same time, not forgetting her grandchildren, that is the children of Piers Griffith and Margaret Mostyn Griffith in one close family circle. Evidence points to this family unit being recusant Catholics, at least on the female side, likewise their poet-priest, sympathetically sharing their religious views. It would seem therefore that Sir Huw Roberts (even within the context of his marriage to a suitable girl) could be part of that related network of old families in Wales still secretly clinging to the Old Faith. Somehow there is a devout, understated Catholic ring-tone in these two elegies to the grand Lady of Mostyn and Penrhyn, a religious sub-text that is later echoed in the Wills of Margaret Griffith and her daughters Dorothy Edwards and Grace Bromhall, neither of whom was ever graced by such poetic laments; nor was Alys Griffith honoured by the poets, at least no elegy to her has been discovered so far.

Queen Elizabeth I (sincerely seeking unity and peace in the religious matters of her reign) had declared that she did *"not seek a window to men's souls"*, so some recusant Catholics were excused from paying fines for not attending church. In North Wales, it was known that the Queen's officers of the law could easily be bribed by rich gentry like Sir Thomas Mostyn to keep their mouths shut, as suggested by Dr Anthony Carr. When the old Queen was nearing the end of her life in 1601 at the time of the Essex Revolt and Lady Catherine's 'Feast at Mostyn', several young men from Welsh Catholic families had been let off lightly; but when the Queen's kinsman James Stuart came to the throne after her death in 1603, times were changing.

As the more rigorously Protestant climate of King James I gripped the land, not only did the monarch set out to trounce pirates like Piers and his crew, but to deal with any religious miscreants to boot, like John Roberts, a Welsh priest condemned to death for treachery, by King James's double agent, John Cecil in 1610. Victims who fell foul of such purges were Catholics, independent thinkers, Puritans, necromancers and the niggling remnants of a host of evils listed in *Daemonologie* and *Malleus Maleficorum*. However well-meaning the 1611 'King James Bible' was, his instant crackdown on superstition and witchcraft (often unjustly) together with his new strategies of legislation, taxes and friendly relations with Spain, albeit in the cause of peace, caused discontent in some quarters and hope to others. There were also rumours of distaste for James's personal habits and for his gentlemen friends including the Machiavellian John Williams, cousin of Piers; people also disapproved of King James's unfair treatment of his wife the Queen, Anne of Denmark, a widely respected Catholic princess.

In this new mood at Court, the Spenserian idyll of spectacle, costume, dance, music, masque and poetry once associated with the glamour of Gloriana had long since gone by 1618, the possible date of Huw's elegy to Lady Catherine. The much maligned King however *did* promote drama at Court, even to excess and funded by the public purse, in his association with Sir Edward Herbert, Earl of Powys and with William Herbert, third Earl of Pembroke, who eventually bankrolled Piers's estate at this time until John Williams could snap it up, the very same Earl of Pembroke who had also been a friend of Shakespeare (died 1616.) King James, an author himself, showed his support for theatre and culture in his patronage of The King's Players at Court and of the revised Welsh Bible in 1620, a revision by Bishop Richard Parry and Dr John Davies of Bishop William Morgan's translation back in 1588, Armada Year, commissioned by the now late lamented Queen Elizabeth.

Huw's *Elegy to Lady Catherine,* like his *Ode the the South Wind,* reveals a somewhat radical approach to women. In the new uncertain, shifting times of the keenly Protestant peace-maker James I, the composition of an elegy by a recusant poet-priest to a prominent lady was a brave act indeed, especially to one from such a well-known old Catholic Family as that of Lady Catherine's late father, Piers Mostyn of Talacre (died c. 1580 but not forgotten.)

We may expect the same unconventional, off-beat angle found in *"Ode to the South Wind".* Huw is lamenting the death of his friend Piers's mother, a religious widow with ancient ancestry in her own right before she ever married two Knights of the Realm. At her home in Gloddaith, a Mostyn property, she seems to have led a separate, independent life from second spouse Sir Thomas Mostyn while he himself kept to Mostyn Hall, as a man known for getting into disagreements with people from time to time, so why not with his wife, who clashed with him several times in law-suits?

To Catherine's credit, it seems she had the *chutzpah* to discreetly brush aside all that wildly colourful personal history attached to her first husband Sir Rhys, Piers's father, after duly taking her time to consider the matter in the manner of great ladies. We are told she looked after the poor and supervised splendid feasts at Penrhyn and Mostyn with great aplomb, no doubt shrewdly taking the measure of a battle-hungry ambitious Lord Essex with his sophisticated hangers-on, before husband Thomas embarked for Ireland in full military splendour, carrying his magnificent sword and Queen Elizabeth's royally sealed secret letters to the command-posts of the Irish Wars.

The personal details given about the life of Lady Catherine Griffith Mostyn in this elegy illustrate her social standing at the time. The poem also evokes the intimate family life she led on two large country estates, often quietly at dull moments, in the midst of that dramatic age where she had lived through the reigns of five monarchs: Henry VIII, Mary I (Bloody Mary), Edward VI, Elizabeth I and the first Stuart King, James I.

There seems to be a new trend in the craft of elegy-writing at work here, despite a raft of missing words in the fragile manuscript. There is less of the high-blown sycophancy of Siôn Cain for instance, and of other past poets of this convention with their impassioned, somewhat excessive praise and poetic licence. In this work there is perhaps more frank and open comment, possibly from the privileged position of Huw the family poet-priest and friend.

There is even a tone of wit and drama in this tribute, as the poet briefly whips through the traditionally expected section about Lady Catherine's ancient ancestry, as a lady of rank, *"from Adam"* onwards, thus blowing away the cobwebs of such tedious recitals as we often find in other laments, especially when we infer from them that they were often read aloud to a live audience. Instead of that, we are given shorter, crisper lines.

> *... descended from Ifor Fychan who cut off the heads of his enemies.*

The poet now gallops through a family link to the powerful Trevors (who are meanwhile mortgaging Piers Griffith up to the hilt and everyone present probably knows this) then on to the chivalrous Earl of Hereford without further delay and next to the Stanleys, supporters of the Tudor Dynasty since the Battle of Bosworth. But the poet wastes no time in hum-drumming out all the details here, because clearly his well-informed audience already knows all that. Or maybe he is just getting tired of life when most of the family poets of old are ageing or already dead.

Significantly it is Catherine's openly Catholic father, the late Piers Mostyn of Talacre, we now hear praised and revered in particular, with echoes of Siôn Cain's traditional stock verse-line, giving us a useful clue to some missing words in this fragment:

Oes wylaw hallt ar ['i hôl hi]

meaning

Bitter tears are shed for [her loss].

Again the fact that Catherine was the *"beautiful, virtuous and wise"* wife of two Knights of the Realm, is part of the poet's tribute to both families. The recently dead, illustrious Sir Thomas Mostyn seems to get barely a mention and Catherine's stepson Roger Mostyn not at all, a man in dispute with her over Sir Thomas's Will in 1618, and who granted his sister Margaret Griffith her £30 per annum on condition she lives apart from Piers Griffith. This suggests a bitter, long-standing family feud, where the Mostyns are determined to uphold their noble status and dissociate themselves from the notoriety of the sea-captain who has blackened the family name in their view. Have the Mostyns extended their displeasure to Huw the poet-priest as well, a man who is less than luke-warm about them in this elegy? At this point, c. 1616-18 and just before his death, Sir Thomas had his son-in-law Piers, Huw's friend, imprisoned in the Fleet for debt, with its iron bars, rattling chains and hollow stone passage-ways.

In contrast, Sir Rhys Griffith, Catherine's first husband and Piers's father is idealised as

the white eagle ... of Penrhyn with its fine poetic patronage (line 39.)

We are also reminded that the chivalrous heritage of Piers's grandfather is still symbolised by

Sir William, a wealthy, splendid knight (line 41.)

In the verse section that traditionally marks respect for the family mourners present, there is an original and lively upturn in the tribute to Catherine's elder son, Piers Griffith, now aged 50 in 1618 and clearly out of prison, if the two elegies date from soon afterwards. These poetic lines show vivid insight into the Pirate's character from a man who knew him well, a contemporary who was not afraid to tick him off from time to time either, for his neglect of his wife. Fragmentary and tantalising, this evidence is worth scrutiny:

> … … … … *man of fine lineage* (1.47)
> … … … … *of royal blood-line*(l. 48)
> *Piers … … Griffith the handsome, gifted*
> … … … … *leading deer of the herd* (l. 49)
> … … … … *Rys, his famous father.* (l. 50)

And where the Welsh manuscript reads:

> … … … …] *liwn hwn heno* (l. 51)
> … … … …] *y gwelais fo.* (l. 52)

Could this be:

> … … … …] *his [ga]lleon tonight* (l. 51)
> … … … …] *I saw him.* (l. 52)?

Possibly slightly older than Piers and once his *socius studiorum* like Thomas Prys, Sir Huw Roberts could hardly have missed the glorious spectacle of the *Grace* sailing by, or for that matter, the *Esperanza*.

What remains of line 53 continues with his description of Piers's home-life:

… … … … Penrhyn set on a hill in splendour (l. 53)
… … … … and he used to return there (l. 54)
… … … … his father at all times (l. 55)
… … … … was a delightfully close, loving family. (l. 56)

As in the poem by Siôn Cain, William Griffith, the second son of Lady Catherine is given sincere commendation:

… … … … … … … William
[Gruffu]*dd, who is deeply sad without his mother.* (l. 58)
[In] *mourning is here weeping,* (l. 59)
… … … mother so dear to him. (l. 60)

Whereas Siôn Cain's elevated classical *cynghanedd* (complex metrical and alliterative verse-patterns) somehow distances the two brothers from us to heroic status above that of ordinary mortals, Huw's psychological insights seem more realistic and familiar despite the missing words.

William's grief for the loss of his mother is doubly emphasised in lines 61, 62 and 63, striking a poignant tone but perhaps Piers, for the moment, is able to contain his grief. William is described as *"golden, famous and strongly built"* (l.64). It is as if the poet feels for this second son, who has long been in Piers's shadow, possibly from boyhood. We are told that William too has achieved fame (*"y bu'r sôn,"* line 66) suggesting *"it was said everywhere".* Indeed the poet calls him the *"second ranking deer"* (line 67) who has journeyed to *"a hundred countries"* (*"cant o wledydd",* line 68.) It is known that William served Queen Elizabeth as a soldier in Ireland and in the Netherlands, and then was in service at the court of King James, a record he probably recalled later about 1660. Siôn Cain rates William highly too, praising him for *"the good management of his own estate",* as if to imply that Piers has not fared so well in this respect.

Both sons together are referred to in the rhyming couplet that links them as *"orphans", "Cold and desolate with neither mother nor father"* (lines 69 and 70.)

In the preceding poem, Siôn Cain makes no mention of their elder sister Alys (who may be dead by now) nor indeed of any female members of the family, apart from his main focus on Lady Catherine. It would be typical of Sir Huw Roberts, a cleric in close touch with the lives of women and children in great houses, to consider their suffering too, amongst the mourners for *"my lady"*; and the fact that he does not refer to Alys whilst assiduously listing the other ladies present, her friends, suggests that Piers and William have lost their sister too by then, or else the poet may have another reason for ignoring the 'lost girl'. The exact date of the elegy may be somewhere within the last lines, now missing.

We are told that Catherine's *"... sisters shed bitter tears"* and *"... there is much grieving"* (lines 71 and 72.)

We imagine

The chill lamentation of Margaret Conway,
[Mary] her sister, how splendid and finely dressed they are!

(lines 73 and 74.)

(G.L.)

The people of the lands of Tegeingl and Ystrad Alun neighbouring the Mostyn and Talacre Estates *"all share a deep sorrow"* for Lady Catherine; and this anguish is tempered only by the mercy of God promised to be freely given. The poet-priest, perhaps officiating at the funeral service, now extends a prayer for the comfort of the bereaved (lines 79 and 80), including the saddened younger generation of the family, referring to the children of William Griffith, to Alys's surviving son Thomas and to Piers's remaining descendants:

God's Will has taken their lovely, kind grandmother,
Jesus has especially chosen her. (lines 80-82)

Lady Catherine has been charitable to poor people and virtuous all her life; this is the clear message of both poets, taking her role as a Knight's consort *"seriously and with dignity, dispensing wine and graciousness at feasts"* with her *"kind, charming presence"* for all ranks of society, *"rich and poor"*.

The elegy concludes in a unique way by paying tribute to Piers's mother as a *"gifted, accomplished woman"*, encouraging of others, *"wise, well-educated and knowledgeable"*; an *"honourable lady"* and a loving, good, *"devout … tender-hearted"* wife and mother.

Her entry into Heaven is described, *"with Daniel's choir"*, her body lying in blissful peace sealed in her tomb. We recall how the boy William was *"mindful of his mother"* and the boy Piers *"helpful"* at their father's funeral back in 1580 before the Knight was entombed.

Piers Griffith was fortunate, it would seem, to be reared by such a remarkable mother, a woman who took the trouble to so carefully select the best clothes for her eldest son going up to Oxford. Did she spoil him, in an age when children were usually brought up very strictly? Her support for him could have been partly the cause of her conflict with husband Sir Thomas and stepson Roger.

Piers's brother William is *"deeply affected"* by his mother's death. Perhaps, in Piers's absences, William remained closer to her. We may recall too the protective loving arms he extended to her at his father's funeral when he and Piers were boys together in Penrhyn. Despite the odd feud over the years recorded in the Penrhyn papers, Piers *did* secure William's estate of Cororion for his brother and his family when the *"notable pirate"* finally sold out to Archbishop John Williams in 1623. When their mother died, this was the final blow. Her death signalled the end of life as they knew it at Penrhyn:

> *The Castle has become desolate and chill, once a place of superb beneficence.*

Like the other 'Ladies of Penrhyn', she remained true to the traditional role of peace-maker within the family, her own rather than that of the Mostyns. No one knows where Lady Catherine Griffith Mostyn of Talacre, Penrhyn, Mostyn and Gloddaith is buried. If she died at her own Gloddaith, where she was mistress of hearth and home during her lifetime on an allowance from Sir Thomas of £300 per annum, the logical place would be Llanrhos Church, as suggested by Shaun Evans, Bangor University Ph.D. research student into the history of the Mostyn Family, but he says no evidence has yet come to light. If she died at Mostyn Hall or at one of the other courts, there is no record of her burial there either, near Sir Thomas at Whitford, Flintshire but perhaps Ursula, his first wife took priority there. If Lady Catherine died during the last days of Piers's Penrhyn about 1618, we may only speculate about her joining Sir Rhys in the Crypt at Llandegai Churchyard. He had left her instructions in 1580 as his capable executrix, for him to be buried with his first wife *"the Lady Phynes"*, so Lady Catherine may have been buried there separately, observing some kind of heavenly etiquette perhaps.

Apart from the suggestion that it might have been *"desolate"* winter time in Siôn Cain's poem referring to a Penrhyn *"empty"* of Lady Catherine, there are no further clues about the date within the verse. Here was a great lady: once a young girl married to the much older Sir Rhys, a Knight imbued with the values of the Age of Chivalry from his father Sir William's day; a lady who mothered a son who took a leading role in the Age of Piracy and lived long enough to see his decline with it into Stuart times; a lady with another son, a soldier who fought in international campaigns; and a dauntless daughter who fought her own corner.

Lady Catherine Griffith Mostyn was a grand lady well aware of the Rise and Fall of the House of Penrhyn.

There remains one nagging question. Can we be certain that Piers actually attended his own mother's funeral? Some believe he did, but sceptics have suggested not, reading between the lofty lines of kindly old family friend and poet Siôn Cain whose plangent,

Portrait of Sir Thomas Mostyn, possibly at the time of his Knighthood by the Earl of Essex in 1599.

Gabriel Goodman, rich Tudor Merchant.

Portrait of an Unknown Young Woman at Gloddaith, (late 16th or early 17th century): possibly Margaret, daughter of Sir Thomas Mostyn and wife to Piers Griffith, or less likely, her sister, Lady Catherine Hanmer.

Gloddaith, near Llandudno, home of Lady Catherine Griffith Mostyn, the Pirate's mother.

The ancient hall of Cochwillan on the Penrhyn Estate, home of Robin ap Griffith and his troop-of-horse off to the Battle of Bosworth. Birthplace of Archbishop John Williams.

Interior of the renovated medieval hall at Cochwillan, famous for welcoming poets like Guto'r Glyn in the 15th century.

Archbishop John Williams (1574-1650) with his hand on the Great Seal. Royal favourite and Chaplain to King James I, Lord Keeper of the Privy Seal, Speaker of the House of Lords, Bishop of Lincoln, Dean of Westminster, Archbishop of York. Attributed to Cornelius Janssen or Gilbert Jackson c.1621. Steegman favours the Studio of Mytens.

Abercegin Creek, where Piers Griffith's pinnace Grace once lay at anchor, also the captured Spanish galleon Esperanza and his local trading vessel, Elizabeth of Beaumaris, skippered by Captain Richard Dobbe.

© Photo: Glenys Mair Lloyd.

A View of Snowdonia, rare 18th century print by Gastineau believed to show part of the estate and the old bastion and tower of Piers Griffith's castle, before later renovations by Wyatt and Hopper, and before the design drawings of Moses Griffith.

Private Collection.

Barbara Gamage, Countess of Leicester and her children, 1596: infant boy, son with sword, and four girls. Her Welsh grandparents were patrons of poets and she was adopted by the pirating Stradling family of Glamorgan, kinsmen of Piers Griffith. She gave birth to eleven children in all; Margaret Mostyn Griffith had ten offspring. Portrait by Marcus Gheeraerts.

Part of the Mostyn Silver Collection.

Edward Herbert, Lord Herbert of
Cherbury, the Duellist (c.1604-1642).
Attributed to Robert Peake (1580-1626).
Private Collection at Powys Castle.

Bridgeman.

Mostyn Coat of Arms 1622.

© Reproduced by kind permission of the Mostyn Estate.

Prince Henry, Prince of Wales (died 1612),
a contemporary of Ellis Prys and William
Griffith. Steegman saw such a miniature at
Plas Newydd, Anglesey.

© National Museum of Wales.

The Galleon Seal with which Margaret and her three daughters each completed the legalities on the Manuscript of Bangor/Mostyn 144, 8 May 1643.

Signature of the Pirate's Wife, Margaret Griffith.

Signatures of the Pirate's daughter, Dorothy Edwards and husband William.

Signatures of daughter Grace Bromhall and husband John.

Signatures of daughter Elizabeth Humphreys and husband John.

Here
lyeth the body of **Peeres Gruffith** Esquire, sonne
& heire to s.r Ree. Gruffyth & grandchild to s.r William
Gruffyth chamberlaine of North-wales, who dyed the
18. of August 1628.

Coat of Arms of Piers Griffith of Penrhyn. © Reproduced by kind permission of the Dean and
Chapter of Westminster.

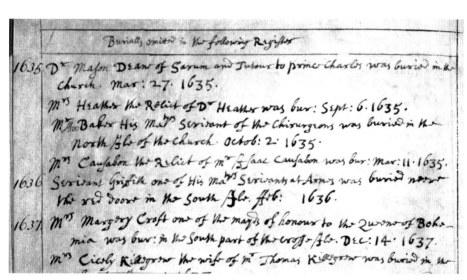

MS Burial Register entry for Piers Griffith at Westminster Abbey 1628.

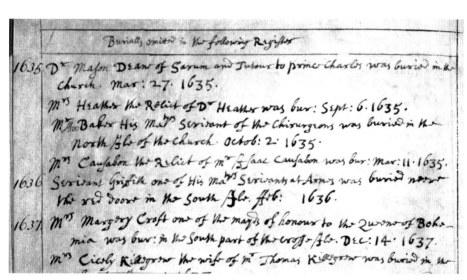

MS Burial Register entry for Piers's London nephew William Griffith, serjeant-at-arms to King James I & King Charles I, 1636.

Westminster Abbey.

§. 34. On the South ſide the Nave is a Table of Arms placed to remember *Peers Gruffith.* one *Peers Gruffith* Eſq; who died in *vid. Ep.*18. the year 1628. Next to which, on the Eaſt ſide the great South door that enters the Cloiſters, is a comely Monument of black and white Marble, with an Epitaph in *Hebrew, Greek,* and *Carola Morland.* vid. *Engliſh for Carola,* Daughter of *Roger Ep.* 20. *Harſnet,* and Wife of *Sir Samuel Morland Baronet,* who died in the year 1674. A little higher is another Monument of black and white Marble, adorned with ſeveral warlike Trophies,

Printed record of Piers Griffith's lost stone inscription at the Abbey, from Henry Keepe's 'Memorials of Westminster'.

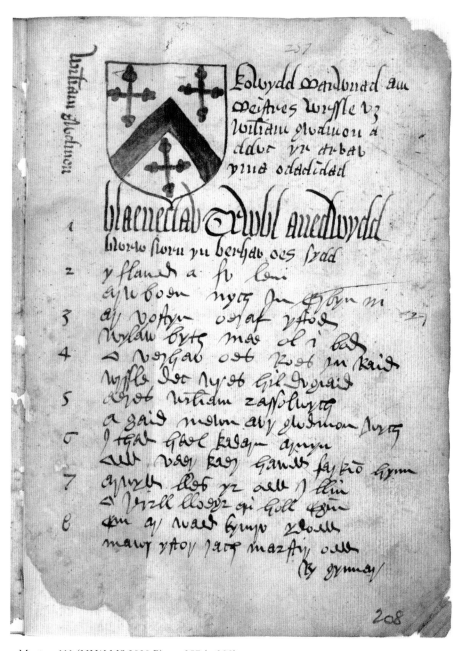

Mostyn 111 (NLW MS 3030 B) no. 257 (p.208)
Opening lines of the cywydd (alliterative poem) : 'Blaenedau, trwbl anedwydd' by Wiliam Cynwal.

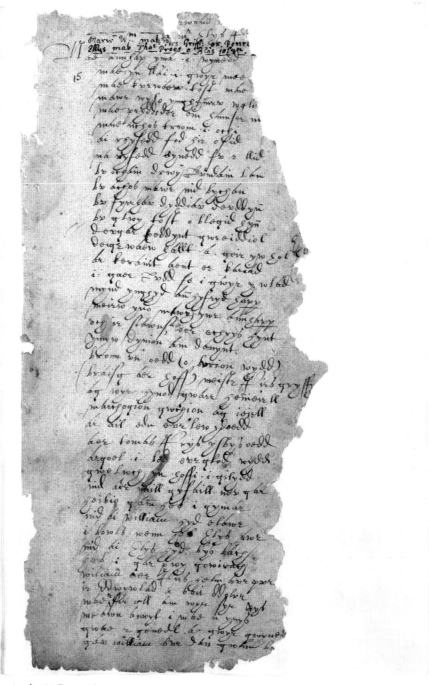

Peniarth 104 D no. 15.
Opening lines of the cywydd (alliterative poem) : 'Mae anhap yma i Wynedd' by Sir Huw Roberts.

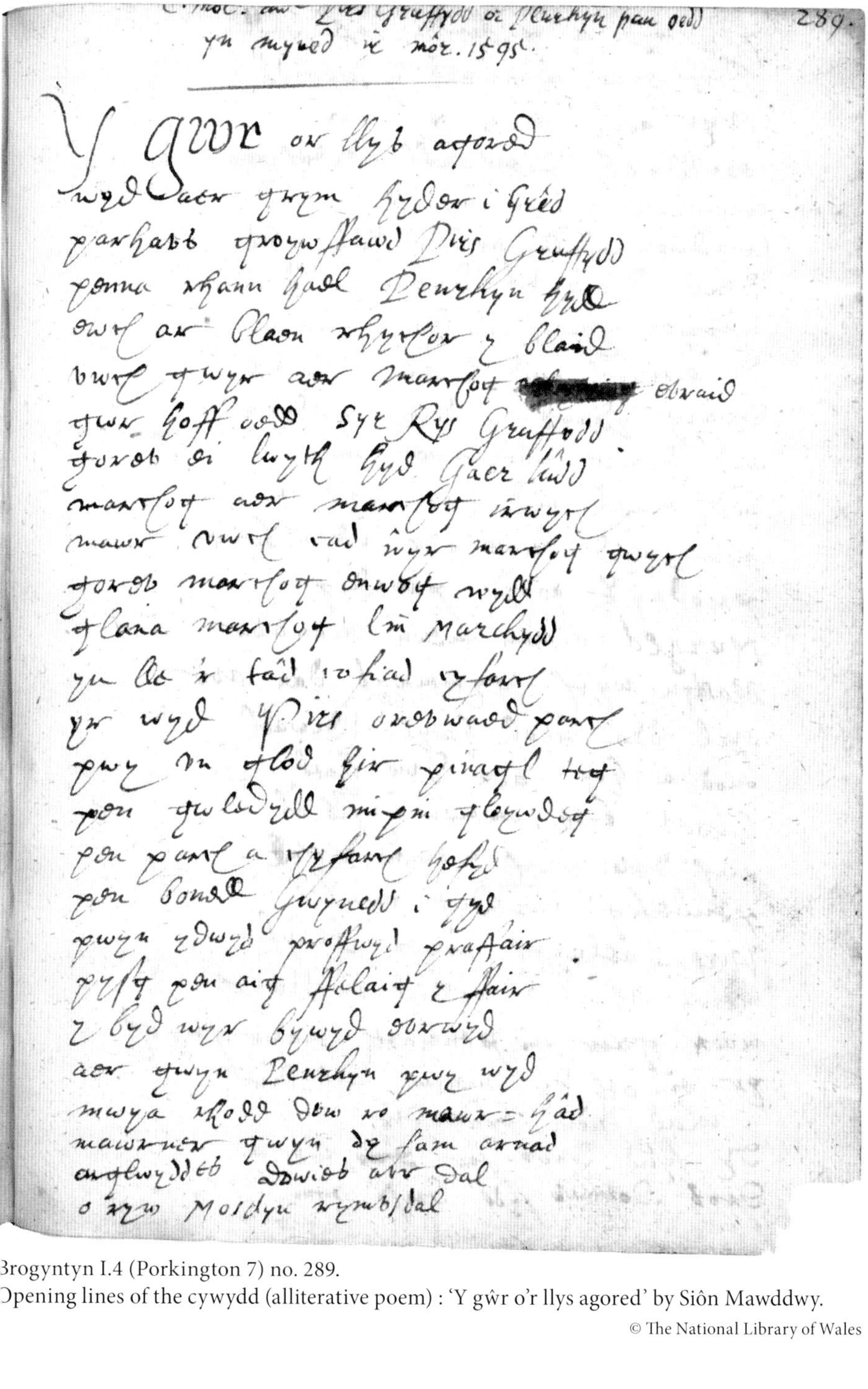

...mol. ... Rys Gruffydd o'r Penrhyn pan oedd
yn myned i'r môr. 1595. 289.

Y gwr o'r llys agored
wyd daer gwyn hyder i gred
parhaus growyw ffawd Rys Gruffydd
penna rhann hael Penrhyn hydd
gwr ar blaen rhyfel y blaid
bwrl gwyr aer marchog [redacted] obraid
gwr hoff oedd Syr Rys Gruffydd
gorau i lwyth hyd Gaer Lludd
marchog aer marchog irwyrl
mawr cwrl vad wyr marchog gwyrl
gorau marchog enwog wydd
glana marchog lu marchydd
yn lle i'r tad yr had rhyfel
yr wyd Syr Rys ordwaed parel
pwy un clod hir pinagl teg
pen gwledydd mi pen gloywdeg
pen parch a rhyfarch hoffed
pen bonedd Gwynedd i gyd
gwyn rodwydd proffwyd praffair
grist pen aig ffelaig y ffair
y byd wyr bywyd dewrwydd
aer gwyn Penrhyn pwy wyd
mwya rhodd duw ro mawrhad
mawrner gwyn dy fam arnad
anglwyddeb ddwiel ar dal
o ryw Moldyn rymusdal

Brogyntyn I.4 (Porkington 7) no. 289.
Opening lines of the cywydd (alliterative poem) : 'Y gŵr o'r llys agored' by Siôn Mawddwy.

© The National Library of Wales

regretful tone of writing elegises the end of an era as much as it eulogises the lady who saw it all happen:

> *… two sons, good men who are neither vain nor boastful,*
> *… these two wise lions.*

Yet the more personal, hopeful tenor of Sir Huw Roberts's tribute to the surviving members of Catherine's family, her grandchildren, and her grieving middle-aged sons Piers and William, offers a new vein of evidence about both brothers and their relationship with their mother.

Chapter 18

Piers Griffith of London

… Strong …
… always vigilant like a hawk, a knight or a soldier, considering
and measuring matters with keen intelligence,
A pearl, upright and valiant, he can be both tough and tender as
occasion demands,
He is the true-blooded ancestral heir, lord of Penrhyn.*

Siôn Cain, Elegy to Lady Catherine Griffith Mostyn,
mother of Piers c.1618

Documents tracing the Captain's movements from this point on until his death in 1628 are thin on the ground. The jig-saw of his life has had to rely on tradition, speculation and random clues, with some new direct evidence from reliable poetic sources, official documents and family papers completing the story. By about 1620 Piers Griffith is referred to in the Penrhyn Papers as *"Piers Griffith of London"*. After removing to the city, he is likely to ponder from time to time on how he had once voyaged, plundered and invested abroad, often on behalf of his merchant contacts in Wales and in the capital of England. It is also tempting to fancy that he may have earmarked some of his stashed-away assets to his surviving daughters, particularly Grace Bromhall, whose husband's kinsmen had important trade-links, land and properties in the Mediterranean and the West Indies.

From the beginning of King James's troubled and often

unpopular reign (1603 to 1624/5) and until Piers dies in 1628, the former lord of Penrhyn lives to witness the rapid development of colonisation in the Americas that Drake, Hawkins, Raleigh and others had first forged in hard-won battles during the reign of Queen Elizabeth I. It is not impossible for him, having taken part in some of these adventurous, land-pirating scenarios, to have secured for himself, like others, some investment there.

In 1607 there is the first permanent settlement in America at Jamestown, Virginia, which develops the export of tobacco. Here the native American Algonquian Princess Pocahontas befriends and saves the life of Captain John Smith. They marry and he proudly brings his beautiful exotic bride to the London court; but she dies in 1617 on the way back to Jamestown which is by then importing Negro slaves from Africa.

In Ireland, plantation settlements of confiscated Rebel land and estates are granted to emigrants from Britain. Piers Griffith has family in Ireland. One relative in Dublin lends him money and interestingly, one kinsman will found the ferry service between Dublin and Anglesey by the mid-seventeenth century.

Griffith has possible links to several dramatic events of his age, both Elizabethan and Stuart. In 1610 Lady Arabella Stuart (King James's cousin and the girl Queen Elizabeth had once favoured as her potential successor, a girl kidnapped by Henry Cavendish from his mother Bess of Hardwicke's house with an armed gang) marries her true love, William Seymour. King James plays a central role here in quashing a potential rebellion. He has the lovers imprisoned and five years later, after many years of suffering and disappointment, Lady Arabella, a royal Tudor descendant, dies young. Her husband is executed.

By 1618, there are more discoveries in North America and in 1615 the costly Thirty Years War starts in Europe. Meanwhile Dutch ships are the first to bring Negro slaves to the Colony of Virginia, so maritime movements are rife. Both Puritans on the one side and Catholics on the other are suffering bigotry and violent persecution. No Catholic can sit on the throne and Catholics are barred from many professions. Puritans have to worship in secret and are persecuted as too extreme. In Wales, the Dolgellau area suffers in particular, with witch-hunts, drownings and terror.

In 1620 the Pilgrim Fathers set sail from Plymouth, Piers's former headquarters, to colonize America, arriving at Cape Cod. By 1623 there is a British settlement in New Hampshire.

Meanwhile in London, King James's close favourite George Villiers (disliked by almost everyone else) is created Duke of Buckingham. Cousin John Williams is another favourite who is part of this royal inner circle and so is the Earl of Pembroke, patron of Shakespeare and a kinsman of the Powys family, the man who has just financed Piers's estate for a time. Meanwhile King James is fast becoming ill-tempered and sick.

In 1624 he arranges for his heir, Charles, the Prince of Wales to be married to the sixteen year old French Princess Henrietta Maria, albeit a Catholic, after James fails to negotiate a Spanish marriage for his son. It is about this time and after James's death that the sister of Piers Griffith's wife Margaret, Lady Catherine Hanmer goes to Court to be lady-in-waiting to the new Queen, crowned in 1625 when Henrietta Maria's seductive influence over her husband King Charles I begins, if not before, for as soon as they meet, it seems they are very much taken with each other.

Again one may assume that Piers is aware of contemporary events. Already Parliament is being tough on the new King and grants him customs duties for one year only. Charles wants to build up the navy to protect British shores from foreign pirates, especially Wales, which may have been one reason why so many of the Welsh later support him in the Civil War, according to some.

In 1626 King Charles I summons a second Parliament which impeaches Buckingham whom he despises and then he dissolves Parliament again. Two years later in 1628, the year Piers dies, Charles calls his third Parliament but the factions of Cromwell and Pym come into open conflict with their king, and Piers probably shares people's concerns. Members of Parliament then present a Petition of Right before the king. They oppose Charles's collection of taxes, then the monarch adjourns Parliament, only to see it reassemble the following year, 1629, to condemn his actions. Piers does not live long enough to see them barring the Commons door to the king and his bodyguard of officers, who possibly include his London kinsman, William Griffith, buried near Piers at Westminster. King Charles dissolves Parliament and rules without it, wisely or not, until these *"troublous times"* lead to the outbreak of Civil War in 1642, when Piers's soldier brother William together with William's two sons will fight on the Royalist side. He will lose them both in battle but he himself apparently survives until the Restoration of King Charles II in 1660.

WILLIAM HERBERT, THIRD EARL OF PEMBROKE 1580-1630

The role of this man in the London life of Piers Griffith is tantalising. He acquires the Penrhyn Estate and Cochwillan for a time until purchaser John Williams can complete his financial transactions. Pembroke, a notorious moneylender as we have seen and a court drama producer, is a member of King James I's Privy Council, "the arena in which the pro – and anti – Spanish factions fought their bitter battles", writes Brian O'Farrell, his biographer. "In 1611 Pembroke had been appointed to this compact body of the King's advisers of about twenty councillors. But with the King's penchant for freely bestowing offices and titles, often without regard to merit, the Council soon grew in numbers and decreased in effectiveness. To counteract this tendency, a small informal group of the Privy Council composed of the King's most trusted advisers, met regularly as a standing committee. This élite group, known as the 'Cabinet Council', assisted the King with all his important business. Pembroke was an influential member of this inner circle.

"Debt is rife, the annual deficit is about £200,000, and King James I himself owes about £680,000." At this time, writers Ben Jonson, John Chapman, John Donne and George Herbert, are all patronised by Pembroke; another poet, Sir John Stradling who is a kinsman of Piers, has "strong political ties with Pembroke. Living in Glamorgan, he is a close neighbour of Pembroke's estates in Cardiff and is involved in Pembroke's overseas ventures. Stradling is a reasoned scholar 'courted by Camden for his learning', and, like many of the Pembroke circle, closely connected by marriage to the Third Earl's entourage. Stradling's *Epigrammatum* is dedicated to Pembroke".

For the last ten years of his life, 1620-1630, Pembroke "received no royal land grants," continues O'Farrell, "but nevertheless, was a net buyer rather than a seller of lands. In 1620 Pembroke purchased one of the largest estates in North Wales". This was from Piers Griffith's trustees as noted, with a down-payment of £1,000 and a settlement of £9,000 by 1622/3, an enormous sum in today's money. Millions.

When the extravagant King James, or rather Buckingham and Prince Charles ask for a contribution to funds, the Third Earl at first refuses, claiming that he is "far in debt … had undertaken his brother Montgomery's debts and for his cousin's, Sir William Herbert of Red Castle [Powys], and that he had enough to do to subsist." Ironically, as part of these inter-twining social circles, the Countess of Montgomery will be buried near Piers at Westminster Abbey the same year, in 1628.

Having been given huge land grants by King James, the biggest in 1617, of a manor and properties in Montgomeryshire and Pembrokeshire, the rich money-lending Third Earl of Pembroke spends his last years buying estates in Overchurch, Wiltshire, Kent, Cranbourne Chase, Cambridgeshire, Talybont in Glamorgan, Crown lands in Wiltshire for a bargain and other properties in Hertfordshire, Lancaster and Staffordshire. Clearly he was a man who benefitted from the misfortune of others. Yet it was Pembroke who perhaps enabled the Captain to move on, rather than plunge into debt, darkness and despair.

Both Pembroke and John Williams, as members of the House of Lords (Williams is the Speaker) dangerously clash with Buckingham. By 1625 Williams falls into disfavour with the new King Charles I who distrusts Buckingham anyway, but Pembroke keeps well in with the young Monarch and stays clear of the influential Buckingham. Perhaps Piers flits in and out of these singeing scenarios or else deems it wiser to keep clear. Perhaps he has his uses for such people, or else he uses them while he can.

Charles reviews the fleet at Plymouth in October 1625 and Piers may be imagined to be part of the entourage or faction pressing for a better navy. But in November, after the failed raid on Cadiz and a diplomatic break with France, King Charles is considered such a bad financial risk that the Amsterdam merchants refuse to take even the Crown Jewels as security.

Pembroke's kinsman, Sir Edward Herbert, Earl of Powys, the famous duellist, is Ambassador to France from 1619 to 1624, during which time he has serious bones to chew with both King James I and his successor King Charles I. In this context, it is possible that Piers may have been pressured by Herbert, his kinsman and his enemy, into some sort of double-edged secret mission or two.

THE PIRATE'S DOMAIN

This is where the quest for Piers Griffith finally ends, within view of the early morning sunlit scene he used to enjoy from his bedchamber window. Someone else may reach entirely different conclusions, or delve deeper and more expertly.

It has been suggested that he went off to London a broken man to escape his debtors and died a beggar on the streets of London. Either that or *cherchez la femme*.

The Penrhyn Estate was entailed on the male heir. Piers was in debt for mortgaging to people such as the Trevors, Middletons, Batemans, Thelwalls, Goodmans, Lloyds and the rich money-lending heiress, Mrs Price of Powys. The Trust who handled the Penrhyn sale included these names and others. The name of the Earl of Pembroke is writ large here. It was he who also bankrolled Piers's associates, including Sir Walter Raleigh up to 1616. Raleigh's wife Bess, being in possession of ravishing beauty and business flair, ran rings around Pembroke, the City financier who also funded Williams and Piers, whom she may have known personally. London was a small place. In social circles, you were either 'in' or 'out'.

The Earl of Pembroke held the Penrhyn Estate in name only until it was bought by Piers's cousin John Williams in 1623, a man whose dark, brooding presence is never far from the drama of Piers Griffith. Ironically, it is Williams (the now wealthy younger son of the nearby Cochwillan estate), who seems to have come to the rescue. Could he possibly be the "*false friend close to home*" Thomas Prys refers to in his subversive poem, "*To a Woodcock*"? The picture would fit.

Piers, having been valued in 1620 at almost 10 million pounds by today's money, now prepared his financial battle-plans. He must have shrewdly set aside money for his wife, daughters, grandchildren and himself, "as one does" was the suggestion. So he would have left for London with plenty of money in his pocket, even after settling his debts. Possibly, there were also gifts of money for his brother William and his family but certainly they were left to themselves at their Cororion estate. His sister Alys was probably no longer alive but she had one surviving son, Thomas who may also have been helped; someone must have paid for the boy's education at school and at Oxford, to study the Law, where he had a successful career. Would Uncle Piers abandon him after doing so much for him and his mother in days gone by? Piers's own coastal farm-house at Abercegin, guarding his hideaway creek, was also exempted from the Big Sale, his personal bolt-hole. He safeguarded the rights to the fish weirs at Aber Ogwen and Gorad-y-Gyt which he gave to the local people, including his tenants. He also secured, before he left, the rights and low rents of all his *cenedl*/people in great numbers, all listed in meticulous detail in the final dealings, so that the urbane, sophisticated John Williams and the canny local tenants knew exactly where they stood from the start.

How could Piers bear to face his last day at Penrhyn, one may wonder, when he bade farewell to all his good companions, some of whom wrote of their loss and longing? Once again he must have sailed away, or set off on horseback for the City as he had before, to Oxford or to the Court at Ludlow, along that familiar old London Road again, (now the A5), past Thomas Prys's Plas Iolyn and other landmarks rich in nostalgic layers of memory. Did he ever look back?

CITY LIFE

By 1624 Piers was perhaps ready to settle down at his London lodging to a good read of, say Captain John Smith's *The General History of Virginia*. Later in 1627 he might have browsed through Francis Bacon's *New Atlantis*, or before his death, *The World Encompassed by Sir Francis Drake* by Francis Fletcher. He would also have been familiar with Francis Bacon's *Historia Naturalis et Experimentalis* published in 1622, and with the '*First Folio*' of Shakespeare published under the patronage of friends in 1623. His old business associate, Lewis Roberts of Beaumaris, son of affluent shopkeeper Gabriel, will not publish *The Merchants Map of Commerce* until 1638 after Piers's death, but the volume was compiled from a lifetime's experience by his family and other traders like Piers.

In London, the former pirate probably remained in touch with his daughter Grace, possibly an occasional visitor to Court from her country home at Northwood Hall with her husband, Piers's son-in-law, John Bromhall, captain of the guard. Piers' sister-in-law Lady Catherine Hanmer, as noted, was also sometimes present at Court as companion to the unfortunate Queen Henrietta and as an eye-witness to key events. And his estranged wife, Margaret Mostyn Griffith was known to have a forgiving nature ...

One may speculate as to whether Piers shrewdly found a way of passing on land and revenues from possible overseas investments and holdings, for example in Barbados, his old, hard-won piratical stomping-ground. Who else would he hope to leave them to but his children, particularly a daughter like Grace and her well-established husband John Bromhall, a couple who may have tried to reunite the family? Surviving daughters Dorothy Edwards and Elizabeth Humphreys were already well set up near Wrexham and Chester. Neither was it impossible for Piers to keep in reserve the proverbial treasure-chest of jewels – gold, silver and pearls. One such unclaimed hoard was recently discovered hidden in a house in the merchant trading area of London, Cheapside. The Will of another 'John Bromhall of Cheshire', a London merchant and possibly a son or relative of Grace and John, shows that he left *"Estates in Barbados"*; but he may have achieved them independently of course. Another possible kinsman, or trading link was a *"John Bromhall of Zante"*, a real-life Merchant of Venice, who left property in both places with a considerable fortune. His Will shows that he lived under the same roof as his *"beloved blackamoor"* slave-girl to whom he left a large quantity of *"gold coins"*.

In London, despite the unhealthy miasma of the place, Piers could, if he wanted, reach out to a network of Welsh friends. There were many Court officials from Wales and other contacts working in government departments. There were constant travellers from Wales visiting the city, some of them reporter-poets, but the 'Old Companions' were dying off.

Piers Griffith probably and wisely kept in touch with John

Williams at his grand house in Deansgate, Westminster Abbey, perhaps even living in one of the grace-and-favour apartments there (or else renting one of the Middleton properties.) An Oxford man of wide interests, Piers surely visited the peaceful haven of the Westminster Library established by cousin John during his time as Dean, with Piers the retired Adventurer perhaps checking out some of his once precious Penrhyn books on all manner of learned subjects. Through Williams too, Piers may have come into contact with his contemporary, the 'Metaphysical' poet John Donne who was made Dean of St Paul's in 1621. The wide range of scientific images, passionate feelings and diverse reflections on life and death in Donne's complex verse and in his popular public sermons would have found a resonance in the enigmatic personality of Piers Griffith.

The rest of Piers's time in Stuart London was perhaps spent visiting friends, not to mention his London Griffith family who later recounted tales of his dynamic career; then there would have been pastimes such as dice, cards, taverns, visiting sports and theatres. Plays performed around this time reflected the milieu of the Stuart Age, a dark Jacobean underworld of uneasy times at Court with its veneer of politics and intrigue, like *The Devil's Law Case* in 1617 by John Webster, or *The Duchess of Malfi* performed in 1623 at the Theatre in Drury Lane before it was published in 1631. Another play of Webster's, *The White Devil*, 1612, was performed at the Red Bull in Clerkenwell and contained yet another famous court scene, like the plays of Ben Jonson who had Welsh friends as did Shakespeare up to his death in 1616. The diary of theatre manager and financier Philip Henslowe contains records of Webster's darker murder-mystery plays together with other popular Jacobean comedies of the 'citizen' kind, often mocking provincials and country cousins. Then there were the powerful performances of 'Revenge Plays' by Kyd, Marlowe and Middleton; dramas by Heywood and Dekker; and also the ever-popular comedies *Westward Ho!* and *Northward Ho!*, collaborations by Webster and Dekker appearing in 1604/5. All these would have had entertainment value for the likes of ex-pirates, Armada veterans and their roistering bloke-ish mates.

Then there was the notable and riveting *Famous History of Sir Thomas Wyatt* performed in 1607. In 1613, Webster's *Elegy on The Death of Prince Henry* was published, a poetic gem Piers would surely have identified with, as with Siôn Phylip's fine poem on the same subject. Webster and Welshman Thomas Middleton collaborated in their theatre production of *Anything for a Quiet Life* about 1621. Other plays were violent, lurid, sinister and blood-thirsty, featuring murders, Venetian courtesans, pandering servants, suspicious foreigners, corrupt magnificos, or shocked-and-dismayed English travellers abroad, as in Ben Jonson's *Volpone*, all scenarios recognisable to well-travelled, cosmopolitan gentlemen like Piers Griffith.

Our man could also be said to be a kindred spirit of his contemporaries like John Webster who "had the courage to face the fact that, though happiness and hope exist, they are indeed often less real than misery and death," wrote Dr Elizabeth Brennan, formerly of Bangor University and an expert on Tudor and Stuart Drama.

> *Integrity of life is fame's best friend,*
> *Which nobly, beyond death, shall crown the end.*

The theatre was the most popular entertainment of the day, meeting the intellectual, emotional and diversionary aspirations of contemporary society. For Piers such plays would have passed the time, at least. Shakespeare had his plays performed at the Theatre in Shoreditch; other playhouses were the Curtain, the Globe and the Rose, where recent archaeological research has revealed that London theatre-goers in Southwark and Bankside during Tudor and Stuart times, ate fast-food at the entertainments which often lasted all day into the evening: walnuts, hazelnuts, raisins, plums, cherries, dried figs and peaches; also sea-food: oysters, cockles, crabs, mussels, periwinkles, whelks, haddock, possibly even caviar/sturgeon. Another favourite seems to have been elderberry and blackberry pie. Fragments of glass goblets suggest that some audiences also quaffed wine with their picnics, like opera-goers today at Glyndebourne.

Fruit rinds found in the theatre areas of London imply that the wealthier members of the audience, seated in the galleries above, not standing in the yard, ate more expensive, imported foods – dried figs, peaches and raisins, probably from Spain, Portugal or France. The smoky atmosphere was open to the sky like a small football arena, which was just as well, for some people seem to have puffed at quantities of tobacco, imported from the New World but also grown later along the Thames. Pumpkins or possibly marrows, both originating in America, were being consumed but these and other products may have been eaten by local citizens too, as well as theatre-goers around the sites.

It is also clear that the Rose's stage area had been considerably refitted since 1592, during Piers' time, extending it right out into the auditorium, so that this 'standing-room only' area would be surrounding the stage on three sides, enabling the people who were watching to be more closely engaged with the actors dramatizing their stories in front of their very eyes. These would have been mainly the poorer people. Research confirms development in other theatres too, showing an important and vivid socio-political interaction centred on the London theatre during troublous times – a milieu which Piers and Thomas – their sons William and Ellis too – must have found lively and inspiring despite the fire risk, not to mention browsing through the fascinating bookseller stalls of St Paul's market or buying bronzed tobacco leaves displayed there in the sunlight.

This would have been the cultured and varied city life of *"Piers*

Griffith of London", Merchant Adventurer retired, one of the legendary sea-dogs of old. After the demise of Penrhyn *"and all its appurtenances"*, this was what perhaps drew him there when almost all else had failed including his marriage. Why not remove to London and "lose himself there", some have suggested, a sort of exile. The metropolis with its taverns and meeting-places was really quite a parochial place in Stuart times; and there, with good companions like Ifan Llwyd Sieffre who signed a document or two for him in *"Westcheape at the house of Thomas Middleton"* (for large financial transactions), he could still be respected as part of what remained of Elizabeth's Age of Piracy, his "brave new world".

ELEGY TO PIERS GRIFFITH OF PENRHYN 1628
by Thomas Prys of Plas Iolyn, pirate-poet

> Before now, it has been generally assumed throughout history
> That certain individuals are blessed from the start by Fate with
> > many gifts and privileges.
> Such a fortunate man would be sure to
> Live a long life on the inherited estate of his forefathers ...

Lines 7-32 follow, where the poet opens this vivid biographical poem with an obtuse preamble before he can bear to face the painful truth of his best friend's death by coming to the point. When he does, his verse is harrowing indeed. But before he can do that, he indulges in a rant against others who have lived absurdly long lives – Biblical patriarchs mainly from Adam to Methusaleh ... "two hundred ... eight hundred years ... even up to a thousand!"

This angry undertone dissolves into a melancholy if not morbid reflection on the transience of life, whether it be short or long, virtuous or not, useful or otherwise. The end is the same. The poet himself has already lost his son Ellis at twenty and at least three small children over the years, immortalised in several haunting elegies he has previously written for them. Now, within six years of his own end, Thomas Prys seems riven by fatalism. Has the news of Piers Griffith's sudden death in London led him finally to a crisis of faith?

The poem continues:

33   And in this day and age, take note,
       Forty is old, very old.
       There are not many who live beyond eighteen years old,
36   The ones who have a weak sickly look about them, they fall down
                                   dead.
       Everyone tries to escape from the Plague, everyone has faith but it
                 is all for nothing despite their efforts,
       In vain do they hope they will not die and follow their neighbours
                       to the grave.
       When the hour of painful sores and symptoms strikes
40   Here is my advice even to the strong, you may as well buy your
                        own shroud now.
       Even if you are blessed with riches
       You cannot extend your life-span, that is the plain truth of the
                            matter.
       Even an emperor with limitless wealth
44   Cannot be given any extra years more than a poor naked cripple.
       Fie on the uncertainty of life that is like the blink of an eyelid
       It barely lasts a second, fie on the world!
       This news has made me ill, chilled me to the bone, and to the
                       depths of my being,
48   This icy shock weighs on me like cold lead;
       I cannot breathe freely under this heavy burden,
       I am suffering such a shuddering pain that it is graven on my mind
                       and will never be gone.
       A wound has struck my breast
52   Like a cold steely blade cutting through my flesh, gone is all hope
                 of a warm, fine summer ahead.
       With a pain like this what is the point of living any more?
       Are not the vanities of this world meaningless?
       Those who in joyous youth are alive today,

56   Tomorrow will be found dead;
      And as for older people, they too
      Will have their thread of life brutally cut short.
      Whatever the pain, why must such suffering be endured without
                               relief?

60   What disease will befall us next, what will happen in the world in
                             future times?
      The news that reached here last night,
      God, give me your Grace, we have been utterly struck down by this.
      It marks the unexpected end of everything between us, *(our*
                      friendship, the purpose of life),

64   The hope of good harvesting this summer has now been
                      completely destroyed.
      The leading Deer of the herd was so precious in the eyes of holy
                         Jesus,
      When he saw Piers Griffith, that he chose him for his own;
      After surviving so many dangers, his life was suddenly wrenched
                    away from him

68   In London he went with his rosary beads to the grave.
      He departed when the thread of his life was cut (by the Fate
                      Lachasis)
      Tragically fallen from existence, when he was barely sixty years old.
      O place Piers the White Swan like a ship on his funeral carriage,

72   Let his body lie in his coffin amidst the choir in the chancel.
      Woe is me that I did not die at the same time, sad with longing is
                  the cold floor where he is buried,
      The mourners who stand in vigil around his grave are bereft, by
                   his grievous and sudden death,
      O that I had departed also to the same tomb that was fully ready to
                  receive him down yonder (in London)

76   Together sharing the same resting-place,
      That is how he departed this life, alas the stars,
      Like our two beloved children, virtuous and tender-hearted;
      Good William, vulnerable in youth

80   And Ellis who followed him.
      Our two brave heirs, exceptionally so,

We were the ones left behind.
We may as well follow them together the same way
84 From the cold troubles of this world to the same grave.

We two went overseas, it is doubtful whether we were right to do so,
You have to face the fact that death is an ever-present danger,
                                    when you sail across the seas,
Venturing far and wide you understand,
88 Risking our lives and wondering whether we would ever return
                                    safely here to dry land.
Even though a certain man of good family deserved in this day
                                    and age
To be appointed a leader over men in an important public office,
It depends on Fate whether the Wheel of Fortune turns in his
                                    favour
92 While others have their lives overthrown.

I am not going to dwell endlessly on the mysterious meaning of
                                    the web of life and drive myself mad,
Whatever is decreed to happen, will happen.
I do not know whether I am doing the right thing by writing this
                                    poem either,
96 Nor whether I am doing him justice in my telling of his life-story;
There was a time when he was alive, may he be blessed for that,
I am enduring anguished cries of sorrow even as I am composing
                                    this elegy for him.
Let us go to lead his Vigil, his funeral cortège,
100 Why should we not go? Is there anyone who is not in tears?
On the life of pure, good Jesus, the chosen one,
The pure breath of life within us and our Redeemer,
One thousand six hundred and twenty eight
104 It was, a record of time passing finely engraved in remembrance,
When Piers died – what worse tragedy could happen?
There is great mourning everywhere, for his death.
O God, more than for anyone else (especially for him),
108 Give light to his dear, generous face.

POETS' CORNER, WESTMINSTER ABBEY

This is where Piers Griffith now lies, beneath the cold stone floor but in good company: John Donne, Ben Jonson and the Earl of Oxford would have been drawn to eminent sea-captains and Armada heroes like Piers Griffith who had sailed with Drake and Raleigh. Curiously, they all knew the Dean, John Williams who, as the King's favourite, was a useful contact at Court. Donne, like Shakespeare, used many geographical images in his early experimental love poetry and in his religious works, with word-images from atlases, compasses, astronomy, anatomy, theology, mathematics and the Classics.

> *At the round earth's imagined corners, blow*
> *Your trumpets, Angels, and arise …*
>
> *Holy Sonnets (2), viii*

Many people went to St Paul's Cathedral for entertainment or enlightenment on Sundays and Saints' Days, to hear John Donne (1572-1631), now Dean, preach his famous sermons. In 1625 he preached before the new King Charles, the congregation possibly including Piers Griffith. It would be strange if such a learned man as Piers were not present there from time to time. If so, one sermon would have sounded ominous to him, preached at the turn of the very year in which the *"notable pirate"* died.

> *Any man's death diminishes me, because I am involved in Mankind;*
> *And therefore never send to know for whom the bell tolls; It tolls for*
> *thee.*
>
> *LXXX Sermons (pub. 1640), xlviii, 25 Jan. 1628/9.*

In his *Holy Sonnets*, there is something of the ring of swordplay in Donne's bold poetic challenge to the lurking presence of his Last Enemy: *"Death, thou shalt die,"* a duel from which one or the other would *"arise"* triumphant. The one-time libertine had become a devout man obsessed with his own oncoming death, even imagining his own autopsy and being reunited with his lost son, William, in eternity.

> *O eloquent, just, and mighty Death! ... thou hast drawn together all the far-stretched greatness, all the pride, cruelty, and ambition of man ...*
>
> A History of the World (1614.) Book V. Ch. vi, 12

wrote Sir Walter Raleigh (1552-1618), another charismatic figure whose life had a certain parallel with that of Piers Griffith.

Sir Walter's verse recalls his life of adventure (with Drake and others, with Piers):

> *... let the diving negro seek*
> *For gems hid in some forlorn creek;*
> *   We all pearls scorn*
> *   Save what the dewy morn*
> *   Congeals upon Each little spire of grass,*
> *   Which careless shepherds beat down as they pass.*

Before Raleigh was executed in Palace Yard in 1618 after his trial for supposed treason, he wrote, "*Gold values all, and all things value gold.*"

⚜

No evidence to date, other than the poetry of Thomas Prys, Sir Huw Roberts and others, offers an insight into the private beliefs of Captain Piers Griffith. A philosophical scepticism, perhaps. Clues from his lost library might well illuminate the truth; but we may speculate that such a heritage library would have included some interesting volumes, expensively bound and typical of the reading tastes of erudite Renaissance gentlemen like the Captain, his father and grandfather. Two former archivists of the Penrhyn Papers have suggested their general impressions of his interest in Alchemy, Astronomy, the Law, Religion, Business, Science, Agriculture and World Exploration.

Under the influence of his Catholic mother, Piers would have felt himself drawn to Catholic religious matters, for she was a learned woman and educated her own children as well as employing tutors. He may have been torn in theological terms between the Protestant and Catholic faiths, like his friend Sir Huw Roberts, married to a Catholic wife.

Piers's cousin Archbishop John Williams possibly commandeered the Penrhyn Library after the grand sale of 1620-23. He was a scholarly book-collector, with a strong theatrical flair. He knew Ben Jonson, Will Shakespeare, the Earl of Pembroke and the flamboyant, vain Sir Edward Herbert, duellist, author, well-travelled diplomat and poet. Have the elusive leather-bound volumes from Penrhyn really drifted into the enclaves of Westminster Abbey Library, a treasure-trove donated by former Dean John Williams? Some books are signed "Griffith", as the Archivist and the Librarian there attest, a hint at provenance.

Piers surely would have been familiar with the following reflective lines by Raleigh:

> *No mortal thing can bear so high a price*
> *But that with mortal thing it may be bought*
> *The corn of Sicil buys the western spice …*
>
> *French wine of us, of them our cloth is sought.*
> *No pearls, no gold, no stones, no coin, no spice.*
> *No cloth, no wine, of Love can pay the price.*

Like other Renaissance men, the poet was familiar with the same legendary, classical and scientific background as Piers. Raleigh seems also aware of the Ancient British history of our island home, of the supposed descent of the Welsh from Brutus the Trojan:

My Muse, indeed, to war inclines her mind;
The famous acts of worthy Brute to write:
To whom the gods this island rule assign'd,
Which long he sought by seas through Neptune's sight.

Curiously, the following verses were found inside Raleigh's personal copy of the Bible at the Gate-house of Westminster Abbey, a place associated with John Williams and with Piers Griffith who just might have passed by during the years before his death:

... such is Time, that takes on trust
Our youth, our joys, our all we have,
And pays us nought but age and dust.
Which in the dark and silent grave,
Shuts up the story of our days!

Thomas Prys had similar thoughts, a man like Piers who could inter-act richly between two cultures, English and Welsh in changing times. Inigo Jones began rebuilding the Banqueting House of Whitehall after a great fire in 1628, the year Piers died. Their associate, Shakespeare (died 1616) and ever the pivotal figure for all such vibrant men of the 'Hamlet Generation', had dedicated his *Phoenix and the Turtle* to Piers's Salusbury kinsman, poet John. Only such a dramatist could sum up the essence of Piers Griffith's shifting mercantile world:

... on the ocean
There where your argosies with portly sail,
Like signiors and rich burghers on the flood,
Or, as it were, the pageants of the sea,
Do overpeer the petty traffickers,
Would scatter all her spices on the stream,
Enrobe the roaring waters with my silks ...
                              I know Antonio

Is sad to think upon his merchandise.
                    The Merchant of Venice Act I, scene i

Poetic evidence for Piers Griffith, like other sung and unsung heroes, is part of a theme about retaining their Welsh identity within the concept of 'Britannia', the ancient Island of Britain, throughout the Tudor and Stuart reigns.

In London at least, Piers could keep in close touch with his Griffith family, particularly his loyal nephew William Griffith (sergeant-at-arms at the courts of King James I and King Charles I) and with his niece Margaret, William's wife. Both admired their valiant uncle Piers sufficiently to arrange to be buried near him at Westminster (as recorded in Henry Keepe's *Memorials*), William at St Peter's and his wife at St Margaret's.

The London family of Griffith thus ensured that Piers had an honourable funeral three days after he died on August 18, 1628. In these candle-lit, shadowy, echoing cloisters far from home, lay the body of Piers Griffith. The Dean, John Williams possibly arranged the service of this distinguished lord whose coffin rested with dignity *"amidst the choir"* in the chancel, as recorded in Thomas Prys's elegy. Also present may have been John Williams's prebendary, Theodore Price of Cors-y-gedol, a cleric who died a devout Catholic according to Williams, later Archbishop of York. Cousin John, by now the new owner of the Adventurer's estate, may even have given the address, followed (a fanciful notion perhaps) by a family tribute from nephew William, with music, psalms and ecclesiastical responses sung in good voice, with garlands of flowers for Piers Griffith in his coffin, the *"Swan of Penrhyn like a ship"*.

Daughter Grace and her husband, captain of the guard at the court of King Charles, may have been part of the cortège, as her father's body took its place amongst his associates in Poets' Corner, near his Sovereign Lady, Queen Elizabeth I on August 21, a month before his sixtieth birthday on September 25, 1628.

Epilogue

"A gentleman of considerable abilities in body and mind"

Henry Keepe's 1683 Footnotes to the Westminster Burial Entry for Piers Griffith read as follows, confirming the evidence of other sources:

> 'Second but eldest surviving son of Sir Rees Griffith, of Penrhyn, Kt. High Sheriff of Caernarvonshire in 1567, by his second wife, Catherine, daughter of Pierce Mostyn, of Talacre, Esq. who remarried Sir Thomas Mostyn, of Mostyn, Kt. He appears to have equipped and sailed a privateer at the period of the Spanish Armada, and afterwards cruised with Drake and Raleigh. In the time of K. James I, he was accused of piracy by the Spanish Ambassador who pressed the charge so strongly that he was compelled to sell his estate to obtain a pardon. He married Margaret daughter of Sir Thomas Mostyn, of Mostyn, Kt. by Ursula, daughter of William Goodman, of Chester, by whom he had three sons, William, Robert and Rees who all died young, and four daughters. See the burial of his kinsman Feb. 1636-7.'

Footnote No. 2 to the 1637 Burial Entries gives details of Piers Griffith's London family, who may have supplied the details of the story to the historian of Abbey records and memorials, or else John Williams may have recorded the details used later by Keepe:

'William Griffith. In his will dated 12 November 1633 and proved 22 February 1636-7 he directed to be buried in Westminster Abbey near his kinsman Peers Griffith, Esq. (see his burial 21 Aug. 1628.) He mentioned his sons, Charles, Thomas and Robert; his daughters, Katherine, Bridget, and Frances (who proved the will); his son-in-law Dr. Nixon; his brother-in-law Mr Maximilian Smythe; his brother Vachan; and his cousin Ellic Sutton ...'

'The Antiquities of St Peter's or the Abbey Church of Westminster' by Joducus Crull also record on page 258:

'More toward the West of this Isle [the south aisle] *on the same Wall, there is a Table of Arms placed to the Remembrance of Peeres Gruffith Esq; who died in 1628 with this Inscription:*

Here lieth the body of Peeres Gruffith Esq; Son and Heir to Sir Ree[s] *Gruffith, and Grandchild to Sir William Gruffith, Chamberlain of North-Wales, who died the Eighteenth of August, 1628.'*

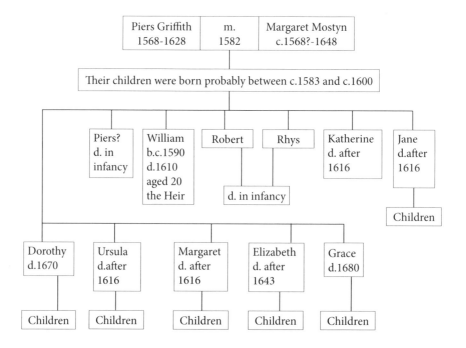

Margaret, Piers's wife, died in 1648 at Erbistock aged at least 80.

Catherine was alive in 1616, according to the Mostyn Papers.

Jane married a Salusbury and was alive in 1616.

Dorothy married William Edwards of Wrexham and died in 1670 aged about 80.

Ursula was alive in 1616 and married a Lloyd.

Margaret, daughter of Piers and Margaret, her namesake, married Humphrey Humphreys and was alive in 1616.

Elizabeth married John Humphreys and was alive in 1643; she may have been one of the youngest of the seven Griffith daughters.

Grace married John Bromhall of Northwood Hall, Wem in Shropshire, a *"Cornet at the Court of King Charles I"*. Grace died in 1680 aged at least 80; her husband died in 1672; she may have been the last child of Piers and Margaret Griffith, born about 1600.

After the death by plague of the last heir, William in 1610, no further children seem to have been born to the couple. Grace and John Bromhall of Northwood Hall had two sons: William who died in 1709 and Thomas who died in 1673, both in London where the family may have continued their connections; in any case Grace had grandchildren, with descendants to the present day, some in Wales.

Business people Dorothy and William Edwards had several children and grandchildren, likewise Jane, Elizabeth and Ursula. So Piers Griffith's family had a continuing time-arc from the Age of Chivalry through to the Age of Piracy and on to the Civil War, the Restoration and beyond.

POSTSCRIPT ON WILLIAM GRIFFITH, THE PIRATE'S BROTHER 1570 – C.1660

William Griffith of Llanllechid, aged 87, an old soldier to Queen Elizabeth, King James and the late king, hath several wounds and lost two sons in the King's service and is most considerable (i.e. worthy of consideration.)

(Source: File 1655 at the Gwynedd Archives, Caernarfon, ed. Norman Tucker.)

This reference to a William Griffith is also quoted in *A Nation Under Siege, The Civil War in Wales 1642-1648* by Peter Gaunt, *Cadw* Welsh Historic Monuments, London HMSO p. 77.

Could the words *"old soldier"* possibly refer to the brother of Piers Griffith? This is the kind of detail that can fascinate, a gem of history that lurks amongst dusty archival files.

In winter, "the humble warriors who had suffered for their king were not wholly forgotten," wrote Norman Tucker in his classic *North Wales and The Civil War* (Gee, 1958.) He added that in 1661, Caernarfon Justices ordered the former military command at Caernarfon Castle *'to call maimed soldiers before them to ascertain if they were worthy of relief'*. 37 names of persons were submitted, including the above entry for a *'William Griffith'*.

If soldier William of Penrhyn, brother of Piers, *was* born in 1570 as it is claimed (or perhaps in 1573/4) and if this is him, he had reached the impressive age of 91 (or 94) by 1661 after the Restoration of the grateful King Charles II. Not impossible. William's Will, like Piers's has proved elusive but there is a *'William Griffith of Penrallt, Bangor'* … Maybe not … or at 87 he was lying about his age.

After toughening out his military campaigns in Ireland, the Netherlands and elsewhere, not to mention during the Civil War, William Griffith may have simply settled down at home on his modest farm estate at Cororion. In old age, despite mourning his sons, he may have proved as invincible and as loyal as the poets had decreed for him as a boy, outliving his wife Ann Owen of Bodeon.

CONCLUSION

Pirate or Privateer?

Piers Griffith was a Merchant Adventurer, not a brigand. A man of honour, not a scoundrel. He was a diplomat, duellist, secret agent, poet and lover, voyager and discoverer. He mingled with the great heroic figures of the Elizabethan Age like Drake, Raleigh, Hawkins, Cumberland, Cavendish and others, in Plymouth and in London, where he witnessed all the glamour of Gloriana. He was acknowledged internationally as such and respected for his achievements. Literally a legend in his own life-time, his fame as a sea-captain lived on long after him, especially around his Penrhyn estate with its ancient princely and chivalrous traditions, where he had been lord of all he surveyed in a destiny of stardom until his downfall.

There were seafarers who spoke of his adventures, men and boys, and people who yearned for him, family who cast the spell of his galleon-crested seal in molten wax on parchment, kept his portrait, his signature, his poetry.

In his personal life he was son, grandson, brother and nephew; a youthful husband, father and grandfather; a popular uncle and friend; a respected lord and protector.

The cause of death is unknown but it seems to have been sudden: old wounds, or a coronary, plague, stroke, 'the sweating sickness', or even the latent onset of cancer after years of exposure to sunny climes, were suggestions from the medical profession.

He was part of Shakespeare's "restless world". He suffered the "slings and arrows of outrageous fortune" and bravely took arms "against a sea of troubles".

It may be said that Piers Griffith did for Wales what Sir Francis Drake and Sir Walter Raleigh did for England in the great Tudor Age of Queen Elizabeth I: dispatch a bloodthirsty, fanatical and merciless Armada of invaders from our shores; explore and map the natural world with its wonders of knowledge, ethnicity, environment, wealth; and establish essential trade for sea-farers providing a pioneering basis for the international communication we take for granted today.

His role-models were a generation of action-men with advanced, expanding ideas. He was willing to follow them to the ends of the earth. Yet like some, he may have over-reached himself with his

> *Vaulting ambition, which o'erleaps itself,*
> *And falls on the other (side.)*

Piers Griffith, a cosmopolitan man who shared in two rich, parallel cultures, remains one of the most charismatic Welsh Elizabethans of the Renaissance.

Timeline for Piers Griffith
1568 – 1628

1568   Born at Old Penrhyn Castle, North Wales as heir to the estate

1570?   Brother William is born. (Sister Alys was born c. 1566)

1570   Piers begins his education with private tutors

1580   His father Sir Rhys Griffith dies

        Valor/Valuation of Estate

        Alys marries W. Williams

1582   Piers's widowed mother, Lady Catherine marries her cousin Thomas Mostyn; at the same time, Piers aged 14, is married to step-sister Margaret Mostyn

1583/4-1586   Piers is sent away to sea for naval training

1586   He goes up to University College, Oxford but drops out about a year later

1587   The Babington Plot

        Cadiz, "singeing the King of Spain's beard"

1588   Piers equips his ship *Grace* and sails with his crew from Porth Penrhyn on 20 April, arriving at Plymouth on 4 May to join Drake, Raleigh and Cavendish against the Spanish Armada

        William Morgan's Welsh translation of the Bible is published

1590   Piers comes of age and starts mortgaging heavily

1599   He follows Drake and Raleigh and others on expeditions to the West Indies, raiding Spanish treasure ships

c.1583 – c.1610   The 10 children of Piers and Margaret are born: 3 sons and 7 daughters. Two infant sons die

1595-1597   Piers departs with Sir Francis Drake on the Commander's Last Voyage

1599   The Earl of Essex arrives at Mostyn Hall for his sea voyage to the Irish Wars and dubs Thomas Mostyn a Knight

1600   Piers brings the captured Spanish galleon *Esperanza* into Abercegin Creek

1601   The Essex Revolt, implicating many young officers from North Wales; Essex is executed, others fined

1603   Piers is arrested at Cork by Captain Plessington of *HMS Tramontana* and heavily fined as "a notable pirate"

Queen Elizabeth I dies

King James I ascends the throne and bans piracy, in diplomatic cahoots with the Spaniard, Don Diego Sarmiento da Acuña, Count of Gondomar

1605   The Catholic Gunpowder Plot against King James I

1608   Piers's mother Lady Catherine is now living apart from her husband Sir Thomas Mostyn

1609   Plague Year in London

1610   Piers's son and heir, William Griffith aged 20, dies in London of the 'Plague' with Ellis, son of Thomas Prys, during the summer celebrations for Henry, Prince of Wales

1611   The 'King James Bible' is published

1612   Death of Henry, Prince of Wales in London, another Plague Year

The Powys family launch into lawsuits against Piers

Duel with Lord Herbert's lawyer in Caernarfon backstreets

Piers is mortgaging heavily

Raleigh plans an expedition but King James is sceptical

1616   Sir Thomas takes Piers to Court for non-payment of the Griffith daughters' dowries and sends him to the Fleet Prison for debt

Margaret is banned from seeing Piers on pain of losing her allowance and leaves Penrhyn with her girls

Piers is desperately mortgaging again

1618   Sir Thomas dies and is buried at Whitford, Holywell after a long delay

Lady Catherine challenges his Will. Lawyer-heir Roger and "*incompetent*" brother Thomas are entangled in legal wrangles

Piers begins business dealings with trustees and Lord Keeper John Williams for sale of Penrhyn Estate

Sir Walter Raleigh is executed in Old Palace Yard, London

1620-21   More Estate dealings for proposed sale

The Third Earl of Pembroke has a finger in the pie

1622/3   Billionaire cousin John Williams pays full balance 'on account' and is the new owner of the Penrhyn Estate, including Cochwillan

1623-28   Piers is now "of London" in documents, immersed in city life

Is he involved in secret diplomatic missions?

Does he ever return to Wales and his last sea-front bastion at Abercegin Farm? Is he entirely alienated from his wife and family?

1628   One month before his sixtieth birthday, Piers Griffith dies in London on August 18 and is buried in Westminster Abbey on August 21, probably attended by his loyal London Griffith family

Is daughter Grace present? Pirate-Poet Thomas Prys, his cousin and friend since childhood, writes him a superb elegy.

Sources for the Poems

Chapter 2: Tudor Favourites

On Requesting a Cloak from Sir Rhys Griffith of Penrhyn / Gofyn Gown by Siôn Tudur. **Transcript Source**: Enid Roberts *Gwaith Siôn Tudur* (1980) i, no. LXXXVI.

Elegy for Sir Rhys Griffith / Marwnad Syr Rhys Gruffydd 1580 by Lewis Menai. **MS Source**: L1 122, 282. Transcript by Dr Dafydd Wyn Wiliam.

Elegy to Ifan Llwyd ab Ynyr, the Bodyguard / Marwnad Ifan Llwyd ab Ynyr, Gŵr y Gard o Faes-y-Porth, Llangeinwen 1591 by Huw Pennant. Transcript by Dr Dafydd Wyn Wiliam.

Chapter 4: Pirates at Plymouth

Pirates at Plymouth / Englynion ymryson rhwng Mr Pyrs Gruffydd a Mr Tomos Prys ym Mhlymwth ynghylch y môr.
MSS Sources: A – B 14964, 7b. B – B 14965, 166. C – Br 4, 293. Ch – N 8330, 434. D – M 112. 560. Transcript by Dr. Dafydd Wyn Wiliam.

Chapter 5: Drake's Last Voyage

To Mr Piers Griffith / I Mr Pyrs Gruffydd 1595 by Ifan Llwyd Sieffre. **MS Source**: Ll.G.C. Br 4, 292. Transcript by Dr. Dafydd Wyn Wiliam.

Praise Poem to Piers Griffith of Penrhyn and Margaret his Wife / Moliant Pyrs Gruffudd o'r Penrhyn a Marged ei wraig 1595 by Siôn Mawddwy.
Transcript Source: J. Dyfrig Davies *Astudiaeth Destunol o waith Siôn Mawddwy*. MA Thesis 1965, no. XXI.

Chapter 6: Spirit of the Age

Pirate Song of the Caribbean / Carol yr India / Bagad o Gymry by Lieutenant Richard Peilin.
MSS Sources: A – Ba(M) 3, A62 a Bl8. B – Brog 6, 132. C – J.G.D. 1, 42. Transcript by Dr. Dafydd Wyn Wiliam.

The Plague and the Rebellion of the Earl of Tyrone / Y Plâg a Chyfodiad Iarll Tirôn by Ifan Llwyd Sieffre 1599-1601.

Transcript Source: Sir T.H. Parry-Williams *Canu Rhydd Cynnar* (1932), no. 98.

Chapter 7: Coded Messages and Hidden Treachery

Ode to the South Wind / Cywydd i yrru'r deheuwynt i gyrchu Mr Pyrs Gruffydd y Prydydd o'r Penrhyn adref at ei wraig 1599 by Sir Huw Roberts.

MSS Sources: A – B 14885, 94 (ll. 1-36). B – B 14898, 101. C – Ba 5946, 364. Ch – C 64, 417. D – Ll 122, 30. Dd – M 162, 64. E – N 3487, 131. F – P 71, 13. Ff – P 184 (i), 60. Transcript by Dr. Dafydd Wyn Wiliam.

On Sending the Dolphin as Ambassador to Piers Griffith / I Yrru y llamhidydd yn gennad at Byrs Gruffydd by Thomas Prys.

Transcript Source: Wiliam Dyfed Rowlands *Cywyddau Tomos Prys o Blas Iolyn*, Ph.D. Thesis 1997, no. LXXX.

On sending the Blackbird to bring Piers Griffith home from the Sea / I yrru'r Fwyalch i nôl Pyrs Gruffydd adref o'r môr by Thomas Prys.

MS Source: Ll. 124, 407. Transcript by Dr. Dafydd Wyn Wiliam.

On Sending the Sea-Salmon as an Ambassador to Wales / I yrru y gleisiad oddi ar y môr yn gennad i Gymru by Thomas Prys.

Transcript Source: Wiliam Dyfed Rowlands *Cywyddau Tomos Prys o Blas Iolyn*, Ph.D. Thesis 1997, no. LXXXVII.

On sending the Woodcock as a Messenger to Piers Griffith / I yrru y cyffylog at Byrs Gruffydd by Thomas Prys.

Transcript Source: Wiliam Dyfed Rowlands *Cywyddau Tomos Prys o Blas Iolyn*, Ph.D. Thesis 1997, no. LXXXII.

I ddangos yr Heldrin a fu ar Domos Prys pan oedd ar y môr by Thomas Prys .

MSS Sources: A-BL Add 14872, 316v; B-BL Add 14876, 41v; C-BL Add 14965, 116r; B-BL Add 31058, 117v; E-Card 1.18, 183; F-Card 37, 138-9 + 143-4; G-Card 47, 61; H-Card 65, 92; I-Card 84, 287; J-He. 214r; K-LlGC 279D, 47; L-LlGC 3021F [=Mos 1], 86; M-LlGC 3031B [=Mos 112], 289 (rhan olaf yn eisiau); N-LlGC 3050D [=Mos 147], 606; O-LlGC 8330, 412; P-L1st – 133E, 651; Q-Pen 104, 41.

Wiliam Dyfed Rowlands *Cywyddau Tomos Prys o Blas Iolyn*, Ph.D. Thesis 1997, no. LXXIX.

Chapter 8: The Earl of Essex Visits Mostyn Hall

The Earl of Essex visits Mostyn Hall / Moliant Syr Tomos Mostyn pan wnaed ef yn Farchog gan Iarll Essex 1599 by Siôn Tudur.

Transcript Source: Enid Roberts *Gwaith Siôn Tudur* (1980) i, no. 27.

Chapter 9: The Esperanza

On Requesting a Spanish Galleon / I ofyn bad hir o Sbaen gan Wiliam Morys o'r Clenennau c.1600 by Thomas Prys.
MSS Sources: A-BL Add 14872, 322ᵛ; B-BL Add 14965, 119ʳ; C-LlGC 279D, 195; D-LlGC 3021F [=Mos1], 89; E-LlGC 3031B [=Mos 112], 302.
See also Wiliam Dyfed Rowlands *Cywyddau Tomos Prys o Blas Iolyn*, Ph.D. Thesis 1997.

Chapter 10: Pirate's Sunset

In the Days of Good Queen Bess / Bess yn Teyrnasu. Anon c.1603.
Transcript Source: Cylchgrawn Alawon Gwerin Cymru, Cyf. 4, 1953 / Journal of the Welsh Folk-Song Society 1953, Vol. 4.

Chapter 11: Plague Years

Elegy to William, the son of Piers Griffith of Penrhyn, and Ellis, son of Thomas Prys of Plas Iolyn / Marwnad 1610 by Sir Huw Roberts.
MS Source: Ll.G.C., P104, 15. Transcript by Dr. Dafydd Wyn Wiliam.
Elegy to William Griffith of Penrhyn and Ellis Prys of Plas Iolyn / Marwnad 1610 by Robert ap Rhys Wyn of Giler.
MS Source: P198, 17. Transcript by Dr. Dafydd Wyn Wiliam.
Elegy to Elis Prys and William Griffith of Penrhyn / Marwnad Elis Prys o Blas Iolyn 1610 by Thomas Prys.
MSS Sources: A-BL Add 38, 53ʳ; B-BL Add 14872, 202ʳ; C-B 52, 318; D-BL Add 14965, 136ʳ; E-BL Add 15010, 52ʳ; F-Brog 5, 273; G-Card 1.19, 106; H-Card 20, 196; I-Card 47, 129; J-Card 64, 319; K-Card 84, 1079; L-CM 5, 610; M-CM 40, 92; N-He 76ᵛ; O-L1st 16, 70; P-L1st 125, 76ᵛ; Q-L1st 133E, 806; R-LlGC 431, 71; S-LlGC 2633C, 51; U-783 22; V-LlGC 3021F [=Mos 1], 108; W-LlGC 3031B [=Mos 112], 370; X-Mos 144, 730; Y¹-LlGC 3050D [=Mos 147], 693; Y²-LlGC 3050D [=Mos 147], 723.
Wiliam Dyfed Rowlands *Cywyddau Tomos Prys o Blas Iolyn*, Ph.D. Thesis 1997, no. LXXIX.
Elegy to William Griffith of Penrhyn and Ellis Prys of Plas Iolyn / Marwnad 1610 by Huw Machno.
Transcript Source: Dr. Nesta Lloyd (ed.) *Blodeugerdd Barddas o'r Ail Ganrif*

ar Bymtheg, 79 / An Anthology of Seventeenth Century Poetry (Barddas, 1993.)

Chapter 12: The Pirate's Wife

Elegy for Mistress Ursula Mostyn / Marwnad Meistres Wrsle Mostyn 1578 by Wiliam Cynwal.

MS: Mostyn III.

Transcript Source: S. Rhiannon Williams *Testun Beirniadol o Gasgliad Llawysgrif Mostyn III o waith Wiliam Cynwal.* M.A. Thesis 1965, no. CX.

Chapter 17: Another Stab-Wound

Elegy to Lady Catherine Griffith Mostyn / Marwnad yr Arglwyddes [Catrin] Mostyn by Siôn Cain after 1618.

MS Source: Ll.G.C. p117, 51. Transcript by Dr. Dafydd Wyn Wiliam.

Elegy to Lady Catherine Griffith Mostyn / Marwnad yr Arglwyddes [Catrin] Mostyn by Sir Huw Roberts after 1618.

MS Source: Ll.G.C. p. 104, 11. Transcript by Dr. Dafydd Wyn Wiliam.

Chapter 18: Piers Griffith of London

Elegy to Piers Griffith of Penrhyn / Marwnad Pyrs Gruffydd o'r Penrhyn by Thomas Prys 1628.

Transcript Source: Dr. Nesta Lloyd (ed.) *Blodeugerdd Barddas o'r Ail Ganrif ar Bymtheg,* 69 / An Anthology of Seventeenth Century Poetry (Barddas, 1993).

NOTE: The Welsh text of the poems is collected in a separate volume: *Y Canu Mawl i Deulu'r Penrhyn,* edited by Dr Dafydd Wyn Wiliam. See Bangor University Archives and The National Library of Wales, Aberystwyth.

Tudor Family Tree 1485-1603 showing the connection to the Stuart Line

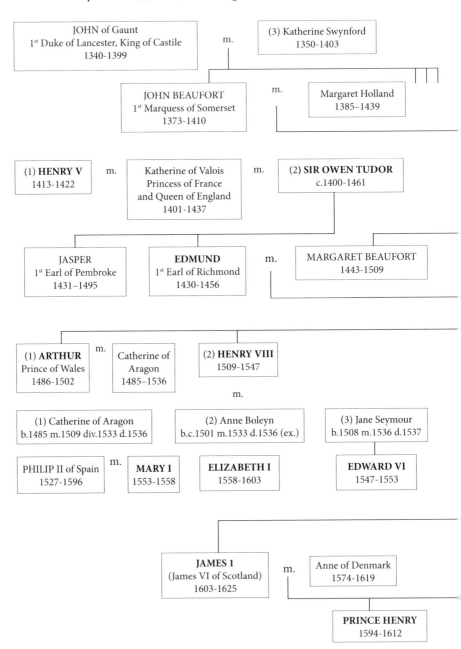

after 1603 and to the family of Lady Jane Grey

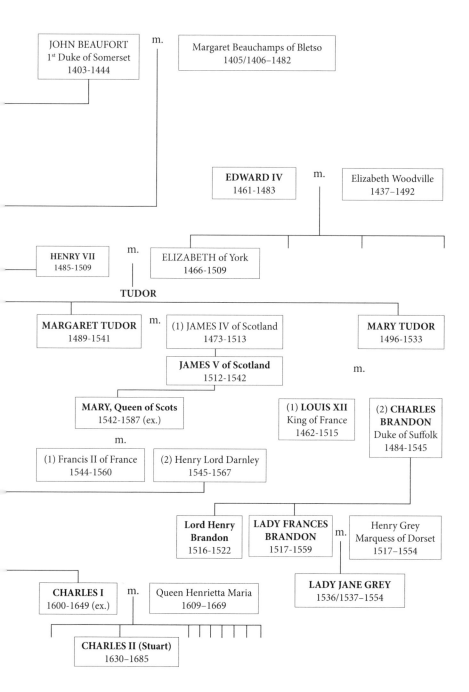

Manuscripts

THE MAIN PRIMARY SOURCES CONSULTED WERE:

The Penrhyn Papers, Mostyn Papers, and Baron Hill Papers at Bangor University Archives and at The National Library of Wales, Aberystwyth. Also studied were the Powys Papers at Aberystwyth. Other sources (piracy charges against Piers Griffith and his crew) are at the Public Records Office, Kew. The Papers of Thomas Prys of Plas Iolyn are at the British Library. Sources for the poetry are either in manuscript form, or are reliably transcribed in theses and in some published anthologies. Details are listed at the end of Part 2.

Mostyn 102 [1581/2, February 6]	(Marriage of Piers aged 14 to Margaret, also of Sir Thomas Mostyn to Lady Catherine Griffith)
Bangor/Mostyn 1340-1341 [1596]	(maintenance of Piers Griffith's son William Preferment of daughters)
Bangor 144 [8 May 1643] and 145	(Margaret Griffith and her daughters Dorothy, Elizabeth and Grace take action against Roger and Thomas Mostyn for non-payment of arrears. Signatures of Margaret Griffith, Piers's widow and daughters Dorothy Edwards, Grace Bromhall and Elizabeth Humphreys and their husbands, with the same wax seal bearing the imprint of a ship)
Bangor/Mostyn 6476	Folio 6A (Piers to Oxford)
NLW Aberystwyth 9054/584 [16 November 1608]	(Letter from Sir Roger Mostyn to Sir John Wynn of Gwydir complaining of the 'troubles' caused by brother-in-law Piers Griffith)

NLW 465/491 [1608]	Gwydir Papers (Sir Thomas Mostyn and his second wife Catherine are living apart)
Penrhyn Papers 134 Bangor [1616, Chancery]	(Sir Thomas Mostyn as grandfather takes Piers to Court for non-payment of his 7 daughters' dowries)
FRO D/M / 3734 [1617]	Flintshire Record Office (The Will of Sir Thomas Mostyn)
Bangor/Mostyn 129-131	(Lady Catherine challenges this Will in the Prerogative Court of Canterbury)
Bangor/Mostyn 114	(Sir Thomas and his son Roger sign a bond of £1,000 for Lady Catherine to 'enjoy Gloddaith' in her life-time)
Bangor/Mostyn 8837 [1580]	(The Will of Sir Rhys Griffith where Lady Catherine his widow is his executrix)
Mostyn 113 [1600, May 8]	
Mostyn 129 [1617/18, March 2]	
Mostyn 131 [1618, September 2]	
Bangor/Baron Hill 850 [27 November 1583]	(Piers is 15 years of age, signing a document on behalf of the Bulkeley family, an act of responsibility, as "Peirs Gruffyth" in the locality)

The Penrhyn Papers

Bangor/Penrhyn 87 [24 November 1598]   ("Perys Gruffyth")

Bangor/Penrhyn 111 [18 January 1601/2]   ("Perys Gruffyth")

Bangor/Penrhyn 93 [18 December 1603]   ("Perys Gruffyth")

Bangor/Penrhyn 112 [2 February 1603/4]   ("Perys Gruffyth")

Bangor/Penrhyn 114 [13 September 1610]   (various mortgages)

Bangor/Penrhyn 118 [1 August 1612]

Bangor/Penrhyn 120 [1 August 1612]

Bangor/Penrhyn 121 [30 December 1612]

Bangor/Penrhyn 122 [30 December 1612]

Bangor/Penrhyn 124 [30 December 1612]

Bangor/Penrhyn 125 [30 December 1612]

Bangor/Penrhyn 126 [1 February 1612/13]

Bangor/Penrhyn 123 [25 March 1612/13]

Bangor/Penrhyn 127 [25 March 1613]

Bangor/Penrhyn 129 [25 March 1613]

Bangor/Penrhyn 133 [4 December 1616]   (Re: Consortium with Evan Lloyd and Sir Richard Trevor as Trustees of Penrhyn. Piers signs as 'Perys Gruffyth' again)

Bangor/Penrhyn 134 [4 December 1616]

Bangor/Penrhyn 135 [4 December 1616]

Bangor/Penrhyn 136 [4 December 1616]

Bangor/Penrhyn 137 [3 September 1617]

Bangor/Penrhyn 151 [12 February 1622/3]   (Re: Coed Howel Dda in Cororion. Signature of brother William Griffith and of Piers Griffith)

Bangor/Penrhyn 152 [1 March 1622/3]   (Lord Keeper John Williams pays an additional £1,000 for Penrhyn with signature and seal: Perys Gruffyth "of London"). Business

transacted in London. See also
Calendar of Gwydir Papers pp
172-3.

Bangor/Penrhyn 159 [1 March 1622/3]
Bangor/Penrhyn 161 [1 March 1622/3]

MSS / DOCUMENTS

Bangor/Penrhyn 114 [13 September1610]
(Ifan Llwyd Sieffre [Evan Lloyd
Jeffrey] signs and stands as surety
for Piers three months after the
death of son William)

Aberystwyth NLW Peniarth 117, 51
(Elegy upon the Death of Lady
Catherine Griffith Mostyn by
Siôn Cain in the poet's own hand)

NLW Peniarth 104, pp 11-14
(Elegy upon the Death of Lady
Catherine by Sir Huw Roberts)

Bangor/Plasnewydd v, 1440 [14 June 1604]
and v, 1444 [14 June 1604]
(Piers is mortgaging to the
Bagnalls of Plas Newydd)

HCA 1, 1/5
HCA 1, 1/60
[1604-1618]
(High Court of Admiralty: Oyer
and Terminer Records, 1533 –
1834, Public Record Office, Kew,
London)

Penrhyn Further Additional Papers

PFA /1 /556 [20 December – year?]
(The Ludlow Letter)

PFA /1 /579 [1569]
(Piers is a year old)
PFA /1 /585 [18 June 1602]

POWYS CASTLE PAPERS

111 39 p.208	(Duel at Caernarfon)
Also MS	
[14 July 1612]	

Schedule of the Powys Castle
Deeds and Documents Vol. I

1134 [7 October 1580]	(Sir Rhys is dead and the Penrhyn Estate is assessed for the new heir, Piers, aged 12 - Wardship of Piers)

11131 [c. 1610]
and 11149,
9195 and 9555

11997-8 [18 June 1610]	(A date very close to the London Plague Tragedy)
9196, 9602, 11128 and 11131	(The Herberts again take Piers to Court)
11997-8	(Bill of Complaint against Piers Griffith)

*   *   *

NOTE:

I am grateful to Dr Wiliam for the following information:

"Born about 1520 Royal Bodyguard, Ifan ap Ynyr, 'the Hawk' is recorded in November 1546 amongst the serjeants-of-the-guard:

Reversion of 6d a day which Yevan Cotmore, (Coetmor) *of the Guard has, for Yevan Lloide* (Llwyd) *of the Guard. At suit of my lady of Suffolk …*

[Source: Letters and Papers Foreign and Domestic of the Reign of Henry VIII (1910), 227.]

"There was a *'Ieuan Lloyd, yeoman of the Chamber'*, who had land dealings in Newborough, Anglesey between 1553-58 (*An Inventory of the Early Chancery Proceedings Concerning Wales*, 1937, 10. ed. E.A. Lewis.) Also a *'Jenn lloyd ap ynyr'* appears on the Rent Roll for the Menai Strait area in 1574 (NLW Carreg-lwyd; 2073.) *An Inventory of the Ancient Monuments in Anglesey* (1937)

328

92 records a half-faded memorial inscription inside the Parish Church of Llangeinwen to *'Evan ... er,'* (*evan ab Yner*, 1591.) His wife was probably Siân, daughter of Maredudd ap Hywel of Llangeinwen, a man who is listed amongst the men of Menai between 1547 and 1573. (P.A.C.F. 72; Ll.C.B. 13969) although who he was, no one knows, not even P.C. Bartrum: *Welsh Genealogies AD 1400-1500 (1983) Llywarch ap Brân* 2 (A)." (D.W. William, 2011.)

BANGOR

MS Ba 7366 – John Thomas, Beaumaris: *Hanes Môn* (A History of Anglesey.)

MS Bangor [Additional 1211] and NLW 19075E, 1769 – Poetry translations by W. Williams and R. Davies, Curate of Llandegai, editor of the *Myvyrian* MS of *Brut y Tywysogion.*

Port Books PRO. 'K.R.'	E 1, 329/4
	E 1, 333/5&9
Esperanza	E 1, 335/14 1, 337/12 1,347/9&10
	E 1, 330/5, 12&16
	E 1, 333/3 1,335/6

THOMAS PRYS

M.A. Thesis 'Barddoniaeth/The Poetry of Thomas Prys, Plas Iolyn' by Wiliam Rowland, Porthmadog, NLW 1911

Mostyn 112
NLW/1998/635/1 Ph.D. Thesis by Wiliam Dyfed Rowlands 'Cywyddau Tomos Prys o Blas Iolyn' 1997.

Family Tree of Thomas Prys from
- Heraldic Visitations of Wales (Lewis Dwnn) Vol. II., pp. 159, 344
- Harleian MS 1969, p. 420
- His Will
- Elegy to Thomas Prys by Huw Machno (Dr Nesta Lloyd ed. Barddas).

A – BL Add 14872, 238^r;
B – BL Add 14898, 17^v;
C – BL Add 14965, 35 ^{r};

12, 230
14, 872

14873, 14874, 14876, 14879, 14881, 14896, 14898, 14965, 14976

NLW Addit. MSS. British Museum
MSS Mostyn MSS 112, 129, 130, 144, 147, 161, 162
Peniarth MSS 91, 93, 104, 119, 124, 151, 184, 195
239, 241
Llanstephan MSS 16, 42, 122, 123, 124, 125, 133, 166,
Cwrtmawr 10, 17, 19, 22,
Cardiff 12, 19, 20, 26, 43, 47, 48, 64, 65, 66

WILLS

Sir Rhys Griffith (two Wills)

Sir Thomas Mostyn

his daughter Margaret Mostyn Griffith

Dorothy Edwards, (and documents relating to her properties) daughter of Piers and Margaret Griffith

Grace Bromhall (and Goods and Chattels) daughter of Piers and Margaret Griffith. The Will of her husband, John Bromhall, has not been found

Thomas Prys

Lady Catherine's Will (circa 1618 if it exists) has not yet come to light, nor has the Will of Piers Griffith (d.1628)

John Bromhall (1)

John Bromhall (2)

Bibliography

Alford, S. (2012). *The Watchers: A Secret History of the Reign of Elizabeth I.*

Andrews, K.R. *Drake's Voyages: A Re-assessment of Their Place in Elizabethan Maritime Expansion.* Plymouth and London.

Anglo, S. (1969). *Spectacle, Pageantry, and Early Tudor Policy.* Oxford.

- ____ (1959). *English Privateering Voyages to the West Indies 1588-1959,* The Hakluyt Society, Second Series CXI. Cambridge.

- ____ (1944). *Elizabethan Privateering: English Privateering during the Spanish War 1585-1603.* Cambridge.

Ariès, P. (1962). *L'Enfant et la vie familiale sous l'ancien régime.* Paris.

- ____ *Centuries of childhood.* New York.

Armada (1988). *Royal Armada, 400 Years.* Greenwich.

Bawlf, S. (2003). *The Secret Voyage of Sir Francis Drake.* New York and London.

Bebb, W.A. (1939). *Cyfnod y Tuduriaid.* Wrecsam a Chaerdydd/Cardiff.

Beck, J. (1969). *Tudor Cheshire.* Chester and London.

Beer, A. (2004). *Bess: The Life of Lady Raleigh, Wife to Sir Walter.* London.

Bernard, G.W. (2010). *Anne Boleyn: Fatal Attractions.* Newhaven and London.

Book of Household Ordinances.

Bossy, J.A. (1975). *The English Catholic Community, 1570-1850.* London.

- ____ (2001). *Under the Molehill. An Elizabethan Spy Story.* Newhaven and London.

- ____ *Giordano Bruno and the Embassy Affair.*

Bowen, D.J. (2002). Y Canu i Gwilym ap Gruffudd (m. 1431) o'r Penrhyn a'i fab Gwilym Fychan (m. 1483), *Dwned,* 8. Aberystwyth.

Bradford, C.A. (1935). *Blanche Parry, Queen Elizabeth's Gentlewoman.* London.

Brereton, T. (2003). *The Book of Welsh Pirates and Buccaneers.* Sain Tathan.

Y Bywgraffiadur Cymreig / The Welsh Dictionary of National Biography.

Butler, J. *Lord Herbert of Chirbury 1582-1648.* (1989). *An Intellectual Biography*: Studies in British History Vol.16. Lampeter, Lewiston and Queenstown.

Calais Chronicle (1846). *The Chronicle of Calais in the Reign of Henry VII and Henry VIII to the Year 1540,* ed. J.G. Nicholls. Camden Society, 1st. Series, 35. London.

Camden, W. (1637, 1695, 1701). *Britain/Britannia.* London.

Carr, A.D. *The Mostyn Family and Estate 1200-1642*, Ph.D. Thesis, University of Wales, Bangor 1975/6.

- ____ (1982). *Medieval Anglesey*. Anglesey Antiquarian Society.

- ____ 1995). *Medieval Wales*. Macmillan Basingstoke.

Chambers, A. (1988). *The Life and Times of Grace O'Malley c. 1530-1603*. Dublin.

Cook, J. (2004). *Pirate Queen:* The Life of Grace O'Malley, 1530-1603. Dublin.

Cooper, J. (2011). *The Queen's Agent: Francis Walsingham at the Court of Elizabeth* I. London.

CSPD (1856-7). *Calendar of State Papers, Domestic:* Edward VI, Elizabeth I, and James I, 12 vols. London.

CSPD (1601-3). *Calendar of State Papers, Domestic,* p. 293.

CSPF, *Elizabeth* (1863-1950). *Calendar of State Papers, Foreign: Elizabeth,* 23 vols. London.

Davies, C. (1995). *Welsh Literature and the Classical Tradition.* Cardiff.

Davies, J. (1990). *Hanes Cymru.* London

- ____ (1993). *A History of Wales.* London.

Dewhurst, J. (1984). 'The Alleged Miscarriages of Catherine of Aragon and Anne Boleyn,' *Medical History,* 28.

Dodd, A.H. (1968). *A History of Caernarvonshire, 1284-1900.* Denbigh.

Doran, S. (2008). *The Tudor Chronicles.* Fully Illustrated. Quercus.

DWNED: *Cylchgrawn hanes a llên Cymru'r Oesoedd Canol,* ISSN 1361-306X (Journal of Welsh medieval historical and literary studies) gol/ed. A. Cynfael Lake & Bleddyn Owen Huws.

Eames, A. (1973). *Ships and Seamen of Anglesey.* Denbigh.

- ____ (2001) *Sea, Power and Sir Gaernarfon 1642-1660, Maritime Wales,* 22. Caernarfon.

Ellis, H. (1824-46). *Original Letters, Illustrative of British History,* 3 series, 11 vols. London.

Ellis, T.P. (1933). *The Catholic Martyrs of Wales. 1535-1680.*

Ellis, S.G. (1985). *Tudor Ireland: Crown, Community and The Conflict of Cultures, 1470-1603).* London.

The New Encyclopaedia Britannica.

Evans, E.V. (1916). 'Welsh Adventures to the West Indies in the Sixteenth Century', *Y Cymmrodor,* XXVI. London.

Fenton, R. *Tours in Wales,* ed. J. Fisher. London 1917.

- ____ (2011) *Sister Queens: Katherine of Aragon and Juana, Queen of Castile.* London.

Fisher, J. (1909). Alumni Oxoniensis.

- ____, Alumni Cantabrigiensis.

Fox, J. (2007). *Jane Boleyn, The Infamous Lady Rochford*. London.

- ____ (2011). *Sister Queens: Katherine of Aragon and Juana, Queen of Castile*. London.

Fraser, A. (1969). *Mary, Queen of Scots*.

- ____ (1992). *The Six Wives of Henry VIII*. London.

- ____ (1996). *The Gunpowder Plot: Terror and Faith in 1605*. London.

- ____ *Cromwell: Our Chief of Men*. London.

- ____ *King Charles II*. London.

- ____ *The Weaker Vessel: Woman's Lot in Seventeenth Century England*. London.

Geiriadur Prifysgol Cymru/University of Wales Dictionary.

Griffith, J.E. *Pedigrees of Anglesey and Caernarvonshire Families*. Denbigh.

Gruffydd, K.Ll. (2004). Piracy, Privateering and maritime Wales during the later Middle Ages, 1 & 2. *Maritime Wales 34, 25*. Caernarfon.

Gruffydd, R.G. (1972). *Argraffwyr Cyntaf Cymru: Gwasgau Dirgel y Catholigion adeg Elisabeth/The Secret Catholic Press in Wales*. Caerdydd/Cardiff.

Griffith, W.P. (2001). 'Tudor Prelude', *The Welsh in London, 1500-2000*, ed. Emrys Jones. Cardiff.

Guy, John. (1988). *Tudor England*. Oxford.

- ____ (1995). *The Reign of Elizabeth I: Court and Culture in the Last Decade*. Cambridge

- ____ (2000a). *The Tudors: A Very Short Introduction*. Oxford.

- ____ (2000b). *Thomas More*. London and New York.

- ____ (2004). *'My Heart is My Own': The Life of Mary Queen of Scots*. London.

- ____ (2008). *A Daughter's Love: Thomas and Margaret More*. London and New York.

- ____ (2000). *The Tudors: A Very Short Introduction, as in the 1984 Oxford Illustrated*

History of Britain. Oxford.

Hakluyt, R. (1926). *The Principal Navigations Voyages, Traffiques & Discoveries of the English Nation*, Everyman Series, 7. London.

Haigh, C.A. (1993). *English Reformations: Religion, Politics and Society and the Tudors*. Oxford and New York.

Harknoll, P. (1968). *A Concise History of the Theatre*. London.

Harris, B. (2002). *English Aristocratic Women 1450-1550: Marriage and Family, Property and Careers*. Oxford and New York.

Hepburn, F. (1997). 'Arthur, Prince of Wales and his Training for Kingship,' *The Historian*, 55 (1997).

Howell, T.B. (1816). *A Complete Collection of State Trials and Proceedings for High Treason and other Crimes and Misdemeanours from the Earliest Period to the Year 1783*, 21 vols. London.

Hunter, J. (2003). *Elizabeth's Spymaster: Francis Walsingham and the Secret War that Saved England*. London.

Hughes, C. *Catrin o Ferain*. (1975). Gomer, Llandysul (Fiction/Novel).

James, C. (2007). Llenwi Pig y Pelican: "Hanes Bagad o Gymru a Aethant yn Amser y Frenhines Elsbeth . . . ir Gorllewyn India", *Llên Cymru 30*.

Johnston, D. (2005). *Llên yr Uchelwyr: Hanes Beirniadol Llenyddiaeth Gymraeg 1300-1525*. Caerdydd/Cardiff.

Jones, D. Glyn (1999). *Un o Wŷr y Medra: Bywyd a Gwaith William Williams, Llandygái (1738-1817)*. Denbigh.

Knights, L.C. (1937). *Drama and Society in the Age of Jonson*. London.

Lake, A. Cynfael (2004). *Gwaith Lewys Morgannwg*. I, II Aberystwyth.

Laver, J. (1969). *Costume and Fashion: A Concise History*. London.

Lee, S. ed. *The Autobiography of Edward, Lord Herbert of Cherbury 1582–1648*.

Lewis, E.A. (1927). *The Welsh Port Books 1550-1603*. Aberystwyth and London.

Lindsay, J. *The Pennants of Jamaica 1665–1800, I & II*. Transactions of the Caernarvonshire Historical Society, 1982 and 1983.

Lloyd, J.E. (1920). *John Thomas: A Forgotten Antiquary*. Journal of the Welsh Bibliographical Society, Vol. II, no. 4 (May 1920).

Lloyd, N. (1993). *Blodeugerdd Barddas o'r Ail Ganrif ar Bymtheg*, ed. / Anthology of Welsh Seventeenth Century Verse. Llandybïe.

Lloyd-Morgan, C. (1996). Elis Gruffydd a Thraddodiad Cymraeg Calais a Chlwyd, *Cof Cenedl, XI* pp. 29-58.

Mendelson, S. and Crawford, P. (1998). *Women in Early Modern England, 1550-1720*. Oxford and New York.

Meirion, D. (2005). *Morladron Cymru / Welsh Pirates*. Talybont.

McDermott, J. (2009). *Martin Frobisher: Elizabethan Privateer*. Newhaven and London.

Miles, E. (2002). *Y Darlun o blant yn llenyddiaeth Gymraeg yr Oesoedd Canol ./ Children in Welsh Medieval Literature*, M.Phil. Swansea.

Montague, C. (2009). *Pirates and Privateers*. Eastbourne.

Mostyn, Rt. Hon. Lord, and Glenn, T.A. (1925). *History of the Family of Mostyn of Mostyn*. London.

Norman, A. (2002). *Sir Francis Drake: Behind the Pirate's Mask*. Devon.

Norris, Herbert (1997). *Tudor Fashion and Costume*. New York.

O'Farrell, B. (2011). *Shakespeare's Patron: William Herbert, Third Earl of Pembroke 1580-1630, Politics, Patronage and Power*. London and New York.

Owen, G.D. (1964). *Elizabethan Wales: The Social Scene*. Caerdydd/Cardiff.

The Oxford English Dictionary of National Biography.

Parry, T., (1962). *The Oxford Book of Welsh Verse*, ed. Oxford.

Parry-Williams, T.H. (1932). *Canu Rhydd Cynnar* / Early Welsh Free Verse. Caerdydd/Cardiff.

Pennant, E.D. (1985). *The Welsh Families of Penrhyn*. Bangor.

Pennant, T. *History of the Parishes of Whitford and Holywell*.

- _____ *Tour in North Wales*.

Pennell, J. and Thomson, H. (1919). *Highways and Byways in North Wales*. London, Madras, Melbourne, New York and Toronto.

Penrhyn Castle *Guidebook* (2010). The National Trust.

Prockter, A. and Taylor, R. (1979). *The A-Z of Elizabethan London*. London.

[Progresses of Elizabeth I](1788-1805). The Progresses, and Public Processions of Queen Elizabeth, ed. J. Nichols, 3 vols. London.

Rees, E.A. (2001). *Welsh Outlaws and Bandits, 1400-1603*. Birmingham.

Roberts, E. (1990). Gwraig Orau o'r Gwragedd. Caernarfon.

- _____ (1980). *Gwaith Siôn Tudur I, II*. Caerdydd/Cardiff.

Roberts, O.E. (1980). *John Dee 1527-1608*. Caernarfon.

Robinson, J. (2002). *Pandora's daughters: The Secret History of Enterprising Women*. London.

Robinson, W.R.B. (2002). 'Prince Arthur in the Marches of Wales, 1493-1502' in *Studia Celtica*, 36.

Rowland, W. (1911). Tomos Prys o Blas Iolyn, M.A. Aberystwyth.

- _____ (1964). *Tomos Prys o Blas Iolyn, 1564-164*. Caerdydd/Cardiff.

Rowlands, W.D. (1998). *Cywyddau Tomos Prys o Blas Iolyn*, Ph.D. Aberystwyth.

Royal Armada 400 Years (1988). National Maritime Museum, Greenwich.

- _____ Nicholas Rodger; *The English Fleet*

- _____ Ian Thompson; *The Invicible Armada*

- _____ Glanmor Williams; *The Most Powerful Monarch in Christendom*.

Royal Book (1790). *A Collection of Ordinances and Regulations for the Government of the Royal Household*. Society of Antiquaries, London.

Scarisbrick, D. (1995). *Tudor and Jacobean Jewellery*. London

Skelton, J. (1529). *An Armorie of Birds*.

Shulman, N. (2011). *Craven with Diamonds: The Many Lives of Thomas Wyatt, Courtier, Poet, Assassin, Spy.* London.

Siddons, M. (1991). *The Development of Welsh Heraldry* (Sources: Wright's *Book of Knights* 1485-1569 and MS BL 46354, f.92 for the Penrhyn Arms).

Starkey, D.R.   (1987a). 'Court History in Perspective', In D.R. Starkey et al., eds., *The English Court from the Wars of the Roses to the Civil War.* London and New York.

- _____ (1987b). 'Intimacy and Innovation: The Rise of the Privy Chamber'.

- _____ 2000). *Elizabeth: Apprenticeship.* London.

- _____ (2004). *Six Wives: The Queens of Henry VIII.* London and New York.

- _____ (2008). *Henry, Virtuous Prince.* London.

Steegman, J. (1957). *A Survey of Portraits in Welsh Houses: Volumes I & II*

Stewart, A. (2004). *The Cradle King: A Life of James VI and I.* London

Stow, John (1956). *Stow's Survey of London.* Ed. H.B. Wheatley. London.

Strong, R.C. (1983). *Artists of the Tudor Court. The Portrait Miniature Rediscovered, 1520-1620.* London.

- _____ 1963). *Portraits of Queen Elizabeth I.* London.

- _____ (1977). *The Cult of Elizabeth: Elizabethan Portraiture and Pageantry.* London.

Thomas, D. (2007). *Hen Longau Sir Gaernarfon* / Old Ships of Caernarfon. Llanrwst.

Thomas, G.C. (1988). *A Welsh Bestiary of Love.* Dublin.

Thwaites, G., Taviner, M., and Gant, V. (1997). 'The English Sweating Sickness, 1485-1551', *New England Journal of Medicine*, 336.

The English Sweating Sickness, 1485-1551: A Viral Pulmonary Disease? *Medical History*, 42.

Tucker, N. *North Wales and The Civil War.*

- _____ (1948) *They Fought in North Wales.* Colwyn Bay.

Turvey, R. (2005). *The Treason and Trial of Sir John Perrot.* Llandybïe.

Vives, J. (2000). *The Education of a Christian Woman: A Sixteenth Century Manual.* Edited and translated by Charles Fantazzi. Chicago and London.

Watkin Jones, E. (1950). Pyrs Gruffydd o'r Penrhyn, *Crynhoad Haf* / Summer Vol, and *Llafar Gwlad*, 8.

Weir, A. (1998). *Elizabeth, the Queen.* London.

Woodward, J. (1997). *The Theatre of Death: The Ritual Management of Royal Funerals in Renaissance England 1570-1625.* Woodbridge.

Williams, D.J. (1942). *Anturiaethau Morwyr Cymru.* Aberystwyth. (Maritime Adventures).

Williams, E.R. (1915). *Some Studies of Elizabethan Wales, The Welsh Outlook*. Newtown.

Williams, G. (1993). *Renewal and Reformation Wales c. 1415-1642*. Oxford.

Williams, G.A. (2000). Beirdd Cymru a'r Goron / Welsh Poets and the Crown, *Cof Cenedl XV*, ed. G.H. Jenkins, Llandysul.

Williams, N. (1975). *The Sea Dogs: Privateers, Plunder and Piracy in the Elizabethan Age*. London

- ____ (1972). *Elizabeth I*. London

Thomas, J. & Williams, W. (1764, 1802). *Observations on the Snowdon Mountains and a Genealogical Account of the Penrhyn Families*. London.

Wynn, J. (1927). *History of The Gwydir Family*, ed. J.G. Jones. Llandysul.

Every effort has been made to contact the agents and publishers of any quoted extracts which have been fully acknowledged within the context of this book and listed in the Bibliography.

❧❦❧

Background Books for Children

Brimacombe, P. (2008). *Elizabethan England*. Linked to Curriculum Stage 3. Illustrated. Jarrold.

Courtauld, S.   *The Queen's Pirate – Francis Drake*
    Illustrated by Vincent Dutrait, Usborne Young Reading Series
    Three. History Consultant: Michael Turner, Founder of the Drake
    Exploration Society.

Ed. Harrison, J., Coppendale, J., Head, H. (2002). *Tudors and Stuarts: British History Series*. Illustrated, Kingfisher, London.

Macdonald, F. (2009). *Tudors: Children in History Series*. Illustrated. Franklin Watts. London and Sydney.

Purkis, S. (2007). *Tudor Children: Four real children, four different times*. *Real Lives* series. Illustrated. Black. London.

Warburton, N.   *Sing for Your Supper*. Illustrated by Martin Cottam. Oxford
    University Press, Tree Tops Series. Stage 14, More Stories A.

Website
Institute of Historical Research, University of London: www.ihr.sas.ac.uk
Author: www.tudors.org

Acknowledgements

My gratitude goes to Marian Griffith for her wizardry at the computer, her photography, patience and professional advice. I am indebted to Dr Dafydd Wyn Wiliam for unlocking the complex meanings of the poems as a basis for my translations, and for guiding me through countless Rent Rolls, documents and manuscripts; also to Dafydd Glyn Jones for his scrutiny.

Many thanks to the staff at:
> The Archives of Bangor University
> The National Library of Wales, Aberystwyth
> The Royal Commission on the Ancient and Historical Monuments of Wales, Aberystwyth
> Cardiff Free Library
> Gwynedd Archives
> Bangor City Library
> Lena Sheil at the Chester City Library
> Flintshire Archives, Hawarden
> Greenwich Maritime Museum
> London Metropolitan Archives
> Plymouth Maritime Museum
> Shrewsbury Town Archives
> *Cadw* at Cardiff
> English Heritage
> Christine Reynolds at The Muniment Room and Library at Westminster Abbey
> The British Museum Exhibition of 'Shakespeare's Restless World' 2012
> Dublin City Archives and Art Gallery
> The Bridgeman Art Library
> Jesus College, 'Hart Hall'/Hertford College and University College, Oxford
> The Verger at the Archives of St. Giles-in-the-Fields
> The Worshipful Society of Apothecaries of London.

Thanks are also due to the following:

Bethan Mair

Richard Douglas Pennant, his brother, Edmond Douglas Pennant of the Penrhyn Estate and their agent Emyr Hughes, who found Alys's house

Lord Powys at Powys Castle

Richard Thomas, Land Agent to Lord Mostyn, PhD student Shaun Evans of the Mostyn Estate and house-keeper Mrs Eirwen Wilson

Sonia Edwards

Mr Ronald Morris,

Dr Ceridwen Lloyd-Morgan

Eirionedd Baskerville

Mr & Mrs Rothwell-Hughes for their inspiring illustrated lectures on Welsh Piracy

Professor John Guy of Clare College, Cambridge

Julia Fox

Dr Mark Nicholls, President and Librarian of St John's College, Cambridge, for his lecture on Archbishop John Williams at Llandegai Church

Dr David Starkey

Rosemary Wynne-Finch and the late Colonel Wynne-Finch of Cefnamwlch, a descendant of Huw Griffith of the East India Company

Michael Powell Siddons of the College of Arms

Aled P. Jones of the BBC

Simon Vilamoura of the University of Santiago di Compostela, Galicia, Spain

Patricia Byron for her knowledge of Tudor Alchemy and Astrology

Eryl Hold

Head Chef Hywel Griffith

Dr Jack Dubberley for his medical knowledge

Mrs Bethan Williams for local details on Hafoty, Llanddona and Cwrt Mawr, Beaumaris

Jill Webb-Jones, Deliah Jones and Pauline Jones for their reader-friendly comments

Ann Williams, Rhian and Gwenan Llewelyn Jones at Llandegai Church

Lawyer Cathryn Williams and her aunt Gwyneth Innes, descendants of Anglesey seafarers and great fans of Frobisher

Will Humphreys for sharing this quest with me around numerous pirate haunts, for his insights into the characters and for his love and generosity.

Finally I should like to thank my family for all their kind love and inspiration. I could not have kept going without them.

PICTURE CREDITS

Front Cover: *Portrait of An Unknown Man*, English School, c.1610, The Bridgeman Art Library. © Rafael Valls Gallery, London.

Inside Cover: *Map of the county of Caernarfon and the city of Bangor* by John Speed 1610. © Bangor University Archives.

Block A

Signature of Piers Griffith aged 14, and *Seal* showing the Penrhyn Coat of Arms, Bangor MS Baron Hill 850. © Bangor University Archives.

William Griffith I (Fychan c.1420-83) and his first wife Alice Dalton. Sir Roland de Velville (died 1535) and his wife, and Lady Alys née Griffith may also be buried here, at Llandegai Church. Royal Commission for Ancient Monuments in Wales.

The Field of the Cloth of Gold, June 7, 1520, after Hans Holbein the Elder (1460/5 – 1524) by Friedrick Bouterwek (1806-67). Versailles/Giraudon. Bridgeman.

The Engagement between the English Fleet and the Spanish Armada in Crescent Formation off the Start Point near Plymouth 1588 (engraving), English School, Brown University Library, Rhode Island, USA. Bridgeman.

Armada 1588, The Battle of Gravelines, possibly by Nicholas Hilliard (1547-1619) showing the leading Spanish vessel, the *Reale*. Reproduced by kind permission of the Worshipful Society of Apothecaries of London.

Queen Elizabeth I (1533-1603), the Armada portrait c.1588, English School, Private Collection. Bridgeman.

Arms of Sir Francis Drake aboard the *Revenge*. By Wikimedia Commons.

The launching of the English fireships on the Spanish fleet off Calais, on the night of 7 August 1588, Flemish School c.1605. © Rafael Valls Gallery. Bridgeman.

Portrait of Sir Francis Drake c. 1583, Anglo-French School, Private Collection. © Photo: Philip Mould Ltd, London. Bridgeman.

Sir Walter Raleigh (1554-1618) 1588, English School, Private Collection. Bridgeman.

Robert Dudley, Earl of Leicester c. 1560-65, favourite of Queen Elizabeth I and commander of the land forces at Tilbury where Thomas Prys witnessed her speech. Attributed to Steven van der Meulen (1543-68). © Wallace Collection, London. Bridgeman.

Sir Richard Hawkins (c.1562-1622) in armour, 1588. © National Maritime Museum, Greenwich.

The Golden Hind in the Pacific Ocean, an imaginative view by Jean-Leon Huens (1921-82).

National Geographic Image Collection. Bridgeman.

Piers Griffith's Pirate's Chest, attributed to Spanish/South American provenance of the 16th century. © Private Collection of the Douglas Pennant Family.

Tudor Allegory, © National Museum of Wales.

Sir Francis Walsingham (c.1532-90) from 'Lodge's British Portraits', 1823 (engraving). English School, (19th century), Private Collection, © Ken Welsh. Bridgeman.

John Owen, private secretary to Walsingham and possibly to Robert Cecil, *"a keeper of secrets"*, kinsman of Piers. Private Collection. See Steegman.

Smugglers' cove at Porth Ysgaden near Cefnamwlch, Llŷn Peninsula. © Photo: Marian Griffith.

Pirate islands in Sunset, Ynys yr Wylan Fawr and Ynys yr Wylan Fach off Aberdaron, near Ynys Enlli. © Photo: Marian Griffith.

Thomas Prys, pirate-poet (c.1565-1632). Artist Unknown c. 1605. © Reproduced by kind permission of the Mostyn Estate.

Signature of Thomas Prys on the manuscript of his poem *Cywydd i yrru y Llamhidydd/ To a Dolphin.* MS HR 142 Cefn Coch MS. A. The National Archives.

Robert Devereux, 2nd Earl of Essex, (1566-1601), favourite of Queen Elizabeth I by William Segar, 1590. © Photo and reproduced by kind permission of the National Gallery of Ireland.

Block B

Portrait of Sir Thomas Mostyn, possibly at the time of his Knighthood by the Earl of Essex in 1599. © Reproduced by kind permission of the Mostyn Estate.

Gabriel Goodman, rich Tudor Merchant. © Photo: National Museum of Wales.

Portrait of an Unknown Young Woman at Gloddaith, (late 16th or early 17th century). © Reproduced by kind permission of the Mostyn Estate.

Gloddaith, near Llandudno, home of Lady Catherine Griffith Mostyn, the Pirate's mother. © Photo: Royal Commission for Ancient and Historic Monuments in Wales/The Mostyn Estate.

Interior of Gloddaith. © Photo: Royal Commission for Ancient and Historic Monuments in Wales/The Mostyn Estate.

The ancient hall of Cochwillan on the Penrhyn Estate, home of Robin ap Griffith and his troop-of-horse off to the Battle of Bosworth. Birthplace of Archbishop John Williams. © Reproduced by kind permission of Richard Douglas Pennant.

Interior of the restored medieval hall at Cochwillan, famous for welcoming poets like Guto'r Glyn in the 15th century. © Richard Douglas Pennant.

Archbishop John Williams (1574-1650) with his hand on the Great Seal. Royal favourite and Chaplain to King James I, Lord Keeper of the Privy Seal, Speaker of the House of Lords, Bishop of Lincoln, Dean of Westminster, Archbishop of York. Attributed to Cornelius Janssen or Gilbert Jackson c. 1621. Steegman favours the Studio of Mytens. © Reproduced by kind permission of the Dean and Chapter of Westminster.

Abercegin Creek, where Piers Griffith's pinnace *Grace* once lay at anchor, also the captured Spanish galleon *Esperanza* and his local trading vessel *Elizabeth* of Beaumaris skippered by Captain Richard Dobbe. © Photo: G.L.

A View of Snowdonia, rare early 18th century print by Gastineau believed to show part of the estate and the old bastion and tower of Piers Griffith's castle, before later renovations by Wyatt and Hopper, and before the design drawings of Moses Griffith. Private Collection.

Barbara Gamage, Countess of Leicester and her children, 1596 (an infant boy, son with sword, and four girls.) Her Welsh grandparents were patrons of poets and she was adopted by the Stradling family of Glamorgan, kinsmen of Piers Griffith. She gave birth to 11 children in all. Portrait by Marcus Gheeraerts. © Reproduced by kind permission of Viscount D'Isle from his private collection at Penshurst Place, Kent, England.

Part of the Mostyn Silver Collection. © Photo: National Museum of Wales, Cardiff.

Edward Herbert, Lord Herbert of Cherbury (c.1604-1642). Attributed to Robert Peake (1580-1626). Private Collection at Powys Castle. Bridgeman.

Mostyn Coat of Arms 1622. © Reproduced by kind permission of the Mostyn Estate.

Prince Henry, Prince of Wales, eldest son of King James I and Queen Anne of Denmark. Henry died 'of the plague' in 1612, two years after William and Ellis. Steegman saw such a miniature at Plas Newydd, Anglesey. © National Museum of Wales.

Signature of the Pirate's Wife, Margaret Griffith with Galleon Seal. (MS Bangor/ Mostyn 144, 8 May 1643).

Signatures of the Pirate's daughter, Dorothy Edwards and husband William. (MS Bangor/ Mostyn 144, 8 May 1643).

Signatures of daughter Grace Bromhall and husband John. (MS Bangor/Mostyn 144, 8 May 1643).

Signatures of daughter Elizabeth Humphreys and husband John. (MS Bangor/ Mostyn 144, 8 May 1643).

© All the above signatures are reproduced by kind permission of Bangor University Archives.

Coat of Arms of Piers Griffith of Penrhyn. © Reproduced by kind permission of the Dean and Chapter of Westminster.

MS Burial Register entry for Piers Griffith at Westminster Abbey 1628.

MS Burial Register entry for Piers's London nephew William Griffith, serjeant-at-arms to King James I and King Charles I, 1636, and for Margaret his wife. © Both images reproduced by kind permission of the Dean and Chapter of Westminster.

Westminster Abbey.

Printed record of Piers Griffith's lost stone inscription at the Abbey with details of his London family, from Henry Keepe's 'Memorials of Westminster'.

© Both images reproduced by kind permission of the Dean and Chapter of Westminster.

Manuscript Images: Mostyn 111 (NLW MS 3030 B) no. 257 (p.208). Opening lines of the *cywydd* (alliterative poem): 'Blaenedau, trwbl anedwydd' by Wiliam Cynwal. © The National Library of Wales.

Peniarth 104 D no. 15. Opening lines of the *cywydd* (alliterative poem): 'Mae anhap yma i Wynedd' by Sir Huw Roberts. © The National Library of Wales.

Brogyntyn I.4 (Porkington 7) no. 289. Opening lines of the *cywydd* (alliterative poem): 'Y gŵr o'r llys agored' by Siôn Mawddwy. © The National Library of Wales.

Back Cover: Armada 1588, The Battle of Gravelines, possibly by Nicholas Hilliard (1547-1619), showing the Reale of Spain.

NOTE:

Front Cover: *Portrait of An Unknown Man*, English School, c.1610, The Bridgeman Art Library, Rafael Valls Gallery, London.

The painting shows a man at the height of fashion, with an expensive fine lawn falling collar and matching cuffs, black velvet doublet, superbly crafted sword and scabbard, trimmed beard and well-cut hair of burnished gold. The tip of his right little finger appears to be missing and he has a slight frown-line between his eyebrows, perhaps the suggestion of a scar. His expression is enigmatic and his eyes are remarkable in their intense, steady gaze. This is a masterly portrait painted from life, capturing the character-essence of the sitter, along with hints at extravagant and sensuous inclinations, seen in his loosely fitting neckline and cuffs. Here is no buttoned-up Puritan. The image shows both a man of action and a man of culture. The right hand has the refined elegance of a Renaissance poet, whereas the left shows the grip of a deadly swordsman. Could the left index finger be pointing subtly at himself ('here I am'), a possible clue about the individual's need for status, a man who keeps stylish company? There is not a whisper of scruffiness nor brutish threat here in this well turned-out figure of the new Stuart age: pristine and privileged, opportunistic even, with a reputation at stake. The centrally focal sword marks him as a person of rank and authority.